I0817022

Praise for Anselm Hollo

"In this posthumous trove of brief, zestful poems, Hollo . . . relates the 'incredible onslaught of being,' seemingly dashing off each of these frenetic, fragmented vignettes in a fit of wild gusto." —*Publishers Weekly*

"Hollo's poems are, for the most part, gentle and sweet and self-effacing, and they often display a restraint that allows the circumstances of the world to unfold naturally." —*Heavy Feather Review*

"The bedrock solidness of Anselm Hollo's poems makes as ever a place of refuge and delight in these meager times. Thank god for his humor, else we'd all be dead." —**Robert Creeley**

"Don't miss anything at all by this strong poet." —*Library Journal*

"Post-hipster wit and lyricist Anselm Hollo has always had the world's lightest touch when it comes to balancing a poem on the invisible wire between sentimental openness and ironic judgment." —*San Francisco Chronicle*

"I await Anselm's new poems with more eagerness than those of any other living poet. His work is 'news that stays news,' a poetic gazette that is one of our times most accurate neural readouts. If you can't remember your way to your heart, Anselm's poems will show you." —**Andrei Codrescu**

"Here is a poet capable of teaching the curious how to read what some would still call avant-garde poetry. These poems are snips and snaps of contemporary life run together with a taut gathering stitch and played off against particular moments and figures in the history of ideas, literature, and politics. This dexterous and often humorous interplay creates moments of surprise, as in 'Why There Is A Cat Curfew In Our House.' The poem, an energetic narrative about a family of raccoons coming in through the cat door late at night, ends with a wry nod to the desire for more: '& if I were a Victorian poet there'd be a moral/but late in my century all I can say/is that she did of course remind me of my mother.' Notes at the back help unlock the references for those who are not content to just go along for the ride." —*Boston Review*

"Hollo is an epic poet . . . Against explosions of carnage and fear, there is a persistence that is as close to heroic as I can imagine. It continues! Improvisational humor, smarter'n paint, counterpoints a profoundly moral pulse. Equity. Compassion. Tenderness. He writes . . . out of hipness that knows staying alive was always a matter of exploiting the unexpected."
—*St. Mark's Poetry Project Newsletter*

"Ironic in-jokey, post-beat hipster and quietly beautiful lyricist, avant-gardist Hollo (*Outlying Districts*) graciously draws readers to his work in these poems through both the copious notes supplied with many of them and the gently funny, probing tone assumed throughout. The opening poem '1991,' an elegy to his sister, moves in a moment from dark reflection, 'At the rites we think of the old days when belief/ made words reach the dead/ a resonance / gone,' to light, 'OK Sis/ now of no fixed address in the kingdom of Dis/ Miz Ubi Sunt,' never failing to carry us along. Hollo often quotes, invokes or directly addresses the poets of his waning generation (Ed Sanders, Robert Creeley, the late Ted Berrigan) or plays himself off poets of all ages and languages, many of whom (Yevtushenko, Brecht, Allen Ginsberg) he has translated into English or Finnish. His preoccupations with literature are woven into reflections in which we spot our more articulate selves; never trite or off-balance, these are poems that sustain." ***—Publishers Weekly***

"Anselm Hollo's *Pick Up the House* is a satisfying, lyrical mix of both old and new poems, including some from his highly praised Toothpaste Press chapbook *Heavy Jars*, gathered together in one volume. Hollo's method is simple and direct. Written in an open colloquial style, his poems invite one to share in his commentary and intuition. Pausing often, he allows us to catch the music and grace in the trivial and seemingly commonplace. . . . This is reflective of Hollo's real talent, a hand so sure and inviting that the reader can be led to the necessary conclusions. But it is in the short lyric where Hollo excels, with a sense of line derived from Williams and Creeley and a sense of humor straight from the New York School, he captures the possibilities of transient moments, becoming both commentator and object of comment. With more jukes and jumps than Michael Jordan, Hollo's poetry continually confounds as well as exceeds the reader's expectations." ***—Independent Publisher***

"For three decades Anselm Hollo has been an important figure on the intercultural poetry scene. In *Outlying Districts* we see how his original work has been enriched, both technically and in content, by the contact he has had with European poets through his impressive translations." **—James Laughlin**

". . . it is in the short lyrics where Hollo excels, with a sense of line derived from Williams and Creeley and a sense of humor straight from the New York school, he captures the possibilities of transient moments, becoming both commentator and object of comment." **—John Stickney, *Small Press***

"Anselm Hollo's so sly and subtle he almost melts in your mind."
—Richard Silberg, *Poetry Flash*

The Collected Poems of Anselm Hollo

The Collected Poems of Anselm Hollo

Edited by John Bloomberg-Rissman
and Yasamin Ghiasi

With a foreword by Jane Dalrymple-Hollo

COFFEE HOUSE PRESS
Minneapolis
2023

Cover design by Alban Fischer
Cover photograph © Jane Dalrymple-Hollo
Book design by Bookmobile

Coffee House Press books are available to the trade through our primary distributor, Consortium Book Sales & Distribution, cbsd.com or (800) 283-3572. For personal orders, catalogs, or other information, write to info@coffeehousepress.org.

Coffee House Press is a nonprofit literary publishing house. Support from private foundations, corporate giving programs, government programs, and generous individuals helps make the publication of our books possible. We gratefully acknowledge their support in detail in the back of this book.

LIBRARY OF CONGRESS CATALOGING-IN-PUBLICATION DATA

Names: Hollo, Anselm, author. | Dalrymple-Hollo, Jane, writer of foreword.
Title: The collected poems of Anselm Hollo / with a foreword by Jane Dalrymple-Hollo.
Other titles: Poems
Description: Minneapolis : Coffee House Press, 2023. | Series: The collected works of Anselm Hollo | Includes first lines index.
Identifiers: LCCN 2022050231 (print) | LCCN 2022050232 (ebook) | ISBN 9781566896856 (hardcover) | ISBN 9781566896863 (epub)
Subjects: LCSH: English poetry--20th century. | LCGFT: Poetry.
Classification: LCC PR6015 .O415 2023 (print) | LCC PR6015 (ebook) | DDC 821/.914—dc23/eng/20230125
LC record available at https://lccn.loc.gov/2022050231
LC ebook record available at https://lccn.loc.gov/2022050232

PRINTED IN CANADA

30 29 28 27 26 25 24 23 1 2 3 4 5 6 7 8

A friendship. A marriage. A promise.

There are moments in life that are indelible, crystalline, beyond everyday meaning.

It was in one, two, perhaps three of those moments that a beloved poet, uneasy that he may miss his train, his long-awaited journey to the beyond, asked his wife to keep a promise. The promise was to make sure there would be a posthumous book, a book of his "Collected Poems."

The book you have in your hands is a realization of that promise. If you had the privilege of getting to know Anselm Hollo in person, you are fortunate. But, even if you are as far away in time as Hipponax, whom he translated, you will always have access to his spirit in the poems residing herein. In this volume, Anselm invites you into the eternally convivial "company of poets."

Jane Dalrymple-Hollo

Dedicated to Josephine, Kaarina, Tamsin and Hannes,

along with all the poets and friends he loved, and who loved him.

"Always treat language like a dangerous toy."

Contents

& It Is a Song

"I occur very infrequently. I have no patience.
Our poor Brother Thankful used to say of this world:
it does not matter."

—BERTOLT BRECHT ("FIRST PSALM")

Heads

In the rain of time

Smoking a pipe /
talking to cobblers /
falling in love /
getting lost in the fog /
/weeping /

smoking a pipe writing a poem on falling in love /
on getting lost in the fog / weeping / tearing it up

smoking a pipe /
writing another /
falling in love again / while fucking another /
smoking a pipe / talking to painters /

talking to them / while fucking / & smoking a pipe thus
inventing Cubism /

listening to gargoyles / clochards & / the bells in your head
as they open your head / to remove a war /

falling madly in love / with a redhead /
fucking madly in bed /
your brain comes loose in your head
the pipe
still smoking
poor Guillaume
lies dead

Pythagoras

At sunset
come stomping
legs pitchy
with blood
through the beanfields

(this is the tale of his death:
the end of his easier symmetries)

and he was drunk
& alone & happy
within and at one
with his spheres

Quietly
he came at sunset
stumbling & singing
hey, hey
toward the end
the beginnings of Rome

and we still have the book
(& the beans: he advised
his disciples against them
and drunkenness & incontinence)

They took him
back to the city
for it to destroy him,

as later itself was
destroyed
by a greater beast.

A warrant is out for the arrest of Henry Miller –

(November 2, 1962)

GET THAT MAN!
what rooftop
chases! Zig-
zag sprints in alleys
smelling of garlic
& good fucks
get that man!
he's alive . . .
skittering
down fire escapes,
the women watching
with big startled tits
rock-drill roar
& torches flash
down into fall-
out shelters –
But all the while he sits on a mountaintop
& smiles at sparrows hatching
at the foot of the ladder to man's heaven
& says, Yes now
they're chasing
everybody.

Our Lady Without Nipples

Edvard Munch: "Madonna" 1902
& de Sade's letter to his wife

In the man's brain in his brain
woman
woman's hair
man's head in woman's hair

the man is
Edvard Munch the foetus
is the man is "two people (the lonely ones)"
the lonely ones

ones
like spermatozoa lonely
in the man's pain

"imagine a rifle
charged with a bullet
growing larger the longer
it remains in the rifle —
if you let the bullet get big
it will break the rifle when it comes"

woman always
woman never
she

and so he painted
pain

"with movements and unimaginable convulsions
the whole time it is going on."

Bury the Falcon

(René Faulques)

A mercenary
    A sword
    for sale
        is a truly free sword

The fallacy of the sword
    for sale
Legio Nostra Patria

        Colleoni:
    an artist's dream
gone to ground
gone to seed
in Katanga

Stragglers among the black roots
engaged in a vague destruction
    an evening prayer
    of bravery, senseless
    useless

            well-paid
        as ever
        this kind of *accidia* was

    A mercenary
        A bird
    A face with a beak
        A face
    Hardly a face
        A face
    Destroying itself

Artaud

His twenty-five pages
on the impossibility
of thought:

"J'puis pas *penser*!"
how terrible for a Frenchman

yet it was feeling he lacked,
choking: "KRR — Ahh!"
And when he broke through
— too late, too far

back in the frightening shadow
streets of childhood
spirits of hairy menace
earth quaking under his bed

and nobody there.   Only the black
decaying Lion of Logic,
red crows of insanity

black owl of death,

drawing him on
with its stare.

From: Loverman

they say she was
this one who sang

dawn   sunrise
set & dusk
    come at night
    smell my musk

dusk   sunrise
set & dawn
loverman loverman   where you gone

dusk   dawn
sun rise & set

dawn   dusk
sun set & rise
on eyes   lies   hope he dies

sunrise   sunset
dawn & dusk
    came &
    left me
    here   a husk

who sang was
beautiful
    his once who sang
    sweet invocations
                    in her ear

Winter Poem

for Gael Turnbull

Whispering
of trees, and birds in the trees
each bird a different song

The legend, cold fires, time
to come, white

Whispering
beaches and rocks and pebbles
the song that was in the waves
each wave a different wave, the same
as the others

The legend, cold fires, white time
to come home

From here on, the voices
will fade, these
were the trees, and trees in the sea
and bird waves across the stars,
in the sky, were pebbles, infinity

Gone,

whispering,
points in time,
silence,
the legend;

a winter's tale.

1961

& I Heard a Man, Telling the Sky

I have spoken kindly
Without causing offence I have spoken kindly, politely
To customs officials wanting to know
The reasons for large amounts of peppermint tea in my pockets
Kindly, a soft-spoken man
To policemen lifting me out of the rain & into the shelter
Of well-built cells
To presidents, ministers, headwaiters & whores
All wanting to sell me what I never asked for
I have replied with a smile & a warm handshake
& a cheerful nod in passing

Nobody can even remember seeing me
Except from the back, a peaceful Chirico puppet
Receding into the calm perspectives of the city
Pushing a red wheelbarrow full of plastic explosives
Crossing borders unnoticed
In the guise of a walking egg
Without causing offence
To rich & poor alike I have hummed lullabies

Tactfully have given away bombs to rebels without private means
& unobtrusively presented Alliance Commanders
With the latest in opiates & relevant literature
Walked at dawn
Apologising for getting them out of bed at this early hour
Caved in at night
Whispering words of admiration for the ingenuity
Of my interrogators
Yes I have spoken so softly & smiled so much
My face has fallen away
This has encouraged me in my endeavours to be affable

I knew I was doing the right thing all along
My smile has increased in intensity
My eyes are fathomless caverns of admiration
& flowers sprout
from my upturned nostrils of bone

Dancing Lumumba

Where have you taken
the tall thin man?
Where have you taken
the man who danced?
Spoke like a bird
but could not fly
spoke like a bird
but could not flee
from you.
No one was there
when you took him
no one was where
you took him but you
no one was there
when your heels came down
& flattened him
like a bird, but you.

See the two breasts
bared here in sorrow:
two breasts.   Two eyes
a woman.   She knew
the man who was tall
& thin, & a thing of grace
but lacked the wings to escape from you.

Until Death Do Us Part . . .

To think of them
from afar
to think of the distance, that air
its broken voices

    thousands of miles, the sea
    and the rivers, returning
    the sun also rising
                                        but then

it was less: the distance
two hundred yards!   They are moving
into the sights, they are moving

    into the eye, wide open,
    opened in the earth
    his earth, to let him in

the suddenly opened eye
the windscreen meshed
into a honeycomb of light —

To think of them
as close: as he was

his head in her lap, her arm
across his chest
as they were floating, floating

        wherever it was
        we were going, we cannot stay
        on the road

yet must drive on
and out of their sight who try
who tried to think of us, as we entered
the dark city

        to be encased in a light
        of diamonds and death,
        dead center of stillness

where there is
no fear

            out of their sights
each into his
her night, now shared
                    forever.

26.11.63/9.4.64

Message from the Border

A messenger,
    bald, his skin burnt onto his bones, he appears on the skyrim
    walking, not slowly nor fast, just walking: his bones move,
    his toe-joints grip the ground: he has been on his way,
    he will soon arrive.

We see him approach,
    we will see him arrive, we are his arrival: we will see
    how he opens his mouth, we will say: no! first — drink this!
    we will see how the water runs down into this sun-crumpled hide,
    filling out a few wrinkles.

And he will open his mouth
    and deliver the message: what will he say?

He will say what the one before him said,
    and the one before that one — he will tell us: The dancers! —
    the dancers — they — are surrounded! by the burning —

So simple it hurts . . . and always the same.
What else could it be?
What else could the messenger say
    these days? The dancers, in the midst of the burning . . . this
    is the messenger's voice, the sound of his horn, abandoned
    for lightness, and speed, now it lies on the sand
    cracked by the heat, blackened — soon charred
    by the black
    heat

1962

Bestiary

From The Book of Rites and Events

Shambling along the veins on its way
to the heart the great beast has arrived in the city
its scalding water on friend & foe

it will pass

& mushrooms will grow
& mushrooms will grow

Anonymous

Ants scurry away from the cloudburst of fiery piss.
What does he know of their poems & rites & deaths?
His head opens: his teeth crash through the walls
of apple city.

Changes Chased

Clouds dark as
& the way it keeps raining

my woman tells me

on those two
white horses
in a line

some people say they were at my funeral

midnight clouds
one way lane

going

slow

my funeral they

the way it keeps white in
that no change wind

They are blobs of starch
I tell her   & now
I will blow you
a wake

she's a river hip woman

                                        she

can take this jive

we watch
the white hearse

                              pass

in the rain

1961

The Red Piano

        A red piano
he says
        a red piano.
I never saw one.
I knew a man who had a red typewriter,
he hardly ever used it.
        A red piano.
Would it seem lighter to carry upstairs
than a black one?
        A red piano, a red piano.
Let us think more musical thoughts.

The Bees

The bees: a   poseur's? memory
Always wanted to stroke one, bumblefur

was saddened by the knowledge they
would die, and I be stung

As you will see I was a charming child
& now I can't eat honey, my road
to a certain (well-known) gate being paved
with teeth already.   & the fact death will lose
its sting & die just like the bee   well
it is something to ponder, in bed
beneath my moonroof

The Lions

I said,
later!
I will give you a poem
a flowerpot of reality...
Later!
I will show you my private lions.

Well It Has Been a Pleasure England

Well it has been a great old
Party the first one said starting
On down the stairs a
Great gettogether the second
One joining in all the others
Pushing out into the stair-
Case following them
On down talking and
Singing and laughing like
Mad supporting each
Other stopping to pick up
This and that on the way
Down the stairs a great
Great long party winding on
Down a merry old dragon of
Chinamen retelling itself
What jokes writing them
Down on the walls for those
Who came after stumbling
And hopping on down so pleased

No one noticed they must've
Been going on down for at
Least a month and well

below

street-

level

A Plant

That a plant
should arouse such affection . . .   A plant,
its seeds to be spaced six inches apart
to sprout in twelve days, to the height of a man
to delight him: a gardener: calumet smoker in the blue air —
a backyard sunset, his plant, in his pipe, the resin
from flowering tops, and it was May when he spaced them,
autumn now,
male & female they grew, sweet resin fills the air
His lungs are blue, clear skies, not black, like his neighbour's
who fears the blackness of skin, the whiteness
of laughter in their faces
who cultivated this plant,
millennia before Voltaire before Raleigh
and who eats potatoes now?
Nothing but guilt in tobacco, he is filled with pity:
black tar in his neighbour's lungs

That a plant . . .   a thing of stalks & leaves
in alkaline soil in freshly turned earth
a miniature vineyard, should arouse
such enmity! but it does
They will send him to war
for it, send him to prison
five cigarettes a day, and death:
his soldier's, neighbours' pay.

The Landlords

Get them all out so we can get in
and stay in, inside. where it grows
from ceiling to floor, from window to door
we float, in a soft rustling fluid of green

Dreaming of those who walk strong through the town
to bring it back here, to keep our tanks warm & full
our beautiful strong-men and grateful green-lidded girls
who also know how to live and let, let live, the insect crowd

Filling its sordid caves with nothing but crowded flesh.
Yet it secretes, prodigiously, this green
this voluptuous green, if you know how to milk it
to the full: our fill.

1963

Song of the Tusk

The elephant
    bogged down
thousands
    of years ago

The fragmentary tusk
    now in a glass case

no no these are untrue statements
it is I
    who am in the glass case
        counting
            the stubs of museum tickets

It is the elephant
    who walks the downs
        who laughs at the Sea
            growling

There is no such thing
    as thousands of years
I drop a stone on your head
    from the elephant's back

Show me
    show me the thousands of years

I walk through the water
    throwing stones at the women on the beach
        the honeymoon women
            their eyes far apart

Frightened
        they close the glass case
                over themselves and their lovers
for thousands of years

The Struggle

A man,
standing
in the road, in the way
of himself

standing, being
himself
too exactly, to tell you

the road or
the ways of
the towns:

                        see him
— waving his arms!

My Ancestors

They sat him down
at table's head
drank to him merrily

hey Old Man Bear
you dead and stuffed with hay

while eating his insides
joined hands and sang
riding the wooden bench

long poems with short lines
to remember them by

Poem for Josephine

Rhinos

can't swim

"I do not have a rancorous spirit"
your sister once said
well I don't either
it is a rhinoceros spirit
though not the Sutta Nipata rhino who always fares lonely
in endless stanzas
gentle creature in yellow monksrobes

I in dusty black mostly
am mostly disturbed by even such
natural parasites as my children
(& yours)
charging them and their mother
mindless enraged & ever more bugged
by being so

short of
breath &
sight

— whoomm
into trees

or walls there being
more of those in a city

And the only time we go to the seashore &
hire a boat I upset it
too upset by your words or was it my
helmsmanship
when you get wet you get wet you get
continuous senseless arguments who
said what at what
bad moment

"when he sailed into the harbour his ship
became a snorting horse"

(round-eyed Korinna saw Hermes)
well our boat
snorting rhinoceros sank

No I do not have the rancorous spirit
            "but the simple heart of a child" I pray
metamorphosis   gods, me   a hippo
swimming midstream, a prince
spouse & her young on his back

    serene   serene

                    such glories

Trobar

Trobar: To Find

Moon in the window window in the frame frame in the wall

Within the frame I sit at my table
        it is not my table
I sit at my table in my house
        & it is not my house
I sit at my table in my house at my window
        & it is not my window &
I see the moon

the moon I can see I sit in the light
she in the window
in the dark my face
is it my face dark in the window under the moon
your face   light in the house
is it your face
is it light is it dark is it the moon

"The moon —

                        in the window?" yes
ma domna
the moon in the frame in the window

                can it be
                can it be ma domna! I'm singing
                    & it is a song

1963

& With Your Hearts Between Your Legs Come Seek Us Where The Rainbow Ends

(Francis Picabia)

Slow to speak
slow to touch

Make it soft & low baby make it soft & low
    if you feel like lying down with me:

    "when the lines are cast,
    the nets are set & waiting
    the tunnies come slipping through the moonlit sea"

soft & low
they go

even their speed a slowness, as it is
with us at night

*

As when a woman in a lonely place
                bends down

    do we speak freely with each other?

As when a woman in a lonely place
and pierces with her breasts
the man
he in return
takes hold of them

    no it is silent silent here
    a silent place

"a piercing embrace"
& rightly named so.

*

As when   the waves

—past
the sly flickering words, through the door

shedding our clothes in the room still talking looking looking away & at
then standing
naked
between us a sudden clearing in space
humming as if to give birth to a sun

Dawn. Dusk. Dawn. Dusk
We could stand here forever
blind
with what is jetting
through

*

Dark blue
Slowly through

Under a blanket in a bedroom today this very minute
we make love with open hands

Dark blue woman by my side
Slowly through mind, through words, back to my hands

Dark blue inside
we are
this very minute   and it cannot move away.

The Sound

"music tonite"
The sound, breath
the horn/pipe
Finger/tips
making them jump the sound
to touch: to touch a child
a different softness

This afternoon I danced
with my baby son

The machine, a
black wheel of sound
turning
as it happens clockwise

there is also a clock
on the windowsill there is
a light
hung in front of the window

shut out the night
to write you these
words, who are

next door
as it happens
reading a play or
trying to iron a shirt
in any case growing
a new child

untouchable as yet
as yet no dance, no prance
(that all? Writing: a spiel)
no: but repose

a black wheel of sound,
turning
clockwise

Three One Four Nineteen Sixty Four

Though in love with
          the newfound vehemence
I am always surprised, surprised
          at getting anywhere when walking
surprised to be ravaged & hurt
          by faces ravaged & hurt

               "The stern travail of thought
               will not be suborned" . . .

                    a little boy
                              rhythmically yelling:
               three/ one/ four!   nineteen/ sixty/ four!
                    3 / 1 / 4   19 / 60 / 4
                         . . . *teraphim*:   oracular image

Surprised at the relative permanence
          of ink
               on paper
          at the tracks on the spoor
               superimposed,
                              surprised

1961

The Arrival

As the wind comes
as the wind goes
slamming doors as it goes
closing valves as it goes
scattering crows as it flies
killing flies as it goes —

And the door kept slamming, slamming itself
to death
and the valve was opening, opening

against the wind opening
with a knitted brow and a scream
it would come, and purple
in the face, the hair
damp and dark and smelling of mushrooms

To birth, to birth
as birth comes, is
a sucking out
an against

the world's weather.

The daughter, new

A
coco-
nut, her head is a

coconut,
she sucks, she
guzzles

her head
full of
cocomilk,

at the breast, her
breast,
and I and

the son
look on,
look on

Observations (1960)

1

Blue flames

He is ten months old and loves
Blue flames.
Bending forward on his elevated
Seat better to see
Blue flames
On the gas cooker and sometimes
Blue flames
Are to be expected anywhere:
Up the trouser's leg of his father
Or in a cupboard when the door is ajar —

2

Knowing the cat is black soft and endowed with great
patience
Grabbing him by the ears and laughing in old-mannish glee

3

On a grey carpet, in a yellow sacklike garment
Gently rocking to Dixieland jazz
And contemplating a sliver of tinfoil,
its ever-changing shape
He sits and radiates the one true way
— a mustard-seed Buddha

4

A lemon in each hand he's marching:
Of mute yellow cymbals
— great sound!

5

When walking

On a fitted carpet.
When walking
On the pavement in front of the house,
When walking
On grass (is best & lifting the feet
like a kitten out on its own for the first time)
— the important thing: not to lose
Sight of Her!

6

Inside his head
— you can see
That through
His eyes
— he shakes his
Other head

Kanya

On the beach

The Sea
come rumbling in-
shore

I don't want to
stay here any
longer

it is a
big rumblygod
I do not
trust

*

A blue
plastic elephant
on yellow wheels

— look, I
can make it
move

*

Mornings

ooo — boomm — bbahh ooo — boomm — bbahh. this is my

heavy dance

but my smile is not

menacing

like Father's

1963

Age: Four

"switch on the light
so it gets dark outside
& we can go
to bed" (Hannes)

*

Yes he wants a gun
like everybody
but at least he
doesn't claim it's
"for protection"

*

B U R S T
the balloon

His face,
poor tribesman . . .

all that joy
he bartered

for this
worthless thing

*

Nursery rhymes
I don't even know
the tunes
so play the record
over & over

he sits
flushed face
eyes glitter
listens
            listens

"ecstasy" to me
the word
now flesh

The Angels

In the dream, we were adam & eve
the first two moles
in earth

and as we made love in the humming darkness
first ecstasies, visions
came into our heads

stories to tell our children, of wonderful beasts
in a region of lights & colours & flames
living and coming together

far beyond any universe we'd ever know

in a room such as this one, where now they lie sleeping
eyeless & warm in the dark.

Song of the Touching

Come let me touch you
— our fingers, sinking

into flesh: it gives way
like the water on a chill

morning, on a stony
beach: come let me touch you

We are sinking but upwards
to a sky as grey

and as hard as the street,
come let me touch you

hovering, see
the earthly bodies
below, giving themselves

to each other: and some
making light of it: few
giving light

My back against cobbles
of stars, I see my hands
falling through you, reaching

for these few,
pulling them up
to your back, to warm you

Come let me touch you

Eating Raisins at Midnight

Past midnight, & me
        eating raisins
                out of a cellophane
                        bag.   "Sultanas."

Once
                a minute a raisin
drops on the floor
beside my

                        chair.   Plop,

plop.

                An innocent
enough activity,

        yet it provides
                me with nourishment
& an awareness of

                                how much
is bound to get lost

always, in time,
    on the

— plop —

way.

Four Stills from "The Poet" (A Film)

for Tom Raworth

1

The poet, drunk, is seen
composing a poem to the
revolutionaries of the world.

It is to be a long poem.

While working on p.9 he realizes
that he is stone cold sober:
he stops, goes back,
reads what he has written
starts crossing out words —
lines — sections —
whole pages.

One line remains,
on page five.   It says:

the heroes, their mouths full of

It is not
a very good line.   Maybe
he only forgot to cross it out.
We cannot
ask him.
He has fallen asleep.

2

The poet,
asleep,
addresses his friends

You, my brethren
	in the dream:
remember the time of night
	we have agreed
to light our pipes of peace

Remember our pact
	be gently mad children
at the appointed hour
	paint the blue sign
on your foreheads

Knowing each other's rooms
	we can then be together
remember
	no one must know
our vow not to grow
	up in their world

3

In the morning,
the poet looks out and sees
a quiet residential neighbourhood

Look at it long enough
				and it won't go away
talk to it long enough
				and it will yawn
scream at it long enough
				and it will dawn
upon you that Rome
			was not overthrown
						in a day

4

He returns

to bed:

there is,

possibly,

someone

there.

Blue Dream Movie in Eleven Takes

One: The seagull, with a flower in its beak.
Three: The wolf, a seagull in his mouth.
Two: The flower, grown out of the dead balls
of a dead soldier
Four: The lady is white like a seagull
Six: The wolf comes loping with his lope
of Lupus-the-Wolf.
Seven: The seagull is dead.
Eight: The lady smiles at her wolf and takes the seagull
Five: The lady is white like a seagull
because she is naked
Nine: The lady takes the dead flower from the seagull's beak
Eleven: The drugged speech of sleep.
Ten: The lady seems beautiful
she becomes
smaller as she approaches
receding
into the daylight
that blasts
my eyelids
wide open

The Numbers Within

Returned to this place
defined by the number of four
there are few of us
but certainly four
after an absence a reunion
now

again

alone
here where I write

absence of three reunion of two
married for seven years & only met
again as two

one into one

now where

alone I write
"returned to this place defined"
I remember the russian poet
his stammer when talking
but suddenly gone as he said
his poem out loud
by was it heart

by heart

how can I remember a line
a thing to touch

by its sound
a stammering in what was before
& did not come to an end

at heart

how write a line that is true
of heads outside of mine
all voices mine a stammering
counterpoint of things
the russian poet & I
spoke of in poems
true voice broken

                                        halting there
how can we speak of these
by what is here at hand
& in the hand   held
                              there

here in the hand an apple its smell in the room
simple exciting

                              a breast in the dark
a beast in the dark & another another another
                                        warm

1964

Air to Dream In

Leave it, leave it

behind the dark
window the owls
calling out to each other
my voice to you
only heard
there in the dark
treetops of the sea

red the moon rose
cooled off shrunk
to a coin in the blue

alone it is if it is
a poem for you

Faces & Forms

'As who should say,
This is my face
This is my form,
Faces and forms, I would put
you down
In a style as of leaves growing'

—LOUIS ZUKOFSKY, "A-2"

For
Her

Matters of Life '64

What buckets or balloons —
full of simple jazz
we need to sustain us:

sleeping in beds

    not alone

& with tulips
on the table

*

Soon as I turn
my back she
dives for the bed —

whale-woman,
wearied
by the Jonah
in her belly

Moving House

Up all night
among the things of this house
    shoes books & paintings
    petalled on the floor

the lightbulb
naked, tired
            you
now shedding clothes
beneath it

in this house
    this flower we plucked
        apart
            all night

Two pale servants
of what we'd made
    with care
            our own

        Poles of the *tipi*
        dragging
        through our dreams

Late: The Aspen Hour

Oh, oh
        we
            are
worn out . . . "I can see leaves,"
you said
        "they're
        everywhere"

I saw
        your nerves
                    veins
        in a talking leaf

When The Air is Right

Out in the air
often as not
we are afraid

"Look there
look out
   outside &
     sideways
warily
   take care . . ."

Though when truly
naked & moving
   towards
   about to know
another

it's a warm
blur, a music for
all the body
twitching in
rabbit-nose pleasure
as the mind
then moves

in hops & skips
   slow-fast
   fast-slow
& closer,
     closer

when the air
   is right

A House A Street A Night

The ears listen the eyes see the nose seeks for smells the skin feels
the pen writes
the car drives by & shadows dance on ceilings
rays of light
follow the straightest course
from 1 point to another
or get deflected & pursue a slightly
crooked line instead
from 1 point to another
innumerable points to innumerable others
a net of light & shadow moves across walls & ceilings
winces
& disappears.

A street
houses with small gardens
first a restaurant yellow light people talk laughter & warm smoke
then a building with shops then houses where people think they live
the street goes uphill
& after all these houses where life is lived
sleep slept food eaten drink drunk near the crest of the hill
there is a house where it has all
stopped

Ears listen eyes look July flowers in the gardens
& there must be a petrol station somewhere
skin wide awake the night
is warm
particles of air
hurrying about not getting anywhere tumbling
around warming each other & my skin

I have to pass this house
& stand in front of it & be inside of it
also
all passing is standing all going
going through passing by

the car
passes a net of shadow & light
slides across walls & ceilings
& is gone
wincing.

The streetsounds heard
here in the room
the windows open though shuttered
shards of noise
someone leaving the restaurant the other end of the street
singing vomiting singing & cursing
cars
tram
almost but not altogether
silent hum
of night & breath

Eyes to follow the lights on the ceiling
eyes
strongly connected back to the brain
eyes not telling a thing
as long as they only stare at the ceiling
I could close them
could turn them to her that lies sleeping
could

The pen
a poor instrument
you may go pen have a good time
look me up some day maybe have something for you to do then
write an address perhaps
tonight
I am outside & inside, I stand
in front of that house
in front of this house
a dark house with shutters
closed on the ground floor

I look at it & know that I'm inside
& that it is inside me
unseparable
lights shadows singing
far-off rumble of the tramway
small tight-flowered shrubs strong smell young smell all belongs
quietly hilarious
dance of brotherhood of air
I stand outside
I lie behind those green shutters & something has happened & is
still happening & will happen until it is gone & passes
wincing
until I am
no more.

Stuttgart 1956

1962, October Dreams

The rain
Heavier on our bodies the year
October: an eye and a mouth: our bodies
Moved through the frightening dark of smiles
On faces unseen. What thoughts in their power-beds
Sleeping   Waving   Coming up for air
Who are they who force us to walk
The streets past houses shaking with steam
& fear? Toward each other my love to walk to walk.
Will they stop us, who are They? Bodies
Rolling, groaning . . . to wake, not to wake
To morning decisions and twitching eyelids, the eyes
are nails of lead in their brains
& heavy, our feet in their sleep, what gestures
Distances, who walks here, on our legs?

*

In his brain
Blockaded by sleep
A child sits in the one small well-lit room.
It is drawing a picture: an island, an eye
Staring, out of the blue ocean face
And he says "Cuba" in his sleep "I never went there,"
The child turns, smiles. It is thinking of Christmas.
He sees a tinplate fire-engine in its mouth.

The Skull

Tyrannosaurus: agreed
that the tyrants of men . . .
But to me, as I see
your skull here, in front of
and six times my own

A black iron skull
with broken charred teeth
and sockets, jagged, broken —

No, it is not
Enough: not the name
to conjure away this vision of
        mindlessness
                powerful! mad
with it, uncomprehending . . .

The balance of terror
is stricken true
in this silent and musty
museum hall

A huge carnivorous frog
        yet not a frog,
                they tell me
I cannot see you a creature
once-lived like myself

I see destruction itself,
      my destruction, as you
            would have seen me —

Nothing, a nothing
but a blind appetite
burning your nostrils and jaws
now frozen and petrified
      still wanting to tear me
to tear a new name
      from my throat

You are terror itself
you are what threatens

and black, a skull
broken, an iron skull.

The Empires

1

The para,
the para-
chute on his back

      In a pack
      they are tailing, a pack
      of heroes

            Head, over-
            head is the sky is the earth
            is the sky over heels
            over head over
            heels, they are falling

            beadlike somersaults

He is falling
he is one
a hero

If the parachute
does not
unfold

If the seed
does not
die

2

Father Robert Davezies
who was sentenced to three years' imprisonment
sheltering & aiding Algerians on the run
from the torture chambers devised by his own
countrymen

Stopping a man with a gun
stopping a man with a wall
these methods we have approved
but stopping a man with love
try that, and they'll stop you
with a gun, or a wall, four walls
a cell, three years, three years for stopping
to love a man

many men, on the run
from guns, men on the run
from walls, or trying to vault them:
three years. Father, three years
in a cell, three years they have stolen
from you — for us all,
three years in a cell

chalked up on what wall, in our minds
that we do not cry out
do not fall on that ground
where stone is said to have sprouted with voice?

to have split with the mouth,
the saxiphrage of the just
the blind voice of dust
        crying out
        to the skies?

Scroll For a Time-Tomb

Behind our bellies
we sit, cross-legged, in the warmth
of our purring black balls,
they rest on our heels,
they are full of good,
good.
                Memories
                                        of a sky:
cracked mud — & small fiery suns,
small changes . . .
                                  Write:
living in tents, underground.
Underscore
                    living.
                                     We know
how sudden & black
in the snow we'll be

high above
the cities of Rome
& all their dead wars.

This time, the scrolls
should be better; gods, heroes & beasts,
we seed them anew.

Where the Shadow

Where the shadow of light
meets the shadow of darkness
the line, the tightrope that leads to the nowhere

a man, a black foetus unfolding in song:

stricken for life with the beauty of harshness
the dialectic of marching along
a long
way from nowhere to nowhere:

Bertolt
Brecht.

Hot Day

After Brecht

Hot day; writing-pad
      on my knee
                I sit
in the pavilion. A green boat
      moves through the willows
            into sight

in the stern
      a fat nun
            thickly wrapt up
in clothes

      in front of her
            wearing a
bathing-suit
      an elderly person
            a priest,
most likely

and on the rowing-seat,
toiling
for all its worth
a child

How like the old days, I
say to myself
how like
the old days!

A Rooftop; A Distraction; A Cloud

The eye

climbing

climbing

as far
as high

as
the cloud

painted onto the sky
to deceive the eye, the cloud,
a lie
a
Juan-les-Pins postcard
from God
?

Return
to sender
if no reply . . .
The eye

goes on, as far
climbing, as high

as it can
        go

O

An
orange on the
    windowsill

the baby is drinking orange-
    juice

    the clock has
        stopped

                the baby

goes on
drinking,

in the window
    she sees two
        suns.

Evensong

After a good day's work
The military scientist sits listening to his HiFi set
But does not realize his depraved, motorcyclist son
Has substituted Ray Charles for Maria Callas.
The military scientist has protruding ears
But they're all clogged up with radioactive dust
And his president's speeches. He sits there, smiling.

Like a little cobalt angel in his open-plan house, in
full view
Of millions of stars, and the desert, a good day's work.

A New Ballade of Lost Ladies

Tell me where
or in what land
are Jean
the glassblown hair
Marlene
her silver breasts

tell me where
that beauty rests
or Zarah
voice to drive them all insane

tell me
whatever
happened
to Baby Jane?

Where is Rosalind
who woke
all cocks to crow
where is Brigitte where Shirley where
did they all go

Ingrid too who sent
the earth a-rockin' & a-rolling
bells were tolling
where the golden mane
of Marilyn tell me where is Baby Jane?

Prince
staring at the flickering screen
of time where once

they all were seen
in splendour   let me tell:
where in a bed are gathered twain
burnt in the brain
are Baby Jane and Baby Jane
and Baby Jane

warm flesh   to crackling film   to ghost
God grant them peace   God give them rest

Prince let us not take to bed
the dead

Hommage A

guillaume

i r
o a
a p l e n
l n i

napolleoninaire

of art
tra la

that long
gone spring

now apple — in — air
et — air — nity

tes yeux

guillaume

Short Lines After a Long Procession

The Drum-Horse
Alexander
o
boom boom
most
memorable horse
huge
shaggy
home
from what crusades

your steps
in perfect measure
hoof & boom & hoof

and he
who was not moved
to weep that day

was moved
to boom
inside
as you loomed up

so slow
so measured
so at ease

in gentle mourning for what grows
grows huge & fierce
grows ugly & unique
grows beautiful & loved   grows
old and has to die
boom boom
to die
one day

under the bells
he stood
and smiled
as you went past
he understood

30 Jan 65

Lady Europe

That woman
she's dead now
last she lay
down on the Indian tribes

That woman
they always
carried
lazy dimples in her back

Now dead as Zeus
& Christopher
her mounts
grew weary

She just spread
out on the ground
slept & gave birth
to sudden monsters

Big & bigger
finally
no one could lift her
so she died

The Cabbages

Driving through the outskirts of Madrid
the British Socialist businessman from Hampstead got so
depressed he didn't see this concealed
crossing so slammed at 80   into some poor guy's donkey-
cart, killing the donkey outright, spilling its owner & some
eighty cabbages in the road

                                        where they rolled to a
stop, eighty green donkey-blood-spattered heads not looking
at anyone, in particular.

The Alarm

6 o'clock
    this morning the horn
        of our neighbour's new MG
went mad

    blared
        for minutes
one long
            howl

    round-eyed
        cradling each other
we waited
    waited

        sun was shining

The World Outside

At times, the world outside
is a big red sailor
with a five-months' load:
when you live in a mailbox,
you have to watch out
for the heavy parcels . . .
But if you seal the slit
no one will ever be able
to clamber out when the horn
is sounded by airmail angels
travelling on a pale green wind
we lie listening for,
having had word.

Night Wind Pieces

i

The wind, let loose in the dark
& the lights of the city, moving:
the city is a great dragon, it is a procession,
it is on the move . . .

But the curtains are drawn, the music unheard —
see: men & women, preparing themselves
for the long journey across a room.

ii

Another night,
    another window

She has been brushing her hair
    fully an hour

The other, behind his dark
    wishing window
eyes spanning the width
    of those uncaring shoulders

Another window,
    another night

Having wiped
    the shrivelling eyes
off her windowsill
    she draws the curtains

The light, round the edges

Eclipse, an eclipse.

Observing

A Black Maria
with a man's face
in the steel-mesh window —

A green van
& a pig's snout
looking out —

Contemplating
their destinations
a head
atop of my blue overcoat.

Successful Legislation

By sentencing everyone
      found in charge of words
in a state of intoxication
      to months of hard labour
on airfields and launching-sites
      we provided
the younger poets
      with worthwhile employment
restored mental vigour
      and physical health
to the elder statesmen
      and greatly furthered
the causes of
      sea-travel
            and peace.

The Lies, the Eyes

"He repented
on his deathbed
seeing the great evil
he and his men had done"

The false consolations
of "history"
as taught
to children

Some of them destined to march
2 by 2 & follow your leader
      who did not die
      in a bed
your leader to a truck in a field

littered with skulls & shoes
later, in that day

The photograph
remembered
the Polish boy 6 or 7
cloth cap on his head
still on the scrawny neck

— burn
two holes
in this page:
his eyes

Les Fleurs

Hello sweet fat
Lady World, you
interested,

have you read
Baudelaire, O
lady let us

in, your
flowerpot, we'll
show you

Love in The Bathroom

This love story begins

with what we all
find so exciting:
a naked woman!

bending over
spitting a milky
water jet into the basin

returning the toothbrush
clack, to the beaker
turning to wipe her mouth
cool body washed

moving now, fast, presenting
structural changes, new formations
pleasing to me as I sit on the can
smoking a pipe in the sun
comes through the blinds

my "zebra belly" remarked
on by the daughter
three years old and well on her way
to that same build
though she can still be held
upon one palm

she's having a shit too,
on her blue plastic pot
and even more
creatively engaged
by threading wooden beads the while

whatever these
two do
is interesting

Discreet Love

(12th century Austrian)

Came to your bed last night,
late, didn't dare
to wake you . . .   But now, you say:

"Damn
your timid balls: am I
        a wild boar,
                or what?"

Lovely,   woman.

Give Me You

Your hand
your breast
give me at least the sight of you
standing there, naked
by the waters' edge in the sun
holding your elbow with your right
supporting it,
the left arm and hand
and your chin, with that hand,
and your face
    looking out
        to sea:
how exactly I know this
pose, its angles and tensions of
bones and flesh, just
                then

Only by having seen
your broad and radiant back in the hush
after love by the
            waters' edge
                    in the sun.

Like This

(von Morungen, 13th century)

O. he says
my lady's belly lights up at night
whiter than any snow of this
or the next year
                    Liars, who claim
I'll not see her again, like this — but true, my eyes
were deceived: I thought
                    surely, it is the moon
                                        but it was day.

Impossible,
she says, never to have him stay
the morning here
                    with me. But when the night
                    goes pale on our skins
we cry: The day! it is here . . .
                    He said it
                    the last time,
                    and it was
                                        day

No counting, he thinks, no counting, and
in our sleep, too —
                    but later, her tears
                    running down, as all
                    must run . . . I tried
what comfort, a man . . .
                    her arms around me.
                    And again
                    it was day

No counting, she says to herself,
no counting the times he has seen me,
like this
                    he pulls down
                    the sheets, he has to
                    see me, all
                    there is, and
a strange thing: he does it again and again . . .
                    But now
                    it is day.

Things

1

A manner of representation

things
in old

ROMA
AMOR

had
wings

2

The pleasure of

knowing
you is
yes she said yes she
said
    as he was
knowing
    knowing
        knowing
            knowing
her

From a Book of Rites & Events

Hey,

come out and see
come out and see

the

HEY!

enormous
animal,

shitting

suns!

HEY!

the

state-
ly roll-
ing

across
the hemi)
sphere's
hey! heaven.

The Fiends

One
by one,
caught out
in their secret gardens:

        sun in his head
leaning against a
Notting Hill lamp-post O hate
to see it go down
that dark cell drain
        hiding it in the TV set
neighbours told them,
"he never turned *it* on"
        or Camden Town basement
sounds laughter & smoke, *eheu*
fugaces O evil fruit
        pushing a pound of it
through Golder's Green
a baby carriage, 2 babies on top
surprised at bobbies
groping around their damp bottoms
O drug fiends.
        Or on the way home on the Circle Line
6 packets of good Ghanaian
fell out his umbrella,
more in the bowler
O noeud de vipères
        & one with her lover man on her mind
                green seeds & leaves
        in her hair O vicious
Cannabis . . .

The Stop

On my way to work
I stop by the Amusement Arcade
slot-machines cigarettes flashing lights &
my old friend
the 6d Rifle Range
put the thin silver into the slot,
      a tinkle,
            the light comes on:

duck   duck   duck   duck   duck
owl   owl   owl   owl   owl
rabbit   rabbit   rabbit   rabbit   rabbit
                              glass

r
i
f
l
e
b
a
r
r
e
l

The trigger, clicking: Electricity, Great Mother
in a playful mood
fifteen shots for sixpence, you get them all, you get
      your money back (something wrong
            with this machine: I always make it)

But now — the glass, as a mirror: mygod
      even her breasts
            as if they were smiling —

The trigger gone soft
      the light out
            the girl vanished

or, her reflection gone
        and in there
                all that's left
is one orphan rabbit
                very upright
                in the gloom

                        On my way
                        to work

Minotaur Poem

½human, ½bull

To say good morning blues how do you do
something is sneaking around the corner
not about the weather
myself I'm feeling pretty bad
not about the climate
you are adorable
but of certain limitations
myself I'll go to spain one of these days
but of no importance
all of you are wonderful people
and to say it is a great pleasure indeed
with a lilt

The Seventh Lady

The Oldtimer Speaking

She could never pass a department store without buying a toothbrush
that is how she caught my eye in Oxford St.
her pockets sprouting with toothbrushes & a big bunch in her hand
she had lovely teeth and couldn't explain it

All over town   All over town
Small bombs of love explode without a sound

She said she was a poor cactus so carelessly potted grown askew
yet she was sweet & thick & coffee-strong
but hated light so at night she caught you unawares with sudden
brutal flowers
her husband had run down the street with cackling ankles

Big bombs go mega-bang! Big bombs go mega-boom!
Small bombs of love are tested in a small dark room

She stood & smiled in doorways of dimlit hotels
leaning her head medusa-like against the neon jamb
but when you stopped to ask her the time of night
she looked at you round-eyed and said O it wasn't you it wasn't you

Some rockets go   Some don't get off the ground
Some drop too soon   Some make it to the moon

She always dreamt of midsummer's nights up north
sitting in a tree in a white nightie
yet even in those dreams only the owls came to nest in her lap
though once a fox stood watching her green-eyed

All over town   All over town
Small hopeless bombs of love explode without a sound

She said I am a stranger born I can never make love to people I know
this is the last time I'll speak to you
please give me the fare to Bergen or Cedar Rapids
that's all I ask of you darling she said adjusting her seams

Bad missiles flop   Good missiles fly
But timid missiles do not even try

She wrote me a letter from Malta saying
"there's always one more of us than we suspect
one morning I wake to find I have forgotten
the toothbrushes my husband & even the owls yes even the owls

Big bombs go mega-boom! Big bombs go mega-bong!
The seventh lady comes to end this song

— so let us test again!   Explode again!
I'm seven ladies!   You are seven men!
And many more   And many more
There is no end to this seven-years' war"

All over town!   All over town!
Small bombs of love explode without a sound

Loverman

"Lemminkäeinen": Kalevala Country

i

Riding July mosquitoes trees
birches, few holy
oaks

Forget not the spells:
oakspell snakespell
spell against dwarfs
(dwell in the ground
sleeping are any
handful earth)
evergreens pines, rocks
grow larger, trees
low, up north.

Riding   thinking   singing
    See her turn, golden
    below the charred beams
slanteye   bluehair
remember how round O these daughters!

Long night 9 moons dark
nipples marshberries
far apart
        long hair, swing
        cross buttocks broad belly
        surprised
                his eyes in the door

turn, golden
charred beams.

His thoughts hardly
thoughts   flames
in the round-cobble fireplace lick softly through

ii

How sad
is the Mechanical Moose!
    Anguish
your lot when the heart
beats like a metronome
    bowels move with the whirr
    & clank of the assembly line
your eyes blur nothing, all is seen
    in meaningless detail.

    Anguish
shines through his eyes
    at night

he believes he is standing still
in suffering contemplation

yet his legs move, the oil flows
        into the bearings & joints
the durable synthetic skin
        creases uncreases on hard flanks & haunches
twigs break, cones crackle, ground thunders
his ears ticking it all away on tape
spools of it coiling in his belly

yet he does hear & is standing still
in his mechanical mind an enormous silent
        effort to wrench one cog to slip
        & clench *another*

but all he is able to do is this,
a drawn-out, wailing sound —

a factory siren in a ghost town, a train
become invisible & immaterial, an error

desolate, hooting across the far plains of the moon.

iii

moom moom
hear my call
moom moom
speak to me
mother   father
lands   sea
moom moom
in your room
I   we   all
hear my call
in you are
toad   star
moom moom
are you far?
moom moom
are you near?
moom moom
moom moom

you are here
I will hear
moom moom
moom moom
moom moom
        moom

The Mural

He wasn't there; nobody was, he said
but as I went down the broken steps
past the green dustbins & on, into the small basement room
I saw it: a mural, a garden of pleasures —

    A jungle, a lake & a plain: the sky electric blue
and it wasn't people peopled the land, but rhinos:
Rhinos, standing sitting & lying down
others in full flight, yet none in an aggressive mood.
Their eyes a friendly red, like the sun over the plain & mountain:
orange, almost, like the fruit on the trees.

    The paint, still firm, no peels, he said
. . . the place was damp & dark. I stood and watched them.
Two, in a corner, pearl-grey rump to rump
nearby a third, looking away as was fitting, up at a swarm of birds
across the great orange (— It made me remember Susan, & first attempts
in time flown past . . . well, like those birds, he said)
then one, jet-black, squirting a steady stream — at life —
its countenance serene & satisfied:
the likes of him should rule the world.
    Farther away, a family of six, or ten —
o there were hundreds! walking into the turquoise lake,
not holding hands, but, asitwere, he said, in unison
of armoured friendliness.

    And, all alone by itself, the beauty! White as snow to cap
the mountains' knees on the horizon — white,
floating through the green grass labyrinth we might get lost in
or run over, by lions jeeps or rhinos, in another time continuum.

He said, I don't know. Who painted it, & anyway
it was not painted. It was a man,
standing in front of that wall one night & shouting, YES!
in a very loud voice: a voice
of oranges, and lemons, and rhinos.

Idylls of The King

i

I want
          to be a
fine lover
     husband
     father
     poet
     critic
     political
      head &
     defender of truth
     champion of liberty
     saviour of the world

        Now the word is you
        want to be
                    all of these, too

     — so there'll be
        2 of us, at least

ii

It's the old story of who sits in a room
waiting for the Great Lens to appear
          above his head
the paper to catch fire

& is me & is here
tonight in this city
"one of the greatest"

& wants to say
& wants to know
                                what makes you love him?

iii

11.45 p.m. . . . . it is receding
or I am
going away
going away where?
going away
receding

this is a crude registration

I wasn't really looking.

iv

See, that's the thing,
he explained
                    with all those guys
they've all had **visions**!
but then we were somewhere else,
talking to an old man
        about the great troubles
                somewhere else again, it was
                    none too clear.

v

bedtime
story read,
goodnights said
— now's the time:

run about —
shout —
open the door —
slam it again — giggle —
jump on, jump off the bed —

let's see him
rush out roaring! o he gets
mad doesn't he? here he comes

vi

The baby
sits in her chair
smiling
shining

on good &
bad alike

what does she care
for all the false republics of this world?

Let's do something about the unequal
distribution of wealth right
now. (Her mood
might change)

vii

Not many
words
in my mouth

when I point North
into my lady's South

(or, we come
first
        words, later)

viii

blessings,

invisible fingertips

no other
way

with words

What I Know of That Country

The men are lying in the shadows
Looking at their empty hands and
Thinking, thinking

Of children, ticking like clocks inside their mothers

Motionless, swelling, in the sun
And listening, listening:

Their breasts, clocks
                    that have lost their hands.

Prayer for an Old Lady

A house was not
    enough
she wanted to be
        the house

A husband
    a houseful of children
        not enough

so she left her body
    & became walls
        to wall us in, in-
            side her

Now her eyes
stare at the point beyond
    the dwindling world

O heave her back
into herself
    now that we've gone
        from her

Some Flowers

for J.

On the low
    black table

        you made the top for
                5 years ago
        when I sawed its legs off
                less competent
        one of them always
                shorter than the other 3 (& so
        it got a little too low
                in the end, kind guests
        referring to it later
                as "in the Japanese style")

stands the tile-red
    pitcher

        we bought in a
                Venetian
        hardware store
                pleased by the good &

clumsy shape,
        archaic
comb's-tooth ornaments
        leaving the sinuous
skeins & outrageous
        chunks of coloured glass
to others
        (we're not that
sinuous either)

& in it, a bunch of tall
    leafy stems

cut off for a street-corner stall
        where I bought them, what are they
I don't know what they are
        you said "you can always ask"
next time I will
        if they still have them, the seasons
so rapidly changing
        would I be a folk-singer
if I knew

& clustered
    right on top
small orange-coloured
    flares

in the twilight
        & at dawn & also in-
between

        or, most of all there,
in the dream
        after falling asleep
at 3 in the morning
        wrapt in your warmth
so simply, at last

        & waking up I thought,
I sang, in my head: it is a

marvellous thing —
    the way
some flowers
    last

        got out of the bed
            you had already left
        the house with the children
            trailing behind you
        down the long stairs
            their voices
        reverberating & fading
            on their way to school

        sat down, alone, in the chair
            facing the table,
        the flowers, the bed
            & the picture above

        of a city, rising
            from the sea

suddenly there in the morning

how many years ago?

The Mosaic Standard from Ur

looks like a wall

and that's a camel
no a horse

it's got a face like a horse

Set of museum postcards
showed them to her
one by one

people
people too

they're sitting   two are
standing up

that's a
bad indian no   a lion
is what it is

What it is
is a pair of eyes
only opened
three years ago

He Points at The Ceiling and Says: Look — Bird!

I tell my son: it is a fly.
I realize this is a lie —
I recant: "It is a bird.
Do you hear? It is a bird.

It's on the wing, and it can sing . . .
Why invent another name?"
Purged of shame I shout the word
It is a bird! It is a bird!

A Free Man

He will punish the wind
for breaking the lamp-post's window.
He has concluded treaties with all the trees.
All cats sparrows pigeons and puppies are
his rightful property.
He can touch them and take them with him whenever
he chooses.
He hits his enemies
when they're down and if they don't get up
he sits on them.

He calls a red light a blue light
or a blue light a red light
if it so pleases him.
He is never lacking in entertainment.
Songs, stories, magical Words.
He takes running jumps at whomever he chooses.
He stops all strangers,
inquiring after their business.

He calls a man a man
being three years old
— our son before history.
He wants to sit *on* a plane.
He tells the stars to take care.
And he will punish the wind
for breaking the lamp-post's window.

And What Else is New

On the beach
my son points with his little spade
at a, as my Grandfather
on the maternal side used to say,
somewhat statuesque lady
                                        and says
she hasn't got a tail has she?
&
what else is new

from Haiku

Exegesis

"... most of them (are) pretty recent ('island,' as vide references to hovercrafts, etc.) — & none too 'purist'; quite a few wd probably be classified only as a sort of surrealist 'senryu.'"

— ANSELM HOLLO

17 x 17

passing the bus queue
she glances back, then tells me
"but you *do* look fierce"

*

on their bawling young
High Street mothers use the slap
lollipop method

*

follow that airplane
of course I *am* high, this is
an emergency

*

giant Scots terrier
I thought I saw was known as
Taxicab Mountain

*

brown photo, legend
"Serene Enjoyment" they suck
pipes bones crumbled back

*

roaring hovercraft
toad shlups out of the Solent
disgorges the pale

*

night train whistles, stars
over a nation under
mad temporal czars

*

round lumps of cells grow
up to love porridge, later
become The Supremes

*

we saw her come out
now she comes out like the sun
each day, charges us too

*

lady I lost my
subway token, we must part
it's faster by air

*

"but it is *our* world"
tiny blue hands and green arms
your thought in my room

*

sweet bouzouki sound
another syntax for heads
up to the aether

*

in you the *in* moon
its rays entwined in my mind's
hair, hangs down right *in*

*

viewing the dragons
there they ride slim through my dreams
Carpaccio's pair

*

slow bloom inside you
the mnemonics of loving,
incessant chatter

*

far shore ferris-wheel
turning glowing humming, love
in our lit up heads

*

switch them to sleep now
the flying foxes swarm out
great, it's flurry time

The Coherences

Introduction

the poet Vallejo invented new ways of walking
sitting lightly on wooden Metro benches
not to wear out his trousers
not to wear out his shoes

in the secret code of his poems
he describes those inventions

I'68

I

The Empress Hotel Poems

i

just get up
and sit down again. then
    you can watch the dust
        settle.
or wait for the Irishman to come round
knock on your door again. twice
    he's asked me
first, the time, and then
"would you know of anyplehs I could get a job sirr —
    lehborin', that is."
they won't take him, he looks too
purgatorial. poor soul
8 days over from Eire
        where they have strikes.

ii

the typewriter banging
better than radio   for company.
sheets of translation pile up. too many
    words, too many
other men's words
    bang thru my head. why don't they learn English
in Finland. why don't they learn Finnish Swedish German
in England, Old & New.
they're just being kind to you, Anselm.
    they don't learn,
        you earn.

iii

the old housekeeper lady downstairs
    likes the stamps. she says could you
let me have them if you're going to throw them away
    anyway. Mr Burroughs she says
    always did that, he always
        gave me the stamps. he got a lot of
            mail, too.

I give them to her. we are
Burroughs Hollo Saarikoski Ball
we are Mrs Hardy's
nice writing gentlemen.

iv

white smoke from Battersea Power Station
rise moon star London city light
beam from the airport
sweeps the sky. I switch the room light
on and off and on, light dark light dark.
it occurs to me
I'm trying to tell you
what goes on inside me.
out there
they'll suspect
a Chinese spy.
ha. Battersea Beast on its back
pushing vapour puffs thru the soles of its feet
for fun.

v

go thru my things
god knows what you'll find. when I'm not here.
I'm not here, in this poem
I'm in another room, writing praises
of their loveliness and terror
the long-haired beings that dance thru my mind
not endlessly, but to be one, at one
with them
I want to be.
I want to be one,
I want her to be one
when the voice begins
she is, and she dances.
I am the voice. I praise.
there is
no mind.

vi

to return and find
2 men in grey suits who have come to look at me thru their eyes
  and say Mr H. is this yours? you know they're illegal
    in this country. oh I didn't know.
  well they are, you better get rid of it. ok.
they go, and I think
  it is a good thing to have more than one room.
what would they say
  if they found what I have
in the other poem.

V'66

Journey

. . . watched you
and you were turning, turning
  from me, and back to me, you were light & dark
    both, in ever-shifting proportion
as were the questions that whirled in my head
    — question answered by question, your voice & mine
following, leading, leading us where, where were we going
  where could we go, if we would, when we would, and what
    were the reasons given, the best way to get there
through the rooms & streets, the blueing desert, enclosed by time

  I watched you,
    trying to read your face
— a wanderer in light halls, dark caves, and held by the wind
  piercing us beyond pleasure or pain, a constant spear
      . . . watched you,
resting, our bodies stretched out on a shield
  in a place with many old gods on the walls;
    did they whisper & hum,
back through their millions of lives, through time?
  I could not hear them, they had nothing to tell me,
    I could not hear them, only your breath

only the songs of your body, your face,
    an intricate chant, an enchantment, yet clear
        in all its relations
and high, high on it, in the place we had reached, a high place,
    I was opened to you, your music, through my eyes
        not watching, but seeing, now, seeing
            you — light in the dark that shines beyond walls or time . . .

V'66

The Going-on Poem

eight p.m. in the backyards of Fulham,
June.   their trees in
        leaf

no junipers, no, shouldn't think so, no;
"A.TUNIC.AND.CLOAK.
SCENTED.WITH JUNIPER."
    what the old Wanderer
        was given . . .

a small boy talking
    earnestly, his voice
blends with the pigeons' coo
— a 'cross-fade' they call it, in radio;
in my ear
they make one sound.

there is a community   of sorts.
where is it. take a walk down Charing Cross Road
and look for it. there is also another group
    who buy film magazines, there are, it seems
        a great number of communities
            but they don't know
        and they don't love each other
                much.

the smallest
    linguistic community:
a tape recorder
    and a man.

        juniper,
smell of memory.
        to give in
to one's mind.
        Winnie the Pooh
going upstairs,
        bump, bumpety, bump.

there are Xtians in Fulham
as I am told by the bell
now calling them to their rites.
has poetry ever been
    anything but trouble.
but I guess they're happy here, no one
    sets himself on fire   no one
        preaches   that sermon.

        MAKE LOVE NOT WAR!
well I wasn't going to
    make war . . .
        then GROOVE FOR PEACE!

it seems
    these days
we have to have reasons
        for everything.

oh I'll just go on doing it
        for love.

when the occasion
presents itself

my greetings   to
        who knows when.

a shooting occurred
between the last two lines.
James Meredith!
the man shouted
James Meredith!
and shot him
in the back.

"the shooting is most unfortunate"
the senator said,
"from every viewpoint. I regret
that it happened," said the senator.

there are few Buddhists
in Mississippi.
the others also
have their reasons.
they have their communities.
it makes a frightening sound.

and, there's no end to it.
continuous screech of
metal fatigue.
yet in my ear, tonight,
the other sound too:
the patient humming lives
of people, not
communities I cannot
understand.
Winnie the Pooh
wrote this poem 30 years later,
still hanging
from his blue balloon,
to get at the honey. they told him
he was soft. he was pleased.
you can't be too soft when a cloud
is what you have to be.

it was a soft tunic, and it smelt
of juniper.

he wore it
next to his skin when he released
another odour in the great hall,
    the reek of their blood.
OYTIZ   returning
to his Queen Bee.
    it never was anything
        but trouble.
you grow up a lonely child
and want to become a hero,
soft and cruel.

that shooting was most unfortunate, too
but not   from every viewpoint,
we do not regret
that it happened.

yes the world is on fire   even here
they burn. I burn
    — sit here, licking the flames
            of honey.

slowly it goes, but it goes.
and if it doesn't go, we make it go.
the little boy's song, now he's in bed
dreaming of the fast planes he will build,
while our slow ones roar by   overhead.

VI'66

Dream Rain Dance

listen to rain swishing down
good empty sound
after all the voices
but only then. a moment's
un-loneliness.
listened
to a friend's voice, remembering
how he told me his dream; months ago.
it was about driving along flat country
straight road towards a herd
of what seemed to be elephants
only their shape
was that of pyramids,
no visible eyes or mouths
no apertures at all, but
as he suddenly knew
they moved in a dance
of three figures only:
sex food companionship.
he was driving towards them, but not getting
any closer. he would never
reach them. felt
regret, but also a sense of
exhilaration: while driving, he found
while driving, he found
he could figure out all the possible
permutations
of their dance: I give you A (food)
you give me B (sex)
he she it withhold C (companionship)
etc. etc. . . .
imagine! he said, about a hundred of them
— and I knew it all, all they could ever
and would ever
do . . .
just like that, in my head. and me
who has trouble with simple sums . . .

it seemed
a sad dream, at the time. now
it is a good deal funnier
than much of what has happened since . . .

"when the sky gets cloudy
and it look like rain
that's a sure sign
the weather's gonna change"
Leadbelly's
sound on the record
we sat nodding to
in companionship one night
— for them, I will type out a copy
containing one more line,
their names.

on record, yes
there have been such as could give it
all
at a time, A, B, C. rare voices
of little mathematical interest.
the true dream: where
is it? your eyes
in the dark. and shimmering
hair, like a cloud
come to rest for a
moment's
un-loneliness.
my arms
were aching
from holding on so long
to my balloon.
it was good to see you
that close, to hear your voice
from no distance at all.

VII'66

The Day's Events

two young girls
with long, red-golden hair
over identical short fur coats (black)
walking, fast
to some pleasurable place.

I enjoy saying it
so slowly.

then a sparrow flies past the cat
'buzzing' it
so close, the cat almost falls off the windowledge
turns, comes back into the room, looking startled.

World War Three
going on all the time.

an old mumble on a park bench.
an eighteen-month-old
stumping up the hill,
seeing only the ground
move away
under its feet.
then seeing a dog,
emitting shouts of joy
trying to catch it.

there is pain,
who can deny it.
there is joy,
who can deny it.

president ★★★★★★★ may be an asshole,
but so are you.

the ultra-intelligent machine
is what we need.

like toys in the nursery fail in their power
when one is, say, five or seven and knows
she is not in the house, in none of the rooms
— when will she be back?

She wants us to love her
in all her daughters
She is her own mothers
She is all her daughters
She wants us
She wants to love us
we can't make it without her
can't get there without her
we're in trouble

what we need to do is write a lot of sentences
and then put them in the right order
if we know the right order.

World War Three
going on
all the time.

not far from here, in a shadow
or cluster of shadows
not my own
a large beast is turning, half-walking
moving a heavy head slowly
a hum as of generators in pain or of pain around it
a brotherly being
tho' of a different order
perhaps a being in love
it hums it sighs and hums in the shadows.

reading the book he sent me
the poet
whose loneliness now is a great book of aspen leaves
vibrating in the light of last summer
uncounted, uncountable, now here, now gone
now gone, like she whom he loved
gone under the leaves, her last summer.

reading, for him.   and for her
        and for all of us gathered together
the praise-words from the Book of the Dead:

"I am in my city.
I have tied up my boat
        in the celestial lake.
I have seen Osiris, my father
        and I have gazed upon my mother.
I have made love.
I am the bull in a turquoise cloud.
O Unen-em-Hetep,
        name meaning 'Existence-in-Peace',
have entered into you,
I have opened my head."

closing the book,
        switching off the light.

going from this room
        to her, to you.

not knowing the right order,
        how could I deny it.

it is there, with the silence,
        between the sentences.

X'66

Instances

i

nice place ya got here
the Messenger said
to her whose island
it was

but the boss
give an order:
let the guy sail
back to his own

ii

there he sat
by the shore
broken nose
missing teeth
balding
old dog

thinking of elsewhere as always
traveling hard in his head

iii

where she was
a moment ago
there is only the wind
whirling up leaves
in her form

long train of leaves
carried by known to be small
though invisible hands
while someone is playing a tune on a reed

iv

o Athenaia
fixup the old dog
make him look good to her
again

eating her famous
celery salads
drinking to her
with new eyes

flexing
his toes
under the table

v

like a trajectory of tons
metal and flesh
hurled down the street
in the living light

his anima
drifting ahead
leading him into it   and through

when he got to the other side
people looked different than he had thought

vi

came up from the cave
patted him   told him
time now
          to go

"who said I wanted to go?"

vii

who walk in back of the back of the real
"beside you"
          the term intersection
a crude imitation of what they are

your known dead are your gods
beautiful but inaccurate
metaphors of themselves

who comes
                                        has words for it
will be worshiped as men on horses
in Malinche's country.

XI'66

Stop Saying Oh Oh

arm's length
and a half
from where I am: you

I can't see you

under the breastbone I am,
unable to hear you
for the continuous trembling

snake, biting its tail

"words, chatter
don't help the sick nor cure them"

but holding you   gives back a voice
and at least half a mind
                              mine, I suppose

breathing,
trying to think of the lights
                                        (love lights)

XI'66

Parting

after Hugo Ball

don't go is what I want you to tell me
the rainless wind from the south
will make me long for you

tell me these are beautiful days
to have you here to look at your mouth
and to listen
                    don't go
tell me life pleases you
tell my voice to go on and on
tell me you will be happy and of good cheer
even when I am gone

tell me I'm stupid
a child or feathers and a small brain
held in your hand
then tell me I know my way back to you
even at night
                    even in the rain
that hides the stars from my sight

XII'66

For The Sea-Sons & Daughters We all Are

sea   the ships
going out
coming in
passing by.

carry
& hold.
there are lights
in the harbours.

going on
going out,
going
on.

hold
the living,
carry
the dead.

see   the lights
lead us on,
to friends
& loves:

hold on   take care
keep warm
fall
      softly
if & when.

XII'66

II

3 Bear Poems

for ever and a day

thinking of how I am always
"a long way from home"
and looking for a bear   to take me to the mountain
the glorious city inside the mountain
where all the lost people go

I remember how the one side of the record went on playing,
two hours   not turned, nor repeating itself

that was in the heart of the mountain

the bear

it was an old dance, and he took a few steps
he was surprised to remember
then stopped   gazing at her
his body felt huge and warm
he did not want to go on   but he liked the tune
                    she was the tune

'after you've gone'

the bear sat down
he felt weak   unable to move
his mind was going so fast
he fell asleep
his mind was going so fast

I'66

The Coherences

i

for whom the
electric
organ   rolls

girls
    born in the fifties
dance
they have souls
                    and carnation pink petticoats

again
    someone died
he wrote
I could not understand it but thought it beautiful

the animals went in two by two
but the *khimaira* went by herhimself

twelve thousand days and nights
these brains have been lived in

ii

now again and now still
moon in the branches
                    Luna 3's remote-control hands
total recall   total loss of total recall
almost coincident shapes

lid   and   lid

eye   eye

iii

a sea   at the end of the street
a burning ship on the sea

the glass door swung
he saw what moved stop
                                        then the eyes
the ball
          in the air he already knew
as the ship approached he reversed the glass it receded
the sedan chair's curtains closed with a rustling sound

fingertip thoughts
the flawless   the flaws

a small lifetime
                    leaftime

iv

how to live in this
                              the last Age
though there is street
                                    and household electricity
I had tried to return from two different places at once
     not knowing I had to be everywhere

"you have such young hands"   and old feet
it had grown more than halfway down her back
a sound as out of three hundred
                                                  Rolling Stones
     as she approached

v

whorls and wakes
drawn through the air
the gestures'
                    dotted lines
who can write on them
     unrepeatable figures
can you tell me the way her foot was gently swinging
     perhaps here I could
                                        he replied in the dream

the eyes
swung open
allowed him to see
shooting star-trail graphs
rhythms of millennial dances
the variations
under all music and song
and even
soundless
speech

I'67

A Poem

it is a poem
but is it the trewf? says the daughter

it is (he said
somewhere inside)
that so many things
tho' not here are true

Battersea Power Station
for instance and you

the proof the trewf?
in the thinking, the loving

fire and heat and smoke
and the light
at the ends of the grid

our fingertips touching
lit up those days

I'67

The Taxicab Came Lurching Round The Turn

for J

back to the old country
car ferry train and jet
engines took over
again
          the pounding
of all those hearts
their imprecise speech
the plaintive music of
how & why

riding the streets "up & downe"
to the cold country   back
and still farther back

thrown thru the air
to where he lay   the father
come to a stop   to stone

how
     dead chief
how cold your hands are

without her warmth
around me he thought
the cold would have entered my heart

the way her hair stood around and above her face
by the gate in that south   where he would soon return.

II'67

Spring Fever Bear Post-Hibernation Poem

is it spring

out of their fevers
gaunt men come

look you new ladies
they have

a new thing

i

it was hot in the dream-hole
there was light in the dream-hole
there was smoke in the dream-hole
music and dark and staggering dreams

ii

they have been in
the within within the within

iii

staggering
in their dreams they have seen
the staggering dreams and
the staggering in the dreams

iv

it is spring
and they are coming
out of their eyes

there is no thing
not new to them now

III'67

Isadora

(lines written after seeing Ken Russell's film)

i

splintering laughter
the burning man-scorpion raises his eyes
the ladies stand up in a circle
nothing but sky and fast-moving cloud behind them

ii

this tribe believes there are those among us who would become angels
later we see them on television and they are ghosts we would have loved to have known
had we known what 'love' meant, or 'angel,' or 'ghost,' or 'tribe.'

III'67

Diana

Pentti Saarikoski

on the steamer
on my way to the island
the sea is as smooth as a mirror

was as smooth as a mirror
I jotted down
"sky summerhouse April
Diana Nemorensis"

there are many small rooms in this ship
with people sitting on benches
and a great many empty cupboards with no doors

it was as smooth as a mirror
I wrote
"in Diana's mirror the moon is a clock
telling a happy time"

I went through the rooms
peered into all the cupboards wrote
"thinking about you
here there are many small rooms
and empty cupboards
I lose my way when I think of you"

Diana
sits in the summerhouse
keeping an eye on the moon
through the crack in the door

VI'67

Buffalo-Isle of Wight Power Cable

i

writing a letter he said
"this instant in time"
but what was that instant
if not where they were

she and the three
like plants with platinum petal hair
sprung from his head

ii

'in the Neverness Motels of the Bitter Country
lovers lie sleeping and loving in fits and starts'

iii

empty
          milky sky
above the building-brick town with its captive dogs
baying at night and in the mornings
the radiation
you opened the door and it hit you

air of metal and transmutations

iv

the cars kept flowing past and into the tower courtyard
but when they stopped no one got out of them
he was waiting for no one
whom did he want to hold
                                        here in the next town
far away too

he had won the race but no one was cheering
slowly he drove up to the starting line

VII'67

Heart's Ease

summer
days and nights

with legs and wheels
to take us   to and fro

VII'67

The Lights Going on in the Rooms Strung Out Back Through the Years

the way
the blue room
(remembered)
lights up

as you turn to
        be held
and to hold me

your
        beholder

VII'67

'All The Way to Morning Town'

falcons,
old songs —

love,
was it

clearer
then?

poets.
horses.

vanishing
animals.

'rocking,
rolling

riding'
rising

a-
way.

IX'67

Love: Discontinuous Consciousness

; by the window
looking out
thru my fingers

listening
to my own breath

singing
old Indian song

    "bear get into car
    car him start to roll
    bear no get out long time him happy
    stay happy roll along"

        like slow bees

        buzz through
        heart's
        laminated matter

            thistles in bloom
            'tween rotting grey crossties

            they are waiting flowers

            they are
            a hugely
            relentless
            tenderness

X'67

Possible Definitions of 'Beauty' & 'Happiness'

babies
cry

all
different

*

fat
woman

light
shadow

*

sleep

wake

room

*

cicadas

think
in
sound

how you walk through my mind

*

myth
her name is

soft soft in the dark

*

XI'67

The One

the one
long hair in my beard
this morning
makes me smile:
it's yours

XI'67

The I.S.S.

one day he was singing
his way through the fields when he saw
a cow stop grazing to listen

he was enchanted
but when he looked closer
he realized she was simply peeing

it was a good story Brancusi
in the bathroom my friend had a pinup
his 'Endless Pillar'
I stood there
peeing and looking
listening to the music my peeing
and looking and listening made

on my independent sound system

XII'67

Meeting Another

when you go fast
there is no time
— LARRY EIGNER

there he was
in his chair

an
incomprehensible

a retching a bawling
a delicate wit

"he knows he is dying"
as we all are
but to talk

'like love being made between fire-engines
the poets talk to each other'

not a word remains
in my memory
but a kind of war

XII'67

The Charge

small metal box I was given
with a length of black string
            the fuse? no
      it won't light
                  no fire
only his ashes of eighty years
into this hole in the ground.

burial
the law demands
in his cold country

can't keep your ancestors
      on a shelf nor give them to wind sun and rain
they must be dug under
mummies bones rotting flesh even ashes go
            into the ground.

hold the string gently
      it slides
across my palm
goes slack. *son*
            bury your father
is the law.

a scholar
he had the face of a chieftain
it haunts me
      the sense of that hole being far too small
to contain what I left there.

XII'67

Walking the Beach with My Daughter's Eyes & the News in My Head

smallest child fewest words
notices
          most
most impressive
stomping along the top of the sea wall

sun haze above the far out tide
acres of watery sand
small packs of dogs and humans
tons of kelp on the beach below
chunks of driftwood half a life saver
a plastic toy gun
block letter labeled STEPHEN
                              AGENT 009

the naked and headless
corpse of a swan

*

in a place named after Simon *Bolivar*
La Paz and CIA *(Washington)* money
paid for his death

so let us have
no epitaphs beyond the true
american
lived fast died young made a beautiful corpse
no monuments no
cities or states
bearing
          his name
no speeches
               muffled reports
like Policeman's Specials on Lake Erie shore
where the late Charlie Pfohl
rode with the Vultures
                                   MC Club

the mortician gave him a head
it had to be paid for
                                        of plaster
it was a necessity

'such flowers   all over the place.'

XII'67
Isle of Wight

Postscript

a face in the dark
        among many
you bend down and kiss it
it asks you a question
it is a delight   you answer

and that is all
        you will ever remember.

I'68

Tumbleweed

Dedication

'no end to troubles' he sd

gave me heart

Webern

1

switch off the light
the trees stand together

easier then
to be in our bodies

growing quietly
'dem tode entgegen'

slow it is
a slow business

to grow a few words
to say love

2

"who will have mercy upon us
if we
        have none"

merci   is thanks
say thanks
for the small mercies

such as the breath
and the hand
                        still moving

Tumbleweed

on 'the day of great routes'
he remembered a head of tumbleweed

yes once we traveled together

tumbleweed
looks like the skeleton of a brain
if a brain had bones

day and night it travels
the great routes
propelled by the wind

looks startling comical even
the first time you see it
but cannot look where it's going
has no eyes

is dead yet moves at speed
sometimes caught up in barbed wire
or meeting its kind at the foot of a wall
until the wind   turns   drives it on

is like something
in the soul

The Hidden Creation

1

"the tracks of your feet
won't come to an end"

2

he had known they were eyes
someone looked out of

3

he'd lost his map case
which love would sustain him?

4

sad nights
in a suitcase

5

she was

6

she was picking up speed

The Monster

1

even though she despised him he would ride with her through that bleak land

Gilles des Rais rode
by Jeanne d'Arc's side

all Paris turned out to see
the monster go

that was later
much later
it was consoling to read the chronicles

2

reference. metaphor. black crowded dreams
never more than a moment's loving

3

the horses' heads bobbing up and down within
his own   their wooden lips drawn back
from rotting wooden teeth
meaning him

meaning him and what would become of him

4

her secret name
he would not say
he would not forget

The Flowers

1

the flowers he
was going to give her

suddenly turned
a fascia of screams

2

how short a walk it was
to the House of Paradise

oh all he gave her
was a bagful of ice

3

how monstrous the diphthongs had grown

4

the door wasn't closed
then why did he push it

5

the train passed very slowly
it took the train a number of years to pass
if not another number of years

6

but on the rollercoaster they went up
and down   and down

7

the scent of jasmine
he gave her
it was a sweetness he wished
his pain his sweat his stopping and starting heart could create

jasmine   jasmine

not a candle
but almost a tree

The Wreck

1

'it became clear to him
that   '

it got very dark and the cartridge stuck in the flare gun
the instruction manual lay soaking in the bilge

the pages
stuck together

what to do now
anyway he knew it wouldn't have said
what to do when stuck in a barrel
becalmed   at sea

stuck   it became clear to him
that was the word
in his throat

2

came out of a tunnel
sneezing sneezing
sound of shattering glass in the street

someone getting out of a cab weeping
or is she laughing
pack of gitanes on the table
an orange candle
Smith-Corona 'the *hard* typewriter that looks *soft*'

horses
have a *hard* time
they can't climb trees like
where would they go in an emergency

well they could always go back where they came from

to be a tunnel
a tunnel has to have an end
a middle and an end

'Rime Riche'

he had gone to some length
such sonnets

to some   as always

who once had the patience
let her hair grow
to an unusual length

he decided to purchase a radio

I   that is
decided to buy a radio
it was that way
(of variable
lengths)

then listened
to himself listening
to how it all rhymed and would go on rhyming

Bouzouki Music

1

Odysseus was
ein Sitzriese

'a sitting giant'

one who looks tall
at table

see him now
through Nausicaa's eyes
shambling forth and into her eyes
out of those shrubs by the shore

2

we love you
by our defects you
tell us apart and
we
love you

3

'he had the funniest legs'
— Calypso

4

a man's legs grow
straight out of his soul

who knows where they take him

5

heel and toe
and soul to sole

all that
            bouzouki music

About Her

outside
some human beings were roaring
to one another

inside and no doubt
contrapuntally he was whispering
to the typewriter's erratic pulse

the words on the paper
the words in his head
never quite the same

the stock cars were tearing round the track
they seemed to be going a great deal faster
than they were 'in fact'

it was a poem in fact
about writing a poem while waiting
for the whole world to come home

Chanson

after Pierre Reverdy

when she wouldn't be there
when he would be gone
from that place and its days
a bird would have to go on
singing
all night

time when the wind
blew across the mountain
white peaks of the mountain
they lay on the sand
hidden by rocks
time, then
nothing else
let a cloud walk by
the cypress trees are a wall
the air full of dust
her hair still damp

when they parted there was still someone
to wait for them and to hear them out
a single friend
under the tree:
the shadow they'd left there
getting very bored now all alone by itself

Any News from Alpha Centauri

1

the dog suddenly punched the back of his knee with its snout
short snap of teeth he stopped shouted hey your dog bit me
in the dark street the other man swayed and will go on swaying
thick weed in the sea of remembered nights
                                                                                an event of no consequence
but for the small marks on his skin in two days they faded
not as persistent as cigarette burns on his hand and arm
the previous summer he'd stayed so drunk he believed himself Orpheus
many a man before him   delusions of a like nature
well dogs never gave *him* no trouble did Kerberos know the good dead
by their smell was he blind as most of them are did cat people ever
enter Hades
                    a little of that goes a long way he thought
walking on in the frosty night with the stars as stately
as ever up there any news from Alpha Centauri
they have their own scene there pretty small pretty quiet
a fortnightly newsletter printed on green gas

2

laughing all over her face her body swung
into it too she was telling him something
she was such a joy he didn't know where to look the cat
came in he looked at the cat but it did not enter this moment
how years had changed them   how they had taken his memory
sometimes he thought his mind away
every instant of waking a new start often so slow
he made many mistakes per hour
the cat lay down in front of the fire
and she had already turned into another
lovesong worksong
                              dark soon in the winter
there was hardly any time to stay
awake to think out a sentence like that
one movement
                        she gathered all objects in out of the light
where they hung in the room about him
how 'years' stood in the air in his place a dumb idol misnamed

3

in the bar there was a photo of Albert Einstein
a photo of Franz Kafka in the rented room

Louisiana Man by Bobbie Gentry in the bar
Mozart and The Mothers in the rented room

eyes and voices   screens of solitude
he remembered the touch of a pair of hands

4

walk in the house of light it said in the Indian legend
walk in the house of light and it walks with you around you
wherever you go

there is only one can give it to you
only she can give it to you
she smiles it stops raining the world will not drown
you walk in the house of light

5

it moves across the big water through many dawns
it goes uphill it stops near the crest of the hill and opens
all its doors

Finnish Folk

after Pentti Saarikoski

go to the lakeshore go
throw in a feather and a stone

the stone   floats

it is the day your son comes home

from Maya: Works 1959–1969

I: 1959–1965

La Noche

The wind   let loose in the dark
& the lights of the city   moving

the city is a great dragon   it is a procession
            it is on the move

but the curtains are drawn
the music unheard

see   men & women   preparing themselves
for the long journey across a room

Man, Animal, Clock of Blood

the animal runs
it eats   it sleeps
it dies
        goes the old song
and then
the great cold
the night   the dark

in the dark the man runs
he stumbles he hurts
    his face   the world is hard on his face   is a she
he is in love with the world

lord of creation   he wears his shoes large
    make way make way
he does not think of that night
he is warm, he will love her if only, whenever
            he finds her

if only he could go without eating
if only he could do without sleep
if only he could hold her forever

he need not die
                    goes the old song
                    in his head

and he keeps on walking & wanting
the beautiful goof   walking &
wanting   make way for the lord
idiot   flower   awkward   man

The Trees at 2 a.m.

one dimming window
across the garden

where the trees
dip & wave

thin veins in winter
black on black

three years we have lived here
with no curtains to hide us

moving more freely
summer nights

leaving the lights on
trusting the leaves

now
    the cold season again

we wrap ourselves
in blankets & darkness

only this
yellow candle
on the floor

Four

1

i don't
    want to eat it
i don't like it
        you
    eat it
i wished you lived in another country
then i would have another daddy
& i would always do what he says

2

one babyfat cheek aflame
the other pale she stands
her hair
down to her nose & cries

    all the old wrongs

        in his eyes he
        glares at her

3

don't walk so fast
when you take her to school
I saw you yesterday
    you made her run all the way
don't think you even noticed

yes well no she didn't complain

but it looks
            cruel

4

i want to run
down the hill

ok but take care
i will but why
don't you run too

oh i'm a bit tired

yes that's because
you sit so much
      at night

Poemology

an apple a day
is 365 apples

a poem a day
is 365 poems
most years

any doctor will tell you
it is easier to eat an apple
than to make a poem

it is also easier
to eat a poem
than to make an apple
but only
just

but here
is what you do
to keep the doctor
out of it:

publish a poem
on your appletree

have an apple
in your next book

That Old Sauna High

to make the vapor-bath
a frame   3 sticks
meet at the top

stretch woolen cloth
take care
the seams are tight

a tent   and into it
a dish
with red-hot stones

then take some hemp-seed
& creep in

the seed
onto those stones:
at once
great smoke!
"gives off a vapor
unsurpassed
by any bath
we have in Greece"

410 B.C.
eyes watering
by candlelight
Uncle Herodotus
penned these instructions

adding "the Scythians
enjoy it so
they *howl* with pleasure"

getting so clean
all clean   inside

Who Walk By

who walk by
    who walk on by
are a tune in my head

o lovely daughters
  to come

    to walk
and talk with him everywhere
        my son

    when he has grown
        to hear
            that tune

In the Octagonal Room

to see
Blake's earth
Mother Christ

1790
the color of
clay

holding small
men to his breasts

to see through
the blood
that flows from

the inner
hinge of
the eyelid

in '62
when darkness
prevails

cruelty
blinds you

where
such clarity
rests

Requiem for a Princess

(Marilyn)

come & see the sleeping beauty wake!
the rocket cavalry charge her
womb-caves; write your name to pulse
forever on these purple walls
be voltage   one out of 500 million
charging her making her

jump & smile   jump & smile

till the lines harden
& in the seething
mirrors she saw   death

*

she made him a bed
drownd in a sack
shot in the back
he sat on her head

paper tits tommyguns boys
mouthing 'love' with gunmetal eyes
plaster the murderous walls
in Berlin anywhere in the world with her
glossy & naked awaiting
rape
            there is no
love in it
                  it is the same
falsity
              stop
stop fucking yourself
dead things with dead things

*

yet she whom they broke
bottles in trampled

across blew up
& out of her mind

is now with the other
who is oviform dark &
seldom shows her eyes

whose crime it was not
whose crime it is not

hear she is singing
to her by the river the black
water o my
daughter:

*

ballooning you rose
sea-born   froth & white softness
into our eyes our mouths
by claws! you had fallen
into   on the dry
land   now yours
are closed
                    & nothing
could ever come out of you

the river the black waters
have you   let you go a-
way   back where
those who are liquid
& no hardness go:
not
        ever
                dust

sea
        rose unborn again
blind breasts will open
in the deep & be
two flowers without name:
awaiting no one.

Out of the 'Kalevala'

1 *hero, riding*

riding
July
mosquitoes
trees

birches   few holy
oaks

forget not the spells:
oak spell snake spell
spell against dwarfs
dwell in the ground
sleeping are any handful earth

evergreens
pines
rocks   grow larger
trees
low   up north

riding thinking singing

    see her turn
    golden
    below the charred beams
slanteye
bluehair
remember how round o those daughters!

long night
9 moons dark
nipples marshberries
far apart

    long hair   swung
    cross buttocks
    broad belly

surprised:
his eyes in the door
turn   golden
charred beams

his thoughts hardly
thoughts   flames
in the round-cobble hearth
lick softly through

2   *troll, chanting*

moom moom
hear my call
moom moom
speak to me
mother   father
lands   sea
moom moom
in your room
I   we   all
hear my call
in you are
toad   star
moom moom
are you far
moom moom
are you near
moom moom
moom moom
you are here
I will hear
moom moom
moom moom
moom moom
          moom

3 *maiden, singing*

they say she was
this one who sang

dawn sunrise
set and dusk
    come at night
    smell my musk

dusk   sunrise
set and dawn
loverman loverman
where you gone

dusk   dawn
sun rise and set
. . .

dawn   dusk
sun set and rise
on eyes   lies   hope he dies

sunrise   sunset
dawn and dusk
        came and
        left me
        here   a husk

    . . .

who sang   was
beautiful
        his once   who sang
        sweet invocations
                        in her ear

The Claim

here
the first cold night in November
reading another
tame poet
his 700-year-old troubles
with a lady whose name has been lost
as immaterial no doubt
but troubles they were
no doubt
cold moon

"her anger has caused me great pain
yet she won't stop fighting me
but hopes that I'll free her
now that I'm leaving
for the Holy Land"

his job
to amuse and delight
and whom? the bishop of Passau
and boon companions

"may god let me burn in Hell
if I do so — come hell-or-high-water
not for one day
will I give up
my claim on her"

imagine
the roars e.g. Arch-
bishop Engelbert the crusader
(visiting / of Cologne)
falls off the chair rolls on the floor
"clever bastard *bi got*!"
("fat asshole I hope
the infidel prick your paunch")

"though well do I know she'll desert me
at the drop of any plumed hat in sight
yet what gain does she think that'll be

not for one day or night
can I lose thought of her"

and she
sitting there with the old enigmatic
some Countess
or Margrave of Meissen's spouse
with little enough to conceal
perhaps a flicker of it
for the old bore
(old boar)
knowing he'd only
made it all up in the Provençal fashion
his job to amuse and delight

so I guess he rode off
good Albreht von Johansdorf

"how love begins
I know full well
but how it ends
I do not know"

fellow
concisionist

to the Colonial Wars

they say he knew Walther
the bird-willow
Vogelweide
who was a success with the ladies
but when sick old and pious
after all the *tandaradei*
lumped them together
and bid Her goodnight
Lady World

it may come to that yet
though it seems a long way
and Albert's my man
(who knew him they say)

but poets make poor friends
November nights any century

hang too much on themselves
and should praise their luck
if they find one to love and fight
cause them great pain and joy
betimes

though if she'll listen to their *vers*
in the mood intended
                                        is doubtful
all of her having finer ears
than even the Walthers
        for the false notes

                which is
                precisely why
                they try

not for the engelberts
even when multiplied five
        or ten thousand in stadium or hall
nor for the other hound-dogs
howling too

                cold moon
        cold moon and how many tonight
on their last Crusades
        and their Bishops and Kings
                hellbent
on really making them
                the last

                "but how it ends
                I do not know"

but how I know
it does not end
until we do.

II: 1966–1967

In the Long View of Human History Man's Reliance on Fossil Fuels Can Be But a Short Episode

the moving houses are very moving
as they move slowly into the sea

The Moving Houses Are Very Moving as They Move Slowly into the Sea

in the long view of human history
(darting from hut to hut)
man's reliance on fossil fuels can be but a short episode

if the earth disappears
there remains all that is not the earth
there remains the joy of being first in one place
and then in one another

Gales and Showers

"o foolish father! o foolish mother"
— BENDEDICT RAWORTH (AGE 2)

bits slamming around inside

WANTED: director
for the center of gravity

breath goes in and out
why worry about it

now let us all stop trying to sound as coherent
as we aren't

o foolish fathers o foolish mothers
your children sit staring at you
small disapproving owls

"WHA' HAPPUND?"

o nothing daddy fell down he'll get up in a minute
I think he's trying to write a poem

having written it he'll proceed at 3000 m.p.h.
to the nearest poetry festival

and we won't see him
for a while

Bang Bang with a Silencer

watching the screens
all that dying

    the mind goes faster
    won't stop to wait for words

        "maybe there will be a time"
        two pairs of feet in the snow
        "you remind me of someone"
        "me"
        "I used to know"

taxi clock ticking

        no connectives or interval music

                airfields and freezing winds

walk faster comrades
into the time that will be

Le Jazz Hot

talked to my father again in a dream he seemed happy
perhaps a little older than the last time   told me
he had discovered something called *'le jazz hot'*
and found it of some interest

Los Sedentarios

most of the time we sit down
to write 'sitting down' down

Mark Twain made a contraption
enabled him to be funny in bed in writing

Goethe and Hemingway
risked varicose veins at the highdesk

sitting down we get
fat round the ass

short poems
not too frequent
are the least fattening

if you're sitting down while reading this
now is the time to get up

III: 1967–1969

Bits of Soft Anxiety

dreamt: crossroads
drove straight ahead
arrived then with some confusion beating of wings sound of great
    engines et cetera
in a strange country where things kept falling on him & out of him
they didn't hurt but caused some anxiety nevertheless
maybe they were just cherryblossoms
maybe it was just his old difficulty of remaining in the upright
    position of the higher primates
maybe it was May
as it was in the other place where he spent most of his happy
    waking time

Your Friend

he said this
he said that
when pressed
as to which
he said nothing at all

in his country the weather
was mostly rainy

he tried to ride horses
they didn't go   or went
too fast

he punched them in the head
he fell off them

he tried to love women
tried to write poems

even his fellow men
their wives their children and cattle
he tried to love

but he didn't know
how or what was
or was good for him
at all

whatever it was
it kept punching him
in the head to make him
fall off

so he blamed them for it
all of them fellow men women
children cattle poems and horses

many a rainy
day you could hear him
yelling 'it's all
your fault'

after that things
were all right for a while
until the next try

Two after Reverdy

1

a painting with no background at all or
a minute's rest then the star
comes down from the ceiling and covers her eye
a silver shutter replaces the other

he put his hand on her hand
sky   through crack in the ceiling
a glitter
            venetian blinds like bars of a pretty cage

and in the street
as they descended

the same words as ever
someone is leaving
                    no time for goodbyes
in the dark there remained
the light of their eyes

2

"what happened
give us the story
let no one else say
another word"

he laughed
the street was dark   gently
night fell on the mind
turning corners

back there
hands joined
kneeling on mounds of stones
all those who forgave him
out of their bursting hearts

starry eyes   names
choked giggles lost
telephone numbers
wham   the wind
scattered them all

on into echoless dark
he looked at the sky
at the wall at the ground at the water

story   regret

all gone
from that corner when he returned

Sunset with Blame

you started it all
    and again
        she said   *you*

        THE BLAME
    came rolling straight at him

            chanted
        I'm yours I'm all yours

        into the sunset
            he rode with it

On The Occasion of Becoming an Echo

the goddess stands in front of her cave
waves me into the drawing   eyes
like an afterthought
dotted in   green

Gaia   drawn by a six-year-old
very clear

many more things in this room
books chair a bed
at least two people
(how many more in their dreams)
but the signals are garbled
garbled

I mean (he says
who is I   who *is* I?)
mean well I want the whole world to love me
not need me at all

the goddess stands in front of her cave
not waving me in   just raising her hands
as if to say 'well   who's to tell you?'
once upon a time
my head says   there was a man he got very tired
he went to sleep and didn't dream
didn't even sleep but was gone

out
and out there
all things were clear

The New Style Western

the two horsemen
on opposite banks of the Rio Grande
shook
their fists
then solemnly turned
their knobble-kneed steeds
and rode away

they would be back
but not in this movie
which was about the strange and amusing ways
prairie dog
owl and rattler have
of living together

The Walking Catfish

1

here
I give you
a *walking catfish*

(it is a present)

2

oh
you don't like it
the catfish *I* gave you?

3

see
it's walking away now

all the way back to Florida

4

(narrative)

we decided to pursue the walking catfish. we found it in the nick of time: it was about to enter the Iowa River, on the north side. after some serious discussion we agreed to let bygones be bygones, and it followed us back on its strong fins.

Found Fellow

for Gary Snyder

knick-knack-minded
I carried him out of the head shop

2 inches tall
2 inches wide   all round

a bear   I thought

making up for enormous belly
with pointed snout face
(the way some fat people do)

wrong   he's a badger
THE badger
likes to drink saké
sing and dance

big belly's for drumming
cock   huge   long as his legs
for making big-bellied girls
(surprising them in their sleep)

"I didn't do nuthin'
badger did it"

whose name is Little Hole-Bear

badger badger burning bright
stomping gladly through the night

holy hole-lover
Japanese
            soul brother

Elegy

the laundry-basket lid is still there
though badly chewed up by the cat
but time has devoured the cat
entirely

The Resemblance

hey did you just see the man who looked like a camel
we saw in the zoo who looked just like a man
we saw in the street who looked at you
just like a camel?

Shu

*

orange Schubert

*

this
my car

Big Battered Shoe

*

****

my white powwow lettuce shoes

****

— *Tamsin Hollo*
(b. 1965)
November 1967

Good Stuff Cookies

2 gods
⅔ cup hidden psychic reality
2 teasp. real world
¾ cup sleep
2 cups sifted all-purpose iridescence
2 teasp. good stuff
½ teasp. pomp & pleasure

beat gods   hidden psychic reality
real world and sleep together
sift together iridescence   good stuff
pomp & pleasure
add to real world mixture
drop by teaspoon
2 inches apart   on cookie sheet
press cookies flat
with bottom of glass   dipped in sleep
bake at 400 F   8 to 10 minutes

2 dozen cookies   good stuff

Love Is All You Need

it was 'one of those days.' everything went wrong & then to top it off, my wife came home complaining of a rough day. I had just burned the potatoes, & all I needed was for her to ask how I could do something so stupid.

as so often happens, we were quickly in the midst of an all-out argument. but one glance at our six children watching was enough to bring me back to my senses. I stopped suddenly & said instead, "oh forget it & put your arms around me. Can't you see that I'm just tired & need a little love?"

it's hard to be in a bad mood when everyone is hugging & kissing you. I can't think of a nicer way to spend the evening.

Frank Bull Moose
Horse Nose Butte, North Dakota

The Finnish Experience

1

the finnish language
so different from all other european tongues
is a great stumbling block
to the exploration of the less frequented parts
of the finnish interior

but the enterprising & intelligent traveler
armed with a handbook or a dictionary
can easily make his way & enjoy
not only scenery & life
which comparatively few tourists have witnessed.
but also excellent sport

in winter he can shoot as many wolves
as he chooses to pursue on a sledge
with a sucking pig as a lure

the pig is kept in a bag
& made to squeak
by twisting his tail

upon which the wolf darts out from the dark forest
& attempts to seize his prey

the traveler then tucks the pig away
& proceeds to take aim

— *Thomas Michell, "Russian Pictures": The Religious Tract Society, London 1889*

2

when my mother was but a young lass from germany, moved to finland for a life with my (then, future) father, they were invited to dinner, a formal academic occasion, & she was seated next to a dignitary chosen for his command of spoken german. it was a long dinner, with many speeches, given in finnish, a ugric language my mother did not understand. the only attempt at conversation her neighbor-at-table managed, was the statement: "this is good pig, is it not" (in german, of course). she is still fond of the story, fifty years later.

Rain

one evening when we were lounging in his apartment in a relaxed mood, sniffing a little cocaine, Charles Baudelaire said to me: "you know, everybody has seen rain falling — most people have, at one time or another, actually noticed it."

I agreed with a chuckle. he continued, "you know, I think we can be fairly confident that it has been raining, on & off, for a very long time!"

having said this, he collapsed on the *chaise-longue,* in a veritable *paroxysme*; but as always, there was a tinge, a definite tinge of bitterness in his merriment.

"it would be absurd to imagine," he said, "that rain could ever have behaved in any way different from that which we observe today . . ."

after a moment's crystalline silence our conversation drifted to other topics — the day's gossip, the inexhaustible genius of Edgar Poe. but when we stood on the fire escape, taking leave, he gazed over my left shoulder into some indefinable distance or abyss and said, almost dreamily: "it is for ever washing the substance of the land into the sea."

A Floor Like San Marcos's Ceiling

& moving a small sheet of glass
over it   with the tips of his fingers

what he had was music

or was it water

like the record he found on the beach
a few seconds later

put it on like a glove
& it sang

he liked the dream
he was me
& all the music was mine

all the music

Out of This World

astonishing
complexities:

a Volkswagen bus
full of greens

*

Iowa City crickets
September nights
don't have that much to say

but say it & say it & say it

"scribble scribble
eh Mr Pound?"

*

Cheyenne,
Wyoming.

a known
town on Mars.

*

ah Anna Bloom
sweet ginger muff

*

young girls walk

jointed
disjointed

no one to plug them in

don't let the exo-skeletals take them

they are the moon

*

"let's make it to the rock hole"
the spirit children sing
& men & women   in their bodies
do   that   thing

*

brother immortal
jellyfish
"brighter than
the brightest star"

what do you know of wars
here on TV

poetry workshops   pills
the Naga question

or Dr Sigmund Freud
the famous hypnotist

there's none could cure you
of your ignorance

I mean that's great

we love you as you are

*

here
in the Upper Devonian Sea
life is quiet
even the thousands of hogs
make but little noise

*

dark blur girl
rushing
past in a car

a lifetime.
where was she going

*

hi —
late summer.
all
is forgiven.

*

Ovidius Naso
wrote a book

Sir Vincent Wigglesworth
created a giant caterpillar

here
I put them together

(you do too)

*

Thales of Miletus
loved
this humid universe

there are
such advantages

to walking on 2 legs

& in carrying
one's brain in one's head

let the galaxies
ride!
Thales

it's been a long time
between drinks

The Swinger

Uca Pugnax
the fiddler crab
keeps time

keeps time with itself
maintains the rhythm
(changing color)

keeps time with the cosmos

keeps
good company
(us)

The Atlantic Fire-Worm

in the good season
time of full moon

the female emerges
surfaces
brilliantly luminous

the male loves that light
o the male loves that light

Gone to Egypt

no clothes on   there's the moon
& he's too old   (ta-ram)

Menelaos
        remembers

    her white
    & strangely cold
        ass
            too often

    "it nibbles my mind

        I watched her

                much"

They

    active mostly at dusk or at night
secretive   living mainly in mind
or underneath stones
    in shore zones

What Happened to a Young Man in a Place Where He Turned to Water

1

no sleep for 12 days

then found himself in a circle of water girls

"come dance with us"

water people
they say
were dancing with him

ahead of the water they came
they were water
the water's soft feathers were theirs

closer they came
& to the very end of the water
closer & closer
their hands were electric

fog people
danced with him they say
where the fog was a wall
they came
they were fog
the fog's soft feathers
were theirs

closer they came
to the very end of the fog
closer & closer
their hands were electric

the moon before him they say
high as a woman's head
or no higher

the sun before him they say
no higher than a man's head
or as high

"come dance with us"

again no sleep for 12 days

2

he woke up and saw
one had stayed

remembered stumbling
over her foot in the dance

they say those two went away
to where the country is great with maize
there they sat down

they went where the country grows pumpkins
tremendous pumpkins
there they lay down

big maize big root big stalk
sweet pumpkin long tendrils wide leaves

where the sun rises
soon as it sets

pollen & dew

3

he came back here where people were living

his mother was angry but she forgave him

he went & hunted the deer with his brother

(White Mountain Apache)

The Twins

the twins were fighting
their mother surprised them

one of them yelling
"life? no such thing!"

the other shouting
"death? no such thing!"

when they saw her
they stopped
fell back into sleep

their argument
open for ever

open
        this world

to life
to death

(Coeur d'Alene)

Song for a Sleeping Brother

my brother has taken sleeping pills
thus   he is sleeping
if he has taken a lot of them
he'll sleep a long time

the sleeping pills do not sleep but dissolve
inside my brother
if he goes on sleeping too long
he will dissolve too

I wish his grief would dissolve
I wish his pain would dissolve

the sleeping pills will be gone
I do not wish my brother to go

The Anvil

> "Can the sight of an ant reach to the
> far-off Pleiades? And can this insect
> lift an anvil?"
>
> — FARID AL-DIN ATTAR

sunday morning
hymns on the radio

my father (dead)
cried over radio hymns
in a house of green sunlight
one early summer

for his father
mother brother
shot dead at 30

muertos *muertos*

none of them went to church much
most of them got to the graveyard all right

one great uncle
hyphenated or no
never died
he disappeared in Arizona

his friend came back
blacksmith
proud with a Springfield rifle

what's the use counting

strokes on the anvil

Two Epitaphs

1 (Juan Agustin Palazuelos)

your friends stand around amazed
to merge in the afternoon light

*

fire on the mountain
                                        my friend
the inn
burnt down
                                        my friend
no more news
in this world
from you   my friend.

2 (David Sandberg)

a letter
on green paper
wrapped round a stick of incense

a pool of blood
on top of the pyramid

these
      in my nostrils

your light
in the Sun's

3

america is
crickets at night

like any place south
both greek & roman
would feel at home in

america is
likewise
nowhere

& they both made it there
for ever now

From the Big Moon (Non-Verbal Songbook)

drums tambourines
and a boss bass guitar

    Big Moon has many houses
    in and out he moves
                                        becomes
    sheer raga sound

one day we'll all
get on Big Moon
be gone

problems polar bears
sick polar bears and all

                        signed yours
                        the convalescent polar bear

He She Because How

one a.m.
          and she has been sleeping
two hours
          is still asleep

didn't marry him 'only to sleep'
but does now
               sleep

because she's tired because
he's been unkind? because

feeling her bones through her sleep
on the floor in their other room

because she's her kind of woman
because he's his kind of man

and because she is sleeping
                              he's writing
moving a few of his smaller bones

words like love and hurt
kindness unkindness blindness
ecstasy jealousy anger
sweetness
           that too
sweetness of making it with you

how do those words hang together
how does his hand move the pen

how do he (plus) she (equals) it hang together
on their still beautiful
(though in his case
                     slightly bent) frames?

two a.m. questions
now make him sleepy too

he'll go wake her up

they won't feel the same

The Great French Poet

François Villon was beautiful people

he went around treating people like shit

at least he had the decency
to disappear

but he keeps cropping up
like in this poem
which is for the people

like in a mouthful
of snow

Going Upstairs

"the colors must be incredible"

speaking of planets
like Jupiter

"it's a known fact"

like candy and coconuts

or heavenly / earthly
love

its ferry moments

breathing them in
he got up
"I'll be back in a minute"

then found himself lost
in a methane world

where sad / unsad
were all different too

Song: Chablis Almadén (4 a.m.)

"this *sprightly* white wine"
he said to himself
drinking it
keeping warm
glad to be in
the whirring house

closing the book
(*not a word* by d. alexander)

his head felt new

and he took it
and laid it
next to hers

put some of her hair on his face

Swirl

Rock Island Line   hoot hoot
owl with sheet metal sound box
travels the night

stately contrast to moth
battling itself to death
on the poet's lightbulb

keep your eyes on the road

reading the works of Dafydd Jones
my head starts swerving

falling apart
coming together

aging
beauties
wood or Armagnac

Josephine's sleeping
remembers her dreams

her

I find hard
to leave
alone

to cease
from touching
talking to her
twenty-four hours a day

owl on my desk
has eyes
two eyes six breasts
is Japanese
wood
is a thing de ce monde

the Tutelar of the Place
spreads her mantle
"now go to sleep
keep your eyes on the road"

Poem with Dragon and Elephant

for Ted Berrigan

sonic boom

dragon trails

"all over this land"

saw red flowers
tulips I thought in a window across the street

a few minutes passed
the elephant fell in love with a millimeter

and they were gone

it made me sneeze
being the past   elegiac tense

there was some green left
the stalks

still stalking you
on vapor trails

all over this head   full of sky

Waiting For a Beautiful Bather

"back in the sixties"   my god!
        the *incredible* string band

shaggy
like Custer
                        my dog

(like he's sixty-four)
(but much hairier
        than a parking meter)

                                                    that
                                            was the english voice

        mr Roger
        MacGuff
how's your television show

it's the inner macguff
we have to combat

        and we do so constantly

faithfully rendering the sound
                                    (la percussion)

the car will run ok   once we put an engine in
        then we can go riding to hounds
(Custer would love that)

                        come on out of that bath

Up

Iowa City night
people walk past the house & sneeze

tomorrow's September
I'm glad
I'm not past sneezing either

red working bandanna round my head
I look at things:

        little green plastic
        brontosaurus

your retail price is ten cents
American Money

glint glint
                  (us wits)

I'm so full of shit
it comes out so pure

                        but then there is you
                        & more every day
                        I can't comprehend it (my
                        sidelong glances
                        at your form)

        I want to be
        the ageing yet lovable beast
        to her beauty
        that is from within her

Wave

for Josephine

white framed your face though you hadn't
just stepped out of a bath

oh the tree
                    branches

a wuthering   a
being *inside* a wave as it travels

and this has traveled with me all day

Tried to Remember Something to Cheer Me

(for the first reader)

great big hand
grabbed the goddam car

threw me all over   the goddam city

days later tried to remember
something to cheer me

"let a cloud walk by
in a toad's golden eye"

(that was nice   I think I wrote that)

& then
I had it:

                    it was a giggle
                    it was a sea
                    anemone

for a second
dear reader
we touch

all the way back to Ibiza.

Llanto & Short Discourse on Method

seasonal changes in shape of head

the tune   any tune   give us a tune
El Che is dead   long live Moomintroll!

the sucking of babes
resounds
in these universes

out there
a granny neighbor descends
into a yellow container

she has her obolos
to take her across the Iowa River

out there is a long way
from say Brazil

they took out 2 of his friends
& blew their brains out

over & out
to you good Lindolf

(who thought he saw Zoroasters bloom
in these verses)

now sits in his valley
& I in mine

it's all falling out
the other end.

the method is to swim jerkily
eat all the algae   microscopic animals
organic debris
swept into mouth by water current
created by waving limbs

Down & Up

buzz

Louis Armstrong (68) says it's a wonderful world
he loves it

easy to *love*
bison & indian
see   there they stomp through the sky

I *loves* you
but i can't find him   buzz   buzz buzz

The World Seen As A Huge Impenetrable Granite Arse
would Wallace Stevens have loved *that*
for a title

buzz
hand
long way off
arm stuck to paper
"enemy fly"

disregard it!

still a few things
unelucidated
might even prove
a great pleasure

buzz 1 minute buzz

"everyone who cares about the industry hopes that each young or new operator to appear on the scene may be the one to bring forth the whole magnificent potential of *kelp* — & thus realize the promise that *kelp* makes in age after age but seldom succeeds in keeping."

buzz 3 minutes buzz

at last
when they thought
the world had to end in that rain

the drummer suddenly changed the song

and she the Sun
raised her face
so pleased at the sight of their dancing

She forgot her grief
and smiled.

Sun Star Hum

under the rule of Augustus
astrology was in fashion

Malampus Tiresias Chalcas Helenus
more celebrated than ever

the light
falls through the green

same as ever

Traveler

he was of the kingdom whose people bring destruction
love to wound kill & mutilate
                                                    for diversion and amusement

over them reigned a red personage
always inclined to hurt strike kill

but sometimes seduced by the fair-faced queen
of the other kingdom
                                    whose people were charming
loved gaiety and festivities
whose natural disposition inclined them
to the good & the beautiful

when they heard of evil & ugliness
they were seized with disgust

a woman reigned over them
all men believed all women were of that kingdom
unfortunately this was not so

so he decided to emigrate
to a kingdom whose people were tiny and slow
who passionately loved the arts of the writer
the sciences of the stars
                                        theurgy   magic
had a taste for subtle occupations & deep works

we haven't had a word from him since
they probably changed him utterly
or dissolved him in *acqua fortis*

As It Is

there are snippets of understanding
& there are snippets of connections between these snippets

at the best   there is a vague memory of details
which have recently been attended to

like reading the Whitehead snippet
recalling a redhead snippet

De Amore

1

love-I   — thou —   me-off-pisset

Hopi Catullus

2

sponges are simple
colonial animals

attached & submerged
they grow

in autumn some sponges
form *gemmules*
small round structures

when the colony dies
in cold weather
they drop to the bottom

& the following spring each gemmule
becomes a new sponge

reading this I can see
old love what it is
we forgot

3

consider time
                              mon amour
      identities of time
a time of days   a time of fishes

drops of time   each drop
      with its own skin of surface time

& when I'm with
                              & partly within you
      it's a moment in time
      'devoid of any temporal spread'

4

the Power Return on the new typewriter

strikes the glass

the wine goes all over the desk

I love you

everything's changed for the best

xi–xii: 69

Sensation No. 27

OR,

THE BOOK CALLED *BOOK*

1969–72

---

it is a well-lit afternoon
& the heart with pleasure fills
flowing through town
in warm things
yes what do you know
it's winter again
but the days are well lit
what's more
they're beginning to stay that way longer
that is a fact
& i am moving
through a town
in a fur hat
the third one in my life
or is it only the second?
the expeditionary force will have to check up on that
back there in the previous frames
while i move forward
steadily, stealthily,
like a feather
i am a father
bearded & warm
& listen to words coming through
the fur hat off a page
in the finnish language:
"when there's nothing else to do
there's always work to do"
my father said that
in one of his notebooks
& it's true
i walk through a town
& up some steps
& through a door
it closes
now you can't see me anymore
but the lights go on, & you know i'm there
right inside, working out

Touring

window of room nine
college city motel
northfield minnesota
& a fraction to the weaker side of a winter's heart
"white country"
peter schjeldahl's book
& this is his home town
& white country is what one sees here
& then one sees a matchbook it says
"thank you for stopping"
one has stopped here one feels the light (la lumiere)
moves faster sliding across these acres of snow (la neige)
one worries about the future of bears
in public in one house
this is known as a poetry reading
then one proceeds to drink gallons of cider in public
in another house
this is known as getting crocked
one remembers the cider junkies of somerset england
exceeding pale eyes in exceeding pale faces
the weird sheen in the paintings of samuel palmer
back in room nine one's brain scanner flickers & zooms
across these endless heartlands of the heart
(el corazon)
the telephone does not function (no funciona)
after the hour (la hora) of eleven p.m.
back in new york & london back in iowa city
back in cuidad de ibiza & paris
one then goes dark
in the college city motel
in northfield minnesota

---

between bouts
i keep in shape
for visitors
from e.g. thibet:
a cock
signifying craving & greed
a snake
signifying wrath & passion
a pig
signifying ignorance & delusion
they just decided to drop in
but i tell them all
gettahellouttahere
the western way

---

in love we loaf
munching love's loaf
it is a fortunate condition
it is a preoccupied porcupine
going about mother maya's business
on an ardent spring night
taking this deep a breath is ardent
like diving
up up & away
keeping the harp in tune
even here, where we are
amerika, no one knows you
but loafing & loving
upon your mighty body
remnant mind & trembling heart
we may yet escape
"planet x goes kablooey"
"bang bang! wowee! that's neat"
no it ain't, son
except in the most particular way it happens
continually, in your skin
your flesh, your bones, your art
which is what keeps it going, you understand

Art & Literature

let me recommend
the "dennison" series of seals
the twenty-five cent booklet
"cat seals" in particular
it contains a wonderful persian
electric blue fur
& amber eyes
it's a classic!
gerry gilbert has created a classic, too
it's called "phone book"
you order it from weed flower press
seven five six bathurst street toronto canada
a dollar and a half, & you should act now!
the grass sits mumbling under the snow
memorizing its survival techniques
must end this now
there's folks drooping in

---

long hours one labors at the desk
to come up with these funny
little chunks
like samson agonistes
all for the birds or anthologists
one has a staggering cold today
but one can read
unlike the unfortunate
eighteen point five million americans
who can't
"the tibetan mysticism of john 'tantric' blofeld"
"wishes lies & dreams"
"american indian lives"
staggering lives
the world loves
"the world anthology"
but no one even likes "british poetry since 1945"
which is just a roomful of music boxes
confidently playing "lara's theme"
but one does like one poem in it
peter pewter's haiku "alone in the kosmos"
it's so brief one quotes:
"i kneel by the infinite sands of the stars.
my hat blows off the planet.
dinner is in doubt."

Old Space Cadet Speaking

let me tell you, the captain knew
exactly what he would do
soon as he reached the destination
he would fuse with her
plumulous essence
& they would become a fine furry plant
later travelers would run their sensors over
to hear it hum
its favorite song
"call me up in dreamland"
by the old minstrel known as "the van"
ultimate consummation of long ethereal affair
he knew he would miss
certain things small addictions
acquired in the colonies
visual images baloney sandwiches
but those would be minor deprivations
hardly bothersome in the vita nuova
he was flying high
he was almost there
& that is where
we leave him to go on hurtling through the great warp
& at our own ineffable goals

---

at this point, the moon
starts to take on a little brown & gray
as opposed to being so very bright
as it appears from earth

*

up in the andes
an old peruvian
in a featherwork mantle
sits listening to his god
his god is playing looney tunes
on the organ of novelty
while down below in iowa city
a small dane is freaking out in a drugstore
shoving & beating on the other customers
yelling this is my drugstore my drugstore
get out get out
the proprietor calls the cops
& they take him out
because it isn't his drugstore
a large unclear device explodes in alaska
furious hurricanes sweep through the banana fields
old man in featherwork mantle
knows the innate beat of all things
he is engaged in expressing unobservable realities
in terms of observable phenomena
a great body
of tender & intimate works
to sleep beside him
later
like a large friendly lioness
who loves me
the old peruvian

---

apollonius
his mother
walks in a meadow
she lies down on the grass &
goes to sleep
some wild swans
at the end of a long flight
approach her & by their cries
& beating of wings
awaken her
so suddenly
he is born

---

on christmas day nineteen seventy
a small english girl from hampstead near london
walked several miles in sub-zero weather
to see the children's cartoon show at the hampstead cinema
but when she got there
it was closed!
the manager of this cinema happened to pass by
& he saw the little girl "crying & frozen almost blue"
he asked her why she was crying
she told him & he took out his keys & they went in
& he seated her in the empty stalls
& went into the projection room
& the show was *on*

*

that day he was the fastest man on earth

---

the performance of the world
can happen only through the energy
put forth in producing it
which is maya — the energy
put forth in producing
the performance of the world

---

on lake titicaca
era of giant tapirs
she stepped out of her craft
oreana
her skin the deep shade of gold
with weird webbed feet
& hands embraced the boss tapir
thus we began
who have two breasts like her
& intelligence
& a womb like hers
& a tool like the tapir's
thus softly we sing of her
our large-eared lady of tiahuanaco
who went back to her star

---

pocket-size water pipe
next to tarot pack with sun on its cover
flanked by some works
by alfred north whitehead & gregory corso
partly obscured by a green glaze jar full of feathers & pencils
now a hand appears in the air
it removes first the pipe
then one of the tomes of whitehead
finally a feather
smoke drifts over the scene
it is peaceful, peaceful
though there is faint hum of fellow beings next door
busy constructing bombs or other
wishes, lies & dreams
everybody
must
get
bombed

---

vibrant mutants of the future,
i love you!
but what can you do with this love
or a twentieth century fossil?
well, anyway
i love you to bring you about
that is what love is all about

---

across the incredible static of time place language
the air of june sings
& heaving the brick though the plate-glass
the people go crazy
head forward trunk back leg up arm down
indefinable heads in bulky suits
traverse the universe
can you see it going on & on
you minute bug
walking across the back of my hand
your life can be measured in minutes & now
i flick you off
that was one of the most exciting days of your life

---

sitting by the door
"making moccasins"
thinking about nothing
the sun is halfways down
at the end of the plain
i am talking to the lake
i am talking to all in the lake
i am not a human being
not only a human being
i am pit river shaman
i am jaime de angulo
i am anselm hollo
dog face
son of maya

---

after verlaine
right now
it is raining in iowa city
but it ain't rainin in my heart
nor on my head
because my head
it wears a big floppy heart, ha ha
it wears a big floppy heart

---

drinking some cheap but good wine
after tu fu
two thirty a.m.
using all this potential
not one minute of my life have i wasted
you drunkard poet uncles
i like you a lot
my nephews don't
they tired of the twang
you been putting out
but here, have some wine!
have a good cry

---

huginn & muninn
odin's twa corbies in orbit
extended his nervous system throughout
they were named after thought
& memory
they were sensational corbies

Impression du Matin

for Ted Berrigan & Alice Notley

hi, folks!
i sing
the cardio-vascular lotus, out of whom spring
channels to the number of one hundred & one
each of these branching
into a hundred channels
& these again into seventy-two thousand smaller channels
"as hair springs
from man's body
& is withdrawn again"
that was the cardio-vascular lotus speaking.
this is anselm,
on a spring day
on jupiter

*

land here!   *everything has been prepared!*

*

o thank you, thank you
now let us walk together
past all those kindly, weathered, mossy stone lions
& hear what the high folks on this planet have to say.

---

september nights
even the mastodons'
incessant farting
sounds muted,
autumnal

---

walked into grandfather
most literally
suddenly sat in his rocking chair
had only one thumb
wished i could stay, write his life
the one i never knew

---

through two layers of glass
the far end of this restaurant
a man
whose head is
a glob
of light
like anybody's
any body
he is formless form
by means of maya
& all her daughters, assumes
innumerable forms
of which i am one, eating out alone

The Discovery of LSD a True Story

the dose of a mere
fifty micrograms totally altered
the consciousness of professor albert hofmann
motel soda works intersection
swerve hit geode albert
inadvertently
inhaled it
blast core city ominous rock
spiraling rites of light
inhaled his consciousness
& exhaled
"phew! wow! pow! *zat* voss somsink!"

---

black elk speaks
black elk speaks & speaks
earth
heaven
walk away
black elk goes on speaking

(for Anne Waldman)

little asterisks cheer up the page
but poetry is blood
is dwarfs' drink
dwarfs' drunken ship kvasir
zonked? what
do you mean,
"zonked?"
can't hear you
i'm zonked
& the great god whose name is amplifier
feeds his strong signal into the goddess
whose name is speaker coil
& the quantity of air that is moved is huge
& the pressure of that air is heavy
& the sound is loud sweet lord it is loud

*

later, i go out & look at the sky.
it is one great asterisk.
& there are ships sailing in it
with lights & joyful singing,
the dwarfs' charter flight to earth
a mighty flotilla
come in to land
this giant night

---

hot moon, & still looking
at you, sideways
on country roads long ago
or a little crosseyed at times
but mostly focused on the continuous & projective field
we compose in our walking & talking dreams
where the lover stands ever
in unintermittent imagination of his belovèd
& electric current gives light
where it meets resistance
sweet resistance, sweet suck & push
suck & push, all we know
ever know as the splendors of paradise

Key Three, Arcana Major

here we go,
zapping about in the folds of her gown
of an ample cut & seed-pod design
her hair so bound in radiant energy
all twelve stars in her crown
it is the empress we live in
snug up against her skin
that once did open
to let us pass & be in
the born world

Nineteen Sixty-Five

sunday morning
naked woman, bending over
spitting a milky water jet into the basin
returning the toothbrush clack to the beaker
turning to wipe her mouth

cool body washed now & moving fast
changes, formations
pleasing to me as i sit on the can
smoking a pipe in the sun
comes through the blinds
my "zebra belly" remarked on by the daughter
three years old & well on her way
to that same build
though she can still be held
upon one palm
& she's in session too
on her blue plastic pot & even more
creatively engaged
she's threading wooden beads the while
whatever these two do
is interesting

"Dune"

beautiful woman, molecules
same as me
you &
your ass
so at home
in rivers
lakes
the sea
you're a very large vision
i believe
the largest vision i ever had
in the light's heart
at the head
of a legion of shaggy dragons
i salute you

---

the low black square

is a table
once upon a time
its legs were longer
but i sawed them off
i sawed & i sawed
one of them always shorter
than the other three & so
it got a little too low
in the end
kind visitors breathed
"ah, japanese"
& on the black square
the tile-red cylinder
is a pitcher we found in venice
we were happy there
in a pitcher we found in venice
there are flowers
they are flowers
they're just some flowers

I call your name
clear as joe brainard's prose
a summer's day
wondering where you are
just want you to know i have not forgotten you
since our meeting in toyland
snow starts falling
white as carpaccio's dog watching his master
write some more on the back of the postage stamp
long before the beatles &
i call your name

---

foghorns on the solent
rumble of rock island line
summer & autumn have passed without you
winter is making ready to occupy this space
vivaldi & coffee
a white man's morning
separated from you, white woman
there is a terrible shortage of you in this house

Double Martini

do you remember
i ask the stewardess
how madly in love we were?
when we were four years old
no, she corrects me
not four but fourteen my dear
fourteen through seventeen
& here we are
twenty years later & in a dream
her memory seems unimpaired
i kiss her fraternally
then go for a walk round the plane
in the surrounding blue
& through the windows i can still see her smiling
smiling, moving along, serving the lords of this world

Zooming

for Tom Raworth

she looked on him &
the moment she looked
there was no part of her
was not filled with love for him
& he too gazed on her
& the same thought came to him

*

"math, son of mathonwy"
two thousand years of formal design
romance, or: the goodies
we do get off
on those
as the big bird goes thundering through the sky
way up above the humpback whale & his cante jondo
the rose & the sword on one word is weird
"hey, miss
may i have another pitcher of gin?"

*

he placed his hand on her shoulder
& she set off & he along with her
until they came to the door of a larger fair chamber
& the maiden opened the chamber
& they came inside & closed the chamber
& no one ever saw them again
but an unceasing flow of wonderful sound poured forth
from that high radio tower
& there's that word now
walks past my window with two humans inside it
as yet unaware of its horrendous designs

the cut-rate shoe store: part of a landscape
otherwise restaurants taxicabs shower curtains
alcohol 'sheer romance'
'hell' & all that
like the more boring
like novelists
now in his sleep he walks past it again
stops stares at hundreds of shoes
all of an unequal shoeness
& sees what he was slow to see then
in the vast supermart of i-love-you
where immediately on arrival
he was handed a credit card

*

oh the gods took pity on me
mercifully they kicked my ass
made me come off it before i got hooked
for ever on third-rate third-person movies

"The Works"

one
it is fine
two
life is good
three
i would like to make love
four
you are trespassing on my territory
five
she's mine
six
how nice it would be to make love
seven
how nice to have made love

*

those are the works of the male grasshopper
i feel exactly the same way.

---

my first miss amerika
lopsided face
long legs
big ass
big heart
pleaded for me & cried
all over the senior citizens
who told her they come in all colors
shapes & sizes
but they are devils
& we must kill them

---

when a poet feels
like a sick owl
he writes
like a sick owl

*

when he was fifteen
sick owl climbed
horse nose butte
& ate some peyote
then he had a vision
he saw this huge owl being sick
all over north dakota
all over the biosphere

---

harrison, lennon, mccartney & starr
music on the roof of apple building
let it be
a farewell to civilization as they, & we, have known it

"Carolina Del Norte"

old platinum wool top black face dusty coat ladies
tottering down the road with big shopping
where i see them
half a second of their long time
then "men at work"
road gang
man with shotgun waves me on
one of the men with no shotguns
gives the black power salute
inhumanities over the radio
in the rented plymouth satellite
purring through some fine countryside
further polluting the planet
few billboards
but one with the stars & stripes & the message
"wallace for seventy-two"
"we don't particularly *care* for crazies here"
nobody said it
how come i heard it
me frodo
queasy rider
through schwarzwald nord-karolina night
hail mother of the gods!
wife of starry heaven, whose eye
is on the sparrow
to you it belongs to give means of life
to mortal men
& to take it away
happy the man whom you delight to honor
freely bestow upon me for this my song
substance that cheers the heart
& now i will remember you
& another song also
"remember me
to one who lives there"
twelve hundred miles in this capsule
three jet-hours in another
let me ride easy
all the way back
to where my hands & eyes are upon her

Antioch Illinois

why are the bronze men chasing hercules?
why does the automobile go grraahhkk! & stop altogether
because things in the sky kah-boom
because the water hose burst

Strange Encounter

megalomaniac
midgets
exist
but uneasily.
yes,
officer.
no,
officer.
my name is
kid sky.
i live in
the elevator.
"you're under arrest."

Wall Poem

the difficulties are great
the difficulties are not great
the handle keeps falling off
the difficulties are awful

---

lights, blinking
up at the plane:
masses of greedy
little creatures
like you & me
using up the earth
for drinks at thirty thousand feet
& mines in haiphong harbor
"no quarter!"
the voice says,
"no quarter!"
& on the ground,
in a well-lit tunnel of sheer desperation
i look to get change for a quarter to make a call
but i don't need it,
here they come, up
two brave co-denizens of hell
to meet me
as if it made sense, &
"hell-o!"
&
"you're thinner"
& yes, i say
yes i am thinner, & my hair's turning gray
& they are deporting me, & there is no way
any of this will ever be made to work again
but it is good to see you

"To Be Born Again"

inside my mother
i make a little fist
& then i punch her
enter another plane
walk right into it
the roaring begins
a few hours later
i stride ashore
"welcome to america"
"th-there's a l-lot of b-bastards out there!"
william carlos williams
one moment please
to adjust machine
two a.m. in bed
says "come on out"
some one in my head
"you've been forgiven"

---

good morning!
when the big grid
shorts out
it's curtains
curtains
going up
on the new world
where horse-borne man
is an awesome thing

On Gopher Hill

at times it seems merely a question of how to abdicate
gracefully to those wide-eyed brothers & sisters
who dwell in the earth
but then i am gripped by tender desire
tender desire has me by the balls again
o wide-eyed
human sisters & brothers
it is merely a question of how to abdicate gracefully
to your embraces
& let *them* wait yet a while

---

the force of being she released in him being
equal to the creation of himself the universe is a place
where he would always want to find her touch
her get lost in the space
ships hailing each other with all the lights on
wires humming & speakers roaring
& a cup of mint tea with honey

---

cloud of dust or roses (rosé) in the head
of that intelligent monkey face man (rilke)
high on another world
another time
country & western time
earrings horseshoes clear lethal fountains
laughter shaking his mother maya's body & his
as he makes her his mistress
for ever or as close
as you get a book
or drive the big white 'car'
with the black 'interior'
through the exterior & its turning leaves

---

winter solstice
night & i burn
a handful of pine
needles
holding you in a high
window summer room
blowing my mind
where it belongs
to you, who knows
where to send it
spinning
white body galaxy
gran cairo
& an archer
on the wall
calendar, shooting the last
days' arrows in the heart

---

in the kitchen
at night
florence
& general electric
are large, square, & white.
florence
is quiet.
the general
occasionally hums
a tone-deaf ditty.
they're getting on.
they have their problems,
'malfunctions,' & such.
but they're still here, to help us.

---

rising to the dawn's cold beams
from the plantation of my dreams
i think of all those gone among
the savage peoples & frozen gases
the other side of the sun

(for Charles Olson)

reading a book
"on growth & form"
to get my head together
& i know it won't grow anymore
the cells are crying & dying
& as to the form well it always was an odd shape
but it's still taping
this book
by d'arcy thompson the dashing biologist
"with the looks of a viking"
& "northern mists"
by carl ortwin sauer
a very clear work
hardly anything else is
i'm tired
of thinking
of things
to say to her
trying not to look at her face
i read "northern mists"
because when i look
it makes me want
to say things & the things
i say
how ever true
are not very clear
it is january
& the world's ill
& the dying of a great being
growth & form
northern mists
& the cave so light so warm
as he reared up
& spread wide his arms

Anselm's Dreams

for Anselm George Berrigan

saint anselm of asota, le bec & cantebury, a.d. 1033–1109, who spent much of
his life attempting
to prove the existence of god by logic, "in plain language & by ordinary
argument, & in a simple
manner of discussion."

*

having heard from his mother, the good ermenberga
that there is one god in heaven above
he imagined, like a boy bred up among mountains
that heaven rested on the mountains
& thus the palace of god was there
& the way up to it was up the mountains
his thoughts ran much upon this

*

& on a certain night he dreamed that he ought to go up to the top of the mountain & hasten to the palace of god, the great king. but before he began to ascend he saw, in the plain which reached to the foot of the mountain, some women reaping corn, who were the king's maidens but did their work very carelessly.

the boy, grieved at their sloth, & re-buking it, settled in his mind to accuse them before the lord. so having pressed on to the top of the mountain, he came into the palace, & there found the king with only his chief butler for company, for all the household had been sent out to gather the harvest, for it was autumn.

so he went in, & the lord called him, & he drew near & sat at his feet. then the lord asked him with gracious kindness, who he was, whence he came, & what he wanted. he answered according to the truth, & then the lord commanded, & bread of the finest was brought to him by the chief butler, & he ate, & was refreshed before the lord & plumb forgot to tell him about the careless reapers.

& therefore, in the morning, when he recalled what he had seen, he believed that he really had been in heaven, & been refreshed by the lord's bread, & so he declared, before others.

*

thirty years later, abbot anselm sat apart in a corner of the church, to weep & pray for his friend.

from heaviness & sorrow he fell asleep & saw certain highly venerable personages enter the room where osbern had died, & sit round for judgment.

& while he was wondering what the verdict would be, osbern himself appeared, like a man just recovering, or pale. three times, he said, had the serpent risen up against him, but three times he fell back, & the bearward of the lord, ursarius domini, stood by his side & chased the serpent away.

*

then anselm awoke & knew that his friend was saved, & that the angels do keep off our foes in the beyond, as the bearwards keep off the bears.

---

grew up in finland
the south of the land
father philosophos & writer
wrote the works of cervantes in finnish
mother a talker & talker
all over the known world
but really my parents
you were giant white rabbit people
very wealthy & powerful
lived in a palace place
under elephant rock
thrones
robes
& a great golden light
strobed out from behind them

"Elephant Rock"

the huge weight
& granite shape of it
ten times the size of our house
billionfold growths
over its back and sides
the only country
ever known as the features of god

Nineteen Thirty-Nine

just sit here telling myself all these stories
when the sun is shining
on the granite & the veins in it & the veins
in the back of my father's hand
pine needles moss & the light the light
a great roaring silence
so spacious & hospitable
to the rising voice of my mind

---

one of the pines has a bend in it
three feet off the ground
the horse's back
about two feet
the neck then stretching straight up
to the sightless head of it
where it becomes so fine
there's no way of telling what goes on there

where was it i
fell asleep in the afternoon
& down
& into a hall
where forceful as ever in her big chair
he who was i there saw her
hum to a thin corner shadow
the brother pale rigid
not a sound then the sister
energy out of a door on the right
but i knew where he lay
went on & entered
the room light & bare
no curtains no books his head on the pillow
hand moving outward
the gesture "be seated"
i started talking, saw myself from the back
leaned forward, talked to his face
intent, bushy-browed
eyes straining to see
into mine
"a question i wanted to ask you"
would never know what it was
but stood there & was
so happy to see him
that twenty-sixth day of april
three months after his death

The Dimensions of The World

father
& son,
playing dominoes
& "casino"
tonight
as twenty-six years ago.
then, son
goes upstairs,
to bed.
"goodnight,
pardner."
& a good night
to you,
father
out there
in earth, water, fire, air

1969–1972

Some Worlds

it is said the chinese believe that the human eye

contains a tiny being of the human shape

which indeed it does, even here in the west

those tiny beings are my dearest readers

---

once in khairouan, south of tunis, a yellow kabyl dog bit me. it was the first time in my life, & i decided that he was right. he was simply expressing, in his own way, that i was in the wrong.

---

thus rainer maria rilke, in a letter to a friend. this rilke was a man who loved dogs & had a profound understanding of them. one of his sonnets to orpheus is not addressed to orpheus at all, but to a dog. it deplores the difficulties of communication between men & dogs, & i wish i could say (now, half a century later) that those problems have been solved, or that these very words are in fact written by a dog. but that would be telling a lie, & should a dog read this at some time in the future, he or she would immediately recognize it as such.

Amazing Grace

people going straight up to heaven

forty of them, in three hours

8.12.72
6–9 a.m.
indianola, iowa

anyone, say, a girl named may
who watches
                    say, humphrey bogart on the late show
go through customs in hong kong
                                        may, years later
if she herself actually goes
    through customs in hong kong
feel she is reliving the past,
                                the past
customs in hong kong

                                oh, absolutely

Gypsy Poem (1)

hey, god, old buddy, why did you
dump me here, & i
built a house, & the bailiffs
came round & tore it down
left me pisspoor
the peasants laugh at me
my woman is freezing to death
under the open sky
hungry & miserable, big tears
cascading down
all the way to her navel

Gypsy Poem (2)

when fall comes, the peasant feels
pretty good
he takes his blunderbuss &
stomps off to the woods
but us gypsies, we weep
for the end of summer

---

writing, damn hard. lake titicaca, the sun. "tell me, rudolf: what is love?" the rain in new york city chews little holes in your shift. she was lying against silken cushions upon a throne artfully constructed from a single large sulphur crystal. she brushed up the room, opened the windows, let fresh air in & made preparations for a delicious repast. the great seventeenth century philosopher & mathematician blaise pascal expressed a fear of the great spaces between the stars. microwave eyeballs. the train passed fairly slowly. she sang a celestial song & began to spin, & the thread seemed to unwind out of her breast

---

in high gravity worlds, structures are short & squat.
low gravity worlds are permitted more delicate forms.

Things to Do in Salzburg

walk, alone
the narrow lane from st. peter's
to cemetery, & abbey tavern
"doctor faustus drank here"
come home late
wine-warm, high on air
think of mozart, don giovanni
think, "i could really stand it here
for quite a while"

in 1926,
as my father.

---

when a proud beast, a complex chemical arrangement
possessed by memory, such as a human, or rabbit dies
        a tremendous amount of energy escapes
        back into the universe

        more than enough to write a thousand great
                poems

---

typewriter humming

yggdrasill growing

this thinking

is this writing

1972–1973

Black Book

Radio Free America

"with the powers of old
we play rock & roll"

the beam extends
from the top of the head
straight out to perfection
with no interference
from other components

it can then be employed to transmit
high priority constructs

*

the dog comes close, lies down, looks worried
or does he remember how sad it was
when there were only the two of us, waiting
for the United States borderguards
to let our Mistress return? a sorry sight
we were, to be sure. & all because of a bad joke
calling itself America, which is not its name

*

attending to certain
forms of insistence
lovers become those forms
& enter the core time
In which the tribe is permitted
to muddle on

*

we've been here long, long enough

to make the visible look the way we like it

World World World

the frightened camper watches the apelike monster
Big Computer is watching you
I am watching a huge
tree-cutting crane
rise up against a Dutch Elm
& cut it down

*

"Almagtig, keek, de ghroote clomp-cameel!"
I'm truly sorry
man's dominion
has broken nature's
social
union

        glassy stare of dying
albatrosses not at all unlike
        glassy stare of
men women & children

this *was* a magnificent specimen of the giraffe
observe its glassy stare

*

it is known that the Pygmy tribes
in Africa actually live in meadows of marijuana
& smoke it all the time
any chance that could be
what stunts their growth?
probably not
the Watussi tribesmen smoke it all the time, too
& they grow seven feet tall

*

"at the lake they found an old blind one
who had been left behind
they gave him food
but a straggler coming along later
shot him as he was crawling
to a spring for water
his bones lay on the ground for years
after the country was settled
his skull hung on a bush"

*

the oysters
brought from Long Island Sound
opened up
at the time the tide would have flooded
Evanston Illinois
if that town had been on the seashore
the scientists were delighted
the oysters were disappointed

*

El Presidente grinning through twenty
seconds of TV footage uttering total gibberish
for edifying experiences we must look elsewhere
out the window for instance
we see a great crabapple tree in full bloom
now of course it's just a tree
someone planted it
a number of years ago
probably a greater number than they had to go
many trees
live in the city
some of them right in front of windows
a gentle breeze animates their extremities

*

we much prefer
the noble face
delighted
with its nobility
to the stupid face
delighted with its stupidity

*

for a fistful of dollars
however small
one is this transplant
heart over fist

"dead skunk in the middle of the road"
in the radio, not on, but in
total privacy, but with a number
of little robots plugged in

as Giorgio Piccardi the astrochemist once remarked
to be subjected to cosmic effects
one does not have to be shot
into space, one does not even have to leave one's room
one is always surrounded by the universe
since the universe is everywhere
as remarks are not literature
& this is a poem:

wear the head as it grows
keep the lights blinking

through Her whose name is Desire & Cherish
all bodies, that they may fit

their faces
that they may fit in their bodies

*

automobile at indeterminate speed into sunset
& in its giant
Council Bluffs rays
the goddess
& all her ladies-in-waiting
                                        waiting

*

Chairman
Mao
Ursula
Andress
on the Bingity
Bangity
Bus

*

A. Wallace Rimington
inventor of the lightshow
continues with us
a beam in the system

*

antlered with desire
in the cryonic pools
between dream & day
we rule all of the heart
the great heart
& the does
walk by
& the nights sing
in the Sunne
The Sunne
a good good mama
a very loud star

1973

Shudder

bending
        over my own
                cigarette smoking
        in the ashtray

the fumes of it
        suddenly throw me back
                        smiling
                into an old

                                    embrace

Marchen (Beginner's Luck)

one day
Ted Berrigan
got kissed
by a toad

he instantly turned
into a tall
beautiful girl!

the toad
in its turn
became Ted Berrigan

it was the first time they tried it

No Money

the last Empress of China
took all the money
& turned it into a giant marble steamboat
that's why there is no money

Classroom

Seas of Tranquility they sort of nod
when you look at them as if to say
in a little while it won't exist
not even on postcards

The Distant Muse

jumped up & down
in the Radar Forest
to attract Her attention

"Sorry Sir
                no message for you"

sometimes He had His doubts

Rima: Dream

despite the label
affixed to her chest
I entered her &
it disappeared
we fucked
in a condition of complicated delight

"6,000 years . . ."

6,000 years of bad fightin' news
sure is enough to give a woman the blues
& quite possibly, or certainly at times
the red mists of rage
swirling in front of the eyes

such idiotic behavior
such *bloody* idiotic behavior

patriarchy's bad news
but so's matriarchy, most probably

way off

4-1-74

Oh, Mama Window

today, you look so neat & bright, today

Seurat, Old Saxophone Joe, Seurat

the air of rhyming: verse & reverse

forever

the poem is fucking

warm spores

Old Saxophone Joe is a pipe
Monsieur Seurat is a painter
well represented in Chicago

Mother's always remarkable

the dead deer appears manufactured

where are my scissors, he shouts

buttermilk, one of life's great pleasures

the smile in the voice
the smile in the voice produced by the body

a simple rhythm, & gaps

the way we appear with

Maximal Polynesian Clarity

Intimations of Immortality

when off a precipitous cliff
Albert Heim, the Swiss mountaineer
fell to his first death
he experienced a series of great clear flashes
a rapid & profuse succession
of images, sharp & distinct
he saw himself looking out the window
of a tall building
his sisters were there, & his beloved mother
& all the rest of his life, performed to perfection
by himself for himself to watch
up in the highest gallery
when suddenly came the realization
"in but a moment, I'll be dead!"
this seemed eminently correct
Albert was still falling
off that precipitous cliff
but felt no trace of anxiety or pain
he saw arching over him
a beautiful Alpine sky
full of violets & roseate clouds
powerful chords of solemn music enveloped him
& he felt himself proceeding, albeit backwards
into this magnificent Heaven
of no anxiety, no grief

Tremendous Wind & Rain

tremendous wind & rain
whipping down the Avenue

on the corner
the plate glass breaks
& the blonde in the ice-blue evening gown
comes tumbling down
into the running man's arms

just as his hat
flies off & is
run over
by our trembling automobile

in New York City
home, for many years
of the Poet Paul Blackburn

now a Resident of Paradise

11-72

Gypsy Poem

(for Josephine Clare)

It's *you* puts the green sprig in my hatband
if *you* should ever leave me
my hat would be a dirty old thing
my heart empty, eyes full of tears
I'd look for green leaves in the woods
but they are the wilting kind
they wouldn't stay green on my hat
where could I find as good a woman
a wife, as beautiful
I'd burn my caravan, cut off my hair
& trot off to the darkest part of the woods
to sleep there in my black sorrow
weep & sleep, until the White Dog comes
to take me back to *you*

Thinking of Il Miglior Fabbro

miniature World Tree
in our Front Room
to ward off the Rampant
Clowns of Apocalypse
(riding hard
on our side)

Snow, in Streets, in Thoughts
halfway round the Globe

so much Water, all subject to Tides, & Memory

according to Dr. Nils-Olaf Jakobsen
the Human soul weighs 21 grams

Alone, & not Conscious at all
Grosspapa goes
                    across the Lagoon

aoi, aoi, a Great Weird

Thrones, Courage — the throne has been transformed
it has turned into a Magnificent Nuptial Couch
the King Embraces His Blushing Beloved
& The People One Another

(Novalis)

nothing is heard but Sweet Names &
the Whispering of Kisses

& in That Temple they shall Dwell Forever
& Guard the Mystery of the World

1972

Indian Summer

on the Wall
                    Vine Leaves
                                        in his Eye

the warmth of their Color

Nature
            he thought   Nature
did I miss out on Nature?
All these Years

Two pigeons were Walking
                                        across a Green Roof
above the Vine Leaves
                                    which were Red

they were too Much
                                like People

he wished they would Go Away

when he Looked Up

1968
                                they were Gone

& there is Talking
                            & No End To Talking

No End To The Things Made Out Of Human Talk

1968

He

One day, when he got loose, he was detected carrying off the liquor jug from the table, holding it with both hands, and trying to move off in a hurry.

He gave the jug up without spilling a drop, all the time making an apologetic chuckle he often used when found out in any mischief, and which always meant, "I know I have done wrong, but don't punish me; in fact, I did not mean to do it — it was accidental!"

Whenever however he saw he was going to be punished, he would change his tone to a shrill, threatening note, showing his teeth, and trying to intimidate.

He had quite an extensive vocabulary of sounds, varying from a gruff bark to a shrill whistle; and we could tell by them without seeing him, when it was he was hungry, eating, frightened, or menacing; doubtless, one of his own species would have understood various minor shades of intonation and expression that we, not entering in to his feelings and wants, passed over as unintelligible.

The Concussed Consciousness

The human animal young can sometimes be seen running round and round, crying and totally distraught, in circles, coils of despair.

It is a terrible thing to see, as is the grown human animal on trial for killing one or several of these young ones; as are the others, then sitting in judgment, all the others.

It is enough to turn one into a nervous, befuddled wreck, barely able to register the most rudimentary perception.

Knife in the Water

The Vampire as Symptom of Industrial-Capitalist Civilization — not as Harmless a Joke as May Appear. "You don't mess with the powers" — or, you do mess with them, every minute: "Strictly Your Own Risk".

Think of those Two, the Beauty & the Wit, so Destroyed one in Body, the other in Spirit for all we know — by the very "Beast," or collective agglomerate of most certainly Human Activity in Exploitation they did their as it then seemed Charming & Elegant Bit to Extend: Roman, & his Sharon, a Rose — "The Fearless Vampire Killers".

Indians

Indians, blown to bits, most spectacularly, on the cover of one of my 5 or 6 "Buffalo Bill" dime novels in Finnish translation. Those covers had a hallucinatory super-reality similar to the (slightly earlier) quality of the pictures in the grade school Bible story book: Abraham and Isaac, Moses parting the Red Sea, or rather, shutting it down again over the Egyptian Cavalry's heads, Jesus and the Little children crawling all over him. And in between there somewhere, the opulent Etching-People in a 3-volume Classical Mythology book including the Iliad and the Odyssey, in German prose translation: they were black and white, thus different, more "ideal"? Such company, for dim yearnings: pictures of a possible outside world.

The big Art Déco cathedral radio
was another story.

Seized with Unrest Winging Through the Dark

(for Philip Whalen)

there was a light on
in a tree out there
but now it's gone

*

The Music gets Louder. It isn't really the Music
Gets Louder, it is the Members of the Orchestra
putting a little more Vim into It
at the Behest of their Conductor

"No that isn't Leopold Stokowski. That is
Bertrand Russell."

*

a breeze of delicate, glasslike creatures

in the dark

intimations of *Frashokerēti,* the next one

the Next World?

*

Recent experiments showing that minute animals can come to life after 6 years in a sealed test tube seem to indicate that they actually die. A spark of life maintained without metabolism or respiration is hard to conceive. Thus the whole subject remains as much a mystery as it was in the 18th century.

*

There Was A Light On
In A Tree Out There
But Now It's Gone

Night's Ticking On, & Away
From All Those Present:

The Light, The Tree,
& You, & Me —
& This Is True.

6-74

Happy Philosopher, Happy House

The Fires Of Autumn
Notoriously Low But Colorful
Are Burning In Me Now
But It Is Winter, & I Am Only 5 Years Old

*

        not so rich,
        not so smart

*

i lie sleeping on the floor

You come in & pat me
    on the top of my head

this makes my day

*

"L'Eternel Retour," Arletty
riding down into the concentric valley
        Her Flashing Thighs
        in 1945, I Think

Sorry Old Greek

"because you are
courteous
shrewd
& prudent"

said Pallas Athena

"10 years"
said Kung

hoonek epatas
essi kai angkhinöos
kai ekhefron

these quiet evenings
with the Enormous

the Baroque Music
is Terrific

*

watching the Spectacle of the Money
come to an End
Things become Clear

the Energy of the World has grown Tired
of our Greed &
Bumbling

It is about to give us
the Bum's Rush

"ah oui
le 'bum's rush'!
c'est une coûtume
Américaine"

it is
undoubtedly
a Procedure

the Mind's
Lateral
Lurch

is the Main Procedure

on the Otherwise
Blank
Page

*

the Proposed Creative
Activity is To Continue

the Great Madrigals
of Sensation

it takes plenty of *tlemosune*

a little *reggae,* too

The Walden Variations

(for Robert Creeley)

White Hair
Fine Fringes
Under the Brim

Old Sunshine on Twigs

Grandpa
a Sturdy
Alchemist

Old Sunshine on Twigs

*

Old Sunshine on Twigs

& on the Pigs
We Ate
Together
He & I

Deaf Alchemist
Loud Grandson

*

Ate Together

Teeth Fell Out

& Died

Old Sun

Baby Anselm

at the Grand
18th Century French
Engraving Dream Party

they meet
fall in love

"how much Time is there?"

"there's only So Much"

it is
so obviously
exciting

he has to laugh

wakes up
right next to her

*

a sharp beam
in the harmonic labyrinth
the woman leaves
the bed & enters
the twisting air

the man
smiles
by himself

in the darkness
there's nothing but leaves

she leaves
he leaves
it leaves

Good Morning

GoodBye

*

wild goose
noise over & on
the Lake at sundown which is
the time
one takes
the walk
on the shore

totally Nuts & Contented

even in November
1973

there are these moments
all one asked for

funny live skunk visions

*

Hawk sits in Green
Post Card Window atop of 3
reams Typing Paper

I, too, am lonely
says the Dog

I, too, have caused
Calamities

says the Man

*

but Chopin
that goddamn Chopin

when still a Mere Toddler
I was known to shout

"that's Chopin
That's by Chopin
That there
in the Radio"

*

came down the back staircase
touching the ceiling
whispering
gods
bless
this house

*

Centuries
Later
Baby Makes Noise &
Women
As Of
Ivory
Bend
Their Lovely
Frames
To Tend It

turn of the year, 73/4

Motes & Paramecia

Motes

for Jan

Song 1

big ball of ivy
green & serious
a chimbley
in the sky

at dusk they spin round it
the high-pitched brothers & sisters

nor is the cop in the helicop-
ter above them lacking

in either the sensuous *or*
the metaphysical dimension

Still Life 1

saw the earth going
into its slow
backflip away from the sun

a somber
burger

Song 2

in the mirror

iaia of kyzikos   saw
iaia of kyzikos
iaia of kyzikos   painted
iaia of kyzikos

Still Life 2

broom: motionless

stare: malevolent

few ways around it

Still Life 3

bad bad federales

Song 3

missing one
heavily
makes one feel
heavily

Life 1

a semi in bagshott

or,

can a tapir do the tango?

(a slight
punch
in the nose)

Song 4

one night in bellona
he ran
because? he was returning
from his mother's house
with the woman she did not
approve

they were, those two,
her berserkers -

& entirely
(devilish bad)
inside
his head

Landscape

zappeln: a place

move
convulsively
leap
(of the heart)

kick sprawl flounder writhe
prance

walk short quick steps
struggle hands & feet
kick & strike about

leave to struggle
leave in lurch

puppet

jumping jack
(a toy)

a place, not only
in the german
dictionary

i know it well

Headline Haiku

scruptious scandinavian
lays off bourbon
before breakfast

Song 5

dark
moves

power
peaceful

dark
deep
religious
green

moves
moves

a heart
in there

a peaceful
heart

dark deep religious
green
moves
moves

o ficus power

deep dark ficus peace

Song 6

riding
the curl
of the whip
"mehr licht! mehr licht!"

these rooms have grown brighter

"adapt
or perish"

not the question

"i used to be scared
but now i am crazy"

back
from the outer banks
& their mutant staff

move around in the sky

& the sea
is a bedtime story

Song 7

in a garden of flexors & extensors
in a cool room to work in

"with peaceful tool"
where the quality of

affection is affection
the soul grows arms to hug itself

in the middle
irregular columns of leisurely horsemen

hector sir launcelot lemminkäinen
quanah parker

move down the main spoke, or
is it up, into the light

most speak of as maybe the sun
flanked by the laughing

jeux d'eau
it is good to see them so

happy at last, the music a
slow *malagueña*

good to see them go
the beautiful, deluded uncles

Song 8

for Tom & Val

the sleeper's
cave

care
core

shrinks &
grows larger

through a
pin
point
light

that opens

to another
side of

the breathing

Bicentennial

we weren't here
a hundred years ago,
nor will we be
a hundred, hence:
& the fireworks were just average

Scriptural 1

for Ted & Alice

boys play.
mind is.
horses travel.
thought roams.
man sees.
money paves.
farmers plough.
birds fly.
i pursued my walk.
night came.
she came to receive their form.
it was flat on top.
his head was covered with a
    brown wig, faded & shrunk from
    time & use, a fringe of thin
    grizzled hair showing below it
    at the sides, & corresponding to
    his ragged whiskers. his ears
    were huge. his eyes were large.
    they were green. they were

i shall only add that when i
awoke i was sorry because i
found that my golden
scales had vanished.

Scriptural 2

distracting particulars
are to be avoided

by the incidental mention
of touching features

like one who draws
the drapery of her couch

around her, & lies down
to pleasant dreams.

Song 9

for Joe & Marta

assateague lantern
hissing the core sound
to lucid murmurs

mottetti, "ditties
& wittie sayings"

hooves & snorts in the distance

Life 2

desire

in the home:

the greatest

Song 10

& as they draw near the rock
whence the road
to the interior
will begin

they are tossed about by a great storm
on the raging sea
            raging
with the great mother's pain

but when it subsides, they see
the horns of the moon:

isis, saying hello

Paramecia

12 Meditations 1967–1976

respectfully dedicated to Philip Whalen

1

A Problem Solved

frequently i have noticed that people are *frowning* for no apparent reason, either while shopping or just walking. it matters not what age — young, middle age, or elderly — most of us are sometimes guilty of this. we work hard to prevent lines & wrinkles by applying all sorts of creams & lotions & then undo this treatment with a furrowed brow! we have to 'think beauty' inside as well as outside — or else spray entire head with one coat of white spray paint, let dry twenty minutes, then brush on one coat of white glue. let dry thoroughly. head is now ready for details: draw in mouth with pen & ink, then color in with brush-on acrylic. mouth should be about one inch above chin. for nice round eyes, i suggest tracing around a nickel. let artwork dry thoroughly, then spray entire head with glaze. result is permanently frownproof head, suitable for day or evening.

your beauty adviser.

2

Message

hello!
i am one of your molecules!

i started out from crab nebula,
but i move about.
i've moved about for millions of years.

i entered your body, perhaps as a factor
in some edible vegetable,
or else i passed into your lungs
as part of the air.

now what intrigues me is this:
at what point, as i entered
the mouth, or was absorbed by
the skin, was i part of the body?

& at what exact moment
(later on) do i cease to be
part of the body
i.e., you?

let me know what you think.

yours,

3

Isle of Wight Vision, 1967

on my way to the high street
i pass many doorways & courtyards

in the corner of my eye
a gigantic scots terrier!

intuitively speaking
his name is wudswooth or hoobsbum

"mcbuth: c'est un nom écossais?"

4

the beetle wakes up.

it is unconscious.

that is all right.

5

From The Log, 1970

> "the sluggishness of two-way radio
> communication over interstellar distances
> tends to make such contact unsatisfactory
> for beings with lifetimes measured in decades
> but for very long-lived beings
> such communication would be much more interesting"
> —SAGAN/ SHKLOVSKY

the core extends all the way out to the surface
the surface extends all the way in to the core
the extent of the core is the extent of the surface
the extent of the surface is the extent of the core
the surface extends all the way out to the core
the core extends all the way in to the surface
the core surfaces and the surface submerges
in the core every moment of our all too brief lives

received october the twelfth
decoded october the fourteenth

origin: alpha centaurus

obviously poetry

of the mystic-elegiac kind.
purposeful matter hovers in the dark

6

in lawrence, kansas
the flustered
faculty member
temporarily in charge of
the visiting god
put his briefcase on top of the car
while unlocking the door.
as we drove off

the case exploded in the street
& we had to stop to retrieve
all that analytical work,
page by puddle-soaked page.

7

New Orc

lackawanna,
a city
of erie county, new york
situated on lake erie
about five miles south of
the center of buffalo
(which see)

it is served by three railroads
& is an important
manufacturing center.
principal industries are
steel, abrasives, cement,
bridges, & ships.
it is,
actually,
hell.
as you proceed across
the bridge leading into it

the air changes
from air to finely atomized offal
the which the damned
have to breathe, all their terrestrial lives.

8

Jet Lag, or; Poem Beginning "i, thor"

for Ted Berrigan

i, thor
lob the great hammer
of my love

into all openings,
nooks & crannies
of the universe —

or, as blaise cendrars found it,
the 'english' phrase
"me, too, boogie!"

common usage
in 1920s
french pacific

9

La Cucaracha

the new members of the orchestra have arrived onstage
to replace the old ones flung into the pit
after a brief tune-up the concert will resume

10

wherever there is a hole
in a metaphysical fabric
you are sure to find a
hundred metaphysicians
attempting to fill it

but above our residence
on earth the sky
is clear, an
uncommitted
avantgardist

11

"katie
who wasn't then
yet
visible"
— gordon brotherston

visible & invisible persons
distributed in space
according to principles unknown
to either group
guessing, nevertheless,
at each other's existence

12

Dragon Mantra

for Jerome Rothenberg

ooh dragons
aahh dragons
here they come
in their lurching wagons
hee hee ho ho hee hee ho ho hee hee ho ho
here they come in their lurching wagons

Lingering Tangos

for Ed Sanders

You

three times as many of you
as when i was born

---

strangely moved
into the image
of a good cave

i sit in this good cave
thinking of all the other bears

going about their early evening

or sitting, thinking, thinking

oh it takes a long long time
for all that thinking to sink in

the house is cracking its joints

winter, but soon the light
winter, but soon the light

"complex environment"
equals
"crazed economy"
equals
dubious sandwich spread
manufactured out the arses of overwrought senators
long departed
from modes of factuality
telescoped into curious positions
infernal contortions
in front of their composite lord of the greedy flies
slurp slurp

up on the ridge, a gaunt man
flapping what look like limp wings
moving at speed

"virgil!   virgil!   wait for me!   virgil!"

here we shall find no corporeal delight

The Beautiful Days of Franz Innerhofer

by the baking oven he
saw her hunchbacked form slide
out ran outside vomited everything
into the toilet the stench
rising was a misnomer his
misconception as his days from
the room's window to the
floor below the couch &
how far ouch so hard
that nothing comes to mind
every time a mouse farts
singing exercises spat into the
kindergarten sister's face children of
his buried there before turning

in the wife remembered manure
knee-deep muck down by the
shack kicked him into the
dirt & then he was
grateful walked through clear light
september nights barking to each
lights an idiot hunk of
bread in his fist to
have to sit there next
to him & eat those
dumplings an avalanche had wiped
out four or five hired
men right there far up
in the woods or even
farther up louder & louder
wasp's nest jumped over puddles
& ditches the farmer mustered
his entire megalomania a hundred
individual cattle in his head
no more prayers emerged from
his lips glad to go
at the cowdung with his
shovel disgust magnified to infernal
proportions evening full of compounded
meannesses then they sat down
around the table & ate

---

they treat you like a dog
you shouldn't have a dog

not easy to be a good monster

---

in a bar called the angel
we spoke to a senior faculty model of human dullness
so extreme you could call it piercing
an example of the educational system's decline
in the era of explosion

---

light comes undulating in
to my eyesight is golden as
the tall glass of *cerveza*
brought me by kirby malone on his break
from the aquarian age
book store on charles street
an act of kindness although
it is apt to make me get drunk
four p.m. celebrating
"the feast of fools"
an excellent tome by harvey cox
first of all jan's happy landing
in the academy of her choice
"not really, but it'll have to do
& joe cardarelli's recent launch
& andrew carrigan's
& susan's & martha's graciousness
& grace, & rosemary's
many more names in the book
& my impending launch &
in memoriam christopher smart
the moon is giving us all these poems
automobile brakes are causing
automobile tires to diminish
corner of madison & howard
repeatedly, this time of day

Avec Poe Dog & T.V.

deliberate wreck of enormous tanker
"enough oil to heat 22,000 homes for a year"
& army bacterial warfare tests
in new york subway back in '68

jay-zuss, poe dog
don't know what the world

elderly man in catonsville liquor store
purchasing gallon of tawny port
"cheaper'n heatin' oil, these days"

"celebrities" shooting *curare* darts

terrifying holidays

without the music
we'd all be shot

---

the academic
desperado's
glasses glint
atop the rod
held in by
sphincter:

"sorry, keed
there's no more job for you"

boring monster

i'd rather work for a cauliflower

---

the infantile dream: to "wake up
& find everything all right again"

no need to elaborate, it is
what we live by
in this country

currently conceived as a sphere of
mostly fast-moving energy
jiving in vast space

*

unimaginably slow haul back to some early moments
of total insight & brimful imagination
though there may be something
enables one to step right through the interstices
but it is rather unlikely, as they say
"in the majority of cases"

On & Off the Road, Baltimore-Ithaca

pale wheatfield
green harvester moving
old model, stately, haggard
riding out
its own process

*

mr. chicken
obstfeld's deli
otto's bookstore
you refreshed me

*

start new life
get lost in
nice place perdix, pennsylvania

*

testing, green, narkissos, odessa
toenails, travails, too long
tomaz salamun, how are you doing?
dealing, no doubt
with mechanistic sub-cartesian cynics
time-servers, status quo heads
mind-clutterers, same in slovenia
& maryland

*

stop &
check the
map for
a *bit*

*

noam chomsky
bertie wooster
ingmar bergman
you refreshed me

*

great black
great black furry mountains
                    in the headlights
both sides of the headlights
       both sides of headlights
                             & taillights

*

boy by the side of the road
walking, seen
from the back
the gait of my son

---

too many constantly in the total
throttle grip of economic neurosis
aware, unaware, yet eating shit without end
pretending the system's 'perfectible'

coloratura snippets through the wall
now it's a goddam trumpet
o turd & tarnation
the joys of having 'musically inclined' neighbors

---

a bunch of gods
struggling acrost the swamp
bent under rain's weight

what kind of info is that
where did you get it

i didn't know it was info

sure it's info hell you know it's info

here comes another contingent
these have hovercraft swampshoes
& geodesic umbrellas

hey wow that's some good info

---

jesus, i don't know how
one does it
i don't think you did, either

*

make coffee
boil egg

put on shoes
walk dog

don't crack

A Top Ten Seventy-Six

20,000 a.d.
beautiful days
spearmint & rosemary
red wagon
the kindness of strangers
small change
alice ordered me to be made
apprenticeship on the couch
presences
all this every day

---

panic person
carries cock
in front
big smile

turkish cigarettes
pale women
incidents
in early life

*

dada dead?
no more'n the bagpipes

In Automobile

the mind's
mild speed

drove three hundred miles
grieving, elated

*

hair, struggling out
of the pate, the face
armpits & pubis

hair, you fink
you don't have to think

*

fast or slow
sporadic spores

---

nightfall image:
lovers, supping
in the concrete pueblos

their windows
lion's eye yellow

lives upon lives, contained
oh, one wishes, graciously

in the greedy o greedy so greedy
land? suppose it still is, a *land*

we can only stay tuned or stunned

---

fourth floor kitchen late afternoon
light rends the heart
earth going backwards
this is the highest
big wheel gondola
it is a moment
you know
the dog's arse is sore
my head is sore
but like chief joseph
i'll fight that particular
pack of pissheads no more

soleil cou coupe

sunset *grand couturier*

greetings you masters
of the sublimely ridiculous sublime

(& greetings mike egan one day
we'll remember that penal colony
with certainly less than affection
but ah so faintly)

Saturday

we sea monsters
came out of the sea
now we be land monsters
trying to become space monsters

---

loving you is a continuous collision
soft & binary
& sometimes we go west
sometimes we go essential
having no need of a cheiromant

(power-mad sorcerers:
who needs them?)

"eccentric" not main mode
but indispensable ingredient

formulations: little forms
as in "the little disturbances of man"

---

unspecified nighttime snack

dogs barking or people
having an altercation, possibly with
some law enforcement agents
through the ages

trudging through unbelievable milton
in its own way as weird as
fennek or lanthorn fish

lew welch, though
his wonderful orchestrations

always liked the accordion

just
enough
there

---

an ever tongue-tied heart
struggling through baltimore in my tattered chemise

---

ephemeral as it is, a cloud is not an illusion
moving in an otherwise clear sky it can rouse the soul
    to a pitch
of pleasure makes it impervious to the certainty of
    crossing over
allows it to occupy itself with meanings
that are more fun, fundamentally

---

there was nothing at all around us
but water when with saint brendan in his coracle
we proceeded across the happily gentle atlantic
subtracting the days we had spent at sea
from the days reckoned; & then, one morning

from Sojourner Microcosms: New & Selected Poems 1959–1977

Author's Note

as the subtitle indicates, the order of this book is chronological: its sections correspond to sequences previously published in book or pamphlet forms. as i seem to average circa 10–20 pages a year, no matter what else is going on, the method of selection has been inclusive rather than exclusive — in other words, i think that the faithful, whoever & wherever they are, will find whatever it was they liked, & not miss very much of what has been left out.

obviously, the head & heart in 1959 are not entirely the same as the head & heart in 1977: i have tried to make allowances for that which seemed possible, & to revise without rewriting "his story" in a stalinist sense. like any familiar, even a ten-year-old work can still seem pretty strange when re-visioned. more & more i begin to see it all as one continuous poem, whether it is a *redimiculum metellarum* (bunting), or an "annotated topography of chance" (spoerri), or both, or whatever metaphorical naming one wants to indulge in.

the book does not include translations that I have felt, still feel, to be part of the process of my own writing — from Aleksandr blok, paul klee, rainer maria gerhardt, paavo haavikko, tuomas anhava, pentti saarikoski, gunnar harding, tomaz salamun, & a number of others. as its publication will coincide with that of a sequence titled *heavy jars,* written in 1974–76 alongside of other work included here, that, too, will have to be seen separately.

cheers. it's been a long time.

—*Anselm Hollo*
Summer Solstice
1977, Baltimore

from *1967–69*

For & From Osip Mandelstam (1891–1938)

my age, my beast, who is there
can look you in the eye
& who can cause his blood to flow through & join
the wrecked vertebrae of this tribe?

*

numbers of twisted
days linked together:

a flute & a spine in the grass

*

angry motor
speeds through gloom
cries out, like cuckoo

from gallery down to stalls
programme is fluttering
like dove

*

who needs a pass for the night who fears
the man with the needle whose master
is the beast

*

as long as there's life in it,
the creature must haul its backbone to the end.

*

no one could ever tempt us to trade it in:
not for a dozen galaxies,
with life everlasting thrown in

at the very end,
in lethal darkness,
we'll remember it.

*

because we buried the sun there
we shall meet again in that city

For Thomas Merton

(in your poem)

first the car wouldn't start
then the car wouldn't stop

the old ladies drowned

someone had fixed the brakes that way

(in your last terrestrial hotel room)

first it was
too light? too warm?

& then
too cold
too dark

someone had fixed the wiring that way

Vodka: Sergei Yesenin Speaking

they drowned my puppies
so i drink a lot of vodka
& sometimes am
a raving madman

it is because they live with me
upon this earth
that men are dear to me

& also because they make vodka & give it to me

what have i done
what have i done

well to tell the truth
i've mostly lain about on the grass
& never stricken animals
our lesser brethren
on the head

i'm glad about that
it's been all right

i drink a lot of vodka
& little by little i depart

but no   that's much too slow
slash slash in red ink i write one more poem

they drowned my puppies

"there are moments when it all fades
you stand between door & hinge
meeting & parting
you realize how we all live
& have lived & die
come & go"

bye bye now
don't take any wooden kopecks

The Anima Abstract

The Anima Abstract

after H. Rider Haggard
& Cornelia Brunner

1

a twin of heroes
setting out
for lost treasure:

leo, "the sun"

& holly, mercurial & saturnine
both: the sun child's
spirit father &
companion: the capacity
to *reflect*

they have a servant, job
a limited person
of narrow & exclusively
old testament opinions

& later, a second shadow
mohammed the helmsman

a masculine quaternity
                    totality
                    self-sufficiency

yet it is yearning
           yearning
for completion

by means of the feminine principle
which has been suppressed
by the conscious mind

& is, therefore, absent

2

this feminine principle
first announces herself
in the message contained in the casket
leo inherits
from his forefathers
but more particularly, from his
(& everybody's) great mother

the five sphinxes in the casket
symbolic of the lost feminine soul
point to the mystery of life
encountered as a task

perhaps a dangerous one,
within
or
without.

the shard inscription
in the inner casket
calls on the heroes
to set forth on a quest

to dark africa, where leo has to find
the white queen & uncover her secret
the pillar of fire

avenge his ancestor
& become
a pharaoh himself.

during the ocean voyage
& as they draw near the rock
from which the road to the interior
will begin
they are tossed about by a great storm
on the raging sea
            raging with the great mother's pain
but when it subsides, they see
the horns of the moon

isis, saying hello

& then comes dawn, like a vision of the bride
preparing herself
for the sacred marriage

3

the emblematic
animals:

unicorn
goose
& buck

lion
& crocodile
& the devil

4

an old wise man
by the name of billali
comes to guide them in

into the crater of an extinct volcano
where the tribesman live, in caves

a black woman,
ustane,
espouses leo

an experience of marriage
as matriarchal
emotionally & consensually
stable
institution.

the tribe knows how to transform
instinct into will

but tends to backslide
into blind urge

the danger of uncontrollable passions
in rebellion
appears as the red-hot pot
slammed down on the sacrificial
victim's head:

hysteria in the male,
"seeing red" —

this regressive condition
occurs whenever a positive
but perhaps unseemly emotion
has been stunted

out of arrogance, rigidity, or perhaps
mere ignorance

the reaction is often belated
& can be entirely
disproportionate:

a senseless, negative outburst,
brought about by some trifle

5

now she,
the white queen,
being a high psychic instance

curbs the dangerous onslaught
of primitive rage

& bids the strangers
come to her
saying she has been waiting for them
a long time

6

on the way to her
leo falls prey to the fever
& deliriously dreams
himself torn in two

he now lives in division

here is ustane, the wife
sanctioned by the collective
a good mirror
for his primitive anima

there, however, is she
the queen of the interior,
all possibility

& she
saves leo,
simultaneously snuffing
the obligations of the marriage
& external commitments
in a wicked fashion:
by killing ustane

it is a vicious circle,
the austere victorian
not permitting the un-prescribed

knowing only either/or
thus condemning
ayesha, the living one,
the queen of the kingdom of kor, the heart

to the realm of the dead

7

she strives for union
with the beloved
but as she is not
a human being
but inner entity, anima mundi,
the nuptials intended
are not of this world

but eleusis' hieros gamos
the ancient solemn mystery
celebrated in temple
by priestess & priest

not to be mistaken
for the external, 'profane' union:

to demarcate the spheres,
protect the mysterium
from ignorant misrepresentation

all initiates
took a vow of silence
on pain and death.

worldly marriage
was a terrestrial reflection
of that sacred act

source of fertility
& life everlasting

performed by the gods
in the highest regions
of the universe

8

thus the goddess, soul
living in kor, hidden
in the innermost heart

inaccessible to the world
hard to find &
even harder to keep

guards as her deepest secret
the pillar of fire
forever gyrating
in earth's womb

pillar of fire
fountain of light & heat

world tree
transcendental phallus

set plumb on center
back to the world of the gods.

the man's anima is the keeper
of the secret of fire
                    heat
                  & light

fertility
creation

& she wants to join him
in his spiritual life
& to be active within it.

first seen as
an incomprehensible impulse
    passing fancy
    wishful image
perhaps even
    philosophical construct

she may yet lead him to herself
who is his psyche, that fire
gaining definite shape
& tangibility:

in the fire of feeling
his spirit is then born,

out of his feminine soul
into reality

9

leo finds the way
of access, but loses it again.

in haggard's own life
the anima, with her irrational temper
"other" wisdom, & need to love
found small welcome

her pagan will
contradicting the fading
victorian worldview too strongly

thus making her appear jealous
power-obsessed, & generally
far too excessive.

by her death
in the fire-bath
she demonstrates to leo
how he too should take the plunge
& be transformed

in a sequel, "ayesha, or:
the return of she"

leo wakes the mummified goddess
embraces her into new life
& this time does not hesitate to join her
fiery intensity.

through his sacrificial love death
the transformation
of consciousness & spirit
the anima, too, is released

from power mania & hubris
from all the entanglements

10

this preoccupation with she
brought sir rider to insights
otherwise rare in this time & place

yet leo & she had to remain
blissful spirits, strictly:

after their fire-change
they did not return to earth

because he would not let them return.

thus haggard found himself unable
to complete the working

to realize, in his own life
what he had seen, in his own words.

the time was not ripe
for the consequences of his experience.

this may well be the reason
why he himself, a remarkable man
was not always able to exercise the influence
that rightly should have been his:

his reform plans were rejected,
& his life-long grieving
over the loss of his only son, who died young,
may have its deepest roots in the fact
that the union of the gods

did not bring forth
a “divine child.”

the possibility of rebirth
through psychic insight

remained a hope for the future,
perhaps to be realized

by a new generation
in a new time.

*

---

pp. 153–158: Cornelia Brunner,
“DieAnima als Schicksalsproblem
des Mannes.” Rascher Verlag,
Zurich & Stuttgart, 1963.

Heavy Jars

Dedication

friends
fit

the words to the song
the song to the words

the words
& the song
the song
& the words

are
the world

Dedication: from Novalis

the scribe is writing
indefatigably

casting now and again
only a sullen glance
at the children

scowling grimly
while handing the pages
to a noble
goddess-like woman

who stands leaning
against an altar

upon which rests
a dark vessel with clear water

she dips the pages
into this water

& when, upon drawing them forth
she sees that some of the writing
has held fast
she gives that page back to the scribe

who then binds it
in a great book

but often seems peevish
when his efforts prove vain
& everything has been obliterated

---

slowly
the eye scans the page

the heart
beats steadily

while the mind winces
in infinitesimal
spasms of
almost pre-natal pleasure

down in the street
it is divided
into three parts:

sidewalk, street proper,
sidewalk, large things
of equally inelastic matter
on either side

these, inhabited
by home grown beings

several of whom are reading too

the karmic revelations
of so many
silly and lovable cells

cojoined in the bliss that feeds
them, and on them, too

thus holding them

(now turn the page)

---

awkward spring
has spilled its
golden ink
all over the angels' bibs

& off
the swan's soft chest
white feathers fall
into the swamp

& so forth

& i thought i was

a big & perfectly sensible dog

walking the other dog

with some dignity

thinking not of form number 0412 dash 70144

but of a city

equal to my desire

In a Tin Can Mirror

"she was a love child
he, a premeditated one

"theirs was a splendid house
color & form & sound
munificently swirling
whirling & twining
within & around, above & below
the flora & fauna of their lives"

well said, but not
what i wanted to say

the music is playing
the dog is sleeping
i am thinking
of one gone upstairs
& why I'm not there

because i am a stupid old fuckup, that's why

& there's this herd of cows
keeps mooing fiercely in my bead

& that's a lie
& you know it

moo, moo, moo

"the hind end of a cow
not all that attractive to us
is bliss to her boyfriends"

same old jungle

same old machete

certainly, always, talking

Landing in the Trees

outside the car
window bright clumps
of hibernating chumps

pop of guns, light rain

driving south
over the washed-out fens

tired
of the single tricycle's squeak
it is time to land
safely, in the park

but the huge nest
we hoped to spot
is gone

into some cave outside our map

huge wings snap

& incidents increase until
they cannot be ignored

in the pyramid
the children get bored

we pull the covers
higher, things brighten

moon slips through blue spruce

a million miles away, bright & loud, like frog

given the heavy jar full of all relevant information, he dropped it on the sidewalk and burst out laughing as the container & its contents shattered & scattered in the raging blizzard. he had been on his way to present it to her, for her to dispose of as she wished, but with the surreptitious expectation that they might "go through it" together. now, the absurdity of the undertaking had become blatantly apparent, & he vowed to tell the next full moon that he abjured such subterfuge for ever: silence & starkness, these were the perennial conditions of birth, & love, & death, the so-called great subjects, the ones no one could ever say anything but the dramatically obvious about.

Helsinki, 1940

exploding, shattering, burning

big lights in the sky

& this was
heaven's gate?

no no it's just the front door
same old front door you know from the daytime
& we're just waiting for a lull in the action
to cross the yard, get down to the shelter
& meet the folks, all the other folks
from all the other apartments

& there was a young woman
at least ten years older
he thought very beautiful

blankets, & wooden beams, & crackling radios & chatter

it was better than heaven, it was
being safe in the earth, surrounded by many

all of whom really felt like living

Yellow Crane Pavillion: from Ts'ui Hao

the yellow crane
comes & carries
him off to live for ever

they build a pavillion
to mark the spot

the yellow crane never comes back

white clouds, millennia,
long, empty, long, slow

clear river light
on each bright han-yang leaf

lush, lush grass on parrot island

sun goes down

where is home now?

mist over water moving

it makes a person think.

---

phantasmagoria
vision
slant light

purple
emerald

meadows
a railroad

a castle
up on
upon a hill

"love you forever" we said

not long after the war

long before
the wars of the heart

pain
in another language
is the staff of life

vision, phantasmagoria, the face
the face, then, there, in the slant light

"what are we being told?"

to kiss her eyes
perhaps
his eyes

as the water goes,
go
go,
as the water goes

---

summer nights
when i won't sleep
i sit & beep
these signals
out to you

oh, i don't want you to weep
just want you to
keep me on!
this sounds like a song

by some miserable creep
but that is only
partially true:
the other part

is really very manly,
independent, capable
& so on

maybe. bullshit. the demands
are entirely self-imposed
& senseless, if met
round anyone else's corner, that
objective place —

yes, they would be that
there, all right.

summer nights
or winter nights
or spring nights
or autumn nights

the wars of the heart

sure as hell aren't righteous

---

the language
comes loose in the head

the lights in the driveway
signal my neighbors' coming & going

it always is 2 a.m.,
as i am

& yet, in the woods there are marvelous places
my daughters go there, every day
bringing home armfuls of mint
& their own fragrant faces

to counter the general grayness & sense of mala suerte
graven on those worn by the males in this tribe

who persist in confronting, confronting
horns lowered
facing the emptiness to be populated with foes

hannes, i love you.
you are my son.
we are the boys.
we are the men.
we do learn to live with the fact
of the language, thus confronting us
with division, which is the nature of all

that moves, is born,
& leads a life,
& gives it on.

---

it is the thinking
no doubt, it is the 'thinking of'
those forms:
the gigantic
breasts, buttocks
equal to them, & yet
the absolute
necessity of *face* —

with, perhaps, a rose?
in her mouth
& arms
upthrown, in the sign —
the sign:
hands joined, or touching

a circle, above & around the head

("hail isis!"
"you don't say?")

"oo-ee, she gives such good head"

professor wilhelm reich
makes one feel like a squiggle
(squiggle)

hello. how do you do. & the folks
all around you, still
'stock-still'

trees in the clearing

& that is the only
time you'll know it is there,
still hanging there, still
in the air
between our bellies & faces:
yet it is
always there

dear, dear. dear

stevie smith, poet

& fellow woman,
where is
the cloud
of energy you were

the gentle wit & in-sight, equal
in every respect
to the most perfect body statistics
i ever respected

no way you are dead

you were such a good head

---

in the little boy's head
the hibiscus stands always in bloom

she better get here soon

---

think
of love, of extensive travels
flat on back

think of henry's
terrible voice on the radio
& in the land, its huge
dazzling cities
where the brick strikes the back of the head

think
get scared

think of the hair, the eyes, the mouth
the breasts, the cunt, the lovely lines of the body
the catalog of paradise

think, am an amplifier
with only one speaker

think of one who knows how to return
the speaker to his senses

be horny lonesome again
pondering silly equations

think of hands
think too much

antiquity, futurity

"voulez-vous coucher avec moi?"

think of oneself as one
not really needing much
but how rare that 'not much' be

& of long travels, of light shining through

habeas corpus,
habeas corpus

drift away, but get ready
to fade in again soon

---

bad sunday

longing, anger, rage

feeling *both* desperate *and* boring

brilliant sunshiney day

i don't want it

i want
deranged jottings!

how to stop envying
the beloved
the beloved's life?

flat on back,
cursing the gods

silly head music:
big cat claws
striking, *pow,* pow, pow

screech, dying mice

general misery
advancing
on saigon of the soul

yes, let's have
that, too.

She'll Be Here

weak-kneed, soft-headed
turns the ignition key
of the mind, then staggers
off to the bathroom, catches
a glimpse of itself

oh dear god

"maybe you deserve it"

Big Dog

i bring you
this head,
full of breath-
takingly beautiful
images of yourself

& put it in
your lap.

now i breathe
more quietly.

now you pat me.

now i sigh.

in a moment or two
i'll get up and
be a man again.

"yass, life as an embryo
was easy street"

"pass the joint"

little men
in head

backyard
suddenly populated:
two tiny girls,
one miniature schnauzer

& now they scamper
downhill, to the urban
removal parking lot

millions of cars on the road

in one of them,
that very moment
the best-beloved
hurtling towards

(what on earth is it
transforms the speaker
when she is around?)

&, beyond parking lot, long freight

rumbles, the porch
trembles, in time

up above, lake seneca, bluer
than the sky

& now you are reading these words

& now you have read these words

& now you are here

& now you are here

---

thanks to the vintner
become simple again
ecstatic

as the season's
temper
just happened

because of one
happening
in me, as well as around

i sense the movement again,
of the one great body

& find it bearable

---

signor vivaldi,
signorina truelove

i thank you
for the clarity of your temporal notions

they are a help

---

it is hot

the picture, it flies
off the wall like a bat

up & down & around it we go
on the convolute ladders of light

wavering foci
in the great boogie-woogie of creation
insistent
beyond notions of size or reason

continuously propelling
the mind's components
through a kind of wind tunnel without walls

& with no particular purpose
other than the absolutely sensational:

a voice, both gracious & warm, in the other room

another, from another universe
crying for its mate in the yard

& what did you just say

---

weaving the soul
back into the body
in the ongoing proposition
of a waking life

there are two of you there,
quite effortlessly
proving the world

---

coleus
& corn plant
on the windowledge

new friends
under the sun

past them, he sees the neighbors'
purple rose bush
in gigantic bloom

in the tinkle of time
we shall be
released
back into the realm
of photosynthesis

& that's a thought,
a mandragoric thought
sweet monster babe

---

tick-tock: years pass:
the language turns foreign:
words like heart, & ease
& dwelling, & heart's-ease

all i have of that flower
is its name,
a love of it

but then there is the blue dragonfly
landing, over & over
on the back of your knee

by flowing water, surrounded by
a multitude of green
subscribers to creation

& i am suddenly filled with joy
& pride in the opposable thumb,
glad to be dwelling here with you

in the language of our amazing species

---

flowering weeds
tall as trees
in windy sunlight

when i was born,
i yelled & screamed

yesterday's news, if mythic

both ends, it is tough

but here in the middle
the mind waves

in tune with the wild
heads of camomile
archangels

Dedication: A Toke for Li Po

born in pa-hsi province
of szechwan
lived muchos años
at the court of the emperor

ming huang, but was banished
as a result of falling
in disfavor? with the empress
kao li-shih, & wandered about china thereafter

only occasionally attached to a patron
leading a 'dissolute' life, addicted? to drink
writing the poems about the joys of that life

notably wine, & woman, & all the rest
& agitation of the sensational universe

came to his death by falling
out of a boat & drowning
in an attempt to have intimate intercourse
with the moon
in the water

one of those of
whom it is said:

"he took the charge well"

iowa city / geneva / east lansing / ann arbor / baltimore
1974–1976

Lunch in Fur

for Meret Oppenheim

"the wise sense of priorities of black 3-legged hound dog thunder
if only we could remember it when we do not
i should not say that i want to be a dog so much as i wish that i
could just remember dog sense of beauty about life
not mad dog or kicked dog but regular dog that would be enough
remembered"

— JOE CARDARELLI

---

memory   rain   pride   wind

she's not here now to say
your hair looks lovely

tears soak his head
he cannot sleep

night deepens   he taps to the f.m. tunes
driving the sky car of the recalcitrant self
through other lives   there is smell of burning

leaning by incense   he sits till dawn
having talked all day   & then kept silent

stuffed white devil
stuffy chinese

john coltrane had a love supreme

note tacked onto a surface says
bring the form

bring the form   to the crazy weaving

---

kicking manhattan to pieces every night
her face softened as she saw the visitor
utter a shrill mocking laugh & crumble
the cactus roared & powdery substance
timely & shapely   blew away

remember the fun we had ramming
the fresh cigars between the teeth
before the infernal biochemical clock
covered us with its rampaging goo

maybe we better get back to the office
the world's largest cluster of oversize lungs

the mind travels wildly among its planes
think of the fun i missed when i was sealed up
i'll get even for that   i'd rather loaf than work
but i have to eat   especially at my age
the only way i can work is to practice astrology
since that's all i know how to do   but at night
you should see this kid at night

the frail silver-haired woman darted across the black lawn
dashed into the cottage then quickly tipped
a bottle of the red medicine to her blue lips

---

po chü-yi heard them   lawrence warned us against them
the chattering parrots in the painted halls   of orc

heart embittered by understanding
sisters   brothers   stranded in strange lands

flesh & blood   cast adrift on the road
as we watch the bright moon   there should be tears

there will be a day when the dust starts flying
even at the bottom of the sea

---

animation subsides into terminal slapstick
it is a como se dice cathartic
flying kick in the rump-shaped ego
which then immediately changes
outward aspect to weeping brain

the cathari believed in something they called
but knew wouldn't necessarily come when called
were right about that
while insane on who we are with our bodies

"they started it all! they started it all!"
& yes we burned them (salut brother blackburn)
had our revenge   now have our consequences

how many goddamn worlds for the one
they thought they had

---

instead of all these gnomic numbers
why the hell not
be sensible?
european tradition ostensible
writer of matter presumed corrective
to big business hirelings' behavior

while appearing to be a possible friendly
ainu   educable in prevalent direction

why is the one at the end so hard to write
while the ones in the beginning weren't easy
they got done   now we are done
with the time we had being
together not too together
in our separate heads
side by side in shared beds
twenty-seven moons

people have gone on loving
someones   all their lives   after less trial time
but then those someones had probably died

live with each other
die on each other
that's what people do
been doing it for quite some time now

many sets   of rules & runes
yet luna still draws the threads
& stricken we weave
through brambles & haunted woods
charred-eyed   terrified
cast into ourselves   burp   well yes
the people are crazy & suspicious

the captain of my soul is my foot
& her sister   the other foot

---

the emotional honesty of any ant is not absolute
nor is the wind around the house
as long as it doesn't blow it down

what we don't say we don't know   we can say
see the ship sinking   see captain rat
paddling off into the sunset

satisfied that the earth is round in english
i take hold of my towel without any doubts
& dry my neck my chest my armpits cock & balls & ass & feet

saying good morning to someone in the middle of a conversation
in the middle of the night is a rare pleasure
we have experienced it many times   we can't get enough of it

---

something about writing to a woman
& quote unquote
the thing is when
you live with another
you   go on   around

& the way is the way
people transmit
ways   of making love

& he was told   start working the reason
we do not like to stay alone
anywhere   in this universe

---

maternity home with
big black bronze
statue of sheepdog
in front who
knows the connection
but as we
walk past someone
points at it
says that is
where you were
born
        that is someone
quite possibly my

---

window i had not felt
down the corridor hoping
sound would come from her
soon as i built for her
looking at her   presently out of bed
besides not be there i fell
into an immaterial
agitation
sound that would work only in the slightest
gust   now it presses my slumbers
just when she was to tremble   the softer chamber
was it quite anyone
an approach
most beautiful
installed in a frame at ten paces

an example of careening verse yes
the only trouble careening is that you have to
come to a stop

the car is in the ditch
the head is up the ass
the heart keeps on beating   under protest
& the crazed soul keeps crying out for forgiveness
it has been wanting
far too long
in stubborn refusal to see that it is
itself   both the forgiver   & the forgiven

clumsy   but it says what it says

---

in the marshall minnesota quickstop
burger joint   i encounter objects
on objects   glass on table   purse on chair
refracted light on more refracted light

how obsessive   this universe
how bone-aching lonely to boot
(bones aching inside of boot)

then it starts coming back   the way
you say the word "whole"
& "yes i like it"
dear master of odin house

how it is both the hole we fall into
& the one we come out of
the one we should visit with understanding

how it all rocks & rolls right through the pain
making the light come through

forty-three years   such wonderful
if also horrifying times
& they stay with you   crowd up around you

if not always affectionate   always insistent
they'll never leave you

---

big sunny room   tall windows   random prolific green
the people recline on carpets & cushions
silent & smiling   but for one in the middle
holding a book & reading it
interrupting himself every once in a while
with a hearty laugh story or diminishing howl
glasses glinting   grey hair & beard bristling
hands touching air   striking   caressing

"these are the interior adventures of henry little-song"
a redhead in jade gown moves about the room
showing us color snapshots of her kittens
important enough   as all of it has to be
here in the golden eternity
where the people are almost perfect in their affection
as the glorious orang-outang
calmly munching her vegetarian   lunch   in fur

time to wake up   time to wait for the return
of the perennially astounding body
thin silvery gentle this time

"take your shoes off   do not fear
bring that bottle over here"

so many rooms in my lady's abode

With Ruth in Mind

ruth

1. the quality of being compassionate; pitifulness; the feeling of sorrow for another, compassion, pity.

2. contrition, repentance; remorse. now rare.

3. sorrow, grief, distress; lamentation.

4. matter or occasion of sorrow or regret.

5. a native vehicle or carriage.

6. to awaken, rouse.

definitions culled from the oxford english dictionary, which also tells us that most, if not all, of them are archaic &/or obsolete.

Or, To Hocus the Animals of the Pursuers by Changing Their Dream Cassettes (Old Thibetan Trick)

for Tom Raworth

cold & windy   cloud with delicate
cottonwool monkey face   drifting by
frittering   violins   on the radio
tape   drifting by   the magnetic heads

& into the spaces   between other heads
magnetic   electric
from here to everywhere
possibly back   & on out

what is it like what is it like
some   recall a   musical theme
by having the score's image
appear before them   then reading it

it is conceivable that what we call
remembering   in a human being
consists in her seeing herself
(mind's eye)   looking up things   in a book

thus what she reads in that book
is what she remembers
wittgenstein zettel (scrap)   six fifty-three
estuche ingles el papél marca bambú

"is the baby out yet"   "no not yet"
when they listen to it   it must dimly remind them
cats to mozart   tape drifting   zettel drifting
someone blown clean down the block

shrieking with merriment shock

*

time travel back again   hopelessly stranger
tremulous listener
heart embedded in cliffside
sea lions bark at it   hungry & curious

many friends quite crazy
plant on table trembling
many-talk-in-head   my name

*

the bats are hibernating so now
the birds   hunt   the twilight
later gigantic   motorized   beetles
scour   the night

*

poe dog   recquiescat   morning glory
blooms but an hour
cause & effect   dynamic
we have no sure means of knowing

duration between   each death & rebirth
the seeds of karma   dynamite
little paws folded   big paws folded
stagecoach takes corner   plenty of dust

the idiot wars of the young
the idiot wars of the old
master babe mandragora
shrieks when torn out

shrieks when rammed back
needs warmth inbetween
appearing   reappearing
uttering language in   extracurricular states

*

goth space   general restlessness
wolfed down bread & meat
among the boulders in the huge scarred seam
a dwarfish person of the queen's retinue

adorned on the upper side with a strongly accented
border of interneural spots
he said nothing but waited
playing with the hilt of his dagger

they usually keep a considerable distance above ground
he thought   above the surface of things
as one who had never seen a mirror might wonder
in what depths of it lay the face she saw

hillsides open meadows disused quarries
seaside cliffs narrow valleys
running down to the sea open downs cornfields
roadsides borders of woods even the woods themselves

apelike he silently disappeared
into the darkness   we are pleased to announce
he had three concubines   famous for their beauty
apelike he disappeared silently into the darkness

this is a fine bright form she thought for my clansmen
live far apart both on the upper & under sides

*

we'll find a way she whispered never fear but kiss me
notwithstanding the abruptness of this introduction
set like a stone he took a deep breath
paler shades & two oblique lines

rather less oblique than usual
in one swift rush all was clear to him
it had the appearance of being sunk some way beneath
north toward the high mountain village

there is a hill track branching off
her hair streamed out like the wings of a raven
of a uniform deep green almost shining
he began to flee from her

but ever she followed him chuckling
sitting on flowers in the hot sun
moving the hind wings wheel-like in evident enjoyment
at the first light of morning

pairing usually takes place in the morning
from neck to ankles she was covered by her head
holding itself upright on a tall culm of grass
the people came out staring & pointing

their whispers rising like surf all about her

*

the wind kept hitting the house & shimmering
in the moonlight he approached
it was impossible to guess in what respect
the form approached obscurity since the description

flatly contradicted every peculiarity of the latter concept
large instead of small & peculiarly bright blue
her features blurred & swayed before him
throughout the room there were broad grins

like fire in dry grass
the larva winced & contracted
directly an ant's foot touched it
a bead would appear & at once be imbibed

his words welled up like stones in the pool of faces
& since she saw no tangible manifestation
of his presence nor any attribute of him
she found it hard to concentrate & slowly closed

antennae waving over & upon him
dawn & the braying of horns

*

melancholia   early developments in physical existence
cause us to experience certain attacks of paralysis
one has only to turn over the stones to see this
& then get into the chariot   with quick   uneven steps

thinking   gloomy & wild is the air of this place

*

slow sinews   how heavy with smoke
how like an orchestra heard through a truck
"head through a truck"   now millions of miniature
guitar picks carved from a wood called grenadilla

strike the roof of that truck
no teeth are not strong enough for solid truth
"immaculate interest in truth is not for human"
who is that guy   it must be his truck

big hulking poet name of thorhall the hunter
back from the dead to taste the wine of vinland
having dined off beached whale his comrades perished
for supper he'll have a chunk of his truck

*

heat waves raced & shimmered round the basin's rim
in limpid space suffused with sunny beams
& then the axe was loud   so good it was to be crazy
mused the archon   look   the mutant metaphors

take wing
wiping the milk off their whiskers

*

having meditated much on airy things
unimaginable distances & cosmic pie
i think i know what the white poodle dog thinks
perched in his window across the street

he doesn't   i like him
he's both eminent & reasonable

*

o eldritch cries of the wind among turret tops
stared at the dark faint outline of hills to the east
intoxicated in the glimmering starlight
lying back upon a low couch

spring you get for free she thought & mostly it doesn't
turn out too well but then life's strength lies embedded
in a fresh coarse evenness
dense like any good production of mnemosyne

on her knee the flare pistol lodged securely in its holster
a prime star shell in the breach
permanent event in the stream of change
followed by another & another

yet slowness & sun have stayed with me
in calm & gentle absurdity she thought
slowly the ice of the unformed universe dissolves
saw the dark blot against the white stair waver

move down to merge with the shadows   "why are you here"
afraid it might be the ultimate horror
foretold in legend   "completely normal person"
but it was just a máquina working by springs

moving talking laughing on its way to the shop
toward morning we begin to feel insubstantial
our knees cease to shake we wrap ourselves in our cloaks
& walk to the grove of oaks

twisted & windblown   clutching the stony planet
with roots of authority   purple & scarlet

*

frequent narrative climaxes   moments
of great suspense   & moments out to lunch
may be saved by one's ability to characterize
one's mythic role   by comic ineptitude

the slow finn in the houses of those-who-cannot speak
not the swift one   gliding through hermetic glens
from dawn to dusk he sat in his chair   gazing out
at the ghostless panorama of disintegrating cones

zapotec killers stare   stone-eyed & deified
there must be a way out of this shirt
p.g. wodehouse probes the drift of cloud
the thing says this   o bless all humble

the thing also says   that's not a shirt
trees & language   in & out of the hat
sure-footed he flows from tussock to tussock
uttering cries of revenge

mighty breathing   sacred rapture   frantic screams
sounds good   thanks   tremulous frenzy   thanks
concealed behind a canopy of palms
whence issue strains of delicate music

from an invisible angklung   she leans
across the table towards her companion
unfurls herself double time as fighting breaks out
among the maniacal jitterbugs

retract periscope
i will return   for my change   another evening

*

who sold you that machine gun a warlock a mind
open to total disaster   enlightened
facts & figures mere ghosts
occasionally encountered as described

this is the song of irgud   we're living in zomboid
where drowsiness lays its thick fingers upon us
even while we are trying to get the money
to be ready to hand it on when it is our turn

he looked about at the faces of his counselors
intent & it seemed to him full of accusation
he began to speak in a sharper tone   a quaver
clenched pale shaking fingers in snowy beard

mysterious indeed were the ways
there were invisible cities   rites of the goddess
outside & above   or were there
well there are tangible & intangible gifts

but not on a silver platter
the worm starts under a similar pressure
meeting in vortex of tattered posters quietly flapping
back & back   before it goes forward

incorrigible intimist mon âme
to hocus the animals of pursuers by changing
their dream cassettes   old thibetan trick
joseph cornell knew it well

Dragons & Gazelles

"late at night
when it is very still
& the obligatory daily
dreams have been dreamt

the gazelles & the dragons
begin to stir"

— CARL SAGAN

in homage to
Olaf Stapledon & Carl Sagan

the wars had bred a great number of contractors

after rinsing his mouth
with the liquor he drank a full cup & saw
as he took up the lamp to retreat
to the brink of a little cliff

gazing
into the pool beneath her
a woman of his world

she inspected the ship & waved
tearfully
from the port office balcony

besmeared with soot & charcoal
overgrown with hair
bent double with the nature of his errors
disfigured too by odd & fantastic dress
individual human
was impulsive & affectionate
but as time passed the wars had bred a great many
a change came over him
he now kept his dog
at a distance
he said what the devil's noise
is this in the ward what
a man & a woman together
in the same cell
that is against rule

& now his crude nervous organization
subsequent obtuseness & callousness of mentality
would protect him for ever
from suffering the full agony
appropriate to short-sighted world disgust
yet there had been times when there was no occasion
to regard the world as hostile to life

or themselves as deformed

when they perceived
that the perfect sphere of their thought
was but a bubble adrift in chaos
yet an elegant bubble
the system was true
in its own joyful
& frankly insincere way

adolescents were encouraged to study
the ancient problems of philosophy
to convince themselves
of the futility of proving themselves
beyond the universe of light

*

"neither utilitarian nor humanistic
nor religious but aesthetic

"music
spoken lyric
epic verse
& the supreme art of winged dance
were constantly practices

"the rest vanished

"for close on a hundred million terrestrial years
we endured"

*

on the evening of which we treat
the new & highly decorated suite of rooms
was for the first time illuminated
with a brilliance visible ten miles off
had not oaken shutters
carefully secured with bolt & padlock
mantled with long curtains of silk & velvet
deeply fringed with gold
prevented the slightest gleam
from being seen
without

*

motel room
perfect ex-con environment
all actions magical

listening to the radio he thought man
there must be some people here

one of the "misters" said
a student said
whoever touches a poem
touches a man

across mucho physical space & time to be sure
strange to have been operating on the margins
then move into center
a curious picture
"teaching high school
better than psychotherapy"

alaska washington d.c.
san francisco new york the drunkest
places every moment
takes me farther from you my love

if i see you sad
my heart is torn
if gay & foolish with friends
i reproach you

your playful habit of pinching
people's this & that
i envy you
your beautiful hat of existence

*

at length they approached the metropolis
with dreams they loved to sell
dragons of eden   mere poets
as sottish as & as mere

while learned in several sciences
having reasonable
philosophical & in some measure
mathematical heads
their seething brains & foaming genitals
still tracked
presented with a trace
they barking bounded down the trail
both joyously & accurately

the town was not particularly
attractive in appearance
& everywhere reeked of sulphur from the swamp
yet was the habitat of the winged ones

*

while new ideas flourished in the empire
ideas they remained until strains of them floated
to the colonies
to be adopted in paradise
where women in midlife sought satisfaction
men in midlife sought it too
while women were no longer ridiculous
choosing young lovers hello xenia
the older man with the younger cucumber
was seen as trying to fool mother nature

glorious results were promised
but by now
large tracts of the higher education had been usurped
by the reptilians

& they wanted her
beautiful & brilliant everybody wanted her
she talked only in metaphors striking ones
never said tiresome things was dazzling
no one was ever sure with her
they never found her

she & her decimated kin had moved on
into the fourfold frequencies

Over There by the Hibiscus

for Carla Harryman

"there is this young, well, forever young lady i'd like you to meet."

"you mean the one over there by the hibiscus? i know her.
that's ms. imagination. hey, she's a winner in my book."

"& you, in hers?"

"oh, i don't know. i'm just a witchy thing."

begin then sisters of the sacred well
& somehow loudly sweep the string
pow
there goes another transformer

*

waiting for the ones who would build
the cities they saw in dreams
instead of the grotesques that surrounded them
they would still attempt to cultivate certain emotions

patterns of "message waiting"
in the self-contained life support unit
"desk" "local" "long distance" "shri yantra"
"motorola quasar color viewer"

birds like flutes winding down
around the watchers' shoulders
patient & smooth
waiting was being with them

time curving in
the way
a human
face moves   with its body   stupendous

let me hold your
hand   sure   let me
see   here it is

*

night night

voices across the street
mildly delirious
your knuckles against my chest
not only yours   not only mine
not only against

*

marveled at the delicate variousness
of her rooms' appurtenances
was also astounded by the crudity of her tastes
their similarity to his own

*

say that tree used to be a horse
only when we desire a climb or a ride
we have to be clear
clearly yes that is a tree m'sieu
c'est un cheval bien sûr

*

such pain within young face
freaked   still beautiful

body giving in
to devastation's beckoning

"spare change?"   "sure"

fate has no irony
she has a mind of her own

the text keeps flying off the page

*

beer is continuum
shots are little hammer blows

winds sweep the earth   they sure do
in process of re-definition
(sitting there stoned
having 'insights')

to fall in love with this wonderful witch!
what a fate!
but to stay with her!
what a drag!
because you are a drag!
"you" in the general sense!
though come to think of it
in the specific one too!

how is it "love" tends to turn us
into total idiots

as does hate

the indifferent being
merely partial

sleep on it

do whales ever feel sorry for themselves?

going a little nuts
hearing just about anything on the radio as "revelation"

"let go!   goddammit let go!"

air personalities
fighting or possibly pleading

quite possibly both

"this is the killer speaking"

chantilly lace

coffee coffee

*

sweet early industrial period songs fill the aural
while the visual & the pulmonary are filled
with the late industrial

the cerebral visceral
hurries right back to the beaver
her blessing song   its innumerable yet consistent
certainly structured forms   right now

would i believe it if the telephone rang
& if it then sang
& what would i do then
who cannot carry a tune   want to be carried by it

francis gary powers
dead in helicopter crash

"tail rotor fell off"
progressive news
"we do not have
either the technology
or the time"

felt shitty   now sleepy

stare over rooves of baltimore

tale told by an idiot full of sound & fury

novel composed of & including
unqualified insults
commissioned by customers

*

legions of monumental
resurrected   gunfighters
on judgment day
surely there will be a universe
for that   dear heinrich heine
who said rest assured
you'll find what you think you need there
"the eskimo will find his polar bear
the polar bear will find no eskimo"
all that was horrible once
will be beautiful now
reversibly   up & down the gyrating ladders

"treat yourself to some horse pussy boys"
with all the gusto involved
in pumping metals

& this is a homage to the "western"
cette forme magnifique de la culture américaine

somewhat occasioned by the anticipated loss
of a good woman being
as hard to find as a good man being

*

go sing the praises
of the real i'm in
here busy communing
with a small cactus & three
oranges on a blue-green cloth
in an invisible wicker basket

helicopters of the occupying
wobble by in the wind

that's probably it
but so is this

water makes music
in the shape of anselm
& all who are or have been
good to him   for no or little reward

o bossa supernova

no stopping any time

*

two bulls as gateposts the twang of the bowstring
"is this where we pay the parking fines"
no this is where we stare at the wall until a window appears
to step through & sit on a sunny bed
hugging our knees or stretching scratching a little talking
or singing the song of the eggs & the women

conch shell egg
white woman
gold egg
black woman with locks of leather
iron egg
black woman with nine leather faces
carnelian egg
brown woman with azure-blue locks
turquoise egg
blue woman with six faces like stars
crystal egg
white woman with two turquoise faces
copper egg
red woman with nine terrifying heads
jewel egg
blue-green two-headed woman
stone egg
dark red woman with iron locks

good old thibetan rock & roll
"no this is two-eleven *west* madison   you want to go east"

yes she was here
that is her footprint

a questing ant ran over his finger & stopped she wondered
how she could be so content to hear him speak of ants
had the past years been too busy for music
they were remarkably handsome forms of the species
gentille & parfit   he certainly hoped this was true
found himself staring into the missing mirror
found himself here & there

*

stone ravens   staying with fiends
how many of her were there
all the pages
blown back   into his lap

"& what is your name"
"my name is 'lap'"

looked into the missing mirror & saw the footprint
knew she had come to baltimore   understood
her gentillezza
                              thought of internally happy andrei
the notion of the big house   outside of the big house
they had spoken of   inside another one

tambourines in the street
sleep on it   how is it love tends to

whales as continuum   sweeping the seas
redefining the world

separate heads   living & dying   knowing
the footprint   the missing-mirror

saying   i could certainly use
a few nice surprises

*

i think i
know i
feel i
think

i wish i knew who it was
called i wish i knew who it was
called i wish i knew who it was
called

please kill engine trying impossible effort

*

now i can't find you i see you
everywhere oldest
trick in that god's bag
to divert myself i consider "the application

of our 'moral' notions to beings
such as fish who produce hundreds
nay thousands of eggs in one year"
mr. whitehead finds that diverting

m. stendhal too is quite diverting
they can both go to hell i want to see you
where i can find you
it might be possible to breathe there or difficult not to

wrote that six months ago found it again today
no more certain who you is than it was then

*

flitting through the great maze
from one clarity pattern to the one next to it
not higher but what about love
the mockingbird is the most loving

it listens all day half asleep the other half listening
then it stays up all night
sings all the other birds' songs for them
now they are sleeping

i see that you know
how from a certain angle
your three-quarter profile
pierces my heart with a flight of crystal

hummingbirds
ah the impossible dream
he was fucking the fucking bird
she was fucking the male chauvinist pig bird

*

inclinations
turn us into natural forces
they interfere
with human lives

thus one might say
of passionate human beings
that they "fall"

as inclinations only become effective
after a time of relative resistance

papa novalis
in the "notebooks"
page one hundred & fifty-two

grunts & cackles next door

what is the minimum
daily requirement or allowance
what   the maximum

*

stare at blue fingernail caused by emotional
car door aberration   faltering under eyes that try
hard to see who is there

the newborn dream more than half their sleeping time
what do they see   what waves come waltzing in

it is not is   it late too
that was who anyway
mean memory funny maybe alive yes thank you
think yes you

assignment suffered   rest entitled
bite mosquito   leave ready

world begetting baby magic
oblique recognition broadly some person
in a sense raging

triple consciousness moving
hand over hand into the quadruple

when do we first see our watchers

*

"ask questions   yes yes   ask questions"
hans hofmann   beaming at student
rock dove climbing through air
far less effort than this one's

struggle through the dense particles
of yearning time   only occasionally
punctuated by some brief & enchanting
south of the border tune

o brother   o sister   o sisters o brothers
forgive me for taking so long to perceive
that lives do fit into tiny spaces
until they don't but move out

in every direction so
they cannot possibly fit
anywhere anymore
more than the heady spirits of helium

until recaptured & coaxed inside a blue balloon
quickly ascending to its maker
& the total equality of blue

*

THEIR CONDITION IS SINGULAR

who live as leaves by the sea

from Finite Continued

for Hannes,
who knows
so much of this,
too

One

Curious Data: A Poem in Fifty Little Parts

for George Mattingly & Lucy Farber

i say
with passion
i know that this is a foot
but what
does it mean

ludwig wittgenstein
with passion

winter & silly shoes

*

cough cough

what smokes a pipe

*

what smokes a pipe
is a man
inhaling
the results of the combustion
of dry shreds
of vegetable matter

of of & of

oh scribble & sleep

*

stare:
photograph of magnolia
blossom
ancient chinese artifact

nervous hallway laughter

it's never been nowt
but bits & pieces

*

i cannot be making
a mistaking
i mean a mistake
about the fact
that i have just had lunch

ludwig wittgenstein
having had lunch

*

t.v. newsman advocates moments
of silence

*

can't tell you anything
you don't know

so pick up your body your body
& let's go

ludwig wittgenstein
restless for peace

*

rare bird may have taken
wrong turn
one of only 100 whooping
cranes
believed left in the world

*

mutant returns from college
to family dairy farm

all deities reside
in the human breast

*

personality

construct of conditioned
reflexes

ginsberg helms
conversation on lsd

helms: it disintegrates
the personality

*

george schneeman's painted shirt
brightens this winter's snows

black & white by
turns

            gorgeous reds &
            grays

*

high continuum sun or
tender sax

*

harveys send harmony
ideogram from seattle
ted his poem composed
of first lines from sojourner
carla a transcript
of her reading &
interesting footnotes

*

cover of newport in new york 72
reminiscent of first
manhattan elations

fifty-part poem
curious idea

*

the odyssey caper
by ludwig wittgenstein

*

what goes where
it all goes everywhere

*

alice gracefully stumbling
a little
gravel path by lake arlene

curious data

*

we are looking
for a convenient opportunity
to meet the survivors

elsewhere in the news
they're feeding the cows concrete
to increase their mineral

*

what a poor reverie
it only leads to
the siesta

gaston bachelard

*

one sees presences coming
already there are infra-presences
dense voids
on the way to becoming presences

*

ulrike meinhof
editor of "konkret"
in the fifties   published
some of my works & translations
of gregory corso

*

strongly recommend piero
heliczer to guggenheim
foundation
he'll know what to do with your money

*

the thing about insights
they don't stay put

will you vacuum when i'm gone

*

little crow & other lakota chieftains
killed 20 a day   for 40 days
then   38 lakota were hanged
at mankato   minnesota
before   the state college   there

let them eat grass
some fool had said

grass ate them all

*

no no that's not
the federales
that's
the liberales

bureau-lovers

*

somewhere out there someone
is singing en mi
corazón no longer will it
rain

*

keep my face on my eyes

charlie chaplin died today

*

vicente huidobro the poet
him long dead too
but in his poem
his head still sit
on smoke

*

the thought of scotland
yard paused for a moment
space is not
the a priori condition
of all visual knowledge

how to drink out of an empty glass

*

scandinavic gringos as horrible
as wasp

absolutely other consciousness necessary
absolutely necessary

*

yes i have reveled
with the great lords & ladies of the tribe
like ludwig wittgenstein

*

the food moves slowly
across the field

dead
it will be fast
food

*

fuck inspiration in no
via ass of venus
or mars if you
prefer

*

to explain
the flower
you have to explain
the fertilizer

*

to make a living
here it seems you
have to be a
capitalist sympathizer

*

wit is but a
wink at the power

i now seek joy
in the thud

you can't buy it

*

what smokes a pipe
is a foot but
just had lunch ludwig
i say with passion
what does it mean

*

construct of condition
advocates moments of whooping
& mutant footnotes

*

if this neither looks
nor sounds like poetry to you
well i didn't get
my money back either

*

this version of world
enough to make one
shrink right down into
one's vegetable shoes

*

lee anderson falls by
we get borracho
thinking of highly sober
philip in san miguel
perhaps soberly high

winter solstice now past
quién sabe we might
just make it through

the fragged seventies

*

comical chemical baltimore sunsets

absolutely other consciousness

*

the street's diagnostic
equipment
its lights
come on

*

a helpful smile
in every aisle

a threatening fist
in every cyst

*

enter chorus singing

we industrialized travelers are

strange coots

you & me baby

*

bodhi tex says
not even the dead
can disappear

where
after all
would they go

*

notebook cover squeaks
between letters of application
& supplication i reduce
body temperature by writing
some other words too

like lick your sweet nipples

*

total mind joy silence

*

eh bien old smoke
time for a nap

*

we must sleep
if we are not to find ourselves
helplessly strange

What Wonders in That Circle Lie Or, The Toad Story: A Poem or a Story

oh mark the beauty of his eye
what wonders in that circle lie
so clear so bright our fathers said
he wears a jewel in his head
— THE BOSS

we stand at the edge of a pond
under a maple brilliant with its fringes of red keys
a marshy place yellow with cowslips
& back from the water broad spreading leaves
of skunk cabbage & unrolling fronds
of cinnamon fern

when near at hand there is a sweet tremulous call
continues for several seconds then stops
abruptly

there it is again from another direction
slightly different in pitch & now
it comes in from all quarters
many voices

it is not difficult to locate the singers
they are toads

the sounds are such that they influence us to loiter

the sustained note is not only
high-pitched & tremulous
it seems to have a dual character
as though a low note were droned
while a high one was whistled

this song has been compared to the slow
opening movement of beethoven's moonlight sonata

the simplicity & quiet joyousness of it all take hold upon us

humbly & thoughtfully we continue our walk

*

lose tail!
leave pond!
hallelujah!

but sometimes that day
of the toads' final transformation
coincides with a day of gentle rain

a happy coincidence it seems for them
but likely to prove rather tragic instead

they cover the sidewalks & roadways
& before each individual of the migrating multitude
finds a sheltered corner he can call home

many hundreds have lost their lives
under the wheels of carriages & the feet
of hurrying pedestrians

*

hold the toad gently
in your hand
so that his hind feet are without support

& hear him talk

he is annoyed
he demands to be released
his tone is not irritated however
it is instead a gentle chirping sound

he twists his head about
& looks at you brightly

he pushes with his hands
he wiggles his feet

all the time he is talking
the chirping notes
coming thick & fast

*

toads live to be very old

authentic record tells the story
of one that lived to be thirty-six
& was then killed
by accident

other conditions being right
the toad can live for some time without food

this may be stretched into months
possibly years
(two years in limestone)

if the temperature is continually such that the toad
can go on hibernating

the toad does not eat lettuce.
but it is not beneath his dignity
to sit & feast
on the plant lice that live on
the lettuce

*

the toad is fitted for his place in life by what he does
as well as what he is
let an enemy seize him roughly
& he is a dead toad

playing dead saves him many a time
he will lie on his back
with scarcely any perceptible motion
for minutes at a time

even breathing
seems suspended

suddenly one leg is thrust out
then another
the eyes open wide

& in an instant more the toad has turned over
& is ready for new emergencies

*

a toad never has the pleasure of drinking
water in the usual way

all the water he gets is absorbed through his skin

a toad kept in a dry place grows thin & distressed
is likely to die within a few days
whereas one provided with plenty of moisture remains plump
& contented as weeks go by
even when there is little food

when drinking he sprawls in shallow water
or on a wet surface & has a blissful expression
in his marvelous eyes

in midsummer when pools & springs are dry
toads often travel long distances
to spend the night on the wet ground about a well

in their search they sometimes unwittingly fall into wells
to lead a most somber existence
feeding on the few low forms of life that live there
& on unfortunates who become prisoners the same way

release may come if the well has a bucket
but more likely their fate is a tragic one

their crushed bodies have been taken from pumps
into which they have been sucked

they have sometimes been found hibernating in old wells
where they must have been for ten or fifteen years
judging by the amount of debris under which they are buried

*

when cold autumn days come
he shuts the door by backing
his way farther in

& lies there with his toes drawn under him
his head bent down all secure he sleeps

the days grow colder & still he sleeps
his house yet more protected by leaves & snow

the winds blow
but he does not feel them

he is cold
we should call him frozen perhaps
he is so stiff & cold

but if the heart is not frozen
he wakes up some warm spring day
when the ferns are unrolling

& scarcely knows that he has slept more than a day

what a change

it is such a pleasure to eat
it is so delightful to move

it is such satisfaction to soak in the water of spring rains

once again he becomes a social creature
& finds himself going with many others

& now at the pond & now in the water
he can contain himself no longer
but bursts into that spring song
beautiful to himself & to his companions

*

see: the frog book: north american toads & frogs, with a study
of the habits & life histories of those of the northeastern
states by mary c. dickerson. doubleday, page & co., 1906.

Two

Mescalito

walked past
the back of my head
while holding
i was
another
equally hairéd head

he did walk past
wearing a big rubber raincoat
& what are known as
"wellington" boots

slosh
slosh

&
out
the
door

oh, yes

*

sir arthur conan doyle & his contemporaries misunderstood the nature of 'ordeal poison,' re-clarified by glover, leary, castaneda, & others: 'ordeal potion' would seem a less biased description, or pseudonym, for one of the initial manifestations of spirit guides, allies, forgotten gods — or as rilke has them in his aphoristic "can you still play the old songs:"

*

can you still play the old songs o play it again sam
the way they weave through my gloom like planes with silver wings
that toward secret casablanca sweep
over the evening sea
& as they come in to land   it is only just spring   spring
& there   on solitary paths   the forgotten gods
are no joke
though patient   & smiling

Teen Angel

streets
he walked
thinking to meet or
merely to see her

once a day   or once
every other
third or
fourth

a madness

buildings   pavements

lines drawn so fine

sweet madness of centuries

there she was   no one else
only i & she

a strange
an isolate
sensibility

eternity
was
my address
then

Behaviorally

it is possible to state
the case for pigeons
as sensibly-behaving
organisms

& against poets
as schizophrenic
humanoids

poets
emit verbal responses
i.e. write verses
that produce
few pellets of food

& even fewer
food surrogates
such as money or fame

thus b.f. skinner has said
without meaning offense   he said
that poets are not
sensible

Pellet: Noon

sudden fists of extreme irritation

Pellet: Man Is the Measure of All Things

protagoras said

fell into the sea & drowned

Pellet: First Love

one leg shorter
she walked into me early

Pellet: Well

the soul is *not* a little man
operating in heart or head
all right but who *is* that little guy

Two for Josephine Clare

JUST PRETEND WE'RE HUMAN

scream scuffle thud
next door   the children
thumping   their mother
upstairs
writing poems

& through it all
the reassuring
beat of creation

PLANH

your
antique
sealskin
jacket

lying
on top of my
prototype
nylon seal
coat

looked
comfortable
together

more comfortable
than we had ever been
inside them

These Machines Were Built for Speed & Anger

september seventy-four   proceeding through realms
of quiet despair   the birdies
keep singing real nice

sometimes i feel like hiding my face in my hair
or covering it   with bags of ice

this makes the jaws feel good where no teeth are
but soon will be again   & then   to smile again

october seventy-four   & "evermore"

Bits of Cottonwood

> *"astrologers meet in secret*
> *room of honeycomb palace*
> *to prepare future events*
> *to translate love into pain"*
>
> — TRISTAN TZARA

a singularity
is a region where gravitational
forces reach infinite strength

where any object
no matter how rugged
must be crushed into nothing

*

but i am just a one-man slightly batty middle-aged
people's studies department

*

he disappears in this region of the universe
& reappears instantaneously
in another region of it

*

dream of monumental slab with words

LARGE
EMPTY
SPACE

who knows what's around it

*

not easy touching
random yet hard
motion of bodies' parts

near exhaustion
generative of speech

*

what do you think i said
what do i think you think you said

*

he picks up the folding trumpet
& hits himself in the face with it
there he says now
let's forget

*

garbled days & garbled nights

*

the spirit that lives in the people
the people
the watch ticking on
the yellow plastic table

well i could cry
I could cry all over you

i'm saying this to make you laugh
not because i would be a battered angel
or early morning rain & a car parking

the power   the information   the difficulty

the most active verb

Southwest Minnesota

for Laurie McElroy

here our antennae bent
but did not break
here we were told
"you talk broken
& once you talk broken
i guess you always do"
here our friends flabbergasted our students
"they just didn't seem like your average
language instructors
the way they didn't
seem to care about sentence
structure
punctuation
or grammar
that doesn't mean
i didn't like them
though i thought these artists were interesting
i was confused
i didn't know how
they could publish
some of the things
they did
who would *buy* them?"
still there were ways it was muy bueno también
not at all like t.v.
but truly philobatic
here comes a letter saying "please tell me
what does it mean
this word 'philobatic'?
i have looked in all major dictionaries
with no success"
well my dear major
success is not it
but "go in love" does it

The Terrorist Smiles

opens small notebook
has another drink
& writes:

no way the feeling
however new
will work in old form
however despised or desired

the higher the technological level
the more denatured the consciousness
used to it

& the more destructive
the collapse of both

may the finite
human carriage enter
good delight

by means of an effective
dialect that confounds
the single-minded
lovers of multiplication

Are you a Catholic? No I'm a Cathode

been x y & z
the past year

who'd rather not be
maker of mildly
revelatory
traditionally grammatical
pseudo-profundities

put on blue suit
be professor of pain &
glamor &
squalor

self-typecaster
basset hound
playing the basset horn

in the whiskey beer bach &
early spring
post-mare's-tail-wintry west
branch iowa sunset

mustard stain on pantsleg

no but it's good to hear
folks clomping up
& down some stairs again
long as they don't beat their children

this music's a little fast

(time to de-program)

Zettel, or, When Everybody Was Falling Out at the Kornblum's

wind sea rages.

*

matter of little weight flies past.

*

milk starts rattling in head.

*

language created by generalized volition, i.e., "windy."

*

"what a nice name for a boy"   "oh boy!"

*

helen of troy had a way with a diphthong.

*

we windows open & close at random,
variable in all our aspects.

*

there goes helen of frog, a large winged animal
i think.   "why, hello, i, what brings you here
this afternoon?"
"we generations keep on humping through the wind."

*

here in cottonwood, the people live in house.

*

"oui, ça, c'est bien normal, ça."

*

he picked up some rocks & dropped them into his heart.
the heart opened a window & threw them into the street
where it became apparent that they were merely compacted noise,
all but one, which he retrieved.

*

las espacios son muy grandes.

*

it takes all the world to make a kin.

*

"you're right, it has to be some kind of non-commercial utterance."

Think of It as Science

for Carla Harryman

suddenly an open space
right in the dark & in it
the rainbow-collared spirit horse
the queen of boogie-woogie

a woman with two dogs
& eyes this is my body
& this the small squat bottle containing
the large liquid wine

& these be the waters
the modern tomato lives in depressed all day
except when suddenly
an open space right in the dark

provides the sense of speak
good spanish no longer a skulking
blossom but one of the greatest
looks up at the snowflakes

& says the bewildering
to the bewildered
who then feel like the precarious
arboreal dwarves they are

this is my body & to some extent
yours it's just the way they think
doesn't give us money
nevertheless we said

i meet you & therefore am
no captive thing

think of it is the science

The Years

for Charles Bukowski

i met her at the west end bar. i mounted.
i felt disgust and horror. i did feel some
pride. i left town. i came back. i had
some beer. i saw it. i opened the bottle
of wine. i saw it. i began to notice.
i could feel the tears. i sat there &
drank my wine. i was fairly drunk. i did
feel some pride. i could barely see. i
was a dog. i lied. i left town. i was
not a very nice fellow. i had some beer.
i came back. i walked toward the truck.
i saw it. i didn't feel it. i got up.
i began to notice. i could look out at
the people. i took my bottle. i looked.
i could barely see. i felt disgust &
horror. i opened the bottle of wine. i
had some beer. i met her at the west end
bar. i mounted. i broke her false teeth.
i was a dog. i saw it. i began to notice.
i left town. i climbed into bed. i sat
there and drank my wine. i didn't feel it.
i was a nice guy.

Vision

here comes a whole crowd of young
& pleasantly middle-aged even old
merrymakers   a little inebriated
but thus full of enthusiasm

up my staircase

oh boy   they'll turn this place

they'll turn this place

Perennial Quatrain

i'm just a little too
old-fashioned to accept that
i'm just a little too
old-fashioned to accept that

For Instance

death, for instance, is a terrible mistake:

it should happen only to the agreeably edible.

Zuk as Horus

(MESSAGE RECEIVED
EARLY HOURS OF
MAY 15, 1978
WEST BRANCH, IOWA)

Dwarf Pantoum

i throw my sock across the room
having thrown my voice across the continent
now is the time to relax
into the good glue of existence

having thrown my voice across the continent
into the good glue of existence
now is the time to relax
i throw my other sock across the room
& go see who's in bed

i'd be a fool to stay out of it

How Are They Songs? They're All About Homing

on route fifty   to the star
the door
is always open
& the light's on   in the hall

o let's
direct our feet
to the alcazar   bar
on madison street

*

she   strode   in

he flew

into her arms

a home-bound hound

Hard as Nails

hard as nails   we are not
& there are no exceptions

but as fragile as "some strange melodious bird"
singing one continuous strain

in which one thought is expressed
deepening in intensity as it evolves in progress

"like a welcome already overshadowed
with the coming farewell"

Unemployed

think of friends envigorates. the signifier becomes not the but a signified. wrote for hours crudely but effectively delving into trash mind. most creatures have some sort of mouth, though not all ingest brussels sprouts. node trak toad trak. they wants to turn your innards out. stroking long hair back wondering if main concern not dream sleep. sudden beauty. go anywhere can you. why do you me old question. toad trak node trak. grotesque shapes our lulus. sweetness the harry. precision freshness & finesse wonderful it delivers economically such fun. we want finished product not petulant papoose. him want finished product too. humorous schubert whose place of birth was in austria at the time. an envigorating prune. the door is always open & the light on in the head. go back to yesterday pretend the time you stopped & didn't get out the door. node trak toad trak. the vicar's van lay vomiting saplings. there's woman there's home. asleep this morning still unemployed.

Dream

late medieval early renaissance "court" — where i am, in some possibly vaguely 'jesterly' capacity — much merrymaking, food drink talk — i have to fight primo carnera look-alike giant whom i keep thinking of as "schmeling" — first fight goes o.k., i lose, of course — re-match more dramatic, involves some stalking — i.e., he's stalking me — a pleasantly aged gray-bearded david ray appears, we sit, talk — then the giant's suddenly next to me, dressed in a tutu, & now has lots of black curly hair & beard — we fight, i lose, he punches my 'bad' shoulder & says, "this'll make it all right with the insurance"

Reverdy

confronted   being   normally hid
shuddered   at essence   feared
was recognized   or not   no matter now

completely dual in form   still dear

sat   thinking   judge   facing himself
knew that not mild

& to hurry   then   long after
futile   fell   thin   waved

obviously
tremendously

see you later   lump it away

when he awoke from his memories
the bar was almost empty

overcast & lugubrious   he got up & paid

the paper notes
tenderness as it was

no longer stretching   into the several
inscrutable now

dizzying then   afternoons

this is not from
for to but
the revery of another pierre

Lecture

for Hans Breder

the *meta-social*
takes us
all the way forward
to *dada & gaga*
mama & soma

the only active
schools of american poetry

unless one considers
the *dominant* school
of *coma*
anything but the *robot* manifestation

of prevailing system of *exploitation*

Iowa City 3:IV:78

At Yaddo

for Josephine Clare

four flights up
in the tower
huge   very white room

splendiferous
mostly arboreal location
thus long spells of
treetops   treetops   treetops

dear madame trask
set up foundation
with some of the crisp

accumulated by messrs
trask & peabody
consecutive hubbies

in their pleasurable
one hopes   labors
as wall street tycoons

half a century later
thirty   of some of us
get to stay here & eat awhile

*

sure is nice
to be treated nice
just because you are one of those nice
writers
who write

things like the gray mist gathered
continually   the roof
sank lower & lower until
he was compelled first to stoop
then to creep on hands & knees

& then get up
& go shoot some pool in the amusement pavilion

Papyrus

history   invisible   calm
thick   with hard blows
shifts   your valuable head
about   in the mud

she did   for you   the friendliest thing

you wanted to   break   the jar   with her

but i promise that
whenever you come
to such as were bitten
by a rabid ape   when small

just go away
lay down   in your tent
& sleep

*

though i was there
for many days
i did not succeed in mastering
the inner topography of the building

my mind was so filled with pictures & songs

Later

bumping into trees
then reassured by total brightness
of universe above
(or "out"   or about)

not raging into battle
stoned on fury mushroom
nor leaning into smoky fatalism

simply walking
towards a light

*

if only
a life,

the one
to hold.

*

the gods know
it's ephemeral.

that's why
they are
the gods.

who gives
a shit
about them.

Pellet: Urban Civilization

no
touching.

touchers
will be
towed away

& made to
justify themselves.

Pellet: The Short Form

It's short enough
to put in your pocket

as you walk around
in search of a socket

Pellet: On Prizes

the retentive fraud
received
the violent ape award

Ho-Hummage to Gabriele D'Annunzio

it gathered up with one deep sweeping ho
all the divine hum of that last ho
of the september hum
it soothed its ho & wrapt it round with hum
exalted it with continual ho
then remained standing there a long hum
the ho of full & perfect hum
diffused all over it

in saying this it was simple & sincere
it had in all ho left its hum behind
on that ho of hum which ho with a little hum
had made the ho of an indefinitely joyous hum

it felt that indefinable ho that the hum of its ho
always called up when it revealed
the vehement & passionate hum to which it was drawn
by limitless ho & hum

it smiled in the surprised ho of a hum before a ho
it seemed to lose the hum of its personal ho
it felt that in its poetic hum its own ho
was not of a far different hum to the ho
of the dead hum wrapped in its opalescent ho

but it was afraid of finding itself alone in a gray hum
& it sat there sat there suffering under the ho of the hum

Winning Entries

translated from "Pastries for Poetry" (an anthology)

NOW MAN

a man
can
hunt.
he balls

big
flesh,
a brief
inning

in
moon
light.
then

rooms tick
old
nothing.
what

say?

THE EYE OF REASON

bedad!   see ark
or eat
tight uniped:

an evening
with food.   ugh,
love. umph.

one lash
of your quick
tongs: me dead dad

hose neck,
stare into space,
hoo doo wha wha diddy.

STADIUM SCHOLAR

slipping each ching, i listen to mocking
flooring over myself, wet as pulp in the spray
from perfect handbook of creative writhing.

Triptych

front oil seal: bad
pinion seal: bad
stabilizer bar: broken
tail pipe: gone
ball joint: bad on left side
needs alignment
tires: bad

*

without the steamboat, ages might have passed without
such a development of her resources as is now
exhibited. the enterprise & industry of the west
would have been unrewarded; the progress of civilization
would have been slow; the trees of the forest
would have overshadowed the sites of flourishing villages;
silence & solitude would have prevailed, where now

the busy hum of men
resounds
(CHAS. FRASER, "THE MORAL INFLUENCE OF STEAM"
HUNT'S MERCHANT MAGAZINE, VOL.14, 1846, P.509)

*

style
        ways of being
                        modes of love & loaf
& the emotions
                    hanging thereby
                                    like enormous
fuzzy caterpillar tails
                        straight down
among the branches of al-qūmar's trees

older than the oligocene
which was when some primates grew
round skulls
                for more efficient brains

fifty
    million
            years

of lovely long-nosed lemurs

on madasgascar
                    al-qūmar
                            island of the moon

T.V. (1)

"for he is ishi   the last of his tribe"

"couldn't help noticing your aftershave"

the brain which takes that in its stride

is yours & mine   & it is late

T.V. (2)

funny
nazis!

twenty-five years
pass.

then,
more funny nazis!

Pellet: The American Economy

fatuously expansive
ultimately expensive

Pellet: The Vikings

hairy marauders
fine human beings

Pellet: Two Schools

home
milk
softball   vs.   street
                       drugs
                       unstable

Pellet: Laurie

"now
let it dream itself
into yoghurt"

Copy Tips, or: Question & Answer Time

> *"copy tips: twelve most persuasive words in the english language: a study team from yale university found them to be: you, money, save, new, results, health, easy, safety, love, discovery, proven, guarantee."*
>
> — LYNCHBURG NEWS & DAILY ADVANCE, 8 OCTOBER 78

would you like
some lovely new easy
(safe proven guaranteed)
results?

would you like
some lovely new easy
(safe proven guaranteed)
health?

would you like
some lovely new easy
(safe proven guaranteed)
love?

would you like
some lovely new easy
(safe proven guaranteed)
money?

would you like
some lovely new easy
(safe proven guaranteed)
discovery?

would you like
some lovely new easy
(safe proven guaranteed)
safety?

would you like
some lovely new easy
(safe proven guaranteed)
ease?

would you like
some lovely new easy
(safe proven guaranteed)
you?

no   i think i'll
        just
    go on being
                difficult
        poor
                poorly
    spendthrift
                endangered
            unproven
                    not guaranteed
        inefficient
                bored
                    old
                        me

oh let the fists of moonlight strike my nose
my melancholy nose

the reek of so many
energetic
enforcers
        of the great greed-law

Or Turned Into A

for Jayne Anne Phillips

years of indifference followed
by years of manic sensitivity
make for a person who understands
too little   or too much

*

first there was one, then there was no one, then there was one, then there were two, then there were three, then there was no one again. when he was one, he felt like no one. there were these people he had known a long time ago as the "pentangle," & here, as he was trying to think some, they were again, they lived in the radio just like the miniature "palm court" orchestras of his childhood.

*

merely human lives, programmed into merely human totally demolitionary set-up.

*

working the ship into orbit, he saw the shining murals blur, then heard innumerable automatic typewriters, murmuring with her many voices. the nature of this new sensibility was not as long as an arm: rather, it appeared as extensive as immeasurable time. when asked, the old vagabond seated on a tall stool opined that things were no worse than usual: "just very busy, pulling down the old buildings, looking for the ancient art." lean, tense, idealistic, he grasped the telephone instrument, moving toward a greater realization of secret harmony or true chaos. the stout woman did not want an android. "saratoga's a pretty cosmopolitan town," she said.

*

looking at her was looking at his ninety-two-year-old grandfather's dreams of great lands & cities by unknown seas, which he had, when told about them, re-dreamt them & populated. the old man had not seen anybody there but had nevertheless felt great calm elation, one year before his death. maybe all the people showed up to greet him then. the grandson, with the notion of his own finiteness, knew that he would never go to tahiti after all.

People in Enviable Hats

did you say
                    will-power-assisted? brakes?
yes
              they work very well
especially for people in hats
(not people wearing them
                                        just people *in* hats)
really do great with them
in this funny
                        lethal   life
though locked in angry dreams
                                                (they shout
they're mine!
                    they're mine!)
& even when
                    their mind is on vacation
& their mouth is working overtime
they're able to resist
                              the high plangent sweetness
the being
                    breathtakingly
                                        perturbed
casually
              they proceed to stuff another elephant
& swagger off
                        to hear what the sphinx has to say
but they do not know
                              the true love of sophy
as distinct from
                        wisdum   they have
no abrazos   no abraxas
they are in fact
                        like unto a pair of
bermuda shorts   adrift
in the bermuda triangle
(& i take it i don't really
                                  dig their scene)

Recent Findings

"The stain of love is upon the world"
— WILLIAM CARLOS WILLIAMS

the it which fumes: a distant beast: a bio-mass resource
knocking into other solids, fumbling, tumbling
in the liquid
                    music's
                              light
"i'm calling george   & i'm going home"

what chaotic
                    late night's
                              wont to scribble

*

thought to take hold of: flashed on lilith: preening: a sign

she was a familiar   did strange things to the gods

or was it she just forgot to remember what she'd forgotten

"a more simple schoolroom"

*

not to take hold of, but most familiar,
now how to lift her: out of memory: back into the world
"stain of love" fading   fading back in

now how to be brave   like "one-man johnson"
not to succumb to bitter   o.d. behavior

eyes far apart   not far away
suddenly close enough
to make one flee
farther than canada   closer to home

*

only mortal
                    hand & eye

enjoys the warm
                    asymmetries

sang the toad
          ah yes
                    sang the toad

After George Macdonald

& when day after day
passed
& the longing to speak to her
grew
& remained
unsatisfied
new doubts arose

perhaps she was tired of him
perhaps
her new studies
filled her mind

with the clear morning light
of the pure intellect

which always threw doubt
distrust
& negation

upon the moonlight of passion

          mysterious
          ever mingled
          with the faint shadows
          of pain

a great longing seized him
to look into that room
once more

Byronics

back in another tall white room
trying to make love to my soul

she is distracted
she has to get up

i am furious
i think kill

then she reappears
wearing a bright blue

furry yet suitable for bathing
hat

*

incredibly wide
gentle madwoman's eyes
as she warbles on
about her great

once upon a time & forever
almost requited
often recited
love for lord byron

*

survived the stepping up of riddles
saw flashes of symbiotic
lives that scampered twanged
then flying leapt into lingo pleasures

Boat Moon Up

boat moon up
                    adrift in
                                  shadows

am to be "all"
                    by my
                              for a why

train   distant beast   i'm braver than you

hanging in
                 upside down
                                    up here

in my   time   bean

Banner

george washington's *feet* are on display at sweet briar college

If

if your child tastes salty
go see the doctor

if the bed break
fix it

if your name is
wyot ordung

you wrote script
of "robot monster"
world's most inept movie

go see the monster

if you like gospel bluegrass
let me just say that simple
piety
        no matter how pretty
never quite made it

if you think
make "an unpretentious
friend
            easy to live with
day after day"

you must be wyot ordung
using a pseudonym:

come see the monster

Joe Giordano's Umbrella

night. rain. food, drink, all gone
into person. person all gone
to sleep. who this? it's
talking. you're right, so it is.
& you is you, right? so it is
time to wake up. no more rain,
umbrella nice & dry. right! light!
food! drink! person! all here!
all now! (no cottage
cheese in the oligocene.) let's go!

The Frenetic Solipsist

it made itself
the navel.
it learned
being it.
then it was it all!
& it took it, yes, all!

(in effect, yes, evidently)

Not the Same

adelheid
worked
for several
years
in a cork

*

as a young girl, adelheid popp, a leader of austria's working women's movement, worked for several years in a cork factory owned by a mr. robert pecker.

*

"my name is
leslie
uggams

& i
practically

grew up

on t.v."

*

who
is
leslie
uggams?

*

she works for the t.v.

owned

by you

& me

My Name Is Rod Magnet

for Ted Berrigan

"sanche de gramont, the distinguished french writer, has undergone an extraordinary transformation . . . he is now ted morgan, an anagram for de gramont . . . he also considered 'rod magnet' . . ."
— N.Y. TIMES BOOK REVIEW

i used to be an elitist
but now i am egalitarian

i used to be chauvinistic
but now i do my bit at the wok

i used to be the strict father
but now i'm not even there

i used to be a hedonist
now want to be immigrant who makes good

my family lived in "france" for a thousand years
hereditary dudes since 1643

& i myself
until my metamorphosis
was a runt

but now i like hamburgers
shopping centers california
wines & wives & anxiety

*

in the morning

it's morning

then, it's something

someone

my heart   your heart

it's very interesting

it is a very great thing

in the ear

winds dance

your america

& mine

*

is it the hit
or the duck?
is it
the sudden light?

*

"it's the atmosphere: viz., issac asimov on 'star wars' bar scene, saying its *verismo* falls down due to absence of respirators — he thinks those monstro max ernst characters shd carry, & take little hits off of —"

*

covered with the magic morel
from brow to jowl

the young chiefs stumble in
start holding forth

moon-women of enchanted nights
did knit such headgear

now we are old   we sit and smile
the sisters bring us good things to eat

*

so how is paradise
                                        the wistfulness
billowing
                                  like a big mess

the randomly variously
                                                  'missed'

like sweden
                                  (well) or stendhal's
orange blossom special

but think, instead, of
                                                guacamole

such a *handsome* word

*

no nor but i mean

no   i didn't say nesting
i said i was merely
resting

nor did i say i was just another poet
i said i was just another boy

but i did say
"flying with captain eros"

i mean flying with captain ears

Aubade

night's ride's over

sun up   radio on

airedale wanda trots by window

time to see
what's there,
not forgetting what won't be

(the what
includes all whos)

so, coffee, here i come

here i come, dear shoes

D.C., August, 1977

she sat, looking
into the unknown (to him) reaches
of her own
where "maybe one day"
as she had just finished
saying (to him)
who stared at the salt
& pepper, made his eyes smart
& hours, days, weeks, months, & years
later, driving back from lunch through tears
he'd still curse his heart, regret his hunch
— foolishly, no doubt: not for the sake of art.

Mr. Ganzfeld

to the memory of Mr. David Lindsay

the old man made
alarming noises
sucking
on his gums

alarming them
(his gums)

then he said tadpoles
he said goddamn tadpoles
just hanging on
to their tails

    (tears, sweat, smudging
    changed
    circumstances

    drastic
    drop
    in in-
    come)

while the voice was calling &
"indescribable hugeness stood in the way"

& someone was trying to make real human conversation
love, & baseball, & like that

we were proceeding
out in the dark

the pipers leading the way

Numbers from Novalis

from the notebooks of Friedrich von Hardenberg
a.k.a. "Novalis," 1772–1801

narratives, disjunctive, yet associative like dreams:
poems, sonorous, replete with handsome words
while lacking all "sense" & "connection"

in which only an occasional line
would fit conventional comprehension

these lines being fragments
of the most disparate entities

such poems can have only a meaning-at-large

no connectives: a concatenation
of marvelous things & events

the world of the faery tale: totally opposed
to the world of "truth"
therefore resembles the latter as powerfully
as chaos resembles
completed creation

*

philosophia: the love of sophy: really
homesickness — the desire
to be at home
everywhere

*

in the world to come
everything like it was
in the world that was
yet everything
quite changed

the future world
is sensible chaos
chaos that has permeated itself:
chaos "squared," or raised to the power
of infinity

Object, Now

for Tom Raworth

large almost spherical shrub whose name its perceiver
realizes he does not know   never has known
as he is circumnavigating the island on which it grows
while his companion is reading postcard
asking for name or brief description
of that very exponent of rooted existence   still glimpsed
in rearview mirror in springtime virginia
so named after pre-industrial despot who wrote a line
or two in her time   *that* time

Her Letters to Her Friends

working on a memorial
often quite boring

though as a job it pays for groceries

not that the subject isn't admirable
she was   but *is* no longer

& the memorial will make her only
infinitesimally more present
if at all

insects stampede in brain

not a bad line but

only plants eat a patio

even better

medium large man in reading glasses
i eat by myself with a fork on a patio
having taken a break
from my work
on memorial

eat plants
not the ones will eat the patio
me too
even sooner

suddenly karl leibknecht stopped & proceeded to execute
a series of weird bounds without cracking a smile

i stared at him rosa luxemburg says astonished
& even a little frightened
what's the matter i said
she says
i translate

i'm so happy was all he said
she says
i translate

this april morning in nineteen-sixteen

With Hastie Joy & Feeble Speed

deecee ten earphones

bottle brush trees in bloom

memory's
selectivity

sometimes appalling

faces
postures
grown dear
over the years

what follows
follows

where are they

            they are away

that's where i've been

poor little thing &
ironical about it

one's imagination of
existence with courtesy
honor
coherence of feeling

poof

as it slides farther & farther out
it tends to the merely charming

In Annie's Garden

after & with Guillaume Apollinaire

had we lived in the year 1760 . . .

(that's the date isn't it annie
on the marble loveseat)

                    in the year 1760
it was my misfortune to be born a german
my good fortune to live close to you

we discussed 'love' a lot
mostly in fractured french

wide-eyed you hung on my arm
while i told you
everything   about pythagoras

but you were also thinking
about the little cafe where we'd stop
in a while for a while

& the fall was very much like this one
crowned with barberries & thorns

with a sweeping gesture i doffed my hat
to ladies we met on our walks
languid   aristocratic   & overweight

in the long evenings
slowly all by myself
i would down a bottle of malmsey or tokay

put on my spanish cloak walk down the road
meet my grandmother
who arrived in her ancient coach
refused to understand german

wrote poems chockfull of mythology
but they were really about your breasts
life in the country   & other ladies
of the district

(many's the time i broke my cane
on the back of some dumb peasant)

(i loved to listen to good music
while chomping on the good ham)

i swore in german "i swear to you"
that time you surprised me sticking my tongue
into a working-class redhead's mouth

but you forgave me
later
in the bilberry woods

as we walked on myself
i hummed a bit to myself

then   we spent a long time
listening
                    to the noises of nightfall

1901
1979

No Complaints

for

Laurie McElroy   Alice Notley

Ted Berrigan   Robert Grenier

friends, sustainers

Frail Old House in Sweet Briar Patch

"just think: with an electronic
dialer
you can call what's-his-name
when you can't even remember
                    what's-his-number"

*

stop, dear mozart: you're making me cry

*

"sure — *i* killed a bunch of chinese —
they're *tall* —
them veetnamese are *small* —"

handsome man in his thirties
clean & with it   pickin' up a sixpack

looks perfectly capable

but is given to these fits of weeping

*

ginkgo tree was here before dinosaurs

*

sometimes i feel like an idiot boychild
longing for mama ocean

oh would you ride with the religious?

oh no i'm just an old crank

now that the old confusions
have been moved out & junked
the heart looks rather empty

"boy   you gotta carry that weight"

i remember it well   that song

& mushrooms have been here all along

*

watch it go by:
"oil is an act of god"   "come home to america"

"you always laughed at these things
it took a little time   but you laughed"

someone in movie   some remarkable dreck
i step into, slip

"you've sublimated that into 'oops-a-daisy'"
says laurie   sunshine, i'll always love you

dreaming, de-programming, then awake
convulsed with rage-mirth at suave golem-blather
chewed ends of blond-gray fu manchu
grown out of middle-aged stone chin

living at certain speeds

affectionately   affectionately

*

tactful translations.   occasional retardations

*

seen the divine
seen the chorizo
seen the radio   heard it too

*

smash bad faith (pretense) says the feathered speaker
sweet shoes goofy grace & heartbreak kid
what happened to us fred   my little arm hurts
in the great dracula organ roar of existence

*

queen anne's lace out my window, virginia

i don't have to go to the bloody store every day

but where else *is* there to go in this bloody place
or any place in this bloody society
this bloody monolith of "store"

& when i say bloody i mean bloody   like joseph spero
mob store operator in kansas city
"accidentally exploded" a while ago

"after all, the old bum is your father"
as buster keaton pointed out a while ago

*

in the great return engagements
between the nineteenth & twentieth centuries
we'll experience many surprises

as for the news, it's still punched in & out
by obedient punks   i know, i was one
for almost a decade

until one day on a very ordinary bus
suddenly deprived of impressions   i became aware
once more   of the painful & weary

& tired of all sensational beauty tips tricks & freebies
it was the time of early to mid-period rolling stones
their diction was excellent then   it was a help
as was herbert marcuse

*

stars stars all around

the air-borne laser lab

new god of all good soviets
good americans

some of them some of us positive roses

like those blooming in wild russian jungle garden
around this house now

sweet jesus jefferson bible bobbie louise o.k.

there's obvious love in some houses

but queen anne's lace no way out cowboy hats no way out

it's time again to come out of the cave

(& go to the store)

*

after wang wei to be sure this is a frail old house
but sturdy table
writing hand bandaged but functional
wine by my elbow
the lady beautiful wise & forbearing
beyond my deserts (1)
beyond my deserts (2)

*

james dean now dead as long as he was alive
to himself an amusing distinction

*

"so you really want to know how it is with me?"
as some poet might say in that strange place
known as translation

in muffed gutturals one strains to hear
the other side of massive airlock glass

well everything's pretty great really

but for poverty illness mortality   & so on

winter is over   that's for sure

*

we tend to think the world sort of stands up
while all it really does is roll around

*

women's laughter through crickets & tree-frogs

*

hum hum twilight's
halloween, year's
dusk   every day   diodoros
of aspendos

sikelianos, jesse james, the whole quote unquote shot

(buenas dias, argentina)

une belle suédoise
une dogfuck in the snow

redeems the vulture cultures

sleazeville collegeville pentagon

hospital follies   a long cold drive

& bathroom mirror says:
"old man, some fucking *sense*"

(remember the professor
whose name translates as garbage)

diodoros   to teeth left, barefoot, grinning
"broad beans? sure, i'll have some"
with the blue blue eyes of a bay scallop

at his best when alone & confused   at large

*

hum hum   "you gotta *serve* somebody"
ah, the new self-righteous righteousness:

"they behaved like sickening pigs."
what a way to speak of your elders.

but when the new self-righteous righteous
speakers & singers look up
they see their "lord."

when they look down
they see shit on their shoes.

"what a self-indulgent jackoff!"
i hear you say

but i do not understand those phonemes

because i am diodoros
of aspendos   pythagorean
of the last days   disguised as a cynic

*

I want to thank my mother
                my family
                my lawyers

& here they come

congaing through my pillow

just like "god"

*

this faded purple box of five thousand
“standard swingline staples number s.f. minus one”
has lasted me through
a marriage or two
almost a dozen addresses phone numbers
defunct checking accounts
seven years & some months
& i still have a couple of hundred left

*

as for belief only one thing to believe
when she or he love you they do   but what do it mean
ah amigo that’s the trick   funny voices in corners
of room-shaped head i’m sorry i got a deadline will you
come back later oil is an act of god

how to get back to conscientious francis scott fitzgerald
or ancestor who ate a cat’s heart   it is four a.m. back on
schedule   more words per square centimeter
conventional even sentimental historical
late mechanized heir to romance

then somewhat speculative & fictional some what
misheard with inner & outer in other words actual by another
not unlike constructive analogous & inconclusive yet mostly
attempts & mentioned synchronous subsequent & compositional
having always held tuning-in possibly acquiring ability

to project voices out there in here & glad to be saying
hasta luego to do without knowing them again
remember my little granite pail   sat up all night roaring
overloaded most of the time   who is this thinks
point now not to country regional hopeless but theoretically

sunlight falling on ten percent united states farmland
supplies total mehitabel joy some ways lord byron
some ways the incredibly blue eyes of a bay scallop
both see through the blob in age of inanition
apple crate art   great difficulties of honesty

some remarkable dreck much of it sublimated into oops-a-daisy
dreaming de-programming surviving three mile island coming up
when you swim underwater this is where you keep your lighter
taps back pocket   john sjoberg   suppose i give you a pill
which makes you draw a picture   or one which gives you

feelings in the stomach   this has been god's minute
the voice is calling & we are lonely for it   in esoteric
lore the lady is the least essential   no kidding   & whose
fault was it pardon me sir whose fault was it yours or hers
common as hell put some heat on it get your ass up here

uprose with hastie joy & feeble speed that agèd sire
the lord of all that land yes well may you stay forever
incredible but know your underwear as it goes through the mangle
combine bottle brush trees with rosa luxemburg's prism &
your own paludal prurience   itspeak kitspeak

otto & myrtle ampersand

*

max jacob: a moment's thought to
max jacob

just a little artist   little motherfucker
caught in the roiling of time hands grabbed him out of —

believed in weeding, they did,
& he was a weed

flowered beyond & above
the greatest french garden

was plucked & destroyed by those hands in black gloves:
regulation s.s., acronym for schutzstaffel

"protective squadron"   protective of what?
of another little artist

little motherfucker, weed
grew like killer kudzu all over europe

was burned off her surface
not much later:

both their seeds
still circling the planet

*

pissing on open grave of last morning's mouse
trapped in the house

three a.m. sweet briar virginia

quiet   madness   insomnia   tequila

old charles laughton horror movie "strange door"

dust whale vacuum cleaner in the corner & now
it's one hundred degrees & i understand nothing
though still attentive just like our cat

to grotesque collective manifestations of regression:
some doddering lopsided smiler
our future leader?
pea-brained predatory type
repeated
several thousand times   gleeful   jumping
updown   blowing whistles   punching
little balloons in the air

back pickets stuffed with truly oily bills

mad baby grins   bubbling   manic brain soup

"america   behave   or be damned"

that's baptist billboard

so

you take a deep breath   & drive on by

*

totally wholly welcome is hokum
but it's nice hokum

people do think of people not here
& sometimes even hear them

many years later there's a pleasant evening
with mr. & mrs. hokum

& maybe mrs. hokum says, on parting:
"we *were*

a little worried about you
back there   for a while"

*

sure been nice to meet all of you people
the complicated simple
the simple complicated
the complicated complicated
the simple simple

not as exciting was it for your ancestors
or was it   confronting red cloud's negotiators

just like you, like them, i've come to the end of the push:
the beach boys' concert

finn proto-shaman half swede a quarter german
quarter pole & various smaller fractions anglo dutch & martian
(inter-galactic viking)

by the light of your campfires
                                        shopping malls
                                        museums
                                        & a few good bars

no way to go now but out

                                        let's figure it out

*

"right side of face hurts more than left"
another pointless statement

thousands upon thousands of those
made in this life until it is over

music fades in & out

beat stays the same

*

now "le beau reste"
as our french sisters say ah oui
where do we go from here

round the page

we'll just go gambolling round the page
once again

& then

let's kill

all the bad guys

let's have

all the good guys

over for dinner

"what's for dinner?"

"bad guys"

Between Novembers 1979 / 1980
Sweet Briar Virginia

Buenas Dias, Argentina

there's this assyrian rite
survives in southern italy:

a year after death,
you dig up bones

& take them home,
& polish them, & talk to them:

"dear aunt maria,
dear uncle gesualdo" etc.

all night, all day,
you polish them, talk to them,

then put them back,
in the ground.

buenas dias, argentina.
buenas dias, cambodia.

buenas dias, russia.
buenas dias, america.

1979

Manifest Destiny

to arrive in front of large video screen,
in pleasantly air-conditioned home with big duck pond in back,
some nice soft drinks by elbow, some good american snacks as well,
at least four hundred grand in the bank, & that's for checking,
an undisclosed amount in investments, & a copacetic evening
watching the latest military *techné*
wipe out poverty everywhere in the world
in its most obvious form, the poor

How To Do It

remembering Milton Klonsky

"*most*
    fun
        friends:
                worst
                      for
                         you"

(albigensian proverb?   original scansion?)

not always true   not in the case of colonel klonsky
of the blakeian host: scholar & visionary gentleman

an hombre funny as you'll ever hear
to make you shed a tear & yet another
of helpless mirth, hopeless delight

*

saluting him now,
envisioning his troops' formation greeting him
to the tune of "klactoveedsedsteen"

us left here humbly mumbles glad
to have been places with you here, gentle milton
never blind to this our oft-times asinine condition

of being alive in this, the be-bop universe
where we do have to know how to do it,
just like willie & eubie blake

which takes up all our time   so

we can never be   on the make

really

9 Dec 81

Hey

for Laurie McElroy

missouri pacific lines calendar:
big black steam locomotive
charges through riverside mists above
october eleventh
any year   any reckoning

    been here before   will be again

kissakatti the cat delighted eating small plate of tuna
wanda agreeable bearhound contemplating the absence of bears
(presence of kissakattis & humans   equally bearable   tho' crazy)

& this as they say writer at red & white oilcloth kitchen table
quite fried & tired   dreaming of power

power to make her feel better   be there tomorrow to reach
make some use of his arms   pacifically   not like locomotive
not running on rails   we aren't
but on our feet
& in our brains   whoo-whoo

so let's get off at that little station in the carinthian
alps of the imagination
a little hot chicken for you
beef goulash stew for me

talk   feel alive in the cold   makes us see our breath

light   & lightly   walking on air as they say

which is what any of us
walk on
ever

fred astaire steps on turd not missing a beat

11 Oct 79

Shark Eats Dog Mind on T.V.

shark eats dog mind on t.v.
no point complaining
about e.g. expensive scotch makes you horribly drunk
so hurt companions & dwell in bad boy poison for months

ding-ding ding-ding they just ate the old man the movie
    was going to be about

now for an oxygen hit   jean simmons
no it's two hundred & twenty-four small spiders
well mostly small
two millimeters up to an inch & a half

any attempt to make this an epic is bound to flop

Poem Beginning with a Line by Edward Thomas

the steam hissed. someone cleared his throat.
it was my father: time to get off train.
summer time
                    for inward world —
rocks. plants. birds. reptiles. mammals
other than ourselves
perceived
                in mute surmise. three months
times ten. a great blank shining space
in life, each year,
quite probably only
                            reason i'm still here.

Songs of The Sentence Cubes

"badfoot:"

white
wife,
walk
fast
leg!
this
man
old;
bad
foot.

"candy:"

big
baby
girls
kiss
small
old
boys

*

why,
we
hear
some
fly
ate
your
new
work?

it
got
your
old
lady,
you
dirty
beast.

later,
man.

it
one
cold
time.

*

had let what kiss taste face
                                                clean forgot

time took it out
                          & how
                                     but slow

Doc Holliday

the silences grow taller
the other end of the line

sporadic punctuation
of human exclamation

"katie?"
"doc?"
"you there?"
"you going?"
"you gone?"

cards, shuffling through
faint honky-tonk

*

saddle up
at least one more time
& ride like hell

in pursuit of unattainable
sanity, joy,
"calme, luxe et volupte"

just hoping the storm
won't rise & blow you under

not too far down, at least
for the tribe

to dig up bones, doings, sayings
of the once happy beast

Nostalgia: Sax Rohmer

the light of the table lamp, softened and enriched by its mosaic shade, gave an appearance of added opulence to the spacious, luxurious workroom, with the soft light playing on rank after rank of rare & costly editions, deepening the tones of the persian carpet, making red morocco more red, purifying the vellum & regilding the gold of the choice bindings, caressing the busts & statuettes surmounting the bookshelves, & twinkling upon these oaken shelves, where petronius arbiter rubbed shoulders with balzac; where omar khayyam leaned confidentially toward philostratus; where mark twain, standing squarely beside thomas carlyle, glared across the room at george meredith, as the table clock ticked on, seeming to hasten its ticking as the hand crept closer to midnight, as the mosaic shade of the lamp poured mingled reds & blues & greens on the pages of manuscript strewn about beneath it, while through the leaded panes of the window above the desk swept a silver beam of moonlight: it poured, searchingly, upon the fur-clad figure swaying by the table. it was richard brautigan.

Dinner with Another Tribe

the distinguished
canadian
poet-anthologist
sure liked that song,
"blood on the saddle!"
when he saw me in tandem
with his ex-colleague's daughter
he insisted
at the dinner party
that the host, a proficient
banjo player & poet
sing it
for *us,*
as it were
right then & there,
in east lansing, michigan.
an old man. & bitter.
just like me, now.
but a worse creep.
who knows,
maybe not.
old gonads play
crazy tricks on
the monads attached.
in any case,
our host
begged off,
saying he did not like that song.

Das Ewig-Weibliche*)

remembering Max Finstein

a heart-shaped face is moving her lips
a pear-shaped person is moving her hips

on her inter-galactic receiver
she hears them   her fans   "c'est si bon"

she loves them   her terrestrial retrievers
named george after george   paul after paul

she comes to visit
& travel on

& when was that   & when was that
oh it was about the time i bought my first hat

April 1982

---

*) "the eternal feminine": goethe:
"das ewig-weibliche
zieht uns hinan" — "the eternal feminine
pulls us upward"

Illustrated Man

for Patti Landi

now i looks at you & is sensible &
not screaming but talking

ceiling falling upstairs   never mind
now is perennial

perennially lonely preposterously grateful
weird & increasingly puppyish

"since love is brittle & precise
against this sharp & crystal pain

we shall be scornful & alert"
that was frances frost speaking

she had a son
paul blackburn   gone

but his ghost lives   & goes on feet
& reads the ground   still unabashed

embodied   as is mine
to make hard music   amiga

so as not to go too soft to melt
into the ground quite yet   yet quite

in energetic duets   muchas gracias
even if rare

still there
to provide some continuous light

The Images of Day Recede

the pleasure principle tends to start squeaking after a while

just like this wood frame canvas chair of mine

does to remind me that nothing related to human

activity is simply automatic, or predictably continuous

Il Miglior Fabbro

to Paul Blackburn & P.G. Wodehouse, over yonder

who said you differ from
my cousin rupert's younger son
anselm who got his chance
in the *canzone* titled
"anselm gets his chance"
who dreamt of myrtle jellaby
because he loved her yet
did not dare inform her uncle
due to meager stipend
feared the wrath of
millionaire philatelist
he lacked the courage & pursued instead
the cautious policy of lying low & hoping for the best
but one bright summer day at breakfast time
found anselm dancing round the table
& so on   a brick in the short ribs
a generous snort of that incredible tonic
"buck-u-uppo"   & so forth
she was one of those tall dark girls
who tend to a certain extent to draw
themselves to their full
height & let their male
vis-à-vis
have it
squarely in the neck

don't you know what ho
cheer up old onion don't lose hope
after all you are
a graduate of the silent films

as was dear mr. wodehouse the last great poet
in the *occitan* tradition

Gehenna

swooning dust continuous hair

the southern coke queen's delicate profile on hospital pillow
wrenched in medieval idiot's heart
befuddled his head for a time

later she turned back into silly disco camel
& he was glad to put many a mile between himself &
her & her vapidly billowing world

(smarmy tunes on flute
are apt to make one puke)

is this the intermission cha-cha no
it's the last waltz on continuous loop

place has come full circle jesus hawks
jesus hawks clawing & loving each other up

let's stay in shape though like national rifles

remember suburban american afterlife
takes place on big deck

Romance

"suddenly in a light shawl
you slipped out of the half-darkened hall —
we disturbed no one,
we did not wake the sleeping servants . . ."

— OSIP MANDELSTROM, TRL. BY DAVID MCDUFF

for Laurie Price

suddenly
    in a bright shawl
you slipped
        in the pitch-dark hall
waking up all the servants
            & twisting your ankle
but i picked you up &
                flung you into my rickshaw
            galloping off
        as all the lights
                    came on
                        in your former home

*

you swept down the hall in a ravishing gown
& i, i swept you up in my arms
& together we rolled down the stairs, & the footmen
gathered us up & deposited us in the taxi
& it took us home, to nubar gulbenkian's place
where we had been staying these past eighteen months.

*

you stumbled, & fell. the pint of vodka slipped
out of your hand & bounced down the chute, alerting
the guards. we looked at each other,
held heads, & kissed:
there was no tomorrow but *they* were fucked too —
the pint contained killer gas. the label
read "no one gets out of here alive."

*

i came shinnying down the vine to you.
your pear-shaped breasts quivered at my descent.
once in your arms, i found myself in the jet
serenely zooming across the gobi desert

*

you stood in the driveway, smiling
& i apologized for not having been there

you said oh no, i was looking at your house
& talking to the animals & all the plants

around your house. & now we are here
& we can go in.

& we went in.

Virginia, 1981

Dove Sta Amore

the days: air

the riddles i talked in
when i saw you again

i wanted
                    i was
shy
     to touch you

  . . . my hand
on your waist as it moved
beside me

  . . .

i raise my hands
to have them remember,
tracing you
                    in words & air

*

the lights going on in the rooms strung back
through the years

    the way
    the blue room
    (remembered)
    lights up

    as you turn to
        be held
    & to hold me

    your
        beholder

1967/68/81

Dirge

comes a time you know every move:

"change the musicians whenever you like"

comes a time "it's all over
                    by the time it hits k.c."

comes a time someone called erik satie
& someone called john lennon
"look-alikes"
are equally dead

comes a time some you gets shot through the lungs
four times to collapse in historic dakota hallway

(someone called panna grady no longer lived there)

comes a time you travel all the way from honolulu
in fellow incarnation
possibly "chapman"

comes a time you don't know nothing

& all the musicians are gone

you missed it: they didn't miss you

8 Dec 80

The Vega

rolled through dragon spasms
of detroit steel
buckling & bending
beyond repair

we got out &
walked away

transforming the yelps
of pain into language
of some interest
(acquired skill)

much harder to say
i love your eyebrows

harder to say
i love you forever

Ten Cheremiss (Mari) Songs

walked
            in the woods: a green leaf
brushed
            against my face

it wasn't a leaf:
                    i had just thought of my lover

*

come, let the two of us
go pull up some leeks!
we'll be together,
one soul around us.

*

a white blanket
                    onto the back of a white horse
a silver saddle
                    on top of the blanket
a down pillow
                    on the saddle
a wax candle
                    on the pillow

you can make a wax candle
longer or shorter.

you can't do that
with your life.

*

at dawn, a dark cloud appeared,
firing lightening-bolts at my father's house.
why do i keep telling my dreams:
who but me understands them?

*

woke up early,
went & carved my name
in the bark of an appletree.
contemplated what i have
& what i do not have.

*

in the dark before dawn
we walk through the woods,
talk, whistle, & sing.
don't listen to those sounds
as if they were songs.
they are the sounds of our pain.

*

i shouldn't have started these red wool mittens.
they're done now,
but my life is over.

*

climbed the hill,
went down into the valley,
followed the white-water stream.
if the dream comes at all, it comes at night,
to allow us to walk in our thoughts, in the hours of daylight.

*

snow coming down,
                                        rain coming down,
there's room for it all
                                        between sky & ground.

& the troubles we have,
they all fit
between heart & liver.

*

you dream that you are traveling through water:
thus, you emerge from grief.

versions based on Finnish translations of these
by Marjuka & Jorma Eronen, 1979.

"mari (over half of pop.) . . . 1965 est. pop. 656,000 . . .
formerly called cheremiss, are a finnic people."
— Columbia-Viking Desk Encyclopedia

No Complaints

six for Robert Grenier

high plains drifting

on the high plains,
when we meet
the inspector
we say, "buenas tardes, inspector"

*

on the phone

"when do you go to bed?"
she asked me.

"when do you go to tibet?"
was what I heard.

"never," was my reply. "i've never
felt like going there."

*

there was some panic on the plane

people were screaming let me off let me off

then one man with an english accent stood up & said

no complaints

*

good
        to do the little
physical
            things
in the only place
sung by
          the ancients
                                          we swim to meet

*

too little & too late

too brittle & too fated

we are but rabbits that pass at dusk

*

parenthesis

the part in her hair had a little bend
      at the end

Notes

frail old house in sweet briar patch

diodoros of aspendos. one of the few survivors (who often masqueraded as cynics) of the anti-pythagorean purges in the 6th century b.c.: "they took part in politics, & their opposition to accepted religion caused them to be persecuted from existence in magna graecia." orthodox followers of pythagoras never partook of beans.

in its cento-like passages, this poem incorporates brief quotes from films, t.v., robert grenier, lorine niedecker, don marquis, john sjoberg, laurie mcelroy, ludwig wittgenstein, the radio, james schuyler, waiter benjamin, de judge, de doc, sir edmund spenser, bob dylan, & probably others.

songs of the sentence cubes

application of a game of the scrabble phylum.

nostalgia: sax rohmer

sax rohmer: popular author of early 20th century a.d., creator of dr. fu manchu.

il miglior fabbro

much of the input derives from wodehouse's lovely short story, "anselm gets his chance." occitan: provençal: troubadour.

gehenna

title: geographical designation of hell (arabic).

romance

mr. gulbenkian: wealthy fellow, patron of investment arts.

dove sta amore

loosely, "where are they now?"

the vega

vega: a star, & for a while, a car.

from Pick Up the House: New & Selected Poems

When having something to do
but not yet being at it
because I'm alone, because of you
I lay down the book, & pick up the house

& move it around until it is
where it is what it is I am doing
that is the something I had to do
because I'm no longer alone, because of you.

—TED BERRIGAN, *CODA: SONG*

Pick Up the House, 1981–1985

In the Mission

for Robert Creeley

God

His
followers
started the place but

God
is not what you think
in the Mission

*

As the song
goes, "The *good*
times, the *bad*
times"

God knows
back there,
in his snug chair
on the favorite floor

of his perishing tower
wistful,
sniffing
a flower:

"*Reminds* me of
all of them"

*

Be a hundred and ten.
Go to sleep.

Say,
"Au revoir."

*

She used to be angry
but now she is sleeping:

"Oh let me dwell in
comfortable-looking
hole in your facial cheek"

*

See See

Five short yellow
dafs — narcissi —
whatever they are,

flowers of spring
tra-la, suddenly
in this long kitchen sing

a scent, sweet, it says,
"Si, si"

. . .

Most of life not
that way,
yet one remembers

when it has been, been seen
and heard and felt and smelled
that way.

*

C & W

Life is complicated
Drains are roaring
Percy B. Shelley
was fond of soaring

In walks a minimalist
He says, "That's boring"

He needs to be kissed
by someone complicated

Another sweet
big head
to remain entertained
and a bit more alive than dead

*

High Cloud

Populous raft of confusion
drifting across the sky
while fur turns gray

*

Rimas

I haven't lost my mind, you know,
although I think, believe, I've found
a woman, most intelligent, most kind,
with whom I then proceed to fight
on what I thought was an auspicious night —
about what, neither of us know.

There is the rain, there is the snow,
the dew, the fog, the mist, the glow,
the atmosphere containing us
and the necessity to catch the bus.
Hers. Mine. Possessive forms of action
giving one little or no traction.

So let it slide, and let's abide and sigh
as dawn is drawing nigh and fires are lit again
throughout the camps of busyness and gain.

I love her eyes: love them when they look at me,
her mouth when it moves, even when not speaking.

*

In the summer, he said, I write short

*

Now that people are wearing hats again,
one can tell them “Go shit in your hat” again

*

Make her laugh: the world
seems like it’s staying

*

“They only made one of these.
Do you deserve it?”

*

Who’s here?

Two powerful Democrats
Many United Beef Workers
Some Undecided Youths

*

“Just white poet trash”
— The Decisive Instrumentality

*

A High Note

leaves one at a loss
for an appropriate quote

and so, remembering, one says, “Hello,”
and says, into dark air, “You’re very nice,”

rolls over, hugs
oneself, and wants you back

*

Back in New York

"My sister, life" — last time I saw her
I begged her not to be as literal as me;
old flames, old blames — none there
that precious funky afternoon: yes,

some lives work: somewhere in here's
this romantic boy, writes letters in his head
and in his heart — which are the faces
he makes, in there, inside himself.

And once in a while he jumps up on shelf
and sits there: looking at you: eyes all one color.

*

Whitman's Secret

You're not gonna sleep
anyway
You're just gonna lay
around and curse

So why not stay up, brother,
and think about everything

And I mean *everything*

*

Her face, absolutely
two sides

and sometimes, in motion,
unearthly harmonious

*

"To bed, to bed,
as Lady Macbeth said"

There was a time
one thought that was funny

An amusing
rhyme

*

Ferocious sociopath
rubs ace of hearts
against his crotch, for luck

Un poco buzzed, observing water's descent
upon phenomena, Thursday, also César
Vallejo's "bad day"

*

Clarification

Not
buying
you:

just
buying
you

a
drink

*

A Kind of a Vow

Make me
a pillow
and I'll
sleep on it
as long as it
takes me

*

Proofreading Discovery

"inextricably
interwoven"

became

"methodically
intentional"

*

Shiva
takes it
apart and
down,

puts it
together
again
in the ground —

("Aahh-yess, Shee-vah take it apart 'n' . . .")

*

Not going to read
any of these
to anyone
over the phone
tonight.

Tonight is the night
anyone's under the covers
with their lovers
present or not,
present or not.

August 1981–August 1982
San Francisco

Mission Aubade

for Tinker Greene

Ambulance howls into receiving bay
Some birds start singing
Folks on the block are getting up
Some are still awake   still alive too

Long Ways

Come a long way,
speak of it now and again:
that is our work.

Twenty-four years ago honeymooned on the Isle
  of Jersey, our son on his way.
Low tide, we walked out to the castle,
warm, apprehensive, expectant, bored.
Slept and woke in the sweet and salt;
sea and light is what I remember.
Dreamt himself into being inside you,
now he has lived the years we had then:
a man, mind, heart, a peaceable builder
  of a future beyond ours.

Go a long way,
travel the seas in darkness and light,
speak of it now and then.

Stars and Stripes Forever

May it always ride in and out again
as in all the stories we love to hear:

horses
        strutting,
ships
      sliding into the harbor —
Lindy
        coming in to land,
Ted rolling out of bed —

greens
        turning to the light,
hands
       insistent in the night;

two people
                playing accurate guitars
on this century's
                      twilight T.V.

Question

Know the various abuses of the locution,
know all the shit one may have to eat in the afterhaze:
yet if you cannot say to another you, "I love you,"
how can you ever say anything anymore anywhere
    in this world?

How It Works

In the suburbs it's quite expensive
to hire an assassin — to get
the witness permanently removed.

In the projects it's quite a bit cheaper.

And elsewhere in not so civilized parts
it's absolutely a bargain.

And that's pretty much how it works.

Valid

Having a *pasaporte,* how much more *valid*
I am than brother Jésus or Pedro
trying to swim the river,
tackle the spiral barbed wire!

Anthropology

"The culture of a people
is an ensemble of texts
which the Anthropologist
strains to read"

over the shoulders of those to whom they properly belong

*

"The essay, whether of thirty pages
or three hundred, has seemed
the natural genre in which to present
cultural interpretations"

and the theories sustaining your jobs   you jokers

Some

Some thing falls
to some floor.

Someone remembers,
makes much of it.

The other one says,
I had no idea.

*

After the telephone
he sat a while trembling
the way dogs do when nervous
when they've perceived something
much larger than their brains

August

Hot sunny Baltimore day,
walking through the park,
holding her hand, touching her waist.
Checking out the zoo,
in and out the gates.
Sun sets.   Oh, Ted, we miss you,
whistling in the dark.

Sorpresa

Cool
    April wind
blowing
    mulberry
petals, belated
                "snowflakes"
in the small
merciful
hours:

Came
    home,
walked into bathroom:

Aahh! Colors!
Pretty shapes!

Your
    summer clothes
shedding their wrinkles
& mothball scent —

doing
    the things
I've been trying to do
ever since you told me

come in   come home

Looking at a Book of Chinese Seals

Wanting to wake you up at 3:00 A.M., knowing
you need rest more than my babble, I try
to calm down, sip tea, and breathe

my way through early morning hits and flashes

to a state approximating the seal that says

paper is too short
for the endless affections

or the one that says

it is a rare virtue
to be able to muddle through
once in a while

or

how can I do without you,
even for a day?

Sixteenth, seventeenth China, not that far away,

which moves me next to you, Particular Woman
half-despairing, sliding into my dreams, resting

yet praying for your dear face next to mine

to be there

to be there, at dawn

Bro Joe

Match, struck, flares
in the dark

Quark
flits through molecule and is gone

to traverse
yet another room

*

Deities' noses twitch in their slumbers,

remember poetry and pinball:

love making no demand for love in return,

para siempre

Page

In measured hand
we write the letter
full of rage

but then,
a little later,
feel our age

and say, Shit —
who's that do?
Some bodies

gun their cars
out of this street.
The sun

also rises. Nancy
and Sluggo
go to it.

Something I Stole & Would Like You to See

Eros
totally involved love at first sight

Ludus
playful love — love as a game

Storge
love from a deep and lasting friendship

Pragma
love with a shopping list

Mania
unbalanced love involving extreme possessiveness

Agape
selfless love making no demand for love in return

Paradiso
all of the above in perfect perennially contradictory balance

See You Tomorrow (We Hope)

YELL! CRY! SHOUT! WEEP! COMPLAIN!
Modes only too easy
in 1983
or any year this fast

in the fastest known century
of an upstart human universe
quite pitifully brief
while possibly unique

"I MEAN," says a lady
calling in on our private
all-night station,
"HOW CAN WE KNOW

THE CUCARACHAS WILL PRODUCE
ANOTHER HENRY JAMES"
or HARRY or FRANK
or JESSE for that matter

Ten trillion cells
exchanging coded info
every micro-instant in her head
(and yours and mine)

Yell shout weep cry complain
trying to hit that note
(can't sing) Oh timid timid time
of weaponry's highly

organized flowering
and wistful pleasure
in the Empire's cities
Crazed pain and its infliction

at outposts and bridgeheads
Broken bones hanks of
disenfranchised hair
by their roadsides

Oh timid timid time
in the Empire's last days
a headline: "RAT BITES FRIEND
EARLY ONE MORNING

LATE IN 1983"
and wistful pleasure
in sometimes cultivated
small spaces:

People
really
aren't
that large

and don't have to
devour
more than
their share

Shed the Fear

Who has a face sees
   the world,
but the world
   is not

to be borne —
   or only
when seen as
   another:

how did this
   come together? How
did I find you?
   So many turns

in the road,
   so few of them
possible!
   How not to spin out

in hairpin turns
   of disbelief . . .
The Sufi martyrs
   insisted:

"The world
   is a wedding."
Why not
   go with them,

in the face of
   present carnage,
centuries
   later.

Sad Little Number

Wandering
through the rooms,
touching things, gazing
in sad drunken nakedness

back in the wilderness
he missed her, his guide

"no clothes on, and no use"

Pup Canto

The body is frail,
even Odysseus',
given to him for a time (no
  mileage charge):
stretched muscles, pinched nerves,
  slipped disks, twisted joints,
    broken bones, ah yes —
There is
    a foot in the water,
alongside the boat

and the toes
        feel pretty good

Amigo, we're buzzing along

A Round for the Trout Fisher

One: Back When There Was Bliss

"Ignorant bliss" —
  not ignorant of but ignoring
Death
  and rightly so,

as death is the cessation of knowing:
  hence what is worth keeping are
the living bodies: many of them

  exploding, imploding,
with anger, hunger,
  splattering
our lordly windshields.

  So stop the car — no, don't:
at any intersection in Brasilia
  you'll be deconstructed

by a fountain of machetes,
  once you step out of
your shell.
  See the world, baby,

but stay in the cage is the password.
  So in our little quite comfy cages
we sit and quiver —

  one dances, one plays the flute.
Friends clack the cymbals,
  shake the tambourine. Once
in a while

  someone remembers
one of those old words:
  Equity. Compassion. Tenderness

and makes them
  iridesce
round the
  edges

Two: Two Scenarios, Or Simple Village Tunes

Well, things came up out of the ground
and GOT them.
Well, things fell down from the sky
and GOT them.
Well, the AIR got so bad, and the WATER,
it GOT them.

WELL, they just didn't
know what to look for:
there were too many things
they'd made, and didn't even
know, besides
the things

they hadn't made, and didn't know, either.

*

And then there were some who said, We don't think
we want to go, we think we want to stay
and look at this place a little longer

Not that it's going to improve by our doing so

Not that it's going to get worse

Just that we haven't really seen it yet

Just that we'd like to look at it a little longer

The Dream of Instant Total Representation

Primaries, conventions, elections —
spectacularly staged surrogates for old dreams
    of powwows by the campfire,
direct votes cast at the forum
    or Anglo-Saxon "thing"

Dreamy memories of just about postnomadic time
when the turnip was the new technology.
While knowing this was long ago, far away,
we'd still like to get next to the headperson
and deliver a speech, at least twice as long
    as anyone else's . . .

Even if telepathy were perfected —
and instant global communication —
where on earth would we find
statespersons, legislators, bureaucrats
able to withstand such an incredible onslaught
    of info? Would the result not be total
overload, fried circuits, the screaming meemies?

Yet each and every ant knows exactly what
    it has to be doing every second,
the whole shebang self-contained
and self-informing —

To paraphrase Blaise Pascal, I'd rather be
    a confused, blundering, warm-blooded
    hairy creature with language
to complain in, to praise with, no matter what,
than nature's prototype for the microchip.

Petit Chanson

One of those quiet moments
when things fall into shape
    and *be*: wind gently blowing
    residual raindrops
    against the window

daytime frazzle collapses
into sweet darkness

and the moment, while officially
3:00 A.M., is all the eternity
one will ever know

On the Occasion of a Poet's Death

The dedication and intensity of the dead
always were greater than ours.
No doubt it seemed that way to them too
as dusk was falling
on their last weary glimpse of a land
populated by twerps.

The disembodied glories of Hades await us.

See You Later

Ascending mountain path
in good company: Ted Berrigan,
seen here the first time after his death —
Duncan McNaughton, still alive in the world I'm adream in,
many others
wearing sturdy United Beloved Nations overcoats, blue-black,
scarves, gloves, goodly shoes,
though there is one fellow with snazzy hat:
turned-up collar prevents me from seeing face
— Tinker Greene perhaps?
                                        Well, anyway, here we go
in bright blue day,
mountain to our right,
sheer drop to miles-away valleys
on our left — the path
beautifully paved, with pale gray, almost square chunks of stone,
the width of it
a person and a half

So we tread lightly and with care
while typically smoking this or that
(Doing this in waking life,
we'd be gasping, stumbling, quite easily gone)

Ted says, "Wouldn't you know it?"
apropos of what? There's also a strong wind,
and I am worrying about the emerald abyss
to my left
                  yet confident we'll all make it
to wherever we're going that seemed
just around the corner
and now is, quite possibly, not merely
atop a mountain
                        but *inside* the mountain,
only to be reached by
an equal number of strides
                                        down: on the inside: no shortcuts.

Hair, beards, coats, scarves flapping
in the emphatic wind

glasses reflecting pale brightness,
we're walking, bullshitting along, just as in
real life. Hey, here's George Kimball III
with a bottle: Thanks, man: who or what "won?"

But careful now, one slip and we won't
feel so great anymore. On we go,
Ted our guide, friend, beloved raconteur . . .

Aeons later, someone, Duncan I think, says "You know,
we're going to give it back to them,"
and I think Oh no, what's this? We're not just proceeding
to the most remote tavern of the universe?

And Ted says "Yes, yes — we're going to
where the pounding of acceptance
meets the pummeling of negation — no, no"
(drags on Chesterfield King)
"which is utter benighted bullshit, of course"

Now there is sleet, even small hail in the wind,
and I remember the waking lifetime we strode
through blizzard in Minnesota, early Iowa morning rain,
and youthful demons on Lower East Side

and I think, There has to be a trick, to end this dream,
the way there are tricks to end a poem

19–20 September 1984

Letter

Dear sister, where was it, where is it *now*,
we sat under a tree, and you were crying, and
I did not have the faintest as to why . . .
But I did. I knew it was because you were in love
with Col. Hercules Wilmot Scott and there was no way
that anyone was going to understand *that*.

Hearing

for Jane

great voices
of the great dead, next
to the great living you
(no TV): such thrills inside
led me here, to you. No
TV. Jonquils, soon dead, out
of season, in howling winds:
winter, cold moon, your warm
belly, rubbed thrice for luck:
clear vision, smile in the morning —
"no war, please."

"Amazing Grace"

for Jane

Ted Berrigan's favorite hymn, more true
than anything I'd heard that year
but for your, my lady's, voice and being,

winging into my life, and so completely seeing
the holes Death had punched into my head —

freeing my heart to love again in ways
forgotten, known again:

the humble rage of love, its tears,
its spasms of joy, its fears, its sighs
and grand designs: amazing grace.

Put In a Quaver, Here and There

It is smooth, fairly
uniformly gray, and of a
topological conformation
not easily described by Euclid:
circa two inches wide,
one inch tall, and half an inch
in thickness.

(I am indulging
in little twinges of nostalgia,
using those ancient
premetric
and soon to be forgotten
measurements.)

It is a rock
found on a beach
called Half Moon Bay
an easy hour's drive south of
San Francisco,
picked out from among a great number
of fellow rocks and pebbles, ground and
washed ashore by the Pacific,
the most intimidating and also most beautiful
body of water
on this planet. The reason
this artifact of an ocean
now sits on my desk,
facing St. Paul Street in Baltimore,
is its sculptural aspect. It has eyes,
nostrils, and a mouth,
all in unexpected places,
making it what the French call
un joli laid —
a beautiful ugly one,
easily seen as the fossil skull of a small
Venusian, landed long ago
on some shore of earth. A miniature
henrymoore, it defies easy recognition,
arrests the eye, and makes one think of
other possible forms.

While knowing well that it's just a large pebble,
pointed out and handed to me by a friend
with whom I'd spent hours and days on that beach,
watching dogs chase pelican shadows across the shallows.

I also know that it is what the ancients knew as
an "object of virtue" — irresistible —

recently traveled to visit its shore of origin
in another friend's purse, as a mascot,
it did, indeed, bring her home safe and sound.

Daniel Spoerri, Swiss artist-philosopher,
friend and disciple of the great Duchamp,
made a book called *An Annotated Topography of Chance*.
This consists of a detailed description of each
and every object found on or around his studio table
on a given date, complete with the history
of these objects' origins,
relationships to present circumstance, what have you:

Looking at my Venusian from Half Moon Beach,
now serving as humble paperweight, I am reminded
of Spoerri's lovely undertaking,
and — what with a post-thunderstorm July sun
shining into my window — encouraged to suggest
to all of you, dear friends, moments of contemplation
vis-a-vis accumulated objects of virtue
in your immediate vicinity: mute witnesses,
they could yet prove to be guides.

In the Voice of Jane to Her Mother

Caught myself
putting away four dresses
I've never worn,
folding them

into a suitcase
to wait for winter, again.
They were my mother's,
before my time —

when I
didn't know her.
She'd hoped
they would fit me:

they never did.
But their fabrics are fine
indeed,
the stuff of dreams:

that a piece of cloth
be revived to new use,
that my mother
be my friend.

Late Night Dream Movies

for Chris Toll

1

The war beneath the seas
is quiet.
St. Paul Street, Baltimore, at 1:30 A.M.,
is not.
But I'd sure as hell rather be here
than in some sinister submarine.
I don't know — why
am I telling you this? Who *are* you?
Yelling, out there. Well, I'm yelling
in here too.

2

Heavyset, self-assured fellow
at marble-top café table
keeps pointing at peacoat
suspended from Martini Rossi parasol
and saying, "You mean you don't *have*
another coat?"
Shivering
in my underwear, I rage back:
"That's the *only* coat I have!"
Grab his lapels, haul off, and,
almost connecting
with his hateful Sidney Greenstreet smirk,
wake up to Jane's startled yet smiling face
and her saying, "You just punched me in the chest?"

3

Now we are in scenic Iowa City,
in a motel
with sliding glass doors fronting on Olympic-size
patio swimming pool: it must be some kind of
conference — here comes Jane, with hardly
any clothes on, followed by patently upset and
expostulating Father — she stops, turns, leans forward,
and tells him, "Why don't you just go suck on a
big fat cigar!" Crash, boom, Rachmaninoff. Next thing
I know, we're sitting at table among dinner debris,
Jane at far end, in some animation,
Dave Beaudoin, looking most proper, on my left,
Father across from us: we're having coffee,
brandy, it is quite warm,
but Papa has been weeping — his shoulders, even, are wet —
and after sympathetic murmurs, and a short pause,
he pulls out a somewhat musket-shaped clarinet from his pocket,
which turns out to be a cigar holder — affixes
big cigar to it, starts puffing — I say,
"But can you play it, too?" He says, "Sure," and gives us
a tune. I think this is quite certainly better
than last night's number, when I was climbing

the scaffolding of a giant roller coaster
in order to get back to my life, my words.

4

The castle, cut off by the tide: we're moving in on it
in these nifty inflatable two-person assault rafts, just
before dawn. Granular silver surrounds us. We're
on time, we'll be there right on time. The Great Electric
Eel is our impartial observer: we'll avoid bloodshed. We
owe it to him. Jane smiles at me through the spray: she is
the most beautiful human I've ever seen.
I squeeze her long fingers: "It'll be all right."
In our wake, light-bearing particles dance.

5

In our dreams
we cry out. Even if
it is merely the computer
brain sorting
recent days' info,
we do cry out, in our dreams:
some things
want to be heard, attended to,
hugged or killed,
known, before termination. Amen.
"Amen?" Yes,
That's an honest word.

A Model

Downstairs
they are improving themselves
by pounding bag.
That's it: pounding bag.

Upstairs
they are engaged in relentless
social as well as existential advance
toward the Great Dark
but not pretentious about it:
they "utilize,"
as they're apt to say,
a pretty good, simple program:

"Keep 'em stoned on the goods."

It may seem monotonous to some
(including us here on the middle floor,
decadents, no doubt,
easily amused, easily bored,
violent and lachrymose by turns:
not properly *grown,* I suppose)

but it certainly keeps those upstairs fellows
in some decent Scotch

Sonnet

There are many places in this world,
some of them inhabited by the totally mad.
She hands them pennies, directs them
to the nearest shelter.
Some we live right close to & somewhat
believe in, as further language.
Remember, too, the ones who died
while telling us they felt great
& the doctors agreed. The sun
shines upon the just & the wicked,
but why should they feel the same way
about how it feels, when no one hands them
a thermometer. As for thought,
I think it went out with Ted. He took
all the thought & sprinkled it all over
the globe, which is now clogging up
the toilet of this Star Wars universe.

An Autobiography

"Go there!"   "Stay here!"
                    "Stay there!"   "Come here!"
What changes
                    is nothing but anywhere
they want you,
                    and you want them to want you
there: and then
                       there you are. Were.
Formerly there,
                     now here. What do you know.
What a way to live. To have lived.
Nowhere. "One, very small,
                                to go."

De Amor y Otras Cosas

Being chased out into the night
can be the beginning of a new life:

us human beings
ain't always benign,

but sometimes
                 She is

And that's the difference between
"So be that way"
and "So be it."

*

How to join them,
the disparate, desperate "halves of the world"?

In the great sea smell of woman of man,

                          of them together

*

Breathing, next to you
someone's telling you
you're not *all* there is —

"Surprise! Surprise."
Laugh. Hurt
a little. Wonder

when it was you were
infinite, all-understanding
of, just, you.

*

Sunday: mission bells at six in the morning,
over thousands of small heavens and hells,
well, mostly purgatories. Give us a big kiss.

*

She changes. She does
what you did not expect her to do.
She'll always do that. It is
her way.

*

In places
there's a face
in place.

*

Saw her walking down the street one day

Remember grabbing ahold of small tree —

Midafternoon, sober, delighted, not knowing *what* to do
but to walk on.

*

Things
burn
off:

See
what's
left.

*

Sound of the summer's last cricket
haunting, that night. but all thoughts
of oblivion
banished
by your smile

as you moved close, and held, and whirred and pirouetted

your way into my soul, that rarely seen cousin
who lives in the house of memory

*

I love
your
back. I don't
have anywhere
to go back to
except for
your
back.

*

Time fills up. faster
and faster

But we
do
try to last

*

Sweet of you to say,
"Well, it'll give you a chance
to spend some time at *your* house,"
while knowing, as you must,
that any house I'm in where you are not
quite soon seems empty
until you walk in the door

*

This man who'd come down from the trees
had a lot of trouble with keys
but when he looked up again

he saw a tall woman
at the top of a stair
looking

and not looking one bit perturbed
by his frankly deplorable condition
(far past "mint")

and in her Greyte Kindnesse
she took him in
and even looked at his book

*

"What is love?" Well, we love
the sight of
                    the species
as it dances
                    at dusk

We would not want to miss it
for ever
            or ever

*

The faces
we make, making love,
are the only ones
will change our faces
over the years
into the ones we deserve

*

Insect-clock seasons pass, but the great pleasure
humans provide one another when so minded
is as close to perennial as creation gets

*

The dances of dusk are slow, because the dancers are.
Yet the dancers perceive them as fast,
excruciatingly fast,
and valiantly marshal their strength and cunning.

*

Voice, smile, hands moving

Hands moving, above all, most eloquently
in the rhetoric of *making*

Such a pleasure, to watch
the highly developed organism *moving*

and, as they say, *doing*

"Oh, doing it right"

*

Los gatos, eating their kind of food.
You, sleeping. Me, buzzed by
Never-so-glad-ever: no more opera now but
some urgent intelligent weirdly impassioned human life —

Never anywhere as this now: generosity: home: how is it
voluptas has become a word again?

*

How was it when this world's people
thought things were *solid*?

In the light, they are

*

The rich extended and exercised gentle paws.
The poor went to the scribe and said,
"Write: 'I miss you. Come soon.'"

And that was the beginning of poetry,
in Egypt.

Encouragement From Two Hundred Years Ago

from the German of Reiner Kunze

At God's
feet, if God
has feet,

sitting
at his
feet, there's

BACH —

not
the Magistrate of Leipzig

Outlying Districts

for Jane

from her querimonious querido

Outlying Districts

Holliday, Dr. John Henry, 86–7, 150
Hollo, Anselm, 189
"Home on the Range," 175

— FROM THE INDEX TO GREAT PLAINS
BY IAN FRAZIER (NEW YORK, 1989, FSG)

Things to Do at 453 South 1300 East, Winter '86

Read ten thousand lines
by the poets of Finland

translate two hundred and twenty-six

then sit & stare
across to where sky meets dead sea
out beyond the polis
of this valley

Think of "SIERRA PLUG, the *Ecological* Chaw"

see hundreds of erstwhile
(*very* erstwhile) trees go up in smog
from the assholes of fast little vehicles

get up and eat some fast little vehicle

That mixed choir's really raving away on the radio

Now contemplate the wish baskets in the Xmas tree
slow down past the speed of light

see them go up & down up & down
floating across the desert & over the mountains

Feel gentleness invade you with the thought of her
who brought you here

& here she is   no need to write now

Diary

One day's
big event was when

the cardboard
box I had set on

top of logs burning
in the grate toppled out

of the fireplace in a lively
state of combustion

Viento

Big Wind
BANGS
against shoebox house

Down in Santa Fe Phil Whalen tells us
                    Duerden couldn't *stand* it

yet it is what goes
every second,
through each one of our cells

blowing each instant through every thing
& every thing through each instant

slow through rocks,
                                        fast through the protein

even faster through the medium called "air"
which lives above "water" a medium with "earth" in it

upon which stands our house
using both "water" & "air"
day & night, adding "fire"

in the form of candles, kerosene stove,
& just the way we look

fast through the protein,
                                        slow through rocks

certainly using itself to the max every second, no?

Yet, surely this is a place
quite marked by our little quirks

one of which, "love": an intangible tango

Local Color

Another plane staggers in.
And there, in the middle distance,

the dirigible *Mark Strand.*
Its captain seems to be waving.

Up here on the mountaintop
everything looks just hunky-dory.

It'll all be gone
in a blink of your eye.

It will be followed by
Jefferson and / or Donald Duck.

"Dig yields wealth of knowledge on Utah's ancients"

Aahh, the ancients, the lovely ancients

they lived in villages
they made handsome pots
they salted the deer
(plenty of salt around here)

they strode in & out of their heads
all over these hills

they raised the young
humored the old
buried the dead
& kept out the cold

They were terrific!
unlike present millions
of even more clever-brained
forked bags of water

now zapping by in their steel
& plastic shells
out there

And that was Mr Cheapo Nostalgia speaking

though sentiment
                    swings either way:

good luck to the living

Direct Address

Bright sun   double yellow
line down the middle   a red one
on the far curbside   drums on the radio

Man in too short check pants glides by like daffodil
& I sit here thinking the Vice President
then thinking the Vice President
needs a new job & a bandido moustache

Who's speaking   "The Finnish-American Poet?"
no no   the poet of the precise non sequitur
in his middle years
in the days of The Great Condom Revival

Hello how are ya   ça va, ça va
*Every*body's a genius at least once a year

0600 hrs

for Simon Pettet
shamelessly cannibalizing his versions
of the French Romantics

In the middle of the party
                                        balancing her purse
on classical leg . . . fried . . .
                                        Be always
my queen, star-studded . . . my face, still red
                    in the black grapes . . . your dainty
        foot in the trellis . . .
"Tie him up while I slip into something becoming"
        Moaned
under those heavy rocks, Eskimo
                    for some few moments more
in the multinational record company offices
WAKE UP! O lake! O silent rocks! O caves! Dark
forest! Let it be! Let it be! I rise! I fall

in the lake! and the skies are screaming
under the scarf of Iris
and a dignified fellow in two-tone suede hat passes
on his way to the Chinese collection, like clockwork

The Phone

"Hi! My name is Scott Cary. I just bought *Up Late*
and read your poems in it
and read in the notes that you live
in Salt Lake City. So I wanted to tell you I think
you're really a good poet."

"Well, thank you. (Pause.) Did you enjoy
the rest of the anthology?"

"Well, I just got it. (Pause.) I'm sitting here reading it
in a restaurant."

"I see." (Pause.)

"Well — what do you do for money?"

(Pause.) "That's — *my* business, isn't it?"

"Hee-hee . . . (Pause.) Well, maybe see you around."

"Take it easy."

A little later,

THE DOOR:

"Hi! My name is
Casanova
Hamilton.
What's yours?"

"No
Sale."

— time to hit the streets for a spell —

Pocatello, Idaho

thin man whacking

away at tire with mattock

in 7-11 parking lot

9 p.m.

Saturday night

we
saw
that
sight

Feeling Somewhat Lost, Like Any "Old Wisdom"

lost with the wisdom like grizzled
old rider of motorbike
parked
by the side of Wyoming road

has he taken his wisdom on a final hike
across that scrubby *melancholia*?

saw him stuff eggs of hen & bits of pig
into still handsome face
at the truck stop only minutes ago
& now he's gone

there stands
his chopper
monument

well he's probably just taking a shit
he'll be back & pass you at eighty-five miles an hour
old wisdom intact

In This Court of Entrance Stood the Gigantic Remains of a Supposition . . .

Where the sun sets on the purple sage
the buffalo roam no more, no more

& the cowboy poet is mostly a crashing bore
& the state's economy is up Shitski Prospekt

the great god Morton Thiokol belches
with the great god Moroni
after the meal they've made of Ute & Shoshoni

& any human being of finer sensibilities

(an "intellectual"
of sorts & a city boy
even though you've spent
much of your grown-up life
in small country towns
you're still grateful
even amazed that these People of the Country
don't gang up on you & kill you

— NASO

Anti-Lullaby

Wake up from a dream
of a large herd (very verbal)
of porcine politicos

assembled for imminent charge off cliff

Well, that's . . . that's almost interesting

The sun also has risen
& we better get on with it

"early in de mawnin' an de road is gettin' light"

So let's tango on down
            the shining path
to breakfast
            at the Café Spartacus

So There's This Little Man

down the street "little"
in that he ain't "big"
has an argument with his woman
gets his gun

a little .22-caliber gun
& hops in the truck
his wife calls the cops afraid
he'll hurt himself

so they give chase
& corner him up a canyon
he's still upset he points
the gun at his head

he doesn't speak the lingo too well
he waves his arms & another
little man in a uniform
shoots him dead

(then there's the other kind
of little man
who runs big errands
for the truly big men

& if he keeps his mouth buttoned
may live to retire
as a part-time landshark
in Agent Haven

"The ass waggeth his ears"

Seems like some of these
younger ones grew up
still believing that old
hype about this being
"a *fast* world"

        the world ain't fast

it's big & sluggish & doesn't
give a shit about your microbial jerking around

        widescreen night stars

        smudge planes slow

        astronomical corkscrew aesthetics

as chemically complicated as poetry equals curved speech

"They drove cars fast — Neon was young —"

for Tom Raworth

There was was there not a time
one sallied forth

big provider hunter
irately affectionate
vis-à-vis wife & bairns

(nostalgically fond in thought
of the bucolic founding friggers

Whereas now
one despondently feels
all that to have been just rotten
rearguard imperialist stuff

Well izzat so
Well tell me it ain't

(enter smiling young neo-imperialist critic
bearing gigantic laurels

The Tenth of May (1988)

Jane is out being a delegate
        when she comes home
we'll light the candle & have some spinach spaghetti
with Mr. Paul Newman his sauce
his good cause sauce & smiling face on the label

I do add a dash of Worcestershire
        a little garlic & some white pepper

oh Eros we thank thee for thy gifts
this day the day
        of the great book burnings in Deutschland
                fifty-five years ago

Bright Moments

when it all makes sense
"deciphers"
a great crystal forest
enchanting

terrifying
because it seems only a sneeze away
from incomprehensible chaos
whose lineaments we are

only beginning to
decipher

"whose lineaments
we are"

well you go out there
& then come back in-
to the midst of whatever
awful things

the people who 'make' money
make a *lot* of money
make money off of

but here walks a portly or is it potty? bearded person
carrying shopping bag moving along
up the street in big white sneakers
having descended from stately vintage Checker Cab

it is God
forever unemployed
but really *muy contento*

The Endowment

of the W. C. Fields
          College for Boys & Girls

"where no religion
     whatsoever
          will be taught"

he left $800,000
          ($10,000 to wife

& wife & lawyers
     took it all

          thus saving these States
     from generations
          of smart atheists

In the Land of Art

the artists
work on the art farm.

They store the art they make
in the art barn.

Once in a while, they take some out
& take it to the art store.

When the art store sells some,
they take their share
& put it in the art bank.

Then they take their art checkbooks
& go to the art inn
to have a good time.

Or take each other to an art movie
or an art dance.

They wash their clothes at the art laundromat
unless they are successful & rich & have
their own art washer & dryer
in their art basement.

When the artists take a trip
(an art trip)
they stay at the art hotel.

When they get sick, they go to the art hospital.
& when they die, they're buried
in the art cemetery.

& that's the life of the artists
in the land of art.

Don't Drop the Yule Log on Your Foot

the clock strikes three
can't think of words for this space
(he feels like a louse)

in Point Barrow, Alaska
it must be time to go to the bar
but we're not there
(not in bars much anymore

these
do not seem like the right words

The ocean of savage lusts
in which the wounded shark
gnashes
at his own tail
is not our home
— William Carlos Williams to José Garcia Villa

Shut up!
I don't feel good!
— tall bearded man, wild eyes
wearing blue sleeping bag down the street
arguing with his anima
or mama, more likely

a small herd of medical personnel
may or may not catch up to him later
(the case, no doubt
with all of us

It is the seed that floats ashore
one word, one tiny, even microscopic word
which alone can save us

where is it, where is it

do send it along if you see it

Professional Armaments

—for Carl Rakosi, who wrote "OK"

December 5, 1988: the phone rings to inform me, in the voice of a male fellow human, that there is a package addressed to myself but to the wrong address, consisting of two books in the Swedish language, at the premises of an enterprise called *Professional Armaments* in the township of Murray, Utah. Could I come and pick it up? Sure, I say, but couldn't you just re-address it to me here in nearby Salt Lake City? The voice indicates strong doubts as to the feasibility of this, so I drive some miles in foggy weather and arrive at *Professional Armaments.*

It is a large, brightly lit store crammed to the rafters with weaponry, enough to outfit a small army: there are cases, shelves, and wall displays of handguns, assault rifles, machine guns, rocket launchers, stun guns, tear gas canisters, handcuffs, leg irons, truncheons, knives, bulletproof armor, you name it. Two soberly garbed gentlemen stand at the other end of the counter discussing the purchase of three dozen infrared nightscopes. A pleasantly schoolmarmish female employee hands me my package.

Back in the car I discover that the grievously misaddressed books are autobiographical works by my friend Mia Berner, the widow of fellow poet Pentti Saarikoski (see "Bro Hipponax" for his posthumous communication), whose *Tiarnia Trilogy* I have just finished translating. Mia's books deal with her childhood and youth in the late Thirties and early Forties; the second volume concludes with a scene in which she, a teenage girl, is rowing a boat carrying, besides her, two heavily armed plainclothes policemen, Norwegian collaborators with the Nazi occupation forces, and her lover, whom these agents have arrested at an island hideout and are now taking into custody. She tells one of them to stop gesticulating with his carbine — the barrel is getting in the way of her rowing.

On the Occasion of & as an Introduction to Robert Creeley's Reading at Kulttuuritalo ("The House of Culture") in Helsinki, Finland on Valentine's Day '89

time & again when I falter & half believe
those always articulate dogmatics
who say our words can never be our own

but are merely signs
devised by controllers
(the controllers being the other dogmatics
on top of the heap)

thus
they say
anything one might say
is merely a reflection
of those historico-socio-economic conditions
that make one this deluded
miserable
little pile of shit

that presumes to have thoughts
feelings
epiphanies *recognitions*
of use to others as species fellows

I think of the way a hawk's
or a gopher's days are an investigation
of its world

the way the days & words
of Robert Creeley's poems are
an investigation
of our human universe

se on saatanan hyvā runoilija
se panee psyyken lepattelemaan

a bloody great poet / he makes the psyche flutter

like the little white curtain
in the candle-lit window
at the end of the booby-trapped garden path

"and Today's Credo is . . ."

Don't feel like hiding in the archetypes

Don't trust the stuff that's supposed to give you
The Grand Shivers
(take top off head, etc.

But what about melodious?

Melodious
I have trouble with

So I guess this avuncular
vernacular
will have to do

Too Much Money or Was It Honey

The decadent aesthete deals brilliantly with the disgusting
but the brilliant decadent
then deals disgustingly with the aesthete

They're both in line for The Farting Rosebush Award
and they are, both of them, you

Bro Hipponax / An Inscription: Pentti Saarikoski / 1937–1983

WHEN I WAS EIGHTEEN
I WROTE BETTER POEMS
THAN DID YOU
WHEN YOU WERE EIGHTEEN

NOW, IN OUR FIFTIES,
I AM DEAD
& YOU
MUST GO ON WRITING
AS BEST YOU CAN

Tarp

for Kit Robinson

Warm & soft
or cold & hard

the taco of existence
lies in front of the bard

who remembers
here in the dark

the barf on your shoes
shaped like a backwards question mark

& as you blink off
the snow keeps falling

over The Searchers
& their dim expectations

In the "Hip" Little Bookshop

catering to the local
writing workshop's needs & tastes
(works by the faculty
& their friends

predictable stylish "fiction"
predictable stylish "poems"

I mutter to myself "but this is
just shit, it looks like books
but it's just shit"

I feel embarrassed
but I don't wake up

it isn't just a bad dream

but out in the street
in the front yards
there are these hyacinths
& daffodils

goddamn little crowd pleasers

Lord Lytton Goes to Language School

"I write for exertion in proud minds. I am, it is true, generally, and think without object. Reputed clever, fools are afraid as I actively interfere with thinking. It is necessary to block head. My mind is legitimate in its destiny of exertion. I began severe thought: what was once put must be connected with paper. Days pass. Ideas become myself, the likeness of rapidity fused with method. A week. No object but intellectual want, overcharged like most writings of the thick and confused. I turn into a Dalmatian."

"It was all about . . ."

poor communications

mistaken identity

voyages   battles   sieges & potions

returns

black sails

& dying

in love

after a busy life

Or, What I Remember of Tristan & Isolde

Cricket Poetics

for Kaarina Hollo

"Here   here"
the crickets again

the real thing not young Kevin's
hi-tech alarm clock
in the trunk of our car

in the Moab desert
strongly proposed
(by myself)
as mysterious
Desert Cricket

well   investigation
oftentimes proves us wrong

but "here   here"
an invisible legion

& that's what we are
the poets

an invisible legion

almost as audible

sometimes

Who Wrote This

being a poet these days is a little like
playing the harmonica
— JOHN CHAMBERLAIN

when we were little poets
we told ourselves
one day
we'll have a big book
just like the big poets

& now
we have big books
but are we big poets now
don't make me laugh ha ha

though even Charles Olson
has not been the same
since the academics ate him

o I do not wish to remember
have trouble recalling
find it hard to believe

what a day it was
flags were flying
bands were playing
& all the lovely ladies
had flowers in their hair

(& that was first written
by Munro Leaf
author of *Ferdinand the Bull*
a great poem

Wordsworth Briefly Revisited

do you behold these steep & lofty cliffs
with huge & black projection overbrowed
as fall upon us often when we look
amid the heart of many thousand mists

that hulk which labors in the deadly swell
within the sonnet's scanty plot of ground
& all its aching joys are now no more
as slips the book from hand to floor

In The Library of Poets' Recordings

the dead speakers
we can hear
but the dead listeners
can not be retrieved

Ah Yes

The time I thought I heard a master tell me
that there was "a lot of cunt" in my poems

& felt a little flustered & flattered or maybe not or both

then realized he'd said "a lot of *fun*"

Letter to Uncle O.

for Andrei Codrescu

Dear Publius Ovidius
"The Nose"
missing ah missing the rose
of Rome
for ten years of letters in verse

in one of them, startled to find yourself
calling drear Tomis "home"
— a shantytown by the frozen Black Sea
where people grow fur & look daggers

& no spreak-a-da Latin
but something called Getic
Getic! or at best broken Greek
& winter is a year long

while you pen song upon song
to send
where you once were young
listing your poet friends by name
& even some whose names you can't recall

praising that lovely sodality
of once-upon-a-time
a welcome break for your reader
who's 2,000 years too late

to do a thing about the ostensible reason
for your lengthy *Tristia* or *Drearies*:
the Emperor's pardon

because that emperor lives
only within the rose
of a city more perennial

where dream & memory converse
carouse & conjure
breathlessly deathless

(& who could pardon himself that way
    except now & again
        between the lines

The Missing Page

It was a poem, the jittery sort

"about" struggling through rush hour
traffic in downtown Baltimore

then, seeing you

there, on the far side of the river

of steel & plastic & sentient bags of water

cloaked & hatted   smiling

perhaps in disbelief at seeing me pass
the second time, in midstream, unable
to pull ashore to let you embark

(it also had some quote from a Godard
— just clumsy artifice)

The thing, the thing was

"how do you say?" immense

                    yearning & delight

Clearly & Dearly

for JDH, 15:X:88

"gone wrong"
so many ways
(not heeding parental
or much of any other
advice

a determined
irregular
in the navies of utterance
no rank no commission
follower of admirals Loser & Loser
in the literary campaigns)

I feel remarkably cheerful
(considering)
because it is your birthday today

& we are quite clearly afloat
in the uncharted archipelago
of Being-Here

& because
having found you
is clearly & dearly one thing
I done right

Response to Colorado Daily's Poll Question: "What is the meaning of life?"

life is a leaf
stuck to her nose
very brief-
ly, just a mo

Idyll

water
the yard o
wild domestic

Alla Petrarca

Downtown
Madison, Wisconsin at night
is pretty quiet. Returning

from the dinner for scholars of Finnish
in black plastic boots that seem to be shrinking
I listen to their heels on the sidewalk and feel like

a German Romantic
a hundred and fifty years younger, enveloped
in my sense of missing you, oh fairest of ladies!

back home in Boulder,
Colorado. It is storybook time, as when we saw
that gown in the window in Stockholm Old Town

yesterday? Or the day before?
We who are of this gender, what can we do —
we know it must be a burden to you

to appear in our visions as the *summum bonum*
the great female sun our souls do yearn for
but at least you don't have to do it in person

every time. My feet hurt but I am so glad

(receding footsteps)

Chansons d'Antan

Greenery waves in wind
o eerie

underwater light

et les chansons d'antan

weave of keyboard & saw & Bromige
says the marimba
makes them stagger *un peu*
on the wide curving steps
(the men
of a certain age

my son my son why hast thou forsaken the world

two oranges in a silver bowl

& if the dinosaurs
"became birds"
what will we "become"

So

— in memoriam Kalevi Lappalainen (1940–1988)

a lifetime ago
we sat in small
Helsinki cafe

('Dutch genre dark'
as I remember)

discussing the translation
of then current idioms

the term “high”
in particular

as in “boy am I ever high”
or “it’s a good high”
or just “to be high”

& you came up with
“to be up on a branch”

we giggled
two cartoon birdies
up on our little branch

then went back to our chosen lands

& now
it really is
a lifetime gone

& how would you translate that

La Mort

probably
another
of those appointments
one keeps putting off

knowing
one has to keep them
one day

“If I
refuse to go
to the dentist

maybe I won’t
have to die”

Nice Curly Hair

It come to the Pope
& to the nightcrawler too

death
is shit

equals loose molecules
(whether it's violins or grenades)

but & I quote the distinctive charm
of YZ's poems

resides in their unselfconscious mastery
of universal late 20th century modes

unquote informed
by her warm young life

so
Fuck Death

is what one must say at all points
of one's silly little existence right?

right right
do not go gentle into that *buenas noches*

in Tashkent or Nacogdoches
wherever whoever you are make a fuss

a Big Fuss
before the Big Foot comes down

Jeremiah Digest

hair falls off head
head falls off body

nothing new under the sun

but evolution
must have slowed
to a *crawl*

Old Love or War Poem

I
know
where
you are!
I
can
see the
bushes
moving!

“Sales figures are up”

(for Robert Grenier)

i.e., there’re more of these human
figures
up & about & paying for things
by making more things to buy

strafed
the curb

while turning into the parking
lot with a head cold & sadness
en mi corazón

due to word of two
true friends who were also lovers
living together for many years

but now are an item no more no more
so there are more of us
than ever before

but two
people imagined happy together
less

& I meant to say “bumped”
“bumped the curb”

but I said *strafed*
didn’ I

Sonnet

Morning strides through these poems
be they turds of protest or histories of the alphabet
social symbolic or just produce
metaphysical grovel   stirrings in the eaves

old baboons at work on our investigations i.e.
"curving rhythmical accidents which loop
    into old choral & liturgical songs
into certain kinds of modern music
even into tunes from banal popular song"

that was Leonardo   Leonardo Sinisgalli speaking

we speak together   then we say
"I always quite misunderstood you"

how grotesque this world
even without us

just two guys struggling with a big sheet
on the stony side of the street

No Detachment

Step out   snow and sunshine
walking   feels good
two blocks   bank machine
working!   good
on to local market
salad stuff   good
head back   small detour
bookshop   browse   my book still there
good   or bad   not sold   buy
last Sunday's New York Times Book Review
more Joyce Carol Oates   oh well
all right   stop   red light
plastic shopping bag on left wrist
shake wrist a little   make sure
watch still on   back home
tuna snack share with cats   good
sudden good god! realization
watch is gone

retrace steps   look everywhere
house   street   call bookshop
wretched day   watch gone
nice watch gone   rage   confusion   dry
tears   mutter mutter   what's the use
snow   sunshine   life is shit
Roman numerals   lovely
picked out with Jane Dalrymple
me protesting excessive elegance   expense
growl sigh yes
                              an evil iguana tongue
flashed out of the Void today

"He the old guy"

he sure enjoys this cutlery he used to eat with when a kid
aahh, yes
"Chimborazo, Cotopaxi"
carried him away

& it seems only yesterday
into the arms of a wondrous wise woman
where he purrs & chortles
like Caligula in his finest moments

he used to be a shortwave broadcaster in London
but now
he is a star surfer in Salt Lake City Utah
& like Caligula & Christ

(as shamelessly subjective)
he too will be gone one day
in crocus time
in some part of the universe

aahh, yes
but he does like
these imitation bone handles
& the Zeppelin Era spikiness of the forks

La Vida

para Janey, mi vida

Through swirls & eddies of footfalls
converging, diverging

some soft, some percussive
she walks to work

thinks of the two
happy young people

glimpsed in the car behind her
& how they *glowed*

among thousands streaming along in their shells
under big plumes of dark smoke under heaven

later says "If I wrote poems
those are things I would write about"

& I say, well, that — that's a *movie* —
but later think, no

it isn't, it's *life*
It's life, all right

Brother (D. H.) Lawrence

& all the eerie
'previous' states of mind

in which one was rushing
around inside

of a roughly
spherical tangle of self-
generated messages

& turned up high, for sure,
to the point of despair

ah, the *drama* of it all!

which was exactly what Brother
Lawrence had warned one against

but better reception
came only much later

such as the one
one is enjoying

this radio morning —
his birthday: a hundred and three —

with Ellen Burstyn, an actress
reading his number on The Turtle

Glenwood Springs

Under Doc Holliday's
weary eyes

    last scanned
just before Checkout Time
in that fake Vienna hotel

my lady, rising
                out of steam
(but not at all
"out of steam"

straight, lovely
                as mountains

Minigolf

In the Spring of '88, Anselm and Jane
played a round of miniature golf
somewhere between New
Orleans and Biloxi. Anselm
kept the scorecard and named poems
written during the remainder of the year
after each obstacle on the course —
thus, *Minigolf*, sporadically
annotated, became a kind of record of
the Game of that Year.

The Way

The way you got to be the way you were
just a moment ago

is the way of "the moment"
a big old notion in which you can never

find yourself
so stagger on on your quest

for the other big old notion
"the now"

as in *right* now
as you just were right then

Castle

"These be the spears the imperium braved" points at

wrought-iron fence symbolic reminder of assegais dense

in the air of (his) head supported by feet (his) on

American lawn modeled on those of an England there

Pinball

Woke up & was being
a nice human being again

baffled but cheerful among the other
480,000 non-Mormons

in this administrative space

& once again quite able
to sit around the old oaken table

the dinner was cooked to perfection

the bang
will follow the flash

yes nukes
have indeed led to a worldwide upsurge

of mad religiosity
don't you think blink blink

Alligator

To live there
in Baton Rouge

one of the globe's
greatest concentrations

of massive
man-made
pollution

takes *guts*!
big guts!
big *reptilian* guts!

"He wrote that
because he didn't get the job"

Who said that?! — I'll — I'll — @#*!!#@**!!! —

Elephant

Ted Berrigan says this to you:

"We are each free to shed big crystal tears on
The dirt-covered ground, tied together only
By white clouds and some mud we can find, if we try,
In the darksome orange shadows of the big blue swamp"

He says this to you in his forty-seventh sonnet on page 47
of his great book THE SONNETS

Which you'd do well to read at least once a week here

"on the vast salt deserts of America
Where Snow White sleeps among the silent dwarfs"

Boy, this one was easy.
But, "how long can a quote get, he sd, eyeing me . . ."
Now locate *that* quote.

Pygmy Hut

Heavy drops
fell from the trees
& made a
plopping
sound
as they hit
the poodles

(shouldn't that be 'puddles'

(no
not puddles
poodles

Heavy drops
fell from the trees
& made a
plopping
sound
as they hit
the poodles

This is sort of a French poem.
It has, how do you say, *l'espace.*

Around the World

My first introduction
to the "Valentine" concept

was an American animated cartoon
preceding a Hopalong Cassidy movie

I'd dragged my mother to in Stockholm
in 1943 or 4

Valentine's Day
is a bit like May Day in Red Square

both are celebrations of cherished ideas
but considering

their flawed realizations
over time
the celebrations seem a little overdone

Hills

Don't just sit there she said
like a lumpy fog

feeling lonely & sorry for
some imagined self

There's no need to feel lonely
there's lots of people out there

Yes I know he said but I'm still lonely
for my friends
my *dead* friends

Oh come on she said

You're just indulging in the midway crankies
past-midlife lumpies & grumpies

come on let's go climb some *hills*

The Jump

Drive to the Beef & Bourbon
in Bowling Green Ohio

with Andrew Carrigan & Tom Raworth
in nineteen seventy-something

have a T-bone steak
have a couple of beers & six shots of bourbon

then jump back to the present
(nineteen eighty-something)

grinning & shaking your head
pleased that we're all still alive

(as of the date of this writing)

Rocket

Teacher, teacher
— I don't like this assignment

I never liked rockets
& the one on the minigolf course
somewhere between New Orleans & Biloxi
where all this started
wasn't going anywhere anyway

& that evening felt definitely pre-rocket
at least the way we think of them now
(to do with Buck Rogers or nuclear wipeout)

much more like balloon
post-chaise & brigantine

Kinder & gentler,
like no CIA?

Glance

it,
there

The managers of this establishment
have come here from another part of the universe

their cooking smells good so never mind the incense
slightly too sweet

wafting into the lobby from the room
behind the reception desk

where they conduct their private lives
(now would this be greater 'in meter'?

no it wouldn't)
at the local joke shop

we purchase some joke beach towels
to go to the beach

which is a joke
— thin sheets of water stretching for miles

then we hear thunder see lightning no joke!
& retire

to our private lives
back at the inn

they do intertwine
as we do

it,
there

Somewhere between New Orleans & Biloxi

Champ

so it all goes back to some big goofy guy

holding forth on the universe

in a lit-from-within

transparent

cube of the past

yeah

that's right

Something Norse-Tibetan about this one. *Lineage.*

Lighthouse

The house
in North Platte, Nebraska
is not a lighthouse.

This house
is dark. The curtains are drawn.
Colonel Cody's
not at home.

They're not expecting him back
anytime soon.

Adieux sentimentaux to my childhood's hero,
now immortalized on a postcard stamp.

The Curve

missed
due to alcohol it was
still there
on the other side of the ditch

Somewhere between Marshall and Cottonwood, Minnesota.
Far as I know, it's still there.

Snail

Ess Enn A Eye Ell.
Snail.

Ee Vee Oh Ell You Tee Eye Oh Enn.
Evolution.

Snail
Evolution.

Tic-Toc

or,
lowercase
on joel
& roy

thought he looked a bit jerky
sounded a little too sweet

that evening
at the folk song society
near primrose hill

a young american singer
in red shirt & jeans
i was young too
& had a young son

& all of us in that room went on
to all we went on to
on this orb

in my case even to liking
roy orbison's songs
"pretty woman"
in particular

it being a very particular
song about a
very general
idea

one also much entertained
by the late great american poet
joel oppenheimer
whose "dutiful son"
i was reading then

ave atque vale

Chicken Coop

it's winter he's feeling mean she's tired

he makes a crack about her command of geography

she pretends to stab his wrist with a fork

he brings his fork down hard

on her plate of Rasta-style beans

both

burst into tears

Strind-
berg.

Berg-
man.

Ragna-
rök, etc.

Nordic Angst.
Weird Genes.

The Fish

in the tank
on the plate
in the mammals' mouths

at 2 a.m.
in Japantown, San Francisco
was

dazzling
quite tasty
kept them awake & talking some more

Present: Jane Dalrymple; Lynne Wildey; Robert Grenier; Kush: an interesting fellow who talked a lot but whose name the author can't remember; the author

The Dada Letter

One afternoon in northern Europe, probably in the year 1939, a boychild one now sees wearing a blue velvet Little Lord Fauntleroy suit with lace collar and cuffs, is walking down a chiaroscuro corridor in a haut-bourgeois six-story apartment building —

What Dadaists are still alive are dealing with their life-movies in various ways, suggested by other labels:

Surrealism
Socialism
Psychoanalysisism

within the increasingly hallucinatory public film, Herr Adolf Hitler's "millennial epic" BOY FROM AUSTRIAN BOONIES MAKES GOOD — The boychild's parents, who met in the Twenties in the capital of the former Austro-Hungarian Empire, never were Dadaists, although they did have the works of Hugo Ball on their shelves —

There really had been no Viennese Dada, the way there was a

Berlin Dada a
Zurich Dada a

Cologne Dada a
Paris Dada a
New York Dada and a
Hannover MERZ —

Vienna and London had their Neo-Dadas many years later, after another World War, and the boychild would have some first-hand experience of those —

Speaking of hands, that boychild (one afternoon probably in 1939) is, in his right hand, carrying a glass plate with a doughnut on it —

When one says "doughnut" here, one is referring to the European kind without a hole, just a ball of fried dough covered in refined white sugar, known in some Teuton-speaking lands as a "Berliner" — whence the essentially Dadaist delight of the inhabitants of Berlin at a Post-Dada United States President's enthusiastic confession that he, too, was just a ball of fried white dough —

This, too, was later — now in '39, the boychild's left hand is most likely engaged in picking his nose or trying to detach the pretty lace collar from his Little Lord Fauntleroy suit —

*

Young Post-Dada Krissie from next door just called to say that there is an Amnesty International special on Channel 2, on women prisoners of conscience — she is a member of Amnesty International, as are Jane and I, and a mover and shaker in the local (Salt Lake City) high school cadres of that organization — a bright sweet blonde young thing who reminds me of my daughters at her age — and *that* seems like an eternity ago — her fellow Amnestyites, on the other hand, affect Modified Punk, that Post- or Neo-Dada marriage of S & M Biker Chic with Seven Nations tonsorial fashions, first consummated in London — where those daughters were
born, in the era of Love and Beatles —

I tell her that it is good of her to point this out but that we don't have a television set, as both Jane and I are somewhat afraid of having attention spans totally destroyed and adrenalin levels artificially but permanently raised by daily exposure to that 'medium of the day' — she says that I'm welcome to come over and watch the program on women prisoners of conscience, or prisoners of conscience who are also women — and then I have to tell her thank you but I am at this very moment struggling to get some kind of fix on this lecture I am supposed to give at the Jack Kerouac School of Disembodied Poetics in Boulder, Colorado, in about two weeks' time, on

Dada

Neo-Dada

and Post-Dada — ridiculous idea, I say, isn't it — don't know what possessed me, it wasn't the money — and am tempted to quote the pertinent line from Allen Ginsberg's still-reverberating HOWL: "who threw potato salad at CCNY lecturers on Dadaism" — but don't — but say that maybe she can tell me later about the program — then feel like a prick, sigh, and return to the keyboard of composition to stare at the words "pretty lace collar of his Little Lord Fauntleroy suit" —

I notice that I have typed "worlds" instead of "words" — this makes me think of Gertrude Stein, without a doubt the great Dadaist in the American language — I need to quote a poem of hers — but back to that moment one afternoon probably in 1939 when the boychild, walking down a chiaroscuro corridor in a haut-bourgeois six-story apartment building, executes, with his right hand, a gesture somewhat similar to the Fascist salute — one cannot say why but one remembers that he is or now rather was in his right hand carrying a glass plate with a doughnut on it —

When one says "doughnut" here — OK you heard that one already — CUT to Grand Pre-Dada Marcel Proust eating a doughnut —

"now rather was," since the Berliner is now launched on a trajectory through the slightly stale but pleasantly lavender-smelling or is it lily-of-the-valley (the boy child's mother's favorite perfume) air of the corridor —

*

While on a recent expedition to my study or office to get Volume Six of the Yale Edition of the Unpublished Writings of Gertrude Stein, I noted that the indoor temperature had dropped to 79 degrees, thanks to judicious use of the window fan, and also that the radio was playing one of those south-of-the-border classics about living out the Twilight of Empire in a sun-drenched tequila coma — and instantly thought of David Bromige, because of his lines in *Red Hats,* a recent work:

"For those who learned to drink in the 50's, vibraphones will inevitably bring on a slight stagger. Down the steep steps he slipped with many abrasions, only to find the Club Serendipitee, where caught some GREAT sounds being improv'd by those cats. Then this chick, see . . ."

— the book Red Hats is so tightly bound, "perfect-bound" I suppose, that I have to type with one hand while the other holds the book open —

As the doughnut is now flying through that lily-of-the-valley and / or lavender air, the boychild is left holding

only the glass plate
which he stops to contemplate

— and how is that for *rime riche* — the doughnut meanwhile vanishing into the chiaroscuro with what Sir Edward Bulwer-Lytton might have described as an inaudible thud —

The Pope just called — he wanted to know if there was any substance to rumors that his invisible guru — whom he referred to as Our Lord — would prefer Salt Lake City to Rome for his Second Coming —

I of course pooh-poohed said rumors and told the dear Vicar that his boss had told me, at a recent poetry and rock'n'roll conference in Gothenburg, Sweden, which he was attending incognito in the guise of a pale and sweating Finnish blues singer, that he was no longer interested in religion of the paternalistic sort —

After a brief pause, the pontiff drily remarked that I must have been reading that dear but over-educated Ernesto Cardenal again — I said, no no, I had actually been reading David Bromige, the wonderfully erudite North American poet and bon-vivant saint of *eiron* —

"The *eiron,* or ironical man, is a man who professes that he does not have, or has in less measure than the world supposes, the good qualities which he does in fact possess" —

Yes, yes, that's from Aristotle, says the Vicar, a mite impatiently — well have a nice day, one gathers it is quite hot out there —

eiron = semper dada

I say well have a good one too — don't let the population figures get you down —

*

The doughnut has come to rest in a corner of the corridor and the boychild in the blue velvet suit is left holding the glass plate — momentarily at a loss as to what should be his further course of action — possibly even *right* action, a concept that's been looming on his psychic horizon for some time now, being often discussed by his parents — who have Hugo Ball's works on their shelf —

Hugo Ball, saint of Zurich Dada, and later ascetic mystic who performed his *sound poems* in a costume made out of big cardboard tubes — looking a bit like the Pope drawn by Wyndham Lewis — spouting things like "jolifanto bambla ô falli bambla" — and

"hej tatta gorem
anlogo bung
blago bung" — and also said "spit out words, *the* dreary, lame, empty language of society" — rousing stuff SEMPER DADA! —from Ball's Russian soul brother Velemir Khlebnikov — to beast-language Post-Dada American Michael McClure — and yet

one has gone back to replacing the *zaum* words with the other kind — those shared with the dreary lame empty language of society — hasn't one — ah, a vast flood of nostalgia washed o'er me — as the indoor temperature resumed its relentless climb — what "one" needed right then was an ecologically sound air conditioner — and maybe a videotape of Post-Dada Tom Stoppard's snotty little "Travesties" — T. Tzara's and V. I. Lenin's café chess playing days in Zurich —

on the other hand, this would have set one back an hour or two in the task of composing the lecture one had in some weak moment consented to give — to this really hip audience of fellow poets just about ready to launch the potato salad —

one paused briefly to correct the spelling of "doughnut" by means of "Word Search and Change," a "feature" of one's writing implement — ah, there — one is now old enough to comfortably enjoy being a little old-fashioned —

then one is captivated by the thought that one could change the word "doughnut" to let's see, how about "Stinger missile" —

"as the Stinger missile is now flying through that lily-of-the-valley air" — well it probably is, somewhere on this semper dada globe —

where was one —

"the doughnut has come to rest
some corner of blue velvet hall
in his left the glass a loss
expatiating parents loom" — yes, the old *scramble* — proto L=A=N = G = U =A= G = E strategy — how one wrote some of one's poems in 1969 Neo-Dada Iowa City-in the good company — semper dada! amigos Actualistas! — even though twenty years later, it is still "venceremos" only in the future tense -vis-à-vis or should one say versus The Big Smirk
o jolifanto bambla —

one does stare at the words —

*

The word INTERMISSION — written when one got up from the writing of this piece three days ago — at a loss what else to say —

during this grand intermission — when all of us seem at a loss as to what should be the further course of action — "possibly right action" —

during the intermission at the phantom opera that occasionally haunts this city by the dead inland sea —

I go to the "rest room" in my grey CIA suit — then re-emerge into chandelier chatter — thinking, Dada is dead but Opera lives — ah wistful wistful —

smile politely at the one Michael Jackson look-alike — among all the Burl Ives and Deborah Kerr look-alikes navigating around and saying things —

who is that tall beauty standing there all by herself — my heart leaps up as I behold — the gentle, intelligent curve of her neck and silver-streaked hair — and know it is Jane — once again thank the gods we're permitted this time — in the great intermission —

in a place where only a few have to disappear before their time — although some of the best have done so — still few, compared to other places one might name — ruled by the grim Anti- or Idi Amin Dada of los desaparecidos — now back to our movie:

having raised his hand in a vehement gesture — who knows why — on his way from the kitchen and mother — who is power — to father in his study (or office) — who is culture —

with the doughnut on the glass plate — perhaps to ward off some phantom of a five-year-old imagination —

and thus having caused the doughnut to disappear from the plate — the boychild of 1939 decides that right action is no longer possible in this particular case — and so —

lets the plate, too, go
into the chiaroscuro —

it is an act of Proto-Dada devil-may-care despair — and is (luckily) found amusing by both mother power and father culture — as power and culture had found amusing the paper wars between Dadas and Surrealists — now amply documented and catalogued — analyzed and deconstructed — by numerous degree candidates in American institutions of well they say learning —

anlogo bung
blago bung

so, Dad didn't get his doughnut — the plate, miraculously, did not break —

so the boychild grew up and out of those corridors — and once he'd outgrown Buffalo Bill and Jean-Jacques Rousseau — discovered Kurt Schwitters and Marcel Duchamp — the heroes of Dada — and lived through a heady period of Neo-Dada-when it seemed like John Cage and Jasper Johns — to mention but two — would lead the world — into art forever — but no, you can't stop here —

Arcana Gardens

Arcana Gardens

the cat's apprehensive inside her head
'things' are really hopping   a cat

with   wings now that would be a thing
there's this lady now writes her verses

with built-in lacunae   there still remain 'things'
& things to delete

contained in the changing light
moving the frame & things

from room to room I miss you
when you're gone all day

yet when you're home there's times I'm lost again
inside the side
        shows of my head

in this picture we see an oligarch
flying in his recliner

*

the practice of poetry:
doing it when called upon

oh blast this doglike devotion to the US of A
get ready for MacCommunism

the light inside the body
at the end of long flexible tube

I'm so bit-ter . . .
I'm so pret-ty . . .

            go on up
            or off

bluejay on woodpile
first prize: dinner in Des Moines

second prize: two dinners in Des Moines
well I'm heading for the bedding

the old legacy was a bottle of no anxiety
& one of no grief   those made you high for a while

then laid you low
weird white sugar architecture of that church in Buffalo

the blackness of Gothenburg   permanent diaspora
the ideal state

when the mind / body committee decides
a habit has become immoderate   it's a good idea
          to let it go

*

had to invent religion   ideas of karma afterworld etc.
in order to enjoy ever more highly

structured existence? (requires 'security' 'stability'
less general random viciousness)

an epic of prayers   poetry what you read
when you exercise the *skill* of reading

when tired of record of operatic soprano
(on radio) stuck on the two little words *da capo*

the world is bigger than your head or even mine

*

oh it's just like magazines used to be — with poems
by Ted in them

(who wants them to *like* their poetry
as long as they *read* it)

well it's time to be drizzling on
truckloads of stuff to keep us within the framework

but writers of small language groups
their admirable stubbornness

clings to the 'absoluteness'
of their particular language

their words   by extension that's of course true
of everybody

(don't know if I'll ever feel like writing 'about' the times
in life I was a total idiot asshole?)

"I want a longer attention span"
"he wants a longer dick?"

Finns: some general sense of shaggy folks tough
eking out a precarious   up there up Norf

"my metaphor machine is bigger than yours"
all greed relative?   love work that sails close
    to its own parody

stand up a berserker   end up a beseecher
in the vast stone forest of the world's war memorials

the ghosts of generals stumble about
dishevelled confused   graffiti on the great moving wall

moving toward The Wall   résumés for god
Papa wanted me to marry the Finnish language

Mama   chemistry   (her father's life)
both kept me away from Finnish-speaking women
    with all their might

so I went to Germania & married a German speaker
but couldn't make a living in those countries

so ended up in England   thus changing
my great love affair with the English (specifically
    American)

language into a lifetime commitment / marriage

*

old staples-through-the-side books   they *work*
people pay more attention to the right-hand page

each text gets equal weight   maybe the species
(homo sap) doesn't spend enough time

looking at admiring coveting what it eats (anymore)
thought while watching cat watching birds

at feeder on other side of glass   "he had trouble
announcing a formal presence"   gazing at red orange
& green

in slowly steaming pan it occurs to me not at all suddenly
that one I grieve for may well be content

to be living completely alone in a universe
of the greatest possible distances

Bertolucci's last emperor of China
a life just like everybody's

the emperor child   the live-forever young man
the long haul to the end

*

"killed by orthodox reality" (Peter Handke)
a Linnéan classification of poets?

re-reading Corso: *that* tradition   the sixties out of the fifties
so sturdy later poetry much more nervous

viz. Grenier's frontispiece for Phantom Anthems
Nerve Man   yet in him as in Berrigan

still that cheek
    & glint

when it degenerates into homily exhortation
or some disguise of those (story or antistory with moral)

it loses the power to drive us happily crazy for a minute
or two totally out
    of our gourds for one of those

        eternal moments
    of *le merveilleux*

*

cut to Pearl Street in Boulder where frisky yuppies
& even aging hippies go shopping for earrings

we just have this little bit of the haul to do
the forms formalities with which we 'stave off' death &
    thought of it

the common customary ones   & then the 'deeper' ones
such as some music   some poems

walking in the wild word woods   first reading Corso
say or EP for that matter   that old strut

that old fiddling while Rome burns canto strut

*

weird inverted Puritan desire to prove one's mettle
through suffering   stoically & wittily

behind the idea of giving readings
drunk stoned on speed mushrooms acid

(handed down by that Welshman   possibly farther back)
like the embarrassed drunk father

only when drunk is he able
to admit non-utilitarian emotion

& LDS part of that mind-boggling Anglo appropriation
of chosen people ism

via King James Bible   also still active in Aryan
Nations types who claim that Anglos

& "Northern Europeans"
are the true descendants of Israel

but the true inhabitants of these deserts & mountains
be lizard coyote   Paiute & Ute & Shoshoni
    (Bear River Massacre)

present-day natives displaying their wounds
(kid in front of Rio Grande Station) & scars

you go out there then you come back in
where the well-meant sentiment meets the hopeful cliché

Hemingway   a bounder & proud of it
the beauty of a genuinely *playful* life

possible?
isn't it?

*

composing from notebooks   a mobile with side shows
"& here we see"   here I see cryptic entry Actual Filth
    "Is that actual filth?"

some poems seem most effortful   as if their author
had labored   over them

ten hours a day seven days a week   & that's
what's wrong with them   "naphthaline"

mothballs of my childhood   naphtha = crude oil
right (check) trudge trudge (glasses in other room etc.)

o be *glad!* you have
many rooms to walk

instead of having to write all your poems in another life at
Mutant State University   "your own medicine"

my mother used to say   "just you wait until *you*
have children" etc.

really just a young 23-year-old American poet (came here
in '66)

or should we start with '51   London   38 in that case

& here we see
the analytical
bent

*

Orff's Carmina Burana quite lovely but also quite like
a bunch of young Nazis roaring

well I can't do everything at once
bet you could if you tried

yelling at each other in front of the computer
the sublime just fell asleep & died

but the utter & certainly quite wonderful *craziness*
of 'analytical language' (Situationist texts

Derrida Heidegger before them for sure) such gorgeous
kudzu lingo   dog noise pollution

"I hope you're not *confusing* the computer"
was it an hour ago I sat there in London wondering

about Ted Berrigan   this tough young American poet &
critic in the pages of KULCHUR magazine

"the testament of beauty" & what was that all about
well I'm sure it had its share of dog noise pollution

a little vulgar eloquence   yes lowercase american
is what I am   a big invisible fish
on a chops *gig*

"like playing for eight hours a day at Disneyland"
so little has been written about x

because x's work cannot be paraphrased   this
is the goal of all poetry   it is indeed

impossible to ascertain what x is really writing about or rather
it is that x rarely writes about

but is a manifestation
on the page
                    in the air

*

dance of dada   dance of death
it only writes itself little by little

a walk through the desert of many faces
by the fountain of six patina'd frogs

the houseboy was told off for sweeping *around*
the outside doormats   in the city of New Or*leens*

let's only be classified when dead
& then perhaps resumed
       in Spanish dark

& if a little myth comes with the territory
that's always nice   & cleanly temporal

human rights day? the day no government's able
to raise an army

for quite some time the way was to fall in love
& you can put quotes around all of the above

over & over
                    hi ho hi ho

child's (my) vision of work as somehow
martially? pleasurable

being a poet gives one permission to be a crank & even
a crank in print

but you my species
you're trying to overwhelm the planet
        by numbers?

*

hooked on English   I make six cents a word
no epiphany sans community

the dick came striding down the hall
"goddamn fucking greek deities again"

old Mozart . . . young Cassandra . . . owls
swoop through the canyon at night

aah am I supposed to say aah?   is this
the 'aah experience'?

who you asking?   dunno
is Robt. Bly around?

we pay the state to kill all those we'd rather not think about
but "a real house with stairs & everything"

you deserve it dear daughter
far more than all the bigdick religious entrepreneurs

who've stuck together
across the centuries

        Sam's Bar & Mosque
                (a hypothetical place)

*

living like happy savages with no t.v.   Arcana Gardens
& he's fifty-five   my goodness   let's dangle on
                down the street

poetry bookshelves   dear elephant graveyard
Science & Democracy

"even just *thinking* about it
ups your production of benign neuropeptides"

all the words this critter can say
when awed by all the worlds   up there

Cygnus XI HDE 22 68 68
Black jewel of the Northern Cross   down here

DIAMONDS GUNS TV's   in the Pavlovian pawn shop
string 'em out

them colored lights
then turn 'em off again

*

up on into what's this all about
this critter makes up its own rules

at the speed
of greed

last night my love got up out of bed & banged
her head on the doorjamb

this evening there's a report on UFO sightings in
Guatemala & it's been very
        windy
                all day

*

ah Babylon I exalt thee above thy detractors
Babylon is The Old Days   The Babylon All Stars

jazz in the ruins
before the ruins

"hey man I just walked out in my slippers"
when I say I wrote that   it is my intention to state

that someone using this same body did write that
then   yes here we see him

his brain   made that metaphor
mid rock & fern adream   with Chingachgook & Cody

but that man in Angola
said to have killed two priests for criticizing his poems

    boy
        that man must write
    some Satanic Verses

*

Colonel Walden at Pulkovo   lauded by Lenin
in John Reed's *Ten Days that Shook the World*

heard on tape on the way to Taos
"HEY THAT'S MY GRAND-UNCLE"

don't burn that flag
boil it & eat it with hot sauce

because I had spent 35 minutes in the bookstore
I felt I had to pay 6.50 for this magazine

I didn't really need then walked on
in the rain past more people resting

dying or dead on the sidewalk
Die Welt frisst was der Fall ist

(the world eats what falls down)
give the homeless $45,000 per capita

& make them sole subject of *all* U.S. news for a year
& let every township in the U.S.

have a simulated four-year oil boom
in alphabetical order

with acid trips among
    the gnomes

*

on the sidewalk a large
dog turd shaped like the male
    procreative organ

"none shall be permitted to retain their shape"
well sir you may be right   Roxie Powell of Baltimore

calls in the early a.m. he's working on a novel
whose heroes are Appearance & Reality

more power to him he did insist we go find you my love
down in the bookbinder's Hades (climate controlled)

for the rest of the story   see page

*

see page   & then see page
page after page
as it goes along

until "one day" it stops
with a squeal or a pop   but for now let's go on

to sing the praises of a brown-eyed girl
"I met in a country town"
                    & love
as light & filigreed but also mud-heavy
        as the old songs

with our glasses slightly askew on our noses

    "time for your Van Morrison sir"

from Space Baltic: The Science Fiction Poems 1962–1987

A Note

The earliest of these writings go back to the early Sixties, in London. The most recent ones, at the end of the book (which is arranged more or less chronologically), were written in Salt Lake City, Utah. One way or another they have to do with space, and spaces, and being both spaced out and spaced in, as well as just plain spaced, in ways at least inspired by, if not necessarily up to the standards of, the best spectacular, I meant to say speculative fiction.

The Baltic is a body of water in northeastern Europe, on the shores of which I was born and spent my early years. That, at least, is my cover story. Whatever inhabitable space realm it was that I really came from, it must have had many of the characteristics of the milieu of the itinerant minority of Anglo, Dutch, Finnish, German, Polish, Swedish etc. provenance that first appeared in the sixteenth and seventeenth centuries, the heyday of the Hanseatic trade ports. An unsettled colonialist world with *pretensions* to respectability and stability that were a terrific incentive for any live offspring to get the hell out of there and see what it was like somespace else.

So, what we have here is a bunch of entries from the log of the *Space Baltic*. Some of them, e.g. *The Coherences,* seem to be more or less straight transmission transcripts, and I am as much in the *chiaroscuro* about their "meaning" as I was when they first arrived. The poet Jack Spicer spoke of the poet as radio receiver, and mine must have been tuned to some distant base, possibly the same one that came through ten years later and was transcribed as *Or, to Hocus the Animals of the Pursuers by Changing Their Dream Cassettes (Old Thibetan Trick).* Others take a more terrestrial American fix on things, but — as Adrian Mitchell pointed out many years ago —the "Venusian" keeps showing through. Well, let 'im.

Egon Schiele

dreamed
the general music of all that lives
a jittery old hurdy-gurdy
but the forest
he said
lives without noise
it contemplates
itself
in mimesis

& he watched the passage of the "rutting people"
did not want to be inside them he said
tied himself to the oval wall of the park
to the thin-footed children

the pale white girls
they showed him their legs
red garters
"hiss, raucous Circe"
but he thought of the distant worlds
the artists
are easily aroused
he said

with long strides & anger-eyes
ran through wet streets
the birds in whose eyes
he saw himself pink with glittering eyes
the birds
were dead

the artists are easily aroused he said
& speak their own language
the world
is their paradise

they need not premeditate
they say it
it has to be thus

he said
yellow
yellow surfaces
intersect steeply
a saturate green
& now they grow closer & show us
here
their yellow atoms he said

End of the Range

weep ye protein herders weep
on dead willow hang the mushroom hat
there's no more natives to slaughter
& the foreigners are fighting back

Two Parts

1

Listen to me,
Señorita:

when your heart
caws like a crow
groans
like a god on the dole

remember
to remember Poetry
the secret language
the one no parents ever know

2

No kidding
didn't know people wrote like that anymore

where did you get that?

The Place of the Great Sacred Secret Obscenities

you don't say

Yeah   it's like this great bunch of perennial hooligans
puking long streams of it

Dark Matter

Big be-
scribed boulder
slowly rotates in the — in the —

My sister
got nervous
when we were only ten minutes early.

That was in
the other time. Now,
the idea is simply

to steer it
on down the road,
with some precision & finesse, too.

Angel Wings

High
on the Great
Plan

the believers
glow
in their pods . . .

Well,
"it's all
a web
of words"

the master
(actually,
Bob
Creeley)

said
in a dream
I saw

in Salt
Lake City,
Utah

Irritable Aliens

Texas, Texas Jack Omohundro —
your famous cowboy president —
where he buried?
take us there, pronto

Let Me Sleep More in My Girl's Arms

Thousands of miles
this year. Now warm here

two cocoons breathe in
dark air & sometimes

dazzling dreams
until the stir of dawn:

"Good Morning,
Your Solar Eminence!"

"Yes, time
to unfold again —"

Home on the Shelf

Yet another
Collected Poems by a friend

In the end
will we all just stand there
doing the Megalith or / and
"We shall be changed"

as foretold by bass-baritones
in Handel's Messiah

Oh yes yes yes
changed
into billions of unrelated particles

some perhaps frying
in the grease of the kind
of Chinese-American restaurant
where your best bet is the "chicken-fried steak"

some flying
better than that, in the bones of a hummingbird

Dear Slovenian Bard

A long sentence: "Son, write longer lines"
a green pegasus, dancers, yaks

sing, masters of the Serbo-Croat pibroch
sing, balalaika in the teeth of adversity

(but don't you think it's time for Comrade Blank
to retire, with the understanding: *no more poems!*)

sing, you "few buckets of water tied up
in a complicated sort of figleaf" (EP)

great solar, you stir, wake each
exile man, mormon, clits and toes

and tiger faces in the fire, Colonel North
got to the shredder in time to deconstruct *l'histoire un peu*

dig, with man, up feeling
here, with Doctor Who, in Deseret

somewhat in the manner of
Tomaž Šalamun

Space Baltic

Far, far
            in the future I see

an ancient gringo baron

showing his little grand-nephew
some dusty glass-case memorabilia

in the more than half-ruined manor:

". . . yeah . . . yeah . . . we used to call that a *foot*-ball . . ."

Cloud Watch

Ah dear friends   gone into the dot of the giant
    question mark   what to tell you   that the sun
        shines upon the just & the wicked
    as it did when you had some time here   question mark

that the soul still gets the gulps & shivers
        at the sight of grace
    & that such grace still exists
in the street   at the dentist's   in bed   three dots

    that the oligarchs drool
        & twitch "uncontrollably"
    at the sight of god I mean gold   exclamation point
while most of the populace goes on slaving & whoring
                                        for grub & shelter

                that your musics
                    amigos
            still play in our hearts

Young Voice

That's it   we've had it
    with the finely crafted
        carefully torqued & loaded
or airily musical   like "Machine Age"
    (our last romantic period)

        no more priceless *aperçus*
    quick crystal hallucinations
            old jokes in new threads

We write for our *compadres*
    in the Last Chance Saloon of the Universe

        But no   no   that's not it either

Answering

An assignment given by Chris Toll of Open 24 Hrs:
"poem with the words quark, quasars, vacuum cleaner,
Mu, Buddha, and Chevrolet."

the Buddha
is in
in the vacuum cleaner

he has his little quarks

& sure they knew
about quasars in Mu

there may be some
in that Chevrolet

now remember one thing
the task of the poet

is not to comfort
but to give comfort
to the Enemy

Enjoy

enjoy your termites & bourbon

Gig

Thick clouds of smoke we roll up to the terminal
they're burning old planes our host is there
Inanna too is there we drive through a flickering landscape
post-Holocaust Ernst to the Hotel Splendide

a refurbished relic from the Booming Forties
where our host has reserved two chambers for us
at astounding expense to be borne by us
the visiting poets the Splendide

sits all by itself in a rubble-strewn landscape
in the piano bar Mars & Venus await us
pleasantly high they cheer us up when the desk clerk
won't take our checks while on the other hand wanting

shekels up front relents after phone call decides
to take a chance on these weirdos & then
it's out in the murky rain for some grub
& a Byzantine film about the end of this planet

Tomorrow we'll perform in the Muses' Temple
next to the burnt-out Pic 'n Pay

Near Miss Haiku:
Praises Laments Aphorisms Reports

For Dear Miz Haiku

"Meas nugas" my Trifles, said Anselm.

— EZRA POUND, *CANTO CV*

Don't Eat That Trilobite

ah, Cyrano's
dream of true eloquence

eloquence
true as a sword

et cetera et cetera
— gimme a break!

. . . but it was
a good one . . .

Frog / Man

One
is obliged to
think. The other
is merely
croaking

Cuando Something El Sol

in Paris
Idaho

these days
no longer do they
eat or sleep

cloud shadows
proud shadows?

a long
drawn-out wail

herding
the distance

the long
distant whale

Exciting Moments of The Past #631

sit in shrub
wait for errant lover
thinking of politics
in 1956

Modifications

as in "with some *modifications*
all this could work"

(makes sweeping gesture
indicating "this")

Godlike

when you suddenly
feel like talking

about the times
in your life when you were

a total idiot asshole you resist
the impulse

& just sit there
at the head of the table

beaming

Italics

for Joe Cardarelli

when young I was awed by authority
figures

even imitation
authority figures (people

who *yearned*
to be *thought* authority figures

I used to resent that reaction
in myself

& believed that it was
my fault

in some sense or at least
my mistake

but now I know
that I was not to blame

those people
really *are* awful

as for the rest
make sure you're reading

what you *think* you're reading

Post Modern For Ever

. . . some kind of
incredibly

wobbly &
woefully wasteful

transmission
over time

seems to be
what all these lifetimes & efforts

yes "lifetime" (lifetome?) efforts
are

so to speak
for . . .

The last of the Montforts
bids you read & pass on without comment

oh bloody Brahms
but well on the other

hand we could say
hand?

yes! hand!
well yes no we could say

"now we've got a theory
now we can get serious"

Rosalie

La Sorrels

Song has it all,
inside & out:

thought's feeling,
feeling's thought —

"on wings of" which we "fly"
through subatomic

air (earth, water, fire)
with you, the likes of you

The Art Through the Ages

Used to be only too easy to know
what to expect

from any poem
in the book

in the limp floral binding
then for a while

it wasn't so easy
but now it's much easier again

they've just left out
the love-dove *schmaltz*

& put in more boring details
about their picturesque

relatives
dead but picturesque

well sort of picturesque
but really

quite dead

The Older Artist

Kid's written a 200-page lament
over lost love: now what to tell him?

All the tears in China
won't bring her back.

Time
chips our mugs.

Dive-bombing hairbrush
scores bull's-eye in toilet.

It's a tough world.

Guilty Your Honor guilty
of much haphazardous waste

& too many shoes.

More Irritable Aliens

Deadwood, Deadwood Dick Nixon —

your famous cowboy president —

where he buried?

take us there, pronto

For Ted

It is 0200 hrs July 8, 1983
& I am "lost"

for two three hours
in Man-Eating District

drunk, hot, almost shitting my pants
"Hollo found dead in alley

on eve of Berrigan's funeral"
but "live" *(vivere)*

to pity myself some more
& to compose

some regrettably maudlin verse
to recite at the service

five years later
I don't know what to say

except that I'm trying to be less sloppy
while still munching my daily

ofttimes with dread
in this best of all possible

where sometimes your lines
leap off the page

to make me laugh so hard I almost shit my pants

Monumentally Self-Deluded

always wondered what that would be like

A Tradition

for the Cowboy Poets who would rhyme this better

soon as THE BULLET
had STRUCK
Mr. Hick-
OCK

"Wild Bill" a winsome
murderer
that morning
in the polis of Deadwud

Captain Jack Crawfud
THE COWBOY POET

took to THE HILLS
to write THE ELEGY

Great Moments of The Past #663

"My fellow Florentines! Lend me your ears!
(jumps on table)

"The Renaissance
has just begun!"

Mr. Erroll Flynn
as Michelangelo

or was it Michelangelo's buddy? but yes
aahh . . . to hear that for the very first time

& not even think of it
as funny

but simply
smashing

An English

o raging for romance he was
singing of naught but "thee" & "thine"

a shabby old Petrarch of Baltimore
back then in seventy-nine

he wrote a poem "with ruth in mind"
& she was kind but only kind

& she was a very sensible person
at least then

No Plan

for Hannes Hollo

Hug grief, hug joy, or hog 'em both:
no *one* way to go.

Eyes look, arms reach, grief teaches:
so does joy.

No Plan
finds either, both, for ever —

far as *ever* goes

After Ungaretti

Darrell Gray in memoriam

the coin
fell through
the beggar's
palm

they called him
Allah Jehovah

they were never quite the same again, *tu sais*

it got them
right in the video

Hells

UNIVERSAL HELL

A world of people who read nothing
but The Instructions
so they can "work" their world

which they insist
is your world, too

LOCAL HELL

When the churches
of institutionalized ethnicities
call the idiot faithful to war

all of us deracinated mongrels
best look for a place to hide

In the Posited Universe

giddy
            on Blue Mountain Jamaican

you do
            love the idea
such as it is

wrung out of your brains

            "still on the scene"

& keep on walking
                        not long before sunset

            — bird in big hurry —

Things to Do (For the Aspiring Young Writers at Asterisk Senior High)

read a lot write a lot
stop to *think*

(once a month or so)
then go on up

or off
or in to see what's to eat

be happy but don't forget to be sad
be weird

not as weird as you want
but as weird as you are

(that's harder)
make sure you're reading

what you think you're reading
avoid the well-meant

sentiment and the hopeful cliché
write little write big

small or tall thin or wide
look at it all

this amazing flyspeck in the universe
that it all came together

is truly awesome
& we're really only seeing its awesomeness

now that we've seriously interfered with it
be baffled but cheerful

hence baffling
(at times)

write the poem of the great manly statement
write the poem of the great womanly statement

then write the poem to your man or woman friend
when you've read everything in the library

& everything in the regular bookstore
find the weird bookstore the weird library

or start one of those "well I can't do everything at once"
bet you could if you tried

practice vulgar eloquence
but remember your manners

doubt everything
then doubt your doubt

& hug your friend that bundle of contradictions
Don't get classified in your lifetime

read read read
work for the night is coming

search & change
stop trying to overwhelm the planet by numbers

(the Hutu & the Tutsi are at it again)

Laureates in Salt Lake City: A Cultural Evening

brisk dark clear November night
in Salt Lake City Utah 1955 hrs

as friend Randy Silverman and I approach
the Fine Arts Building on the U of U campus

ready & eager to attend a poetry reading
given by the winner of this year's Nobel Prize

for Literature: Joseph Brodsky
emigre poet from Leningrad

it seems the reading is already underway
a gentleman posted on the Fine Arts steps

tells us to "follow the cable to additional seating"
we follow The Cable which is taped to the sidewalk

& looks like it ends in a brick wall
but snakes around a clever comer

& does indeed lead us into a large auditorium
where a couple of hundred people are watching

the U of U's own heartthrob Mark Strand
twenty feet tall & in full color on a huge screen

reading from a translation of Brodsky's works
he reads calmly & clearly

visible only from the waist up behind a lectern
très soigné in grey herringbone sports coat

blue shirt blue-green tie & lucite reading glasses
the poem appears to be an extended meditation

on the evanescence of human delight
circa twenty minutes into the poem Strand

slows down gives gas slows down again
halts briefly & somewhat incredulously

enunciates the words
"*. . . kipper soil rickshaw headline . . .*"

he smiles clears his throat looks at the audience
& now the only about twelve-foot-tall Joseph Brodsky

balding bespectacled and clad in sensible mole gear
comes on-screen to explain that Mark

is reading from galleys with corrections & emendations
& that this may give rise

to some occasional difficulty
the two poets

have a short confab in electronic garble
then Brodsky blips off the screen again

Strand adjusts eyewear & vigorously
recommences:

"*. . . kipper soil rickshaw headline . . .*"
isolated cackles

can be heard over the loudspeakers
while audience in *this* hall

aware that its reactions are not fed back to the poets
indulge in hearty waves of guffaw

the effect is similar to an amusing malfunction
in an elegant eighteenth-century writing of speaking

automaton: "It's stuck!" Gospodin Brodsky
reappears looking a little ruffled

in a controlled sort of way
more new wave crackle babble

Strand back on camera saying
"Well I guess that's what it says"

then segues into the next line which says
something perfectly normal like

"while your eyes misted over in sardonic regret"
then Brodsky reads the same poem in Russian

no waving of the arms no thrusting out of chest or pelvis
no heavenward glance

although he does occasionally sneak a hand
under the lapel of earth-toned sports coat

to rub earth-toned sweater in region of heart
Russian language sounds great when *intoned*

like muezzin rabbi or southern baptist preacher
back to Mark & the English version

of a long poem about winter in the streets
winter in the soul

having grown up in Helsinki
roughly same latitude as Leningrad

I empathize with gray-black slusho yucko
perennial darkness wet socks imagery

while thinking that I can take or leave
the interwoven existential fatigue

& pervasive though cleverly restrained
feeling sorry for poor lonesome self

now Strand reaches the end of a long galley page
in midsentence & comes to a halt

the next page does not seem to connect with its predecessor
Brodsky surfaces the two poets shuffle

through stack of stuff on the lectern the camera follows
Brodsky scuttling to low coffee table

stage right where there are more books & folders
but no second page

Brodsky reads again
Randy takes brief nap

the couple to my left say things like
"yes well you see it's those wide open spaces

& all that ice & snow with only the odd black spruce
sticking out of it"   then Strand returns triumphant

having found missing second page of winter poem!
Brodsky smiles sweet little smile

a character in German 1830's genre painter
Spitzweg's scenes: book worm unofficial scholar

in garret & suggests that audience
simply wind itself back to about five minutes ago

which we do sliding back into dark sleeting realms
of the psyche where rarely is heard an encouraging word

things get a little brighter with a conversation between the poet
(Brodsky) & the emperor Tiberius

across as they say space & time
affirming their shared membership in the species

if not much else
Randy wakes up

the wind-up poem is set in Venice
not the sunny one of Thomas Mann

but rather the glum rainy backdrop
of *Across the River and Into the Trees*

empty beercans clatter across puddled Piazza San Marco
all is vanity saith the preacher

then it's time to go home
musing on after-image of Brodsky & Strand

waving goodbye on the giant screen
surrounded by little holograms

of flying kippers dark soil
nostalgic rickshaws & fading headlines

Reading Up On "Year" For the New Year

year: *eir*: from *ei,* "to go" —
so, we who *eir* or *ir*

are the ones who keep moving
through *hora*

(clear Greek
for "time gone by")

& this is to say
with, say, Ovidius:

"Hanc ad horum!"
"This time again!"

& with all you lovers
throughout

the system to shout:
ENCORE! ENCORE!

How I Composed Some of My Items

to the lady who discovered that "wasp sex myths 1 & 2"
were lifted from "the sensuous woman"
& of course GUY DEBORD *who defined "détournement"*
— satire by appropriation

took

what appeared

really stupid

where it stood on its page

(if one knew how to read beyond
the level of Instructions)

& put it
where it appeared

sublimely ridiculous

*

MEMO

now devise the right strategy

to avoid being sent to Re-education Camp

Wordies April 1990

for Robbie Burns
& Janey

Abundance
dances:

Warhol's Red Sphinx Lenin
Kandinsky's homage to Klee

on our kitchen walls

& Les Enfants du Paradis
last night . . . Arletty's smile . . .

Yes to wake up to beauty
right next to it
is such imperial privilege

possibly even imperialist?
well of course!
as was the whole troubadour shot
sexist! pedestalist! et cetera

even though it disdained
the patriarchal *mainstream* the
as Sanders & Kupferberg have it
great River of Shit

down which proceeds *die Geschichte*
History
as "tales of the tribe"
incitements to endless vendetta

invincible
abundant

unlike the Bread of Equality & its dreamers
& the dreamers of
Dark Ladies
always there

across the room

those Dreamers
(& even Freddie)
are but background vocalists
in the grand Symphony of Dread

hey that's not a bad note to end on
thus
to be resisted

So let's see there is always that glimpse
of the lives of the gods
on their *terrasse*
presiding over
a groans — and — whinnies — of — *jouissance* universe

a stage for Salomeh Abundance

& Lenin's Red Sphinx head

Letter of Application Found in Typewriter

in homage to don marquis' immortal archy

4 september 1988
quote professor unquote benedict dickson
chair or table
department ob english
de university ob de souf
swanee river
dear prof
responding to your
open parenthesis rather pompous i must say
close parenthesis announcement
in the current affiliated riting programs
job list that basically worthless publication
although it did get me one miserable little job
at honey suckle virginia
where i tried to talk about poetry
to a bunch of airhead southern debs
for a couple of years and otherwise
stayed mostly drunk and stoned
between trips to civilization
i hasten to join
the no doubt legion of excellent applicants
and nominees for your cushy
quote new endowed chair for a writer-teacher unquote
at your rich and racist institution
my current résumé
enclosed
indicates the vast range
of my qualifications and teaching experiences
in other socalled liberal arts colleges
both undergraduate and graduate
over the past quarter century
while the long list
of colleges and universities
may seem indicative of incurable *wanderlust*
it is really the result
of a basically antiacademic
and even generally asocial disposition
which has made my sojourns at places

such as honey suckle and alphaville u
quite finite due to my impatience
with upstart that is american
academics socalled
and their ridiculous pretensions
which i have always endeavored to counteract
by boycotting faculty meetings
cussing and talking dirty
dressing poorly
acting crazy at faculty dinners
missing classes a lot
smoking cigars and cigarettes in class
when indeed there
and abusing both legal and illegal
substances although i have slowed down
some in that last respect
due to the appearance
near the end of my checkered career
of a veritable angel in human form
viz my wife louise
her family
the landed
and armed
delangoustes
have been members and residents
of the sangrail community adjacent to your campus
for three generations keeping a vigilant eye
on you effete intellectuals
i would also like to mention
that i think your poet laureate
richard punt weller
is a boring old fart
and has always been that way
even when quite young
and i must say that the poetry
produced by your colleagues and contemporaries
down there
is a mighty river of neo-classical drivel
matched in its tediousness only
by the tributaries of *soi-disant* critical material
produced by those same guys
and printed in publications

like your swaney review
hoping to hear from you when
you have mended your ways
sincerely yours
archibald bollenweavil
open parenthesis socialist alien close parenthesis

An Eek

& a cry from the shower
"come here come here"

"what is it?"
"I think it's a FIRE BRAT"

for a moment I see a ferocious
torchwielding child out of Brueghel

instead of the elegant
centipede so named

now quickly dispatched to the great outdoors
then return to my book

or rather Mr Stuart Kaminsky's
book "Buried Caesars"

in which I read "Nature and I
got along okay

but we weren't exactly pals"
(feeling as fortunate as any Caesar

or St. George rewarded
with a damp kiss

Paradiso Terrestre

small lemon yellow butterfly

          & Mr. Sidney Bechet

playing the tunes

      of a more confident time

& what sits here

      observing these

is poet

   or hawk

a flying suitcase

      full of mice or dice

The Patched Fool

for Alec & Ian Hamilton Finlay

so now

it's the latter end of this play

so sing

the ballad of this dream

or:

"The next time you hear
a stewardess
using onomatopoeia,
fasten your seatbelt"

— "Dr. Science" on KGNU radio

in eloquence of confusion
synesthesia lights up
with mucho infolded
irony & passion

— passion ivy oh ouch?

"oh I got it all wrong"

what else is there to say

"it's all in that bag"

surely there is a joke
of which that
's
the punchline

Americains

"No better 'n cockroaches" — bus driver 5 a.m.
    between Frisco & Grand Junction
referring to drug dealers users & ho-mo-sexuals
    including victims of AIDS

*

Grand Junction bus depot: square-faced native american
sits next to mexican vaquero type
conversing
with elfin tall black man
    chiffon rag round his head
        holding young fast-asleep daughter

can't hear what soft-spoken black man is saying
but the rocky native american is barking

    "Yeah, that's STUPID!
        that's really STUPID!"

vaquero smiles steady no comprendo smile

old refined lady
    is telling vietnamese man
        about her childhood in Butte Montana

*

Straight, No Chaser

La Vie Littéraire

for decades on end
Y had made X feel like an "old fogey"

no that's not right
for decades on end when X read
the astounding works of Y

X had felt
like an "old fogey"

well X still felt like an "old fogey"
X was in fact an "old fogey"
& so was Y

they were
both of them
"old fogies"

Wild West Workshop Poem

when after muchos años
& by the book "high noon" encounters

scarred but victorious Ned returned
to the Famous Gunfighters' School

Old Byrum cackled "hell, boy, who would've thought
you'd take all that stuff so seriously —

we just pop 'em in the back
whenever we get a chance"

Near Miss Haiku

order out of chaos equals frogs

*

"here come the faster
'n a rattler poets"

o for the day
we hear that cry

*

the competition
for World's Most Virtuous Nation
has been called off
(offer no longer valid)

*

Modern Jazz Quartet
after all these years —
a bit like when the man smiles
& says "well done"

*

Max Bruch
violin piece
full of glowing
inwardness
made him wipe a tear
for his parents & think
(well)
"one hopes they had their moments"

*

"he probably was a horrible guy"
"nooo, he wasn't"
"OK he probably wasn't a horrible guy"

*

"You can say things *again*."

"You sure can."

*

she had this in-
credible
urge
to tell
the
whole
story
all
the
time

*

early moments of mother
must've been something!
she could never live up to them later

*

having picked it out of
an enormous pile of bodies
the reader
opens the book .

The Assignment

the idea was to fit some words into one
space then a few more
into another

there were so many to choose from
it made one dizzy
dizzy

          looking up at the wagon
     of the stars

*

window   word
(word)   (window)

*

concision
aposiopesis
jumpcuts
anacoluthon
quotes
sadness
acceleration
euphoria

*

the letter from Helsinki
addressed to "*Orebard* Avenue"

arrived here on Orchard in Boulder
Colorado

               land of plentiful ore

     and yes a few bards

under the dragon of stars

Here Goes

for Jack Collom

a magick meta-fax transmission
of twenty thousand *cucarachas*

to the Mop Room
of the National Endowment
for the Arts

12th January 1990
1300 hrs
— wind picks up sudden —
ho-ly hiatus!

SOME
Negative
Energy

well hell I didn't really mean it hey
Operator hey
make that rose petals

twenty thousand *rose petals*

OK?

& that's for giving a fellowship
to a most
deserving
subversive

Two Prayer Flags

(i)

she's out
she's out there

there
one moment

somewhere else
the next

"hurtling through space"

think of it
think of god

then think of ink
dear ink my consolation

(ii)

we don't know what it is
lives in our front yard
under a small mound
now covered with snow

entryway facing south

probably has been living there
longer than we in this house

we've never seen it
it may no longer be there
but if it is

we hope for its own sake
it has some other it
with which
to hibernate
            & the gods willing

wake up
    in the spring
    & perhaps for a moment
    before getting on with existence
join
in a flash of amazement:

what a world   what a world

Vernal Ideogrammic with Names

reading thinking about it
morphic resonance sounds even better in French
"resonance morphique" Ball or Padgett
could tell me if that's correct

rain rain spring early et cetera just like me mythical Ireland

tulips & myrtle myrtle? something with little blue fleurs

less brain & some awful slippage of perception
by these are some of us trapped

but how to get people off symbolism
so lost in weak brag
these days of grudge & flag

just spit on your gods & I'll spit on mine

using same body I writes
"the road salt pyramids"
Tom Raworth called the Church of Lot's Wife

another spring it was in a-historic present
on the road in southern Utah

smoked whitefish pickled lampreys my father's favorites
he long gone now
as is the "inventor" of present whitey universe
        Philo T. Farnsworth of Utah

The Flag's at Half-Mast in Arcana Gardens

3 "Sonnets" for Steve Carey, in memoriam

love wafts by   waving some plumage
never had no message   never will
"none shall be permitted to retain their shape"
ah Babylon I exalt thee above thy detractors

dance of dada   dance of death
"killed by orthodox reality"   Peter Handke *ist* still alive
he rode the train he rode the plane
the bus the car the boat the horse

it only writes itself little by little
no epiphany sans community
Babylon in The Old Days   The Babylon All Stars
17,000 Days & Nights that Shook the World

jazz in the ruins   before the ruins
George Shearing an angel   Stephane Grappelli a god
we meet again on the island of Verba Buena

•

a ride through the desert of many faces
the forms formalities with which we "stave off" death
& thought of it   so sturdy
yet still that cheek & glint   the lively dogsled music

admit one non-utilitarian emotion
admit a thousand   old Mozart . . . young Cassandra . . . owls
at the speed of greed the brain made metaphor
mid rock & fem adream   with Chingachgook & Cody

this evening a report on UFO sightings in Guatemala
ups one's production of benign neuropeptides
they swoop through the canyon at night in Spanish dark
& the sublime just fell asleep & died

our existence   if you pay it any attention
unbelievably distressing   time a huge lizard
but you gotta dance like nobody's watchin'

•

ride the wild word woods *avec Le Merveilleux*
gaze at red orange & green
delight in the *skill* of reading   bluejay on woodpile
contained in the changing light

move frame & things from room to room
no grief   love work that sails
close to its own parody   that old strut
that old fiddling while Rome burns canto strut

a vulgar eloquence   the way was to fall in love
light filigreed but also mud-heavy in the old songs
"straight no chaser" & "translate your head"
shoe creaks   paper rustles   dog talks

wind picks up sudden   it can't be paraphrased
think of them flying into the sun
they he you sang the ballad   of this dream

Ghost Dance

for the ghost dancers
who gave me these words:
Pentti Saarikoski & J.A. Hollo

let the ones gone ahead
speak to the ones coming up behind you

in fast high beam montage of verses old recent & pending
in a-historic present an uncharted music

jumpcuts rekindled translations web of verba seeds & stems
not just to express some righteous sentiments

as at those times one is keenly aware that Mr. Hank Williams Sr.
said it all

LIFE IS SWEET. DEATH IS NOT. THAT'S ALL SHE WROUGHT

but the quick jot & the moves of thought

the text
a continuation of life
by whatever means

one has to write a little about everything or everything
about a little

so much stuff quite a task to arrange the space
to achieve a degree of comfort for each item

even fragments are rare
whole poems no longer found

*

we are witnessing
he said the decline of vowels

we're learning to speak without opening our mouths
as our children already know how to do

they have been taught to read
better to understand the rules & regulations

& they have been taught to write
so they can fill out the forms

new thoughts won't be needed for a long time
glued into the web of their paradigm

in homes the color of what a person who eats
regularly & well   shits

& sleeps & sees a dream which is the universe
brain cells   too many shoes   burnt-out stars

today the deer came to the yard
to eat the shrubs   that is their work   their task

*

the afternoon was one to bring Herakleitos to mind
the world felt familiar like a shoulder

on which one has leaned before
(who *wants* to go to war?)

to be sure it is as the French poet says he said
that we are born among human beings

& die disconsolate
among the gods

an old man came to your table
thought you were a friend of his youth

& you talked   easily   about the old days
while a jet plane cracked the sky

thinking   is remembering
under the vaults in the cool library far away in silence

but you don't even know the wind
when you can't see the smoke of others

*

philosophies & politics snap like dry twigs   power
over fellow humans is costly

chieftains sink into the sediment   night turns
like the emperor when he can't fall asleep

sleep is the foundation of the universe
cool grove   where philosophers congregate

but trees have other things to do
nothing sublime about present wars

hiding their faces men crawl into vehicles
whose engines provide the only light

on roads growing ever darker
in countries that have no Sophokles

thirty thousand slaves were required he said
    in the silver mines of Laurion
to create the material conditions for Sophokles' works

at the beginning of the ideologies
of never-ending growth

well now the world is this size
but the great need so many legs   they stumble

*

as long as wars are described as exciting experiences
there won't be an end to them

the end never finds its end
a hand is a hand but what is a concept

doing thinking & will remain just facial expressions
decide in advance explain later

they built sea monsters of wood & set sail for foreign lands
to kill the inhabitants steal their vessels & weapons

indeed it was a symbiosis of ideas
& econo-political ambitions

Lenin lies in his mausoleum
so definitively dead

he was Marx's mistake   as Stalin was Lenin's
but Stalin made no mistakes

the renewal of machinery is a luxury
which has to be saved for the day
          it becomes
                              inevitable

& crises are important because
they demonstrate that that day has come

*

go through day go through night same effort
all for the wind to snatch your words away

Homer he said was thought of as blind
because he saw so precisely

always looking for words
bloodthirsty cold & dirty he was

as any & all of us   then night came
      long-fingered night

no mail is delivered to the dwellings of death

*

solitude   the cities
you walk through the shadow called responsibility
you can feel it in your toes & eyelashes

birds appear   in the fine evening air

Krinagoras praises a toothpick carved from an eagle quill
sends it to Leukios   to thank him for dinner

of this Leukios we know nothing else
he is one of thousands & again thousands

of whom we know nothing else
except that he too rode a horse that had wings & flew

who owns the land whence he came?
who the land that he has become?

languages don't die
    they drift like the Milky Way

"a fistful of salt thrown across heaven's lid"

*

all that is visible is pictograms   a cat walks *on* the road
& *through* the facets of its days

the eye speaks
the eye eats

in my early youth he said I was often astonished
when I heard grown-ups utter sentences
    that did not contain one coherent thought

startled
you say something but it rolls
out of your mouth to the floor   is it a horseshoe what is it?

today a new bird came to the yard
no time to look for it in the book

& the Left has laryngitis
& the Right sounds like a pig

*

every system he said
satisfies pre-programmed needs

in the end   people adapt to the system
& to the "needs" the system creates

"ideas" are used to legitimize the system
since people can't live *only* for organizations
    & "material goals"

thus it was even in the days of the Crusades
& centuries of hierarchies
when the Virgin gave suck to axe-men

centuries as dark   likely again

then as now
reality diverged greatly from the ideal

oil that sinks to the bottom
joins the sediment   decreases production of nutrients

the side effects may remain
for an immeasurably long time

but who wants to go to war
needs oil

the three hags of the moon decide decide
who does not come back from the voyage   & who returns
once more
            on his fair ship

*

not the world & its places
but places & their world

"if I didn't know that I live in that house
I'd think happy people must be living there"

the red fiber of death is the core of the thread of life
it just grows darker

by & by   & in the final darkness
it looks black

the wind rises   you're on your way home

the grains of sand on the road cast long shadows

Blue Ceiling

[1]

racoon sees Cat go in an out Small Door

the mental beanie rotor turns

the mammal ever-blissful when it eats

"ah, Earthlings —"

one might of course say there haven't been any further poets
since Pierre Reverdy

sentence understood only if read at right tempo, said Ludwig
then he wrote it down
and now we're reading it:
"avoid" "arguments" "with" "the" "furniture"

the magus is dead long live the magus
semper bogus
(by now we should all know what people really like)

then tried to wipe a smudge of light off the table
with all the fussiness of an old, er, void
it's all a struggle
cuttin' time
so mighty fine
you won't be able to verify any of this

[2]

life's just a dream remember
poetry just an interruption
of the great conversation
farewell notes those gone
weave through the composition

a father walks in an old apartment
talks: "never admit you're rich or asleep"

as you enter the recording studio
you notice you don't have anything to record

skepsis is contemplation

may you be forever strange
may neither spring nor ashes faze your dailiness

what's ragged should be left ragged

"we want a guided tour!"

slow thoughts down
notice tone and sensation

bus bounces into pothole
with delicacy and precision

[3]

when you met him he was a man
now he is a postage stamp

you can't open the window this is Dallas

"they took my billiard table!"
Mary Queen of Scots complained in 1576

mice fall from the sky

mind suffers body suffers language suffers
thinking urge greater than any other
bugs in throat in the dead of night

but what's past is yours in the vectors of joy

in a café named after Beatles song
person plays home-made instrument
combining tuba violin and gong

the unconscious
slow as hazardous waste
roll through the night

[4]

Americans still know how
they know how
to manufacture a good working handkerchief

"It's real surreal!" said little Laura

fantasies magicks
all come from the child
to work its will on the giants
then it grows up to be a giant itself
and then
there is still
the whole goddamn universe

"It's never enough, is it?"

the poet you hardly knew
looks dear and old like you
not like you but old like you
and dear to you
on the cover of his "Kings"
not like think dark peacoated figure
glimpsed from a cab this spring
strode past Brompton Oratory
large take-out coffee in hand
his double from half a lifetime ago

[5]

and the closetful of magical toys
shrank
to old shoebox of objects broken and shoddy
now having neither
you have both

slowly they walk across the sunny parking lot

they
are your friends

". . . mad as Cassandra
who was as sane as the lot of them"
in the footsteps of Jesus Tom and Jerry
perfect their running-in-the-air trick
proceed
at speed
off the edge of cliff
perform their mid-air miracles
then plummet back-pedal hover and soar
over America
not to answer the question she asks

but to return
the question
to her
to change it
and return it
to her who asks
shall be the whole of the teaching

[6]

green rhubarb leaf-dragon
dormant under snow
beneath red studio wall
"merely a matter belief"

in December
or *any* time and (whaddayaknow)
so is the snow
the red the green

the wall the house the art
what keeps it all
from flying apart
if not the love that moves
the sun and other stars

and around midnight
racoon lady
stops
just short of the doorway, peeks in —

trundles back out
tells her companion:

"No good, he's still there
in his chair
reading Harper's"

Dec 91 / Jan 92
Boulder, Colorado

Notes

"never admit you're rich or asleep": "I have never yet known a man to admit that he was either rich or asleep" — P. 177, Patrick O'Brian, *Master and Commander*

"what's ragged should be left ragged" — p. 45 Ludwig Wittgenstein, *Culture and Value*

"mad as Cassandra . . .": "the wind mad as Cassandra/who was as sane as the lot of 'em" — p.475, Ezra Pound, *The Cantos*

"the love that moves . . ." — Dante Alighieri, end of *Paradiso*

Among others who "weave through the composition," or compost, are the late ethno-magico-musicologist and film-maker Harry Smith, one of the world's great curve-ball conversationalists, and the very much alive Ron Padgett, poet of Paris and New York.

High Beam

Notes

Inhabited Eyes: "falcon-eyed Montcorbier" – François Villon

A Town Dedicated . . . title borrowed from a health-food magazine article on Boulder, Colorado

O Keats Where Is Thy Sting: *"nell' mezzo cammin"* — "in the middle of (life's) road" — Dante

Schiller's Rotten Apples: legend has it that German *Romantisch* poet Friedrich Schiller (1759–1805) kept rotting apples in his desk drawer and would occasionally sniff them "for inspiration." "Chet" — the one and only

Questions: "Josef Hellström" — Joe Hill

Blue March '91

brute metal glee
momentarily done careening about that Gulf

wind blows dustballs and spiders
out of the walls

> *to sort*
> *black socks*
> *in the dark*
> *is your task*

the Species invented Time
and probably Space

its function to be their recorder
until the End

> *young beauty*
> *picks up spider*
> *re-locates it*
> *in flowerpot*

Inhabited Eyes

falcon-eyed Montcorbier
gone complicated after much dying

sang about April
in nimble remembering

calligrapher Berrigan
carved the Iowa rain

The Comparative Avec

brief local media fame "on the air"
avec Swami Eddie Ananda
in Boulder, Colorado
as ephemeral
as a plateful of tasty shark
avec a side of nimble Nepalese noodles
in Boulder, Colorado

A Town Dedicated to The Pursuit of Fitness & Inner Peace

says the headline   so that's where we are
that's why they're building
fifty new houses
right next door

now the telephone wants to tell me about a deal
on cleaning our carpets & upholstered things

I tell it "we don't have any"
then replace it quite gently
in what I believe is called its cradle

yes among those alive today
we're truly fortunate
to be living these charmingly specialized lives
in "a town
dedicated to the pursuit of fitness & inner peace"

unlike the majority of the planet's towns
which remain dedicated
to plain old pursuit of food
& staying alive   a few moments longer

yes fortunate   if a bit haunted by Kafka's Fear
of waking up in less delightful state
but that comes & goes
just like the battles of light & darkness

old hats bursting out of their secret closets
to be stuffed back in   to reappear thirty years later
empty as ever (no brains) but plenty of clout

very fit for his age
the Senator
enjoys
his inner peace

O Keats Where is Thy Sting

"thorn stuck in paw
bullet lodged in leg
bee buzzing in ear"

ah, *nell' mezzo cammin*
to steal one's script back
re-write it for better & worse —

once again it is time
for our jitterbug lesson

In the Raging Balance

i.m. Jack Clarke

Energy, the man said, equals
Eternal Delight. Does our return to it
mean shedding all that was our art?
Task of The Living: to ask questions
of The Dead. You did it well, you
Weird and Funny Dude! I thank you
and wish you a good Eternal Night
in Tunisia or wherever you've taken
The Show. "The winds on the moon
blow so cold, so cold" could be a refrain
but isn't nor will this last line rhyme
with anything but tears then again why
should it be the last line and come to
think of it it couldn't possibly be

Schiller's Rotting Apples

think thoughts think
desire: wanting that thinks & feels

ah the ukuleles of yesteryear
praise the lord & pass the graham crackers

watch the last dukes of reaction
jet round the empire the vampires they are
while listening to Chet

Chet the great
cool cat

cat fell out the window
cat went splat

shadow moves up & down tree

life is of course utterly

A Chipmunk Called The Present

OK boss off to the supermercado

time for your daily
contact with civilians at large

grazing there in the aisles
with relative ease quite peaceful digging it all

three seconds at a time

Questions

Josef Hellström & Emiliano Zapata
met? In Mexico, 1911? hung out
with Ambrose Bierce?

    our heads
    the "heaven"
    where they engage in lively debate

Chicago

up and down he went
in the pink elevator
                    in the pink hotel

where pink (and, well, some rather ashen)
Elders
      dwelled

went up & down
as all their lives before
                    but now
in these
        "controlled circumstances"

they had, in fact, *become*
"controlled substances"

this occurred to him
as he stepped out of the pink elevator
to meet young friends
                    under the grand chandelier
where they sat chatting
with some Elders
                  in clown masks & wild paper wigs

Note Found on Meditator

war bonnets horseman a waving forest of lances

        a lovely sight

    if you don't care for what they're attacking

it's John Wayne they're attacking OK no problem

        beauty

knows no ideologically correct routines

        beauty knows nothing at all

that's why she asks all these questions

Born Today

for Jane

is to be one to the one
closest to you
who shares the air
& other elements
right there   next to you

two bodies wrapped in darkness
among millions of other bodies
shrouded in darkness & smoke
war bloodshed & chaos
      voices rising out of the dirt

one to the one   without whom one
wouldn't be one
      who saves one when lost
in regions of the past
raging at bygone constellations
                  pursued by a swarm of angst gnats
      who saves one by her sight & sound & touch
to notice
            that gravity's strong on this planet
notice
        there's a half-ton of apples in that tree
notice   cricket jumping on cedar branch
        feline humor   magpie elegance
in sum
          this world
born not so long ago
with maybe not that far to go
            still roaming
      the contradictory corridors
of a universe or two

wind turns pages   then shuts book
he looks up   she looks up from piano keys

            hold that frame

West Is Left on the Map

?

trace my life on the map
a new geographical treatise
every day

check the table of contents
let's see
where will I be tomorrow

— MIHAIL COSMA

Worstward Ho

— SAMUEL BECKETT

---

wee terrible human race
soon to go down   or else into space

let it go let it bleed
into stellar fuzz   the light of another sun

whatever it ever was
fights among capos

a puff of dust where the lampshade bloom'd

Marlene forever young

like Marx or Helen's ankles
at the gates of dusk

or a recital
of Etruscan tunes   what a treat

        "poems in 2091
        objects of monkish interest"
        sez Vidal
        Gore, not Peire

    like poor but civilized urban existence
    another thing of the past

Petrus Kalm (1716–1779), a native of Finland, went west
& later wrote in his "Travels in North America":

"once this old white man went to the woods with one of the savages
& they came upon
                    a speckled red snake
the old man reached for a stick but the savage begged him
in the name of all that was sacred
                                not to hurt this snake

saying it was
                    one of his gods
so the old man picked up a sturdy branch & killed the snake
& told the savage:
'when you said to me
                                that this creature
                                                            was your god
you left me no choice but to kill it'"

& if that old man had not been so old
he would have killed that savage too
                                                    no doubt

yes   that's what's wrong with them:

n o

d o u b t

watch out

for the wailing Fundees
& *their* "god"

their god grows out of the muzzle of a gun

Odyss   on the old plate
looked so comfortable in his body   old enough
to fit a few words together

bare twigs
  cracks in the sky
long lines short lines no lines

let us sit down & enjoy a really empty experience

write what? to a tree?

"dear: chords of night: one is not rhymes
but civil fur   come to bliss late"

this creature called god
   left one no ma

boat sails into sun

west
      is left on the map

an endless warble of dreams

Was there a time when thou, too, wert an optimist,

Falling about in fits of pseudo-mystical glee?

Sho 'nuff — when Goddess Utopia roared in mine head

& I refused to be of time & place . . . Well, I still do,

Still wince at epithets that smack of Church or Nation

& would prefer to be, not just *El Hombre,* but *El Animal*

Invisible — one of those invisible beasties of the Lapps . . .

A follower of Lingo Rapture: she is never opaque,

Turn as she may — Mother Discourse, ever transparent

Even when terrorized by vagaries of head & heart.

Sad, dignified as the winds on the moon

— minimalist intensity! Ah, well, the fire went west

& whims and winds took hat & head. Without

A head, no cigarette. Without a heart, big trouble.

---

remember Bear's Head who saw
between midnight & dawn 1833
ten thousand meteors
cascade across the heavens
from the constellation we call The Lion

remember Bear's Head who saw
a comet in the sky
between midnight & dawn 1858

remember Bear's Head who that same winter
in dreamtime
between midnight & dawn
saw canyon waters rise
& flood the land
& wash away his people Arapaho
saw
when the flood subsided
only the white men remain

remember him
who saw these things between midnight & dawn
in this place Boulder
on this planet Earth

all hail

to Mother Mail

3:30 p.m. the view is
Flatirons above trees &
neighbors across the street
in the window a rear end
of squirrel for half a nervous second
of its life (my life, your life) & that
does of course include
the front end too, my front end
is waiting for the mail
Great Mother Mistress MAIL
be praised: you bring the best, you bring
the worst, but "Lots of mail! I feel pretty
good!" said Ted in a poem, "I open
a beautiful letter from you. When
we are both dead, that letter will be
Part Two of this poem." Give us
our mail fix today & every day
oh I can remember when it came
twice a day, a dear old man
bending to pick it up off the mat
after it shot
through the slot
in our apartment door
in Helsinki, Finland
in the early years
of the millennium

"so what's the diff
between a hopeful sort who believes he'll go to 'Heaven'
& a hopeful sort who believes his descendants
will colonize the universe?"

asked Tattered Old Bird
minor warlock
invisible when at the top of his form

& the tribes unfurl the old demon banners:
oh let the dark ages begin again so we can join
our dimwit ancestors in gore & glory

most of the populace blank
resigned to the neo-feudal

Geronimo stern: "YOU FOOLS"

God is a speckled snake

cat turns mouse into mouse dust

"have a nice day"
said Tattered Old Bird
"have a nice dog have a whole bunch of fine gods dogs & days
in view of the indignities that await us
that doesn't seem too much to wish for
on the way to the old *pulvis et umbra* *il faut s'amuser, non?*"

& the shades they are a-massing
at the gates of ghostly Troy

---

trying not to be
pissed off because
the truck won't start
(too cold)

I pick up a book
peed upon
by long-dead cat
in distant other life

& see the stain's
still there —
of the cat
not a whiff

but find the poems
of the late urban ironists
still pungent & deeply
amusing

so let the truck rust
the book
take me back
to streets once walked
nights
talked
dusk to dawn
in the Eolian cities —

"borne
deposited
produced
eroded
by the wind"

think "son"
night's sleep gone

"we know you're in there"
locked inside
a crowded hippocampus world

of drums & demons
distance   absence

haunted years
of wish & rage

in mislaid brain
& slaughtered time

so the ghoul weeps
he the ghoul
weeps so
for his son

come out please come out
arise
take up thy bed   rejoin
whatever we might be
outside this maze

walking through a geometry
in a gold & green light
reading a sculptor's notes:

to create latent motion
you set up something
one would expect to move
but it doesn't
it remains
in the same place & position
& it keeps doing that

as eye & mind
repeat the event that does not occur
again & again

you might call it a raging balance

space
is mostly
light

what's tactile
reaches out   grabs
the 8 corners
of the room   (Ivan Liljander)

in Heaven which was the darkest corner
of the tavern right next to Diogenes
we hung out over cappuccinos
& munched on tasty raw veggies

I told The Old Dog
people on Earth had finally managed
to kick the nasty expensive habit
of raising & eating cows

Diog' said Pythagoras
would have liked to hear that
personally he said
being the first citizen of the world
I've never been one to proscribe anyone's habits

then we leaned back to listen to Gerry
Mulligan play "Waltzing Matilda"

& as delighted as I surely was
to hang out with my favorite Cynic
I was homesick for Earth
& wished you were there with us

(not worried at all
you wouldn't know how to deal
with The Old Dog
who wasn't really a misanthrope
merely defined
anthropos
very strictly)

then opened my eyes
to the light & your eyebrows
& the golden light of your eyes

---

for him her face
goes out of focus
before his does for her

so that when she's
in focus for him
quite adorably he

seems sadly distant
to her but they refuse
to be terrorized

by that or any
other contradiction

---

though but a weave of dust and shade
caught in the chandelle of our days

who writing shovels grief's doubloons
I can say this: hello! dear woman I name Dream

dear called *Because*
with you, a thousand years would not be long enough

Notes

Mihail Cosma — author of the poem titled ? (1927): Romanian poet, b. 1902 in Tirgu-Onca. d. 1968 in Paris. Contributor to the avant-garde journals *75 HP, Punct, Discontinuité,* and others. From 1928 on, Cosma wrote and published his poetry in French, and also translated Tristan Tzara's Romanian *Primele Poeme* into French. These biographical details, and the poem, gleaned from Manfred Peter Hein's remarkable anthology *Auf der Karte Europsa ein Fleck* (A Spot on the Map of Europe; Ammann Verlag, Zurich 1991), a treasury of poems written by members of the East European avant-garde between 1910 and 1930.

Worstward Ho — Samuel Beckett's prose poem (Grove Press, New York 1983). Should be recited at every presidential inauguration from now on.

"fights among capos" — capo: (Cosa Nostra) boss.

"Gore, not Peire" — "If novels and poems fail to interest the Agora today, by the year 2091 such artifacts will not exist at all except as objects of monkish interest. This is neither a good nor a bad thing. It is simply not a famous thing." (Gore Vidal, in "Screening History," The New York Times Book Review 30 August 1992.) For Peire, see Paul Blackburn's wonderful *Proensa: An Anthology of Troubadour Poetry,* University of California Press 1978.

"Odyss   on the old plate" — in my late sister's copy of Gustav Schwab's *Die schönsten Sagen des klassischen Altertums* (The Most Beautiful Tales of Classical Antiquity), 1925 edition.

"watch out / for the wailing Fundees" — an ideological mega-gang that seems to be multiplying all over the globe. Its members are particularly fond of killing the *already born,* when and wherever they have reason to suspect that these are championing the cause of rational existence governed by the Golden Rule.

"one of those invisible beasties" — in the first novel written and published in the Saame (Lapp) language, author Johan Turi mentions the "invisible animals of Saameland."

"remember Bear's Head" — Bear's (or Bear) Head was a Southern Arapaho of the mid-19th century; see pp. 63–66 in: *Chief Left Hand. Southern Arapaho* by Margaret Coel, University of Oklahoma Press 1981.

"pulviset umbra" — dust and shade (we are); "il faut s'amuser, non" — one must amuse oneself, no?

"said Ted in a poem" — "Today in Ann Arbor (for Jayne Nodland)," in *So Going Around Cities,* Blue Wind Press, Berkeley 1980.

"think 'son' / *walking through a geometry*" — the lines on the right, which may be read as more or less aleatory "marginalia" *or* heard and seen to resonate with the lines West, come from a page of aphorisms by the Swedish sculptor Ivan Liljander that I picked up in 1992 at a posthumous exhibition of his quietly radiant three-dimensional abstractions at the Thielska Gallieret in Stockholm.

"in Heaven which was the darkest corner" — see *Herakleitos and Diogenes* translated from the Greek by Guy Davenport, Grey Fox Press 1979.

"Gerry Mulligan's rendition of Waltzing Matilda" — *I Giganti del Jazz* #49, 1976.

"caught in the chandelle of our days" — chandelle: abrupt steep climb of airplane propelled by the plane's momentum.

Survival Dancing

For Ye Raven's Mistris

&

In Memoriam Sir Orfeo Joe

The title of this sequence was found on a laundromat bulletin board in upstate New York, in the early summer of 1994:

SURVIVAL DANCING
8 PM, MAPLEWOOD PARK C.C.
MAY 12, 19, 26, JUNE 2, 9
CALL BILL 273-0126

Canto Arastra

opera creatures   technicolor elves
love to roam in profusion
make home in voices   shouting at no one
dotty shamans   pathos & farce transmitters
many birds singing waters gardens in Spain

but time's grindstone jaws
surely crunch graybeards
& smoky lamplit ore
in fatal history's central city
sweep twenty years from day

end of tube proclaims gone
lineage guests broken drum virtuosi
gone from free-bop survival dancing

now patriots of the dark
watch earth go silent movie

no poetry no pinball
no dream no pathos confusion
time was a placid pig
now is a shorter drift

ride ice hold terror
endure shadow
light dim flares underground

faster than bubble life travels
metaphysicks away from the sun

dark balance   every moment
all gone   & going   things

In the Music Composed by Nutritious Algae

thought lined up pale winter
white sky
tall smooth car
loaded with motionless wings

staircase time
high speed nail into decades
curious shades of what happened
in small misunderstood group of being
engine loiters in thought

toss coin choose stairs a door with home
black hole of childhood
upholstered in cobblestones
mystery & exactitude of human nostrils

store babbling thought
see shadow body years ago
mumbling wooded mantra
gilded leisure morning

face down on tops of forest
begin to look at colors
they are air

then, mouth, what happens?
how did very good happen?
question, indeed

Kindly Water Other Level

two found together   construct regard
place comb in hand   part knot exactly
look out windows   collect words

longing walk
bounces special

speak out strange
once daily

"she went right
clearing fence"

a few
still make sense

sing
awe
in joy's wise space

lie in bed
smell gigantic steamships
hug great-grandmother
wake up at dawn
well rested calm
afloat

a vivid weightless bean

Beginning & Ending with Lines from Christina Rossetti

strange voices sing among the planets
faint insect talk next door
cartoon mind   cartoon cantos
all the broken drums
La Châtelaine
hushes

her bandogs
& some of us speak weird(ly?)
(no; just weird)
but there is time
all around the time
there is
your pleasure is my pleasure Earth
between walls of crickets
lips move in fluffed-up night
warm shrubs on slopes
dazzled heart thump rhododendron
grown old yet still green

At This Point in l'Histoire

opaque air
            ways to live
in a country of shadows
cold iron horse forests

done with hanging loose
jump out of a sad speak
wrap bliss in tremulous pebbles

            "& how did the French
            revolution begin?"
            (vertical agitation)

laughs lakes willows lady
nests in dry wind on shore
book open
            on mirror
"a nice walk with the dog"
fast insect talk next door

Fair Poetry Eats Trembling Matter

Remote Omar
                    lyrical bug
            or bearded time cloud
our public flits through earth
            belovèd yard of Allah

"Your century
                    or mine?"
            My century
                                My pleasure

"My dear that's dashing! Positively Valhallian!"
                                                    — Christina *Plutarch?*
            or was it Ted for lunch with Rossetti . . .

all now remain in waters far from kin

            remains of enormous gringos
            punctuated by The Other

Was That Really a Sonnet?

"human being"
has government

                        (thought
                        you were so tiny

"real thoroughbred infinity"
this, we don't have in life

nevertheless &
thanks to you
I'm me once in a while

living this moment in English

"he tossed his clothes
into the past tense"

presence: really tough job
compared to natural flutter

Now on to Ghazal Gulch

"When did you last see your criteria?"
"Sometime . . . last winter . . . a minute ago . . ."

Pursue   the saying mind
please train of thought   throw samples

All breathe in some air
but someone needs to till the night

Shows him the miniature city: "Pity, really a pity
. . . possible hole in invention . . ."

Sorry I thought you person
I think I run in to them

(you look
other, stroking
her

Tiny figures
from the past
troop by
in pork pie hats

And why not
think of them as
"souls free of the body"

Gods Walked Animals Talked

trees in windy room
cicadas *possessed*

tall shadow weeds
          you page the heart
when was "think" first a sound?
walk through mind's middle
                    human or rabbit
waves in tune with head

          eye coneflower
bright burning cells
          glad stomp & squeak
what progress after hawk?

megalith or mound
millions covered with snow
          or the great grease
of the longer than we
                    (in living no t.v.)

best bet out of season
bones of gods
               posited universe
          wake up
smile in the giddy blue
join in the flash of was

                    brains still on

The Word Thing

the brilliantly non-objective
appeared within
the century (big introductory note
(a.k.a. Francis Ponge) many repeated preludes
& fun with angry young

century of the plunderbund
but book an object still recognized
words in tacit envelope
perpetuate
occasional whiff

trees suddenly active *meme*
in seasons' natural pedantry

method is effortless:
translation of autonomous objects
from adept to zygote
in rhapsodic rises & falls

next click, human language —
quite soon, physical density!
voice of things also includes
steely twinkle in eye

ingenious it is
to have refined ear
ah, ancient ocher in graves

aureous bodement, enigmagist fogbow
century of the plunderbund
nevertheless, satispassion
tmesis & terribilità

Si, Si, e.e.

warm legend, blue shadow:
"green day made gold tree"
light pulls love
in courtly poem
under other
tongue-sky, soul-grid, water, heart

years don't mark snow
nor skeletons' faces

sky train wind, nude moving *so*
words walk road
body, scene
(traverse child tiger light

but desert lives across targets
annuls cities
                    disquieted
leaves'
          memory: fire, war

muscle, take book, describe profile
thought follows
see for instance:
invisible nothing

eye forge battle blade
                                        fall, shadow
                                        ashes, fall

(& yes, they wore great big hats, size extra large

As Leaves Sweep Past

sister & Joe & Mistah Rilke
gone on "home"
                    small remote fish
on yesterday's pile of ashes

now, more people berserk
difficult demons, shattered dogs

no relief
          from this irony circus
end of tube essayistic
art a dead snakeskin
stuffed with live ants
          (& they return from your past
          grins on their silly mugs

eye meets moment, frame turns
sense looks to say what sense may say

          there, then, it hits:
          "you must change
          your terrible habits"

mocking gaze haunts myth
lyrical bug looks inside
happy to see old cloud
way up in the flying dust

& Time Trots By

sad glad hairy drives
top notch roaring suspense
oh the shaggy years

hero food horny young sentences
hot hero food pronto
pronto   tilted charm never scratchy

(mad hatter at the bar
sometimes a ranting satan
rebuffed by furious foot)

life does it
think of it
enjoy a think of it
among the consequences

drive down Countdown Street
summer sad rearranged
by each day's killing power

beauty death power fear
remember
reside in sky with ears

art
loves
funny details

therefore is
a dreaming
& yes   joy!

elitist
for sure

At Evenfall

recall enormous heave of moment
la vie en rose
before some Mallarméan blows it into the *vide* or *abime*

(but *timing egg in storm*
beats driving car through rock
— Albanian proverb

sun shadows fields cast loose
drum vibes in ground moths flutter
"O Lady Time, summer was great"

but now no house of letters stands
Elizabethanly enjoying given song
paradox knots each graduate

yet she'll stay up to read & write long letters
& on still tree-lined streets attend her musings
do art   eat well   never please wicked money

always treat language like a dangerous toy

Notes

Cantro Arastra

"arastra": Millstone(s) used to grind up ore; probably from Spanish *arar,* to till. First noted both word and object on a drive to Central City, Colorado, an old mining town now abandoned to slot machines, with Joe Cardarelli in late April, 1994. Four months later, Joe, a lovely poet, painter, and dear friend, suddenly departed from the human universe. *Survival Dancing* is dedicated to his memory.

Beginning & Ending With Lines From Christina Rossetti

"La Chatelaine": The mistress of a château.

"her bandogs": Dogs kept tied to serve as watchdogs or because of their ferocity.

The medievalism harks back to a dream Paul Blackburn once told me, and to my reading of William Watson's excellent novels *The Knight on the Bridge* and *Beltran in Exile.* And, as we all know, we are presently living in a re-make of the Middle Ages.

At This Point in l'Histoire

"& how did the French / revolution begin?": Alas, that day (in was it 1946?) I had not memorized the relevant page in my history textbook; all I was able to come up with, under the history teacher's stern gaze, was the first sentence of that descriptive prose: "On the fourteenth of July, all the church bells of Paris began to toll . . ."

Fair Poetry Eats Trembling Matter

"Remote Omar": Apart from its enjoyable interior resonance, the line refers to Persian poet Omar Khayyam (?-c. 1133) who was memorably Englished by Edward Fitzgerald (1809–1883) and later quoted by Ogden Nash (1902–1971) in his lines "I myself am more and more inclined to agree with Omar and Satchel Paige [c. 1906–1982] as I grow older: / Don't try to rewrite what the moving finger has writ, and don't ever look over your shoulder."

"... Positively Valhallian": Valhalla was the pleasure dome to which slain Scandinavian warriors were transported from the battlefield by large and fierce angelic females, known as *Valkyries,* for continuous after-hours entertainment until the end of the world (a.k.a. *Ragnarök*).

"— Christina *Plutarch?*": Clearly, a brief moment of confusion on the intergalactic internet — possibly even a flashback a future when Christina Rosetti (1830–1894) and Mestrius Plutarchus (c. 48-c. 121), both of them writers on philosophical subjects, may seem practically contemporary. A prolific educational author whose influence extended well into medieval times, Plutarch spent the last thirty years of his life as a priest at Delphi. Rossetti was a celibate priestess of the High Anglican deity, her last work being *The Face of the Deep: A Devotional Commentary on the Apocalypse.*

"or was it Ted for lunch with Rossetti . . .": The Rossetti of this line could also be Christina's brother, Dante Gabriel (1828–82), poet, painter, and translator, whose turbulent career as a member of the Pre-Raphaelite Brotherhood would seem more compatible with the life and times of New York School member Ted *Berrigan* (1934–1983), poet of major verbal leaps and bounds both at, and even when out to, lunch. The scribe suspects however, that it is Christina, to whose sonnets a younger critic has recently compared Ted's work (happily available again in a Penguin *Selected Poems*). Unlike either Christina or Dante Gabriel, Ted liked to refer to friends in his poems by their first names. The scribe regrets any possible confusion arising out of his adoption of this practice; now that you know which Ted is intended, you should hasten to the nearest book emporium and acquire a copy of the *Selected.* It will restore *some* sanity to your life.

Commentary: The 'author,' who is quite postmodernly used to dwelling inside inverted commas, and prefers the term 'scribe,' is invoking a number of temporal precursors and considering the ways in which their "fair poetry" ("fair" in *any* sense) ingests their "trembling matter" and possibly survives for a while (until Ragnarök) in some non-corporeal form, while the corporeal ones are transmuted into "bug" or "cloud," and the "public" also "flits through earth." The play on "remain" and "remains" in the last three lines may, tangentially, refer to theoretical and canonical arguments of recent years.

Was That Really a Sonnet?

No names in this one, but three sets of full quotation marks. Most days, it can seem quite hard to utter the term "human being" with a straight face. As for whether it "has government," well, this country presently seems in the clutches of what Ezra Pound describes in Canto LXII (paraphrasing John Adams): "republican jealousy which seeks to cut off all power / from fear of abuses does / quite as much harm as a despotism" (*The Cantos*, p. 344). "Real thoroughbred infinity" is an equally nice but questionable notion, and "he tossed his clothes / into the past tense" is a moment of old-time narrative that may indicate the futility of attempts to describe spontaneous abandon. The two *yous* in the text may be one and the same; the *I* claiming to be *me* "once in a while" probably is. The title is really an afterthought and may be spoken by the reader.

The Word Thing

"(a.k.a. Francis Ponge)": 1899–1988, author of *Le parti pris des choses* ("Taking the Side of Things") and many other books of poetic meditation on "word" and "thing."

"century of the plunderbund": *Plunderbund* — a league of commercial, political, or financial interests that exploits the public.

"trees suddenly active *meme*": A *meme* is to your culture as a gene is to your body.

"aureous bodement, enigmagist fogbow": The 'enigmagists' were a loosely knit group of young poets attending the Jack Kerouac School of Disembodied Poetics in 1994–5.

"nevertheless, satispassion / tmesis & terribilità:" *Satispassion* — penitential suffering; *tmesis* — the separation of the elements of a compound word by the interposition of another word or words, e.g. "far effin' out;" *terribilità* — effort or expression of powerful will and immense angry force.

Si, Si, e.e.

cummings, who else.

As Leaves Sweep Past

"art a dead snakeskin": Statement attributed to Ingmar Bergman by Swedish critic Leif Zern in his book *Se Bergman* ("See Bergman"), 1993.

"you must change / your terrible habits": Paraphrase of Rilke's "You must change your life."

"*la vie en rose*": French pop song the scribe remembers from his childhood, sung by a.o. Edith Piaf and the scribe's sister.

". . . blows it into the *vide* or *abîme*": "void" and "abyss," two concepts / words much favored by French Modernist (and even post-Modernist) poets, over American / English "empty" (or e-ness) and "hole."

Rilke's poem *Autumn* is echoed in the lines "O Lady Time, summer was great," "stay up to read . . . ," "still tree-lined streets."

"always treat language like a dangerous toy": "Out of the green trees across snow as pure as salt. It is so pure it treats English like a toy." — Edward Dorn, Afterward to *Sojourner Microcosms*, 1977.

from Corvus

For ye Raven's Mistris:
"Evermore!"

Author's Note

Why "Corvus"?

In the first Middle Ages (our present era being the second), Latinizations of names of non-Latin origin were relatively common. Had I lived then (and especially if I had been born in Hungary instead of Finland), my last name could have been *Corvus* or *Corvinus*: in Hungarian, the raven is *hollo.* And *Hollo* was the name my paternal Finnish great-grandfather adopted after a family dispute whose causes are lost in the murk of time.

The word has no lexical meaning in Finnish; it was simply the traditional name of a piece of land he owned. Finnish and Hungarian belong to the Finno-Ugric / Ural-Altaic family of languages and share a relatively small proto-vocabulary; but the modern Finnish for raven is *korppi,* borrowed from Latin *corvus* via Swedish *korpen.* Both *raven* and *corvus* derive from the Indo-European root *ker,* "to cry out." (Joseph T. Shipley, *The Origins of English Words,* Baltimore, 1984)

I have always admired that uncompromisingly elegant bird, in all its mythical and legendary manifestations. I even like its *ker,* more appropriate to the poetry of this century than the trills of the nightingale.

My favorites are Odin's two ravens, Huginn and Muninn: after flying all over the world, they return to sit on his shoulders and (no doubt hoarsely) whisper the news into his ears.

As ever, the news is both sad and glad.

1991

i.m. Irina Hollo (1921–1991)

---

morning sun
strikes me pow! in the face
I turn and see

first of all
a small black wall of fur

hear it purr
then see beyond it *you* —

were that five-mile-diameter asteroid
to hit
right now
this very moment
in the age of post-fatalist
neo-feudalism
it would be no big deal
sub specie aeternitatis
"in eternity's sight"

but I'd sure hate to miss
what continuance
of these momentitos of bliss
the gods may still grant us

---

fire stairs dark
                against crimson sky
tall brick walls across the way

moonlit trees & snow a herd of deer
                asleep in the yard

two frames of the window
movie

        only we
        have seen

Lost a tooth had it fixed
took winter's first tumble on icy front step
received the news of my sister's death
all the same day

So you "took and died"
"otti ja kuoli"

Here we say
"up and died"

Where to go in the mind
for language to say
así es la vida
You liked that phrase "such is life"

We do much prefer the suchness of life
to the suchness of death

Older by thirteen years
last one to know me
as a child

Used to think of you there
"among all her things"   Now
we stand here
among all your things

Babble two minutes
in father's tongue
then sit down all pale
(my task at the rites)

At the rites we think of the old days when belief
made words reach the dead

a resonance
gone

OK Sis
now of no fixed address in the Kingdom of Dis
Miz Ubi Sunt

your departure sent us out of our patch in the sun
to fly with the ravens
back to the granite the lilac the moss
my "horse" tree with that bend
country and city of childhood's end

"one of the pines has a bend in it
three feet off the ground

"the horse's back
about two feet
the neck then stretching straight up
to the sightless head of it

"where it becomes so fine
there's no way of telling what goes on there"
1971

looked up at the window of your secret abode
turned
to see what you saw:
boats
gulls
skerries
the Sea
to the Western Lands

In your old cities
Helsinki Stockholm Londinium
you walk to the corner store
walk
on paving stones
smaller feet of yours walked on
past stone walls that sheltered a smaller body

Look up at the sky
out to sea
far seems as far as ever
but there is less time to get there

more time now, in the stone
you have given your time to the stone
cities of stone built by your species fellows
Mr. and Mrs. Brainbrawn
who live and die faster than stone

Think these thoughts
go to the sacred places
the corner stores
light, warm, full of kind
perishable things
for you and you
one foot in front of the other
over the stones

---

aye . . . past
this bubble of assumed person
glassy shapes of the dead *en la noche* drift
beyond glad or sad
fugitives
from all personal referents

and as I step into the King Sooper's
in Boulder, Colorado
I almost trip
over the man in front of me
who's kneeling and bowing to Mecca
while his two ladies wait by the shopping cart

the cricket you hear
is not the cricket you heard
when, and when, and when

---

sat in front of the window

naked

she combed his hair

and he

that instant

achieved

complete

perfect

immortality

Among the more obvious conjectures an analytical reading of this text fragment yields are (a) that the author lived in a dwelling with windows, or at least was familiar with the "window" concept, (b) that he or she was also familiar with the notions of "clothed" and "naked" (= "unclothed"), (c) that people of the period indulged in (sometimes mutual) grooming, possibly with the implements described as "combs."

The second half of the fragment, moving, as it does, into abstraction, presents some difficulty in the realm of what we, for lack of a more precise term, may call "tone": are we to understand the statement literally (in which case the fragment has to originate in a theogony, a work describing the origins of gods — "immortals"), or metaphorically, as a hyperbolic expression of the emotion experienced by the male protagonist of the fragment, at the epiphanal moment described?

When we consider, furthermore, that there was a period around the mid-twentieth century in which some authors of some "metaphysical" texts employed the phrase "instant perfect (or "complete") enlightenment" to describe a state possibly achieved by students of certain systems of thought management, we may even perceive a degree of irony in the substitution of the term "immortality" for the expected term "enlightenment" — an irony which seems to undercut anticipation (or likelihood) of either state described by those terms. If the fragment dates from the period in question, we may assume that the author was a bit of a skeptic in regard to said systems and their vocabulary.

"*the poem machine should not mean machine*
but be machine"

— DARRELL GRAY, AFTER ARCHIBALD MACLEISH

the trouble with

the being born machine is the subsequent trouble
of the being alive machine

and finally
the one of the dying machine
nevertheless there are times
of which it can be said

that we were
                              are and will be
flying
          without benefit of any machine

and when it happens we know it

Some Greeks

Family legend has it that my paternal grandfather, a master cabinetmaker in rural Finland, once became so enthused by the classics that he tried (in vain) to persuade his womenfolk to wear Greek garb while going about their domestic chores — in the summer, presumably, since the climate would have made this rather impractical during the rest of the year. His eldest son, my father, translated Plato, and my father's closest friend was the poet who first performed the *Iliad* and *Odyssey* in Finnish.

When I was ten, my sister lent me her copy of Schwab's three-volume *Tales of Classical Antiquity*, in an original German edition with interesting, faintly comical, engravings of scantily clad "ancient" goddesses and heroines and their consorts and adversaries. I found those tales a lot livelier than the monotheistic Biblical ones I was obliged to study in religion class (no separation of church and state in that time and place). If I had to choose among gangs of deities, I would still feel more at home with the old Greek one than with any other, including the Norse and Finno-Ugric which are presumably "mine" by "ethnic" heritage.

Later, when I read Plato, Sartre, Whitehead, and Wittgenstein, it often seemed to me that the pre-Socratics were still the most serviceable philosophers I had come across. (Permit me to recommend Guy Davenport's and Stanley Lombardo's sharp and scholarly translations of Herakleitos, Empedocles and Parmenides, published by Donald M. Allen, the great unsung Merlin of U.S. poetry, in the mid-seventies.)

Some time ago, I was struck once again by the similar freshness and timeless timeliness of so many of the texts we refer to as *The Greek Anthology* — circa 4,500 poems and fragments of poems written, sung, and spoken in the course of almost two millennia. Kenneth Rexroth's *Poems from the Greek Anthology* may have sparked my first love affair with those works.

My present selection was inspired by another volume, *Jalkapolku* ("The Footpath") by the Finnish poet Pentti Saarikoski (1937–1983). "The Footpath" is Pentti's personal anthology-from-the-Anthology, and his approach, "to let the poems themselves decide how they want to be said *now*," makes him my main collaborator, although I have also consulted other versions by worthy but (to my mind) mostly less inspired poet-translators as well as the hardy perennial Loeb Classical Library.

Like Christopher Logue, who in *War Music* and *Kings* has dared and brilliantly mastered the task of making Homer come alive in late-twentieth-century English, I have no classical Greek. "I was not . . . making a translation in the accepted sense of the word," says Logue, "but what I hoped would turn out to be a poem in English." He calls *War Music* "an *account* of Books 16 to 19 of Homer's *Iliad*." I shall be content if this handful of Greeks, as well as my translation of *The Poems of Hipponax of Ephesus,* are found to be acceptable accounts (or "overdrafts" — Basil Bunting's term) of their originals.

---

where the 3 roads meet
I was surprised to see   the great bronze of Hermes

knocked over flat on the ground:
people used to worship it here . . .

now the invincible guardian
lay flat on the ground

but later that night he appeared by my bed
grinned down at me, said:

"you have to go with the times . . .
that much I learned
when I was a god"

Palladas

          the poet Eutykhides has died —
watch out, you dwellers of the underworld!
here comes Eutykhides with his Odes!
                    it was his last wish
          to be buried
with twenty-five trunks of *text*!

now
Death's grip is truly total —
how can there be
"eternal rest"

when *he* gets to rave on
even in Hades?

Lucilius

someone spoke of your death
Herakleitos and I thought
tears
remembered
our walks in the morning rain

you've long been dust
my Halikarnassian friend
but your "NIGHTINGALES"

live on: omnivorous
as he is
the death-god
he will not touch them.

(POSTSCRIPT)

2,240 years later, I have to admit
I was wrong about the death-god:
he did eat your NIGHTINGALES
he must've liked them better than my EPIGRAMS

Callimachus (& Anselmus)

When Diaphon
was crucified
he saw beside him a man
on a *bigger* cross —
and died
of envy

Lucilius

the only one sober
in a bunch of drunks
he looked high as a kite

Lucian

I love everything about you
except for that indiscriminate eye
that deigns to notice —
well, jerks

Rufinus

o Thaleia how I yearned
to have you stay the night —

now, naked, you lie on my bed
and I feel rather limp

come on you sluggard! get up!

this may be your last
            window of opportunity!

Rufinus

in the dead of night
in pouring rain
I flee from my husband

soaked   I arrive at your door

well   here we are

Philodemos

each morning we're born again
of yesterday nothing remains
what's left   began today —
so, old man,
don't be proud of your years:
what's past isn't yours

Palladas

Hello, Earth?
Yes?
You have Kheridas down there?
You mean Kharidas,
son of Arimmas? Yes, he's here.
May I speak to him?
Yes. Here he is.
Kharidas!
What's it like down there?
It's dark.
What about resurrection?
No such thing.
And the infernal majesties?
They don't exist.
Oh, that's terrible . . .
Well, you can say one thing for this place:
the rents are real low.

Callimachus

Not a Form at All But a State of Mind

"The sonnet . . . is not a form at all but a state of mind. It is the . . . dialogue upon which much writing is founded: a statement then a rejoinder of a sort, perhaps a reply, perhaps a variant of the original — but a comeback of one sort or another."

— WILLIAM CARLOS WILLIAMS

I–XII

I

after reading the tiresome review
from the school of tedious outpourings
the man of letters is writing some letters
"would we all be happier in the factory?"

embittered romantics one and all
"we are but older children, dear,
who fret to find our bedtime near"
in the land of invisible warfare

vast cheering in the distance
hand me my spear   my little secret book
of matches   and footnote fame! oh
give me footnote fame

"but that's how my mind works" he said
desperately singing in harm's way

II

poppy or charms can make us sleep as well
joyful ants nest in the roof of my tree
full of courage and shrewd decisions
given to   marked by melancholy

my most rash eyes want out into the light
in that fierce place where love holds court
and there encamps   spreading his banner
where even wingless soar on balmy winds

in too-thin garments   see with no eyes
shout without a tongue
in a forest alive with whispers
soon-dead deer dash past

strange unrelenting world
I have woven my heart into this net of branches

III

wipe the screen   screw wigs on tight
we grow older our nervous systems decelerate
many thoughts return marked insufficient
postage   "you know how to walk into a bar"

or any box in the postindustrial ruins
most of what we say is in quotes
we like wilderness in nachur
but not our fellow citizens

amor armor amok   emery   immure
yes yes that does describe your arbitrary foci
on a warm wet noon   think "thought experiment"
or murmur "vagaries of the heart"

a comeback of one sort or another
dreams of big live teddy bear that "wants" "you"

IV

it is well known that Mary Magdalene came to Provençe
to live after the crucifixion
but less known that at Maximilien near Marseilles
the tip of her nose used to be on view

no more than that   because she had been cremated
but the tip of her nose remained imperishable
because there   the christ had kissed her
& who is going to pay   any attention to anything

when we aren't here anymore   "& what was it *like*
that *world* of yours?"   so much depends
on Fire Engine Number 5   myth is the practice of memory
dit Joanne Kyger

Johannes Kelpius first american composer
founded a commune called "the woman in the wilderness"

V

the lecturer's heart stepped into the void
the mind slows down the mind speeds up before
it stops   contemplating what's never isolate
"landing a B-52 in a desk drawer"

the man said   spoke of his dying
I believe this is the future site of my plaque
life so short this piece of paper so small
alphabet ends   universe begins

still trudges along in its big shoes
not afraid to include   what seems dull & quotidian
replicas of your thoughts
win free admission to the shores of forgetfulness

at the edge of some divine comedy
the prompter whispers leftover lines

VI

vast cheering in the distance
embittered romantics one and all
on a warm wet noon   think "thought experiment"
or any box in the postindustrial ruins

alphabet ends   universe begins
at the edge of some divine comedy
"the sound like a thousand falling bird beaks
in the brown harpsichord of the grass"

in the last light of evening
and fear has lien upon the heart of me
in a forest alive with whispers
given to   marked by melancholy

a commune called "the woman in the wilderness"
so much depends on Fire Engine Number 5

VII

"days when the giant won't fall for the ruse
days when no kindly mammal speaks to us with human voices"
i dunno man it's tough   & it's never been anything but
many were here but they left again

yet surprised once again
in awkward bliss and bashful ecstasy
let us forgo all pain of crags
here in this pleasant valley of dipthongs

come babe   pass me the delicious
cold cucumber salad
as the axe of the sun descends
we wane away among the peonies

& we have absolutely no complaints
of hours such as these

VIII

"would we all be happier in the factory?"
in the land of invisible warfare
many thoughts return marked insufficient
most of what we say is in quotes

win free admission to the shores of forgetfulness
& we have absolutely no complaints
let us forgo all pain of crags
for a special additional performance

of such as love and whom love tortures
like the eyeglasses of the less fortunate
in that fierce place where love holds court
joyful ants nest in the roof of my tree

myth is the practice of memory
"the pneumatic drill destroys my cities"

IX

underground trees   slow darkness
and fear has lien upon the heart of me
magpie steals silver spoon   it is gone forever
like the eyeglasses of the less fortunate

in a terrifying gray light from the future
the carnival continues   a place where a sad horde
of such as love and whom love tortures
point to the moon and break it

"in the year 1327   at the opening of the first hour
on the sixth of April   I entered the labyrinth"
yesterday's clowns return
for a special additional performance

in the last light of evening
today I think about all those radio waves

X

hand me my spear   my little secret book
desperately singing in harm's way
yes yes that does describe your arbitrary foci
dream of big live teddy bear that "wants" "you"

life so short this piece of paper so small
replicas of your thoughts
& it's never been anything but hours such as these
as we grow older our nervous systems decelerate

in a terrifying gray light from the future
I entered the labyrinth
full of courage and shrewd decisions
in too-thin garments with no eyes

at Maximilien near Marseilles
"at night the streets are tidal like the sea"

XI

"we are but older children, dear"
of matches   and footnote fame!   oh
on a warm wet noon screw wigs on tight
not afraid to include its big shoes

when the cyclops won't fall for the ruse
as the axe of the sun descends
the prompter whispers leftover lines
I think about all those radio waves

where even the wingless soar on balmy winds
shout without a tongue   strange unrelenting world
after the crucifixion   "& what was it *like*   that *world*"
oh footnote fame   the man of letters

"you know how to walk into a bar"
in the year 1327   at the opening of the first hour

XII

"but that's how our minds work" they said
"who fret to find our bedtime time near
in any box in the postindustrial ruins
wipe the screen   amor armor amok   emery   immure

"landing a B-52 in a desk drawer"
the lecturer's heart stepped into the void
where no kindly mammals speak to us
come babe   pass me the delicious dipthongs

the carnival continues   yesterday's clowns return
my most rash eyes want out into the light
I have woven my heart into this nest of branches
spreading its banner of attention

underground trees   slow darkness
murmur "vagaries of the heart"

Small Door at Far End

"time for your take, you assholes"
concern yourselves with what will sell
dead senses rule over a dead mind
the old fall silent and expire

their art consisted merely of the trick
that organizes production for *profit*
rather than for *use* (to find the right size of shoe)
because of you lady I am this way   a stubborn murmur

naked   extremely complex   gigantic
a barrage of labyrinthine winks
present culture not inevitable but offspring
of a particular form   & how *do* you spell "Rousseau"

ask Diogenes   ask Terry Eagleton
ask any intelligent slave

II

always but not unpleasantly torn between
transparent intelligence saying itself
"my poetry is mainly just talk"
economy elegance switching into surprises

& the total Sargasso Sea of signifiers
"they do my *research* for me"
releasing language from rules & structures
demonstrating its restrictions and hierarchies

Eisenstein cantos   Tzara words out of a grab bag
mental & linguistic exercise
think about each word and why it is where it is
moon splashes borrowed light on the wall

across the street of distant galaxies
slowly turning their tails to point to the first letter

III

"le plus souvent il s'agit de tristesse"
it is mostly a question of sadness   the trick's to remember
that *that* is absolutely *no* excuse to be boring
or humorless   or too conveniently absent

not to metamorphose
into moon splashes borrowed light on the wall of sound
keep in mind all of us have lived
are and will be living "interesting times"

of unprecedented   we're beginning to understand
insanely excessive   numbers of human beings on the planet
and therefore   at least quantitatively speaking
unprecedented magnitudes of loss injury oppression

and weltschmerz   "sorrow or sadness
over the present or future woes of the world"

IV

"curiosity — advice to the young — *curiosity*"   EP
to Vanni Ronsisvalle in 1968
slowly turning their tails to point to the first letter
"it is important to keep old hat in secret closet"

concerns charmingly optimistic
bohemie-anarcho-individualistic
oh give me Elysian   give me Eleusinian
city parks where Egil Skallagrimsson

enjoys a nude picnic with Emily Dickinson
satyrs converse with cyborgs
dinosaurs roam across the street
of distant anarchic galaxies

but they have devastated our great cities   & the poets
left there must wear the Star of the Marginal

Lines from Ted: An Ars Poetica

"Plagiarism — Good!   Communism — Bad!

You can't fool anyone
You can't fool anyone that knows anything

But anything that you can use, you should use it"

— TED BERRIGAN AT NAROPA, JULY '82

I

Ho Chi Minh wrote poetry
Richard Nixon didn't have any interest in any art at all
And Richard Nixon had all the chips
Ho Chi Minh didn't have any
                                        seemingly
But of course as it turned out he had them all
It was not because he was a poet and Richard Nixon wasn't
But perhaps because he was a bit more aware of . . . Nature . . . I mean

The President of the United States
                                                    as long as he's in office
Doesn't drive his own car   Ho Chi Minh didn't have that problem

He couldn't find cars very often
When he could he probably found a driver
But usually he was running down some trail looking for a cave
Because enormous airplanes were overhead trying to bomb him
It kept him alert

II

It's true that Form does follow Content
Except that that sentence is gibberish
Those nouns and that verb don't go together
That's like saying the egg follows the picture frame
Which no doubt it does   But not in any way
That we are entirely sure of   except when we say so
We could say form is always and only an extension of content
But then we are liable to sound very peculiar

Only certain people are able to get away with
Saying things like that
Form and Content   That's like saying
If you cut off someone's head and destroy their form
Then you fuck up their content
                    Well that's true that's true
But you don't *know* much more by saying that   I'll tell you

III

I sometimes wonder
                    I sometimes think about how many poets
For example those poets in the universities with suitcoats on
Some of whose work I like very much nevertheless
How many of them broke their own hearts
Fighting against their own natural tempo and pace
        in order to try to write
What was supposedly the right tempo and pace
For English-American literature?
You have to make your work at your own pace
It is made of words
                    One word after another
Some people do it in phrases
Others are beautiful writers of sentences
& some are beautiful writers
        of one word at a time

IV

All this business of keeping score
& knowing who's good and who isn't   Fuck it, man
All those that are no good   Why are you thinking about them
Even if they're famous?   Don't worry
If they're really no good they'll disappear after a while
And even if they don't   So what?
I mean, why are you going to be mad at them?
Because they're taking money out of your pocket?
That's not why you do it
If you want to get some money in your pocket   Get some!
If you have a talent for it you'll get some

If you don't   You got a problem
But just solve it some other way   Ask Allen for some
                                                            Only not this week

V

There is a standard above which you want your poems to be
If you do five hundred above that standard
And they're all very similar
That might not be having done such a great thing
But what I think what happens when a poem works is
That it rises into the air of its own powers
And in doing so has formed a circle
And it becomes something like the sun or a star
Or a planet
                    Or whatever
I like the idea of it being up in the air
            To have no idea is a good idea
            If it helps you to make a poem
I have to go now
I have to go and think about this for a thousand years

VI

The arts are something given to human beings to do
They improve your senses
It is necessary to do more than earn your daily bread
Shelter & food & ability to get the medicine
For your children when they have a cold
It's necessary to be more of a person than that
As Kenneth Koch once said
                                            it would be a very difficult life
To be the only surrealist at the University of Minnesota
            You don't need company to be a Surrealist
            You need company to be alive
We could not be poets if we didn't use words
                    Perhaps there are animal poems too
You can be fat lazy poet & still be a pretty good poet at forty
Survival
                is the hardest test for a poet

VII

You are faster than your consciousness
Just like everyone knows a lot more than they're able to say
"How do I know what I mean until I see what I say?"
Say "ooga-booga" and see if you can think of something to say
Next
        It is a story
But you often leave out all of the plot
                because it's poetry it's song
It's song pierced by intelligence with all that feeling in there
        You *have* to write a lot of garbage
        you may even find a way to include some of the garbage
        in your best poems
And make those poems be more like places that *include* garbage
You can come and sit up here and be a great guy
But you can't make a living

VIII

When you sleep under a tree and have a good night's sleep
You don't say "My new house is a lot better than my old house"
Except if you want to be poetic
I mean it's not a house you know it's a tree
Houses have mice and rats and things like that in them
And trees have crickets under them   For one thing
Because everybody knows something
        But as Frank O'Hara once said
        "I'm assuming everything is all right and difficult"
& Robert Lowell said
"I learned everything from William Carlos Williams"
And Allen said "Good God!   *What did you learn?*"
& I said to Bob Creeley "Bob, how was your day?"
& he said "Well . . . I was reading Shelley"

IX

Once in my life I batted against a pitcher
Who played in the majors
He hit me right in the leg & I went down like I'd been shot

& I had a bruise on my leg this big for about a month
& he wasn't even really good
When I saw that ball coming it was coming so damn fast
I was just looking at it
I saw it was going to hit me right in the leg
I braced to hit his fastball
& it came and hit me in the leg & it hurt horribly
I fell down and said   I didn't say anything
I wasn't Pete Rose
But then   It's time
It's all about time

X

The Real Problems are
Like whether or not you should go
To bed with a certain person
Because they have beautiful handwriting
You know as in Lady Murasaki's book
Whom I once had an adventure with
And by that I mean exactly that
                                        an adventure
No poet worth their salt has less
than a hundred books in their house
Unless they just sold some to pay the rent
But they'll still buy some more next week
The poet Kenneth Patchen was a poet
Of extravagance   The imagination of extravagance
We don't have many of those now

XI

You can become a Black Mountain poet
If you wish   All you have to do
Is find out what a Black Mountain poet is
& you'll never find out by asking a Black Mountain poet
All music is music   That's a good sentence
It doesn't have any meaning
"Take these brains from my pillow"
What's funny? What's so funny?

It isn't funny   Literature is not funny
Poetry is not funny   It's not funny to be a poet
It's not funny to be alive
Though it is pretty funny but
You think it's funny
You should find out how much I'm getting paid

XII

Hip? Try to talk your way out of whatever you did wrong
When you're talking to a policeman
          the farthest you can reach is your *hip* pocket
But the policeman is *not* the guy
          you're supposed to reach in your *hip* pocket for
But somebody up higher
I mean it's difficult to be hip
It's difficult not to be, too
If you learn everything about writing
From some supposed terrible boring Academic poet
That doesn't matter   It's you
It's what you want and how you write
Or if you want to write like some horrifying Beatnik
It still doesn't matter   it's what you write

XIII

If there's a little room up there
A waiting room that you can wait around in
For five hundred years
You can check from time to time to see
What they're saying back there on Earth
And whether you did it or not
                              "He did it"
But as for one's self
One can't use the word *did*
                              ever   See?
Because you're not dead
So it's just like you did that   & you did this
        but did you do it?

But even with Shakespeare
There'll be fifty years when they'll be saying "This guy
You don't have to read this guy   Read *that* guy"

XIV

The poet whose works you love
Who's changed your life
& given it shape   & become a Great Moral Source
Of Support in your life
May just be a prick with a bad character
Don't let that worry you
They just have bad days all the time
If you're vulnerable to never wanting to read their works again
        when you find that out
Then never go any closer to them than this
Because it's the works that are the truth
Every person has a right
Poet or not
            to be judged by their best
The only credit poets get for is for being poets
Then putting their words together   & coming up with poems

Pterodactyls

"Publication date first of October"

I

From Zlatko's Serbo-Croat   via fast translatese French
into "my" English   his journal scrolled up Macintosh screen
these summer months   hoping he lives to see it
I think of him often & of his city's Utopia of *convivencia*

"while you are not safe I am not safe"   Ginsberg in *Howl*
when Sarajevo falls   all of us multi-ethnic bastards
who pray in *all* the temples   like *all* kinds of food
& minds & bodies every color shape & size

we better start digging our foxholes in the fourth dimension
& while we dig let us chant We Piss on the Serb Nation State
We Piss on the Croat Nation State   we piss and shit
on all your godforsaken states

murderous money-making machines for greedy sleazeballs
lording it over slaves who failed to teach their masters

II

tread the fine line between farce and pathos
torque your thoughts in the mental (not metal) bookshelf
hermeto- (not herpeto-) linguistic
shrine to Mr. Hun Tun
professionally known as "The Gourd of Chaos"
walk up & down   walk off & on   sleep off & on
far off   far off in the Gobi Desert   what can you say
you can say   & you won't be far off
"I have my love to keep me warm." & I can say
"'Yes,' he said. 'Yes, of course.'"
then you can sleep it off   & it may well be
what all these pronouns are saying
is merely the tremulous gibberish of just another other
talking to the page with an old child's fingers

III

i.m. Ernest Hemingway

trying to impress felines
strange hairless ape with mad eyes
too tired to explore postmodernism
"a rare   *luckier* kind of guy"
checks in at Perfect Cloud Hotel in Laphroaig
it is 9:15 a.m.   a Fundador brandy, please
yes, he would like to join the Lotophagoi
(old Ez   he wrote it down)
so let's just *decant* it in here
time to wind up the world no more substantial
than a good tune   oh fairer than the evening air
marked by slender delight   what we feel
is what we believe we feel   see say and be loved
despite much dull material to-be-forgiven

IV

for Tomaž Šalamun

a long sentence: "son, write longer lines"
a green Pegasus, dancers, yaks
sing, masters of the universal pibroch
sing, balalaika, in the teeth of adversity

but don't you think it's time for Comrade Blank
to retire, with the understanding: *no more poems!*
sing, you "few buckets of water tied up
in a complicated sort of figleaf" (EP)

great solar, you stir, wake each exile man
marmoset, mormon, clits and toes
& tiger faces in the fire, Colonel North
got to the shredder in time to deconstruct history a bit

dig, with man, up feeling
here, with Doctor Who, in Deseret

Villonelles

I

cloud with delicate
cottonwool monkey face drifting by
tape drifting by the magnetic heads
& into the spaces between other heads

magnetic electric from here to everywhere
possibly back & on out
some recall a musical theme
by having the score's image appear before them

then reading it it is conceivable
that what we call remembering in a human being
consists of her seeing herself (mind's eye)
looking up things up in a book

thus what she reads in that book
is what she remembers Wittgenstein Zettel 653

II

someone blown clean down the block
shrieking with merriment shock
plant on table trembling
many-talk-in-head my name

duration between each death & birth
the seeds of karma dynamite
little paws folded big paws folded
stagecoach takes corner plenty of dust

master babe mandragora
shrieks when torn out shrieks when rammed back in
appearing reappearing
uttering language in extracurricular states

the idiot wars of the young the idiot wars of the old
tape drifting Zettel drifting

III

among the boulders in the huge scarred seam
a dwarfish person of the Queens retinue
trying to speak whereof one cannot
said nothing but waited
playing with the hilt of his dagger
they usually keep a distance above ground
he thought
                    above the surface of things
as one who had never seen a mirror might wonder
in what depths of it lay the face she saw
heat waves raced & shimmered round the basin's rim
we'll find a way she whispered never fear but kiss me
notwithstanding the abruptness of this introduction
set like a stone he took a deep breath

IV

the people came out staring & pointing
their whispers rising like surf all about her
her features blurred & swayed before him
gloomy & wild is the air of this place

spring you get for free she thought & mostly it doesn't
turn out too well but then life's strength lies embedded
in a fresh coarse evenness
dense like any good production of Mnemosyne

slowness & sun have stayed with me
in calm & gentle absurdity she thought
frequent narrative climaxes   moments
of great suspense   & moments out to lunch

may be saved by one's ability to characterize
one's mythic role by comic ineptitude

V

again the owl's hoot pierced the night
wolves came up to the doorsteps of the rich
eager to miss
                    none of their syllables
"did you enter this house for loot or lore?
ghosts do not eat
                         she rose from where she sat
ready to pounce
                      believe nothing I say
                      the town is hot
                      he takes to the road
a thousand *mercis*
                         I've been absent a lifetime
I spread my thanks at your feet

death's dark sack gaped
but you heard the snows
amid the jangling harps of hell
that gibber at each dream of peace

VI

toward morning we begin to feel insubstantial
our knees cease to shake we wrap ourselves in our cloaks
& proceed to the grove of oaks
twisted & windblown   clutching the stony planet

with roots of authority   purple & scarlet
retract periscope   trees & language out of a hat
slowly the ice of the unformed universe dissolves
in the world to come   everything like it was

in the world that was   yet everything quite changed
narratives   disjunctive (yet) associative as dreams
poems   sonorous   replete with handsome words
while lacking all "sense" & "connection"

the future world is sensible chaos   chaos squared
or raised to the power of infinity

Reviewing the Tape

i.m. Piero Heliczer

I

calling 1959 calling 1959   what does he know
a red piano   a fragmentary tusk
he sees men & women preparing themselves
for the long journey across the room

he is in love with the world
it's got a face like a horse
her hair is 365 poems   a tent   & into it
that tune   it's 1790!   oops   he stops   goes back

sleeping is any handful earth
waking returns the toothbrush clack to the beaker
"her anger has caused me great pain"
can't tell which she he is talking about

brown photo   legend
man's reliance on fossil fuels but a short episode

II

no junipers no shouldn't think so no
he wrote   somewhere inside
so slow   a broken nose   repeating itself
into this hole in the ground

no connectives or interval music
it was hot in the dream hole
above the brick town with its captive dogs
the first time you saw it   acres of watery sand

ah to be funny in bed in writing
to be in our bodies
maybe it was just his old difficulty
of remaining in the upright position

of the higher primates
their glimmering moments of loving

III

the instruction manual lay soaking in the bilge
I'm yours I'm all yours   but the signals were garbled
one who looked tall rode away
didn't have much to say

narrative   pomp & pleasure
time in shore zones

ahead of the water they came
wrapped round a stick of incense
he'll sleep a long time
the day your son comes home

a flute & a spine in the grass
too dark   a raving madman
persistent cigarette burns on his hand & arm
november 1967   a hundred farmers plow to lucid murmurs

IV

to disappear   on the floor
in the other room   closing the book
"I'll be back in a minute"   flowers out there

over them reigned a red personage
in autumn some sponges   "i am moving
a fraction to the weaker taking"

this deep a breath is ardent
ultimate consummation of long ethereal affair
sit listening to the gods
approach her   their cries

it is peaceful peaceful
the people go crazy
the manager of this cinema
wears a big floppy heart a ha

V

branching like any body
but here   have some wine
& exhale heaven   snug against her skin
kiss her   ill with love

"him now"   in his sleep he walks past it again
to one who lives there
in the rented satellite
with Officer No Quarter

enters another plane
of the new world   or drives the big white car
through savage people & frozen gases

still taping   his thoughts ran much upon this
wrote the works ever known as
the features of gods

VI

on the horse's back & into a hall
then son   simply expressing   in his own way
that I was wrong   6-9:00 a.m.
through customs in Hong Kong

all the way to her navel
a single large crystal
thinks of Don Giovanni
with no interference from tree-cutting crane

smileful girl   they used to spend maybe an hour
in glamorous roles
in a little while it won't exist

red mists of rage
plate glass breaks   snow streets in thoughts
across a green roof

VII

there is a light on   prudent alchemist
laughs like Leo the sun
crocodile curbs dangerous onslaught
Iaia of Kyzikos   her pagan will to realize

life in the sky   she saw
a tapir do the tango
prance from his mother's house
back where the night begins

in a seven-foot urn
I move about   the beetle wakes up
temporarily in charge of the 1920s

the surface extends all the way out to the core
wherever there is a hole distributed in space
cave equals room equals window

Notes

1991

Irina Hollo, the author's sister, was a talented singer, accomplished linguist, translator, and a dear and steadfast friend.

"that five-mile-diameter asteroid" would effectively wipe out life as we know it on this planet.

"father's tongue": in this case, Finnish.

"Dis": Lord of the Greek underworld.

"Ubi sunt": Where are they (now)?

"King Sooper's": Destroyer-size grocery (*not* corner) store.

"The Trouble With Being Born": the title of a book by the great E. M. Cioran.

SOME GREEKS

PALLADAS: Alexandrian, ca. 355–430 CE. When I first saw the poem beginning "where the 3 roads meet" I thought of Stalin, Mao, Dzherzhinsky, etc., but as my friend, poet and feminist critic Lorna Smedman pointed out to me, it also applies to our late-20th-century efforts to overturn idols representing oppressive patriarchal power as it is manifested in all walks of life, including the arts.

CALLIMACHUS: of Cyrene, ca. 305–240 BCE. Librarian in Alexandria. Erudite and witty poet, regarded as "difficult" — possibly even "cold and cryptic," as a previous owner / marginalia-jotter found a book of my first translations of Pentti Saarikoski. The Herakleitos addressed in the poem is not the philosopher but Herakleitos of Halikarnassos, author of "The Nightingales," presumably one of the great works lost to posterity.

LUCULLUS lived in Rome around 60 CE and is said to have been a friend of Seneca the Stoic.

LUCIAN of Samosata-by-the-Euphrates, ca. 120–185 CE.

RUFINUS: a native of the island of Samos, ca. 130 CE.

PHILODEMOS: ca. 55 BCE, from Gadara in classical Palestine. Lived in Rome.

NOT A FORM AT ALL BUT A STATE OF MIND

Epigraph: Hugh Wittemeyer (ed.), *William Carlos Williams and James Laughlin: Selected Letters* (New York: WW Norton, 1989).

(I) "we are but older children . . .": Lewis Carroll, *To Alice.*

(III) "you know how to walk into a bar": Robert Creeley to the author, one evening in the early seventies.

"amor armor amok emery immure": alternatives to amore provided by "Spell Check."

(IV) "it is well known . . .": from E. S. Bates, *Touring in 1600.*

(V) "landing a B-52 . . .": Scholar, poet, and musician Jack Clarke describing the task of dying to Ed Sanders, in a telephone conversation not long before Jack's takeoff.

(VI) "the sound like a thousand falling bird beaks / in the brown harpsichord of the grass": Piero Heliczer (*The Soap Opera,* London: Trigram Press, 1967), who also wrote

> i cross the street then immediately cross back again
> i never look to left and right when i cross a street
> why else are street crossings put there if not to cross

— and was hit and killed by a truck around the time of my writing of these fourteen-liners; Piero Heliczer (1937–1993), Italian-born American poet, Personist Surrealist, author of *You Could Hear the Snow Dripping and Falling into the Deer's Mouth, The First Battle of the Marne,* and other poetic and cinematic works.

(VII) "days when the giant . . .": lines from Swedish poet Gunnar Harding's poem "Many Were Here But They Left Again." There are other echoes and near-quotes from that magnificent poem in this humble text, and similar embeddings of lines from Cavalcanti (in translations by Ezra Pound and Marc

Cirigliano), Sir Thomas Wyatt, Edwin Denby, Ted Berrigan, Jouni Inkala, and Tom Raworth.

(viii) "the pneumatic drill destroys my cities": Heliczer, *op.cit.*

(ix) "in the year 1327 . . .": Francesco Petrarca, Sonnet 211, translated by Nicholas Kilmer.

(x) "at night the streets are tidal like the sea": Heliczer, *op.cit.*

SMALL DOOR AT FAR END

(ii) "my poetry . . ." and "they do my . . .": Ted Berrigan.

(iii) "le plus souvent . . .": Guillaume Apollinaire.

(iv) "it is important . . .": Ted Berigan.

LINES FROM TED: AN ARS POETICA

The epigraph, and all the lines of this work, derive from a transcript of two workshops given by Ted Berrigan (1934–1983) in July 1982, the Jack Kerouac School of Disembodied Poetics.

It is, naturally, dedicated to him, and also to the memory of Blaise Cendrars, the author of *Kodak* (and many other great works).

PTERODACTYLS

(i) *"Publication date first of October"*: In the summer of 1993 I translated *War Journal* by Zlatko Dizdarevic, the editor of Sarajevo's only surviving newspaper *Oslobodjenje.* The English-language edition of the book was published by Fromm International, New York, in 1994.

convivencia: The period 711–1492 CE, in which Jews, Muslims, and Christians coexisted in the abundant civilization of al-Andalus in what is now Spain.

"The art of being a slave is to rule one's master": Diogenes.

(iv) This was written in Salt Lake City, Utah (=Deseret, in LDS parlance), in the mid 80s, thus quite some time before a certain self-styled Serb "poet" began a war of genocide and extermination against Bosnia and specifically its capital, Sarajevo. Tomaž Šalamun is the greatest living poet of dead Yugoslavia, and now, mercifully, still-alive Slovenia.

"son, write longer lines": my father told me that, a thousand years ago.

VILLONELLES

Ecologically correct — re-cycled, or translated, in large part, from *Or, To Hocus the Animals of the Pursuers by Changing Their Dream Cassettes (Old Thibetan Trick),* first published by Joe Cardarelli's and Kirby and Rosemary Malone's Phantom House Pod Books (Baltimore, 1977).

(iv) "in the world to come . . . power of infinity" paraphrases entries in the notebooks of Novalis (Friedrich von Hardenberg, 1772–1801).

REVIEWING THE TAPE

Ninety-nine percent of the lines in this text were selected by aleatory numerical methods from my *Sojourner Microcosms: Poems 1959–77.*

AHOE (And How on Earth)

"Robin Blaser once said in talking about a serial poem that it's as if you go into a room, a dark room, the light is turned on for a minute, then it's turned off again, and then you go into a different room where a light is turned on and turned off."

— JACK SPICER, FROM THE VANCOUVER LECTURES

"One could also see the face of another large apartment building there, whose windows at night would lighten or go dark in almost a curious narrative. I would imagine, sitting looking out, lives back of those windows, happy, sad, threatened, successful, always a little obscured and changing."

— ROBERT CREELEY, *COMING HOME*

"carve water, caress fire"

for Jane

Turn Off the News

anxiety galops through chatter
fading century's martial insanities
brain struggles to sum up   "shut up"
articulation fails
walking shadow slides across faces

dusk over epitaphs
ash hair rusty litanies

dead friends and rain
paradise is an idiot

bones vines cold day

old vulture in airlock

scorpion dust
sneeze

O Ponder Bone of Fabled Carp

distant in time now,
maman

equals pigeon

duchess of echoes

in hidden ruins'
barefoot patter

memory seizes bundle, rides
horse of no illusion

ear tracks cricket blessings
clods & echoes

translates, fabulates
umbrella afternoons

arrow flashes
the diminutive trembles

in entourage of antennae
gods hammer ears
warlords groan exhausted

caress hair,
lament tangle
in pale fits of ink

And Then There Are These Skaldic Throwbacks

wild Mara mind
        and wicked worm intensity
berserker travel on hushed sands
        longing for opiates of rain
                hawk's angle blue in bateau mist

battlement games
                    grand gears of destiny

pikes under banner
                    wild things pleading
thronged misery refined   laconic bards'

ear tackles era's phrasing in ironic runes

Good Idea, But Will It Work?

these poems

        already fading notes

    pinned to a cactus in a planetarium

announcing a symposium

            of wistful asters

    and non-insectoid sorcerers

            who claimed they could cure this world

                    of its greed-demon vapors

Head Sky Convoy Patter

i.m. Franco Beltrametti

spirit murmur echoes
no letters from the dead

could this be winter
in the fifteenth century?

(in mad orey-eyed paradiso
inner brawler   favorite saber
& that old piece of iron
made to spew lead & belch smoke

Davey Crockett among astronauts
points out earth is far

scholar of cheekbones & urbiculture
glows   hand him his favorite subject
shake out head

red windows   signs between perfect shapes
trees' feet still
glance moves over unknown waves

dreams chase moon
by suitcase steam wharf
face hair head equals passerby
masks float   speak

cloud stairs roof
house folds hums

words' wind   evening   cold birds scatter

tone wall   flag rain   ear beam

leaf tip holds dawn's door

Benign Evening Comedown

untwist antennae
shake out screen
blip on windows
dwell
on this wandering spoke

        in long instant of water murmur
        around us
        anthropoids
        small
        pleased
        and pleased to feel small and pleased

but that's too far back
this is not the sea
just a big puddle of hopeless desire
for a new brain
                for the species

Metaphor Mutaphor

sublunar fish philosophy
in temple pond

far from beaks of ignorance
heads quiet

night softer weave
no more tavern pain

rebel days' bright gallop over
no more perfect knowledge glyphs

but whose system happened?
shuttered minds' dark hole —

raise flag against sad experts
shout *we need windows! this is an order!*

into empty page / hard to read / desert wind

Hey, Dr. Who, Let's Dial 1965

in petaled decade glassy sunlight
tottering bliss in funhouse mirror pills
paludal billowing
                    in pad pavilions
delicate milk
wrote dwarf dream movies:

"Petrarch's Manhattan"
                                        "The Wonders of You"

bodies, faces, chansons of surprise
bits of soft dust
                    soar in sombreros
into befuddled eyebrow thunderclouds
deep breaths make cages quiver
inspired milliseconds
                         tangled raga dark

and what else dreams the rain
                                   dancers receding?

Leaves of Blur

aloft in eyes
quiet electric surprises
                                        (note rush —
old story soundtrack in mind's ear

danced down to the ships to sail
far past sun's orange mane
but we know what became of all that

cling to laconic chirps
weeds across face   glow gulp and write

rain on, past hearts   proud prowl in head
breathe mist on deep lens down the years

seen 'em come seen 'em go
a face or avenue   across blank page

                              (said
                              and
                              undone

Script Mist

hang on to moment, naked, fair
frail as a butterfly — and where
did that come from?
from here, from under the leaves
of 1) lyrical moan, 2) sonorous foam

then the voice said "up and at them, hedgehog"
then it sat on his cool
with dark quark wings
while favorite sirens / mighty old voices
sang fierce and refined epitaphs

scattered and dashing, one does la-la more
at the good times institute
a joint in time
in the great carpentry

An Olive for Satie

easily whelmed by the past
long tangled thinker
traverses lake of mistake
revisiting sighs
& nothing's simplified
but out of that a touch
of animate grace
in thought's audible habitation
to point out earth, high *liebesraum*
& the way to fool's hill
to presence of world in her face

The Opening of the File

blue light
        chandelier blink! delight

pull rock from heavy head

    "ash tree bends to dawn"

page not "blank" but "fresh"

            door at noon

no longer bundle of distress
on slippery field of misfortune

but jovial irony machine
simultaneist presenter
    of elliptoid English:

    vibrant work, sage *gestalt*

ready to bless even depraved progenitors
to be a text to feel outrageous free
    intent on nonsense

        over here the plug
        to another figure there
        astride the request

ah, life in the fictive

hotly used
        in sensation's embrace

Emptier Planet

i.m. Larry Eigner

a face

flies away

while band plays on

a shake of beauty

almost anyhow

once more however

gone

Jungle Finn

hommage à Schwitters

Enemy miss! And hiss, too! Tea yen, à la "see ya." Olé! Inveigh! Then see sally. Zen calf? Aye semper. Kate, in yon car, maté-lickin' men! Ashbery, Hettie, mine tse-tse coo, ten Voznesesnskys. Wry Tio, vow. Noon za-zen, latte, and a cough. Veal in oven, piss on tea; main rue, no den. Neck key, Ma gone. Mm, yass: am a peon. "Coo car sah?" Evokes Thai. Miss it. Yak-San ate Seurat. Ah. Intercontinental Inn Pen sassed? Oh yeah. Tie tacks in Miz Cook's ass. Zen, Homer, and linden. In ark is toe mess, yucks in car doo. La. On Do Di nit. Holà! Ow, key rue non-code Alta. Yon car Ité sue, then. Ashbery Thai Yevtushenko. Hettie, mine tse-tse sees bat! Lola: Wax Pa's doxy. Scene at ten, see bat, Manya wrecks it! Quaalude boo-hoo. Heave at Yahweh scene, olé! Toot, Kim! He zen. Ernie, ark is doity. Hang in, Tilla, oh my coon, tea, hen, ass, tea. A. Vat. Eh? Si. Net Pooh, ooh, net "I." Yatter ate heel. I soothe old lute.

E. Quist

Time Rocking On

fell far from tribe
eagerly bloomed into drift

to wilt
at end of radical dream

ah utopia
                    ah catastrophe
wild duck in eyes

(meant to say
"wild dusk in eyes"

but duck's okay
Ibsen, all that)

end of empire
weird with tears

no human head
                                        on this body politic
yet tree-born dignity
                                                  inheres in a few
pray for quick magic
                                              a new verbarium
pass shell of sigh
                                        & raise to ear

Sur La Terrasse

night train horn
reminder of nameless existence
brief insertions
bright and dark

o undulating gods
in night's open ark
courses of water and war
world's floaty news
an order has crashed
Petrarch in tundra
corpses wrapped in fog

what if long-practiced lyric
prove a dud
all wan and pale

before the unnameable
innumerable
now grazing earth
hoping for timely space ship

poetry this no-thing
drops into notebook air

in sea of air faint voices lift:
"eternity for little me"
dream forest felled at dawn
windless moon

go listen to some Locatelli
adrift in hist'rys drunken boat

Temple Noir

Images distributed about her, unceasingly, like moths: totalized in cognitive map of hair specific to these exercises on the Trail of Death and Ruin, as preface to "adventure moment."

Notice she appeared gowned in actuality, and yet, as the other functions which followed her head leaped into instant anteriority, the dance became problematic.

There was much more to the same effect: precise lugubriousness.

The analytic craze was at its height, shriveling souls with sardonic laconicism in the foyer of instant fame — *her name*: it jerked up with murmured absentation — a coincidence she thought to emphasize, when her eye chanced to imagine this *referentiality* gazing at her, so *dialectical* . . .

Sails of Murmur

rose blade runs through beam
"face your water   cross no wiser"
long bones belch at chortling gators

remember motor hum   barouche in air
raise up favored room of past
erotic morphs
to animate thought's tactile habitation
opiates   echoes   hand them ashore

clarity hardly revisited
species a sneeze in eternity

unnerved by glyph lore
twinge   ride a slow gloom

but in a mouth be pleased
eager for the quiver
if it please the dawn

The Next Fifty Years

turn, tremble at honk
in dazed civil silence

wrong end? wrong beginning?
pain worms in

violent gloomy longings
of porky Agamemnons
in camouflage suits

city stilled   impossible pass

        "lay in *more,*
        master gold grub!"

work as owls, up here
stretch bridge
to where road starts again

Cat-Gods' Channel

we elegant erasers of mice

shall magick into pyramids

these sub-

urbs

you worked

like dogs

to build

inside the mind
she climbs
dazzling as apples, as thought

and so, with ancient yelps, we torch your maps

After the Newscast

past tribal heart's rusty twists
litanies of dagger, ropetree laments

sink or sail into mist
on bluer beam

quiver past
that past

to where the sleepers chirp
echoes of older wiser noise

of city deep in imagination's crystal
intelligence yearns for

so come on up
democracy
it's time

Halo Blade

simple, it said   be mouth
        and will a piece of speak

(god's voices belch and fold)

"thinker of sails, come up again"
tone wall moves on ear beam

you whirl in cylinder of rooms and days
sigh for a place beyond walls

        would it open your piano?
the past strikes many with nothing

they shiver   whelmed by purgatories
pile up habitations, dwell in sprawl

but the words bang your face
into the worlds   soon air and lights arrive

in fits of favorite city
revisited   turning
on to hum impossible dissident idiot love
in walking company
past winding sheets of thought
past violent echoes   hearts drift wiser
        into long tinge remembered

Silent Salad

retune ear
to curiosity
no fear of meaning's underside

remain
allochthonous
in pellucid hauteur

embrace memory
encode mnemonics
in forthcoming volumes:

"Favonian Life"
"American Jesus"
"Toonlight Apocrypha"
and
"Atlantic *Geheimnis*"

tell meaning to vanish
& pray

Secret Cohesive Tactics

Blip off dim sunset. Blip on wild din sunrise!
Rise, Sun! Roar! Screen falls off
Falls off complicated
Fits of unreadable gridlock. Come sane, please?
Slow-lit mind skips out to prance,
Gods' summer legs delight green fool.
Love mind, mouse, moon
& chansons, & cricket chirps.
Chase feast, unwind, let mind ships hover.
Hover, pencil shadow. First snooze, best snooze?
O dark ancestral snooze: spin yarn, hitch smoke —
Flower strange ways. Rise, sun, roar
On serendipitous dill brine,
Gather voice from house now ash and air.

Voice Over Past House

rampant apprehension gone

sneeze twist remember trouble

wise old dog   tulips in bed

red green murmur turn-on

exactly walk

every stalk

come down slowly

write it back long thread

wing down corner zoom through stem

back to moon   or worm song

Caught with a Pronoun

"I have been quite content,
living on the poets' reservation"
—FRIEDERIKE MAYRÖCKER

the nanosecond before choice itself (?) occurs
check spell   uncoil from sheets
having a saying & even meaning
& no body without another

wrapped in deep skin
tangerine notes
that twitter up in mind's air
who for gods' sakes needs a "citational matrix"

let them remain
nailed down by their self-promotion
& me stay here   within the "confines of my agenda"

theory does look gray this morning
corporate colonization of human imagination
not allowed   on this reservation

"Goethe"

Subject! Be
No more subjective
Than old Object
Is Objective!

Things to Do with Life

hang out with quantum generation
watch their terrible elegant dance

apply for job: editor of the universe
write: abrupt paint essential
write: glyph dog curiosity

ask: intergalactic thinking junked?
ask: democracy a blip on the screen?

stay at hotel nouvelle france
23 rue des messageries
with ye raven's mistris

say there, there, surely not a time
for angel wings to be so public
pulse in mountain rhythm
"melancholy, unanswerable"

compose complicated fits
maintain ancient intimate anarch
stare at darkening trees on ridge
observe steadfast lights
look to save day into dark
                words write long laughter

out of once far ago
young splashings in snow
or old now in cherished chateau
where opal lightwave swoops
from *l'oeil de ma Jeanne*

Vibrant Ions

minutes
selves
socks

all one dune

come again?

I will

desire floats
in a cyclone of dizzy cares

The Job

hushed, turned away
from uninspired diatribe platform

certain of being thoughts
alone but tactile

see bodies distilled in tragic nod
hear call: “wake, wizard!
cut time!
dispel this razor air, cold stratagems
and whale anxiety”

in wild incessant years
dusk horses throng

air roars through aeons of babble
whispers laconic protocols

prance advance to glimpse
sprawl in realm of caw

smile on, not quite animate
in glorious timing of blue
and mostly excessive flit

Wings Over Maximus

51 Pegasus a sun
has a planet
half the mass of Jupiter
too close to that sun
to have our kind of life

looks at cigarette burn on mouse pad:
"oh that'll just become familiar"

order in the saloon!

helmeted angel waitresses
out of 1890's Norwegian kitsch

tilted loony toon night

she used to laugh at his jokes
but now he stands there in the cold & dark
howling
at her window

(The Jilted Professor's Lament)

if feeling the absence
equals missing the presence

does missing the absence
equal feeling the presence?

wild surmise
in mild sunrise

"& her name was Solitaire"

Hop Through Intersection

collage dream of arms and the woman
and then through the and comes the *and*
a translation continuous
of moment's magnetic jaws
in country run on the principle
that you fool most of the people most of the time

fill in the stay-alive blanks
of dense wall chart experience

        let sonic awkwardness
        punch breath-holes in thought

write the plural   undermine the panopticon

                as one of the ear

An Or

wild empty leaps?
no, tango breakfast
in autoironic turban

daylight's allegoric air
impenetrable optics
insect creak or blink

rat muddy form
will drink
nocturnal rain decanter

adieu adieu Lili Marlene
(shush please)
or hum a dewy jinx

(or one comma there)

Apocrypha Hipponactea

fly likes smell of shit

*

sweet flesh hope creatures
loiter, does, in browse fest
where dank lads roam on sassy paws
. . .
charmed subject entire[ly?]

*

sillily jot swill slur

*

endure future   crouched in cellars

*

"I got *mine.* But I ain't got *enough!*"

*

toss possible music peony
gentle apparatus
into sudden sea

*

you must assume that this
has nothing to do with you

Il y a

there is self-beast in season
bright dew on grass
there is upon it that it
the sweetness
of festively followed call
of one in flight
there is approaching along a pensive way
a she   seems from the other side   hidden
cultivated
beset by thought

there is dead fish in water
quickly changing into society's givens

there is stood tried to look across invisible sea
(some work for dark)
again away from window
(diligent messengers)

And What's Your Derivational Profile?

"Whammo Ammo, the ammo of choice
for professional revolutionaries"

no thanks I'm on my motley crusade
to reach cells' dwelling (montage universe)

to praise proud trance, not witless boom
but drift & flicker
                    home
        in on beam of noble sorrow's
        anchored overture as heaven sleeps

"come close back once you held me when"
"name no longer on mail box"

water dance, shadow wash, no next time
jump-cuts, the works, vowels of hidden shaking
song of silent movie captions / captains

pick up stems of identity
                                        some time next year

Rundfunk

i.m. Helmut Heissenbuttel 1921–1996

follow blue fern to the eve's hostelry
glance at long broken results of Der Kapitalismus
back ago in mind's ear ghosts imprecate
years more eyes wild ions ah those very devil's years
war's dark harbors inspired many a toad
but a good horse objects to dead fountain
survived arm left on battlefield by fifty years
walk radio lights evening window course Totentag
spy Demeter stoned glad purple thoughts

come up with light and word beams fifty years
at war against smugdom spot in heart for black flag
even though we grow pale into dark nothing
night's rollers turn with tender uneasy weight

Earful of River Wind

back ago far
elevator to grey room

exquisite invisible hat
on transatlantic nakedness

but no instant citadel prospect
so goodbyes in port of old cactus planet

(end of old muse hour)

now paw in air
                    people demand dream

that still glance gnaws years

how many years
does it take to shut up
to learn to shut up

bones under trees
                    in a wrinkled light

down the toilet with old insight stew

September Song

thank you old tree
survivor of long-ago orchard

what's left of you now
is a bushel of apples
pile of dying wood

eat the apples
let wood go back in the ground

sad firs prowl hillsides in night rain
give me pathetic fallacy or give me pun

later in dream grunt coffin dialect
complains about "extreme *ersatz*" and "finite *Reich*"
quite off the meter   way below frogman horizon

next day it's sunny & eighty degrees again

Your Turn

Dewdrop ode   sweet licks
In jokey code   Eat air!
Lose track of nights & days   dear melody
Fly me to Méjico?   no no

No reruns   hands   hair   snow
That's all we have for you today   but to-
Morrow, grace!   Sweet rain
Oaks bees old shoes & watches

Frogs will green again!
Energy roil   waves rock
Bright naked sun haze music play
In this old Pothole City of a brain

Vapors will brim light up slow pensive look
Make neurons dance in World Muse Impulse Book

Red Cats Revisited

wind-up bug
                    'moderne' wail
out of decrepit shop planks
bullets for nails they slung their zeal
new airs: hey, vodka!
bend, man, roll! look, shoes!
even if ings like that um some way yes can't make talk
elegant pants off Hemingway, oh man
the hulk digs buenos articles
immortal suitcase huge, wet, good

and strong, tears, frilly creeds
all that grave poking, mister shriek another
but real time hate returns the sky
perhaps so must to catacomb ground floor

years go inside to lunch in bowl
earth weeps to waters whispers future crumpled dead slow
envelope hereunder feet do perch on marble spout
sky honey-born black steel twigs growl
world bright in tramcar once love ever rushed afloat
see, Master Fu, grave millions step by subway knees
with sacks of air mail for her sky machine

splendid as globe eye vaults the stare
enter hermetic front face mouth
bones glow in toy room there's no door
swarm day to feather chatter take fat family a while
listen to world grief red hot burden
xylophone output hand foot eyelids beds
down woods dark shutters slip
up dawn go houses crows stalk soft

smack motors rain whips rocky eyes
echo in blood pale songs pits wait
all ever round again blue murder hammers
hard trails spurt dust birds shuffle bright
dragonfly stumbles over cloud
profile ancient
                         meet face embossed
tall sputnik midnight snow forgetmenots

stare away bottles
across whirling field
rune posters flap

And a Note:

In 1962 Lawrence Ferlinghetti's City Lights Books published in their Pocket Poets Series a small (64 pages) volume of poems by three Russian poets, in "English versions by Anselm Hollo," titled Red Cats. The back cover stated that "The translator . . . is a young Finnish poet living in London," which was true to the extent that I was twenty-eight years old, born in Finland, and working for the British Broadcasting Corporation in their European services.

In 1961, Ferlinghetti and Allen Ginsberg, with whom I had exchanged letters, became interested in American media reports of the literary "thaw" in Soviet Russia, and Ferlinghetti wrote to ask what I knew about the poets involved in that phenomenon. After some research in the BBC's and the British Museum Library's foreign periodical holdings, I contacted my mother, Iris Walden-Hollo, a native of Riga (when it was part of Czarist Russia) and a fluent Russian speaker, and we collaborated on translations via the German (my first language; my own studies of Russian had never advanced beyond the alphabet).

After checking Mom's German 'literals' against some other translations into Swedish, Finnish, and German, I sent Ferlinghetti twenty-five poems by Yevgeni Yevtushenko, Andrei Voznesensky, and Semyon Kirsanov in English version attempting to approximate what I then thought was 'hip' American English (Gilbert Sorrentino and Ted Berrigan later pointed out a number of embarrassing slips in that diction). Ginsberg came up with the title, "Red Cats," and, well, there it was, with a nice red and white brushwork cover by Ferlinghetti.

Now long out of print (my present copy is the sixth printing of 1968), it has been an amusing if at times irritating albatross; persons who have never read a line of my own work, or any of my later translations from languages I can truthfully say I'm familiar with (Paul Klee and Bertolt Brecht from the German, Paavo Haavkiko and Pentii Saarikoski from the Finnish, Gunnar Harding and Olof Lagercrantz from the Swedish, Jean Genet's Querelle from the French, etc.), have spoken or written to me about the "cats" with a nostalgic enthusiasm I find hard to share. With the possible exception of Voznesensky's The Big Fire at the Architectural College, the poems now strike me as simplistic, sentimental, and not a little hypocritical in their post- and sub-Mayakovskian rhetoric. It is also quite obvious that neither I nor any of their subsequent translators have been able to match whatever purely aural pleasures the originals may offer.

Thus the present text, Red Cats Revisited, may perform a kind of personal exorcism; by chance methods and subsequent editorial intervention, all of its vocabulary (but not a single line or part of a line) was derived from the contents of the Pocket Poets book.

Hang On to Your Spell

restlessly wander alight on dwell in
big puddle oasis stay to magnify leaves
hang on to grief spoon listen
fair voices racked with patient stratagems
plots later afternoon questions old songs
bittersweet numbskull apocrypha
erotic morphs gowns rustling down blue tiles et cetera
entrancing farce in realm of hyperirony
aye forward script keep rolling them forever
red sails & vessels sway unhinged
for same old kumrad ready for the bell
even as gods grow pale
stone birds fall kerplunk from the air

After "IRISH" by Paul Celan

"Mein Irisch Kind,
Wo weilest du?"

grant me
          wayleave

     up the granary ladder
to your *sommeil*

wayleave
          down the Somnus Trail

leave
     to cut peat
                    on Heart's Incline
in the morn

Scripts

species began by accident
spread rose off plate
to make all other life hard
if not impossible

— ERNA MELLY

"5,351 writers of poems listed." Just one great big monologue project? Having one's saying, and even meaning. Love is a beast. The gift to be simple. Only it ain't so simple. Vanish, immediate body. Meld into dreams.

*

Similes out of simile bottle? Gaze verse? Gauze verse? WATCH OUT! *METAPHOR* OVERHEAD! INCOMING *SIMILES!*

*

Mild wind. Wild mind. O servants of sorrow, pray to St. Expedite when *fierce creatures* music gets too loud. Dark station. Mute rain. Taught how to be nothing but remembered face.

*

JOE had Grandpa Orph
grow happily old & gray
with Grandma Eurydice

HOMER his guy sail away
to the Apocryphal Isles

HOMER: *(nods)*

JOE: *(smiles, gently flaps his wings)*

*

Weave
on rickety ladders
between page & brain

once in a while leap off

do whirling dervish number

then you-eff-oh it into starry *noche*

"My script or yours?"

Good Radio
& Good Night

Air

for Janey

"The air, that weightless something
that surrounds your head
and brightens when you laugh"
— TONINO GUERRA

exiles from parallel worlds
we work our arts in this one
carve water, caress fire

the days run faster & faster
winter worms south then north again
now & again anxiety gallops through
wow who am you? are I? here, here

see presence of world in your face
clouds crickets weaving lights & glorious ache
that we be just as mortal as Signorina
Portinari whom Signor Alighieri once saw
(just *once,* so luckier we, to be sure)

& as night falls, house folds around us, hums
faint flutes & tambourines
leave us asway in dreams in world's best bed

Sunset Caboose

"freight train, freight train
going so fast"

old lights depart

brain's, heart's
gregarious troubles
take them out

one by one
to the great compost

but look at the bee
                                        on its way
to what is brought out of light

Notes

TURN OFF THE NEWS

"fading century's martial insanities:" Possibly now worse than any other century's, except in a quantitative sense. But this is where thought tends to fracture.

O PONDER BONE OF FABLED CARP

"maman equals pigeon:" Brief epiphany in the plaza outside the Pompidou Center — the scribe realized how similar his (dear departed) mother's bearing and protective-aggressive behavior was to that of *pigeons.*

The once-upon-a-time modernity of the Pompidou may also have reminded him of certain 'moderne' parts of Stockholm in the nineteen-forties, where *maman* once whacked him across the nose with her umbrella.

AND THEN THERE ARE THESE SKALDIC THROWBACKS . . .

Eurasion "Middle" and "Dark" "Ages" still flash onto the screen with some frequency. Egil Skallagrimsson's life saga stands on the scribe's shelf, next to William Watson's "The Knight on the Bridge" and "The Last of the Templars." There is mucho machismo / in medievalismo, for sure, but there also are records of remarkable women, strong, gifted, and adorable. (It's still OK to say adorable, isn't it?)

GOOD IDEA, BUT WILL IT WORK?

"announcing a symposium:" The (dear) Naropa Institute, among other oases of relative sanity . . .

HEAD SKY CONVOY PATTERN

Franco Beltrametti (1937–1995), Swiss-Italian truly cosmopolitan poet, painter, publisher, world traveler. I only met him once, in Salt Lake City of all places — he was "passing through" — but he was and remains a significant and encouraging constellation in my interior sky.

"Davy Crockett among [the] astronauts:" Ted Berrigan, another great constellation, called himself that in a lecture he gave at 80 Langton Street in San Francisco on 24 June 1981.

The third, open-parenthesis, stanza marks a brief reappearance of the skaldic throwback rage that in the scribe's psyche always accompanies the news of friends' (always) untimely deaths.

BENIGN EVENING COMEDOWN

The middle stanza refers to Elaine Morgan's delightful book *The Descent of Women,* read many years ago.

METAPHOR MUTAPHOR

After its "Chinese" beginning, the poem moves on to consider *la vida,* and its passing, and once again, Utopia . . .

HEY DR. WHO, LET'S DIAL 1965

You were there, too. Some of you.

LEAVES OF BLUR

"old story soundtrack" fading 'like' "mist on deep lens down the years." (Similes perhaps more permissible in footnotes?)

AN OLIVE FOR SATIE

Composer Erik Satie is said to have titled some of his shorter works according to whatever his gaze came to rest on after he had penned the last note.

leibesraum: approximately "love space" — a neologism echoing the lexically 'real' words *Liebestraum* ("dream of love") and *Lebensraum* ("life space" — another German word ruined by the Nazis, who used it to express their idea that their empire should encompass all of Europe).

THE OPENING OF THE FILE

"jovial irony machine:" May have been thinking of Marcel Duchamp. The title refers to both Robert Duncan's *The Opening of the Field* and the personal computer.

JUNGLE FINN

A homage to one of the fathers of "sound poetry," Kurt Schwitters, composed by homophonic translation of text Finnish poet and painter Jyrki Pellinen wrote on the occasion of John Ashbery's reading at the Helsinki Festival. No data available on E. Quist, the presumed author.

SUR LA TERRASSE

"To build the city of Dioce whose terraces are the colour of stars." EP, Canto LXXIV. "Ecbatana, ancient capital of Media Magna, founded in 6th century BC by the legendary first king of the Medes, Deiöeces. According to Herodotus, the city was surrounded by seven concentric walls, each a different color . . ." Edwards and Vasse, "Annotated Index to the Cantos of Ezra Pound," U of CA Press, 1957.

"Petrarch in tundra" — thinking about Osip Mandelshtam.

Locatelli — eighteenth-century composer discovered via Patrick O'Brian's monumental *Aubrey / Maturin* novel(s): his music is in the protagonists' (a sturdy sea captain and his ship's surgeon) repertoire.

TEMPLE NOIR

Written in the scribe's "Cut-Up: Before and After" class. Lives intersecting in the mind.

THE NEXT FIFTY YEARS

"stretch bridge:" Too bad that this now echoes a cliché promoted by the Prez from Arkansaw.

CAT-GODS' CHANNEL

What if cats, etc.? And who is "she [who] climbs?"

HALO BLADE

"in fits of favorite city:" The "New York of the Mind" (as in quite a few of these).

SILENT SALAD

Not sure those "forthcoming volumes" will be written in this dimension.

WINGS OVER MAXIMUS

Zoom shots — from cosmological ("Maximus" / Olson) vistas to 'realtime' flyspecks, on to fantasy, anecdotal recollection of an aging academic's problems, Derrida on absence and presence, and a name from an Ian Fleming novel. Voilà!

APOCRYPHA HIPPONACTEA

See *Hipponax of Ephesus, translated by Anselm Hollo* (Baltimore, Tropos Press 1995). These fragments are "in the manner of."

IL Y A

One impetus for this was the relative untranslatability of Guillaume Apollinaire's poem of the same title, due to the absence of an English locution as loose and comprehensive (at once) as the French "il y a."

RUNDFUNK

One-armed like Blaise Cendrars (the left "left," as they say, on some dismal battlefield in 1942), tall, calm, funny, and erudite, German poet Helmut Heissenbüttel had (as he put it) "a lasting soft spot for the black banner of anarchy. My innermost conviction is anarcho-syndicalist. Never mind that I know it [=anarcho-syndicalism] can never be realized, but that is where my secret love lies."

Rosemarie Waldrop's and Pierrs Joris's translations from his work are excellent: Heissenbuttel is far from 'easy,' somewhere between Clark Coolidge and *Finnegan's Wake* on the translation meter.

AFTER "IRISH' BY PAUL CELAN

Result of Alec Finlay's commission to attempt a translation of Celan's poem "Irisch." Epigraph ("My Irish Child, / Where tarriest thou?") from Wagner's *Tristan und Isolde,* quoted by T.S. Eliot in lines 33–34 of *The Waste Land.*

"Sleep" does not match the weight of "Schlaf" in Celan's poem; recourse was taken to French "sommeil" and Latin "somnus."

SCRIPTS

Erna Melly, author of the epigraph, may be related both to Ern Malley, father figure of modern Australian poetry, and George Melly, the great British jazz and art critic and creator of the comic strip *Flook.* See *The Ern Malley Affair* by Michael Heyward (London, Faber & Faber 1993).

"JOE," here is the poet Joe Cardarelli (1944–1994), author of *The Unknown Story of Orpheus (A Work Unfinished).*

SUNSET CABOOSE

Ideally, the first two lines should be sung in the inimitably nasal voice of Nancy Whiskey. If anyone has a recording of her rendition of *Freight Train,* the scribe would greatly appreciate a copy.

AHOE 2 (Johnny Cash Writes a Letter to Santa Claus)

Arnaut Daniel
(a voice from the past):

". . . who gathers with an ox
who hunts with an ox
to chase a hare
forever, and swims against the current."

Jane:

At least half the time —

Anselm:

And so it was
and is
and this
another little boke
for you.

Passing Vapors

thought hands you strange balloons
Bon giorno!   *Presto!*   you're a farmer
you stumble over a cabbage
but mind bends cliffs   time slides
cleaves hearts   now you are grizzled old earl
playing flute in desert before the Saracens get you
the tune the one about freckled maidens
on the banks of the river Yarn   as the curved blade
takes your head off that morning
the color of quinces   the novel
slides from hand to floor
for fifteen seconds you dream of bombs and cabbage soup
then wake with a start to see any earlier "you"
now purely anecdotal subject

Big Furry Buddha in Back Yard

it's a made-up name
his real name is Bailey
all names are made up

full moon &
our bats are back
bat is flutterer   fluttermouse

verbal tea leaves   interim moments
loony toon galaxy   at bottom of page cup

world symphony much the same
they've just added more instruments
place used to be run by two big bunches of liars
now there is only one big bunch

who cares   full moon &
our bats are back
bat is flutterer   fluttermouse

Lost Original

Mr K. said   in times of great crudity
it is necessary   to be subtle
so please wrap around me
with awkward grace
I may have suffered some Rilke Damage
or do I just have a little trouble
with fantasy tripwires
while engrossed in the sky's lexicon
& hills like purple pachyderms
"there's been a great *upsurgence*"
said the announcer   but I didn't catch
what of   & what of where
does it come from where does it go
still asking   on down the road

Still Here & Here Again Then Here Still

galactic dazzle dream talk & *festina lente*
high bounce transit moon gleam ambient creatures
inside has come outside inviting eye to read
the now   & then, the now
three seconds at a time
edges of moment gleam & turn
where are we now and now where are we now
this place alive with love & skill & care
the feast not moveable but ever on the move
flaring & flashing through the wave barrage

Paint the Vacant Millennia

thought map   sea of paper   details of record
power fog   endless   above

minute written words
                                        dusk pushes window
fate principle consoles (con-soles?)

slender moments   distant abysses
(never thought to use *that* word before)
evaporate backdrop charm

night strides along   endless objects approach
philosophy outside   dark trembling hull
loneliness presence your face branches
(anxiety of dim golden trance)

countless human drift   see twigs turn green
read what cannot be read   great animal faces

Black Hat Up Above

undulant eye script   snakes up to gaze
from mist-fatigued glide   to bright curiosity

midmorning   still certainly dark
universe   (now that's a big word)

        but it begins again
in arcs of green
& tender flinch from implacable codes

o lights on the far shore o sad guitars

ha-ha

                this way to the edge

"woman sues McDonald's
                                                over flying cheeseburger"

Much of It Unconscious Work but Work (Sd Francis Ponge)

pale afterglow on ridge
trees stand above
coal's underfoot pronouncements
same old quiet roar

dreamt younger or as now she may
see image fade to readability

or more like mice asleep for decades
      in time's backdrop corridors

brain twitters

bowstring slaps into wristguard

Hanging With Harpocrates

walk into dark verbarium   hit the switch

of course it's a drug   (addictive)
but you can't test it on rats

dreamchild bounds away
fades to well-behaved courage

take edge off lost music   face
Time's Godzilla Battalions

      step up, handsome thought

but all the days
you hoped would never come   will come

(your bandaged "pirate" mini-teddybear:
what was his name?)

            past composed recomposed

                  a body runs past

Leave It to The Bonóbos

Barrel out of Morpheus City's elliptical traffic, torrid, oneiric, pumped through raven's heart.

Unwind from sheet exorbitant kisses, now back awake in world of Fourteenth Amendment: corporations as "persons" — thanks, Roscoe Conkling.

Golems, are they? They are, and they lord it over that world, determined to win the struggle with its *desdichados* (some of the latter now no longer wrapped in Red Flag but in the ectoplasms of Christ or Mahomet) (or cowering in the crannies of Theory Land — the Circle of Sciolists).

"Quelle époque!"

In gray dust angst, no shoal grace city. Or is it all just moving pictures in a box?

Crystallized Internet

being mystical I was gods
was a visual stuffed
deus ex melodrama
cold as a maiden from hell
mind out of subplot

"Kevin Kline reading Nietzsche in bed
with large automatic weapon"

gibberish
with a few thoughts thrown in
how lovely you are

related frequencies at work
in rattlesnake

colloquially brutal jouissance
of unfettered person

hovering on bushy wings
waiting for goodwill orchestra monoplane

    nonstop sensory triumph
    lit and shot
    in high duality

Sorrow Horse Music

> "*no matter how new age you are*
> *old age is gonna bite your ass.*"
> — UTAH PHILLIPS

creaky human continuum
seduced by daily lot
after remains of the day
(no encounters of the close kind)
on to headlights windings revelations
& things heard naked *la nuit*

veiled nestings   coils feed to antennae
all events occur in different places
& at different times while the i

drop me in a glass
where leaf or mouse is a message
of silent evaporation
forget lucky adjustments
rain high above

("poetry in translation"
— way to easy)

escapes its obligations into this writing
psyches itself to sound right
personal ways of eternal become line
literally filled with thinking

Old Cat Sober Moon

Running into feeling befuddles. A kiss, a moment, spiky, euphoric — then back to evolution. "It are the face on top." And this be nothing but croaks. Wintry mood floats in reason's mineshaft. First shapes, twilight trees, now they are doors. Then fades the sky around one. Looks like a heightened puddle, haloed by symbolic purples, "Cerebral, constructive, American worker will rise!" There was a time one would have ended this with "You don't say?" But that time's over. So let's hear it again: "Cerebral, constructive, American worker will rise!" O, K. All right. Old cat howls, deaf now, at sixteen years, does not know where we are.

Presente or Not

watch stage constantly

"honeycomb
of floating thought"

or just idle prattle
merely panoptic passions

fictional disquiet
in decades of display
which past which present
never document

just secret stuff
you casual somnambule butterfly you
infinite text
no wave jolt kisses
politics in a vase

need coat of alert forms
glimmer intensity of la muerte
writing at small depot of once-again
mind shooting filaments at subject

some small hell & what's it for
posthumous truffles
voice foretold but never close enough
for manifest dream fume

see the words opening
their little beaks
dilemma ardent organic

ever the window
ever idle summer's
secret *fleurs*

Philosophique

what
piped up
song
again

enjoys its
other

*

"feel my book"
"format assistance received"

*

thought maybe that *was* her
so drove round the block
but as I passed her again
she'd aged forty years

*

lampshade
in the spider
night

*

o handsome primates
of the past
your sudden doings

So Fix That Broken Axle

Then is it past screeches of the mighty
"blood actions" Old Bird said
pondering revolted
let us insinuate another song
"Art is my wife & myself"
turn this music on
for identity? slept all evening
monotonous rush and purr
summer hard with the dead
The Edge surely lovely
cannot be a bed
"I am a behind
that grows a mind"
was that a
german joke?
sad-sack protagonist depressed recluse
of sporadic human encounters

> "may note down what he sees
> among the ruins, for he sees
> other things and more than
> others; he is after all dead
> in his own lifetime, and is
> the true survivor" (Kafka)

but one is not that one is floaty yet anchored
"balloon on a string"
ship that sails both oceans and air
elevator that rises
through the clouds
or keeps going down

but no again it is a much smaller but truer
universe

Titled

We call it "titled" (example of good title)
Then use universal program
Characters strung on story
"Unkind Phenomena: A Story"
A certain heft and "boing!"
Words work   to look intended
"It works for wood, and walks on fell"
How long is greatest line?
It sounded full of recent pace
So I think, frogs. So it's very there.
The lovely instances of a kid's 1906.
Hilarious defended his ego:
"I met her in the lobby of the Bukowski Building."
To dream a letter   younger

The Ghostly Screen in Back of Things

high romance out of erasure
and combination: people still really had biplanes
and it was very adventurous
for persons called Beryl to fly them
back when they also had persons called The Original
The Genius   & The Muse
if not kept in the dark
they fade   except in the Wax Museum
where it is pretty dark   you may visit them there
it may bring some adventure into your life
move it forward a couple of centuries
through billions of words as old
as wheat we jokingly call mankind
"singing in moonlight by microphone tree"
if we gave this another title it would read differently

Just Another Bit of Scenery

essence of indescribable intention
one tries to recall
"he studied her body through tears"
actual text does not measure up

then there was the other thought
& the one after the other
it was carried up into the critical sky
but what was the music

did speech give reference to the body
now's the time to light a cigarette
pop in and out   as anyone in their right mind
would   save the words

that might make some interesting sense
next to each other   ambivalent minutes numbered
then hand your best inner sibling
a microphone   "her ass feels hot"

this microphone is a sculpture
so that's one level   now the only thing left
for us to do is this totally childish thing

Say Tango

in the silence of this attic
windows fold into dark

hoarsely the fire whispers
eighteenth century words

the adventure novelist
goes to his encyclopedias
to see what plants used to grow there & so on

while through his head
runs the not entirely impossible phrase

"Arose, aroused, the Duke of Ravebruck . . ."

    but now for a sudden
    something-entirely-different tumble
    into say tango

or some quivery *merde* like that

now Daisy Aldan wouldn't have liked that
she would not have liked that at all

she just wanted M. Le Merveillleux
to settle in nicely for his bedtime read

A Hundred Mule Deer in the Back Yard

i.m. Allen Ginsberg

sleepwalkers' chess   *condensare ad absurdum*
why did we say what just seem to have said
not a thought in our heads
is the thought in my head
meaning
meaning
        is a product
frame form work the old farm
stalking about like some mad Highlander
yet gigglily prudent as a bat's bellybutton
peering at words   "as if all worlds were there"
then think freedom music
not deplorable platforms
think lovely list of things   e.g.
Socialist International Paris 1889 & Erfurt 1891:

        democracy & equal rights for all
            including women

separation of church & state
free education
    including higher education
free medical services
graduated taxes
the eight-hour work day
the right to organize unions

though serious revolvers
they stood no sporting chance

nor does the poet
walk around making hilarious remarks

don't shelve that book yet
I want to remember him a little longer

Ad Quodlibet

wheel around on best days   riding the hum
let coffee fumes spread across Dasein trail
& its perfect unconscious journals
avoid the wrongheaded
even when you can hear them
working up opinions
inside their unpleasant little brains
& the contemporary has aged
at least twenty years
& now has industrial presence of slag heap
just light a fire in the magic bag
spend evening by the well
raise cup of quest to speeding fugitive

We Are Having It Again and Without Sorrow

molecular vessel named I am December
gesticulates its way through mind maze
looking for some opaque you

    archy   old
& after reading les suuréalistes some more

    now mental spin to winding woods
    in ancient jars brain slowly happened
    words come in spurts drool dream at dawn
    history from a tooth
    night grottos of the blessèd matter
    in sleepwalk time no present face

rainy street no stars equals my language

now let us end
            with a discreet representation
      of a real lightbulb
still doing its connotations
          in a city of transparent sepulchers

off to ride
          last waltz railroad in November sun

Life in the Twists

bare freckled skin under black cloak
reminders of turns not taken or not taken well
endless parentheses faraway dogs
nighthawks crouched in basement cafeteria
with Rita Hayworth in her prime
more bitter than instant brewed
in aluminum pot on our way to the program
of was it social uplift or another "summer of love"
between Dubuque and Sioux City

"no let me tell you I am the phantom
of the second life
a wanderer a beautiful stray
on the face of the earth"

shook off the dust & out on her hat

"all that was   ever is
or vice versa . . ."

From the Notebooks of Professor Doppelganger

America still talk bizarre
falls off knocks versions about
stuff odd extensions
this has had bad maintaining

Eve's hand on Adam's inordinate elevation
individual lotus be that way
on day of Utopian items defined

news pinned on heart
as we wheel in to sleep's bright anagrams

she is the model in his dream life class
not having but having the seeing of her

these are our old forms

Give Me Big Shoes

In Western shoes to die and go out in
's an easy religion
(as useful as dead
rat in refrigerator) so delete the messiah strain
but do not question prudent joy
SOMETIMES FIT TO BURST WITH AMOR
think doting think of Thinklife, Inc.:
"this version is the difficult *Sane*"

collective person enmeshed
in last bizarre Utopianism
human time spent maintaining
dictionaries on Platonic porch

response that looks like door
then becomes more intense

snow moon questions dwindle
pick up gaze from window
one among the shapes
begins to play

Hi, Haunting

back then it seemed he had more to say
than could be said in a lifetime
but there was time enough

year is a dome of sadness
"the big sleep"
"these stanzas are done"

the grand narratives are dead
the dead are our grand narratives
the dreadful great

Skid Inside

any of every day
moment hung long
cut into cave

an all night parade
where you kiss people like pretty tarantulas
in the Oklahoma of the self

    Collision Alley
    bent defeat
    precisely your face

what if I glowed
closer to thee
mother of blaze & whippet food?

    in globe of night
    with puddles
    splash of quiet

coins   harbor   mystery   Ribcage Cafe
(obscure play: see illegible)

    out of the texts
    twilight exchanged
    in lopsided mouths' masquerade

Old Aristippus

night morn of glass
                    in cape of age
crystal pagination
adjust wild movement old heart
sleep by one present
                    as by current

ah little oasis phrase:
"seated on his mobile trapeze
the aviator steers his ship
toward the four cardinal points"

then elevate activate leap into leaf
demand expression
                                        demand window too

it's got to be true both ways
live and eat food before enormous general night

goodbye expensive time
                                                  say the murmurous measures

Ultraista Oneiric

dream vortices broadcast
humorous din

from invisible ships of desire
in eddies of luminous sleep

            !Holá!

                  bare feet in pitted mirror
            rarely unfolded planes
      in a blue shade

"where are the arms to go with these eyes?"
sumptuous figures in ample interiors

wave percussion over palpitating globe
swollen dynamics churn merchandise

naked silence   vast theater
      moonlit aerofoil memory
            bounces into unsteady calm

Attention: Selections Come On Tilted

do before reading approach yourself
emanate out as encouraging tale
speak a poem by everybody
stuff not craft   good long stuff
but then tons of blah
the almost whatever just folks
"what's wrong with these filters?"
chillier work stands up on new coasts
pivotal breaks   prior to pleasure
watch the thinking at times
back to a whereabouts
earlier perhaps wholesome denial
of no ideas   "Pluto is good"
then say you are just a line

The World as Fiasco

mais non Henri a dead man
can be a great traveling companion
mind's envelope sails
                                        into destiny's breakfast
today was that day
I was going to be so busy
write cantos escape
crepuscular consumers'
                                        revolving enclosures
on light speed sky trapeze
why *did* the chicken cross the road
Hemingway:
                                  to die   in the rain
so good luck creating an atmosphere
where the honest cop
fears the crooked cop
said the 61-year-old former cop
in a ponytail
beard & earring who looked
more like an aging beat poet
which
        I'm not I'm not

Now O'Clock

"Alone, this sudden darkness in a toybox."
—TED BERRIGAN, SONNET XXIX

mirror black for luck
click into motion our names
are we not paper?

glittering night talk stammered
strange sudden sad but not
old bulldog words drowned in shots
    of whiskey's seamless stairway
that was the wrong ticket that was

    some write "The Visions" but they can't write
    merely disturb the door
    to sudden darkness in toybox

when you return you return to poetry
a person said   this gave her poetry
measured considered worried
slow for some   minute music for others

    the former guard asleep now I did like it
    that them then   remember severely the era
    & its agreement gestures
    it's time it's life it's this like that
    what is a latch? what's wid dis paragraph?
    short tight rural news item   it ain't

wheels   low voices   syntax chant
tight sofa full of tinkling elements
proud semiology it snores

    among accessible presence traps
    some conscious mental quantum tropes of truth

shaped by timing   o tell it to come in

"Tempus? Fuggit!"

unbound from yonder level
        of oceans of presence
    yet crudely modeling such mutations
        just say on   just say off
    pace taken up by events
            population 'explained'
        that quantum clever too
    phenomena! refinement! thanks!
        modern words fail where how
    let the red bury their red
        or remarkable humorous hours as ever
    all day consider utopocalyptic
and then come breathing in and out
        to kiss confusion near the pond-
    erful joke about nonetheless
            scribble scrabble
but parked for breakfast thought continues
        to idle swoop and dazzle
    in loud formations over sound
                                never dim

Johnny Cash Writes a Letter to Santa Claus

now too old to run away
(three months older than Donald Duck)
well they still seem to need me
& feed me at least some of them do
"Are you in the middle of something?"
"No I'm totally marginalized"
but still interested in these critters
walking lyrics to the grand abstruse song
    so singular they are
in their parts   assigned reassigned
& Lyn Hejinian quoted Shklovsky
"Role of Art — to kill Pessimism!"
translation not a matter of one to one
relationships any more than anything else is
Zophus the cat well pleased and even amazed
by his consciousness in successful leap

Notes

AHOE 2 (JOHNNY CASH WRITES A LETTER TO SANTA CLAUS)

This set is a sequel to AHOE (And How On Earth), published in 1997 by Smokeproof Press (Erie, Colorado). The two epigraphs in that volume may be worth repeating here:

"Robin Blaser once said in talking about a serial poem that it's as if you go into a room, a dark room, the light is turned on for a minute, then it's turned off again, and then you go into a different room where the light is turned on and turned off." — Jack Spicer, *From the Vancouver Lectures*

"One could also see the face of another large apartment building there, whose windows at night would lighten or go dark in almost a curious narrative. I would imagine, sitting looking out, lives back of those windows, happy, sad, threatened, successful, always a little obscured and changing," — Robert Creeley, *Coming Home*

HANGING WITH HARPOCRATES

Harpocrates — god of silence (hence, "Harpo" Marx).

LEAVE IT TO THE BONÓBOS

"Bonóbos" — primate cousins who "Make Love Not War."
"Circle of Sciolists" — sciolism: "superficial show of learning."
"Quelle époque" — "what an epoch (we live in)!"

SORROW HORSE MUSIC

Epigraph: Utah Phillips is a wonderful American folk singer and storyteller still roaming the West.

PRESENTE OR NOT

"Glimmer intensity of la muerte": La muerte — Spanish six-letter word. Wonder why I didn't put it in italics.
"secret *fleurs*": French flowers.

SO FIX THAT BROKEN AXLE

"Old Bird": A 'character' in *West is Left on the Map* (CORVUS, Coffee House Press, 1995).

TITLED

"'I met her in the lobby of . . .'": See *the years: for charles bukowski* (FINITE CONTINUED, Blue Wind Press, 1980).

THE GHOSTLY SCREEN IN BACK OF THINGS

"biplanes . . . persons called Beryl": Legend (quite possibly apocryphal) has it that John Ashbery composed his poem *Europe* (in THE TENNIS COURT OATH, Wesleyan, 1962) by means of erasure out of a juvenile novel called BERYL IN HER BIPLANE.

JUST ANOTHER BIT OF SCENERY

"'her ass feels hot'": Translation of L.H.O.O.Q (Duchamp's title for his mustachioed Mona Lisa).

SAY TANGO

"'Arose, aroused. . .": Inspired, no doubt, by a brief dip into the interminable text production of Mrs. Barbara Cartland.
"or some quivery *merde* . . .": French five-letter word.
"now Daisy Aldan . . .": Noted New York editor, art critic, writer of poems, who complained in a review (in a publication hubristically titled *World Literature Today*) of my book OUTLYING DISTRICTS that it contained too many four-letter words and not enough of The Marvelous.

AD QUODLIBET

"disputatio ad quodlibet (Latin)": disputation on anything whatsoever.
"Daein (German)": literally "there-being."

WE ARE HAVING IT AGAIN WITHOUT SORROW

Title from Ernest Hemingway's ACROSS THE RIVER INTO THE TREES: "We are having fun," the girl said. "we are having it again and without sorrow."
"archy": Don Marquis' immortal protagonist in ARCHY AND MEHITABEL.

GIVE ME BIG SHOES

Title from Nike t.v. commercial for hiking shoes, shot in Kenya using Samburu tribesmen. Camera closes in on tribesman who speaks his native language, Maa. As he speaks, the slogan "just DO IT" appears on the screen. Lee Cronk, anthropologist at the U of Cincinnati, says the man is really saying: "I don't want these. Give me big shoes." Says Nike's Elizabeth Dolan: "We thought nobody in America would know what he said."

HI, HAUNTING

"the big sleep" — Raymond Chandler.
"these stanzas are done" — Gertrude Stein.

OLD ARISTIPPUS

Title refers to Aristippus (2), grandson of Socrates' companion, founder of the Cyrenaic school. "he appears to have been the first to teach . . . that immediate pleasure was the only end of action . . . the present moment is the only reality." (Oxford Classical Dictionary, 1992 edn.)
"seated on his mobile trapeze . . .": lines from a poem by poet Rafael Lasso de la Vega (1890–1959), one of the principal proponents of the Dada movement in Spain.

ULTRAISTA ONEIRIC

Title: Spanish Dadas called themselves Ultraistas.
Oneiric: pertaining to the realm of dreaming.
"*!Holá!*": What German tourists shout to indicate their approval at *muy folklórico* performances.
muy folklórico: very ethnic and / or kitschy; mostly kitschy.

"mais non Henri": Henri Michaux, who warned against traveling with a dead man (see also Jim Jarmusch's film DEAD MAN).
"61-year-old former cop": Serpico, testifying to New York city council on police brutality and crooked cops on the twenty-third of September 1997.

"TEMPUS? FUGGIT!"

"utopocalyptic": term coined by poet Michael Heller — "that odd socio-political or cultural product, both fever and exacerbation, in which an individual is torn between idealized hopes and gnawing dread."

rue Wilson Monday

To the School of Continuation

A Note

When I was invited to spend five months in France, in an old hotel long frequented by artists and writers, I decided to write something that would not be your typical "sabbatical poem" — that familiar rumination, by the U.S. American academic (temporary) expatriate, "on" the Mona Lisa, Baudelaire's grave, or "how *different* all this is from back home in Missoula Montana!"

I believe that "rue Wilson Monday" turned out to be something possibly more interesting: A hybrid of day book, informal sonnet sequence (though more "simultaneist" than chronological), and extended, 'laminated' essay-poem. Works I found particularly inspiring in my endeavor were Ted Berrigan's *The Sonnets* and Edward Dorn's *Abhorrences* — books that will make me chuckle and weep to the end of my days.

The book received its title from French poet Guillaume Apollinaire's 1913 poem "Lundi rue Christine" (Monday rue Christine), a Cubist work composed almost entirely out of verbatim speech from various conversations in a cafe.

In "rue Wilson Monday," similar conversations take place in and around my head during that stay (August 1998 / January 1999) at the Hotel Chevillon, an artists' and writers' retreat in the small town of Grez-sur-Loing. Back in 1876, Robert Louis Stevenson came to visit his cousin Robert at this hotel, whose present street address is 114 rue Wilson, "La Rue Grande" (Main Street) back then. There he met Fanny Osbourne, the woman he was to pursue across the Atlantic and the North American continent and eventually marry.

Thus, "Cousin Bob" and "Cousin Louis" put in appearances in this book, as do Charlie Chaplin, Heraclitus, Utah Phillips, Beatrice Portinari, William Holden, Ted Berrigan, Guido Cavalcanti, John Lennon, Bill Clinton, Robert Bly, William Burroughs, Petrarch's Laura, Stéphane Mallarmé, Ben Jonson, Tom Raworth, Aleksandr Herzen, Gertrude Stein, Archy the Vers Libre Cockroach, Oscar Wilde, Damien Hirst, The White Goose of Grez, and a whole bunch of others you may or may not have heard of.

To invite the reader to participate in my often elliptical conversations with these folks, I have provided footnotes, and these too are an integral part of the conversation and the poem.

Boulder Colorado
3 January 2000 C.E.

Those crepes were terrific
The tap is running

— GUILLAUME APOLLINAIRE,
"MONDAY RUE CHRISTINE"

1

carriage purrs man whistles pounds post
in distant rocky dark
reason, weaving, brabbles
cognition digs tunnel through Charlot's suitcase
zoom cog motion   seagull cry
arms around everything
parallel out of someone
else's heaven tunnels
behind doors past
lit-up, frontal, still convinced
climb reviewed
now cautious move to igloo syntax
doodle on   smoke
watch reflections flounce

Charlot: French nickname for Charlie Chaplin in early silent movies.

2

beautiful thoughts
beware of those who write to write beautiful thoughts
upper limit: poet as brain in jar
lower limit: poet as hectoring moralistic asshole
prefer the difficile   the delicately unstable
sealed & farouche   or gamesome pasquinade
but faced with such stirring
Mister Intellectual Rigor marches back in
a staunchly secular sort of guy
deep bits of sky begin to beat
wave summons to water
bird is also just bird said dragonfly
but now there's a kind of drone   card in wrong slot
bits of rough bark fall off trunk

---

difficile: "hard to deal with, stubborn, unreasonable" (English); "difficult" (French). farouche: "marked by shyness and a lack of social graces" (English); "wild, fierce, shy" (French). pasquinade: publicly posted lampoon, satire — from "Pasquino," remains of ancient statue excavated in Rome in 1501, on which people posted satirical compositions in bad Latin.

3

that thar wind is
really movin'
them thar clouds along
what crowing eccentricity made me write that
well now how about the past
past tense of climb   i.e. "clomb"?
CLOMB (an insert):
clomb to the cave
where midget brigands
used to stash
their big false mustachios
wrote this with my French "Red Arrow" pen
& the geese they's a-honkin' down by the river Loing
sounding like Kirby Malone   pronouncing "bain"

"crowing eccentricity": not a typo. Kirby Malone: noted Baltimore poet / performance artist.

4

the stuff of the psyche is a smoke-like substance
says Heraclitus   it is constantly in motion
only movement can know movement ah
this be head-sensitive material
forever in deep shade
we get together to make noises at each other
when we're not there we miss those noises
but hey boss isn't it time to lighten up says archy
you old opsimath you what's that it's one who learns
things late in life & when has it not been
'late in life,' si vales bene est ego valeo
beloved beasts open to so many
'interpretations' we or awe, as in aw shucks
if you are well that is good I am well too

Heraclitus quotes, here as elsewhere, from Guy Davenport's translation. archy: Don Marquis' vers-libertarian cockroach.

5

once again butterfly pulse entire percept
fictional jolt of eye: arms, yarns
hit me adventure come kiss me sadness
as if me had me still
in this ocean of "socio-political & aesthetic"
idiot electric catacomb gibberish
tumbling billows of stuff
something there is in man
wants to be top big banana baboon
but I am not Robert Frost I am a baboon
mad about the planet   even this week
in the America that was   it had that phrasing
ecstatic articulate and beaucoup
beaucoup conscious disquiet

6

now does the blissful somnambule recluster
a dream a flesh-colored dream? say what?
how to identify the ones who tend to war
& what to do about them   discuss
on different color paper free up text
from fuzzy spaces inside head. hey,
are these walls "of" someplace? he stood
a veteran user of mind's ear
for tales of The Device
mortals love noise hurled into gaping flesh
well maybe yes. roll eyes round écriture
distortion makes you enemies
so either "say" things or it's endless postpreface
the elsewhere gunfire problem whose is it

écriture: writing (Fr.)

7

"the ideal story is that of two people
who go into love   step for step
with a fluttered consciousness
like a pair of children venturing together
into a dark room" yeah right but then then
it's LIGHTS! CAMERA! ACTION!
& the relentless Surroundarama
Split-Screen Spectacle of
Everyday Life   & Things to Do
but it's still a terrific idea
since being what or who is also just with
in days & nights of beaucoup conscious disquiet
though sometimes it's not so easy
to reinsert oneself   into the mortal coil

"the ideal story . . .": Robert Louis Stevenson.

8

the general infantilization
that became a groundswell of our century (said Eva)
not that we weren't part of it
when we were young & cruel
"deny yourself nothing"   well that's one theory
only the creature knows its awful secret joys
and the mobile digressive figments collide (said Ann)
and people don't read
poetry because uncertainty
is associated with punishment (said Mark)
is stupid attention better than no attention
what about hissing a poem   instead of the usual
soulful quaver or well-rehearsed scream
when your memory goes forget it (said Utah)

"Eva" — Eva Hesse, Pound's German translator, essayist. "Ann" — Ann Lauterbach.
"Mark" — Mark Wallace. "Utah" — Utah Phillips. Great singers all.

9

yes tribe so richly rhymes with diatribe
but voice in you is home, please give us brains!
Mr. Meter, meet Mr. Foot
the voice in you is home
"thou art too elliptical"
but what's not foible anymore?
farewell Bay Area it's been unreal
now text participants will perform
a simultaneous vote of thanks
so get thee to the poem office
before time goes antique
on seascape's rainy nakedness
(spoken in cóntent absolutely)
how sings her my head such uncanny apples

10

most beautiful order of the world
still just a random gathering of things
insignificant in themselves
says Heraclitus
but man's bootstraps, his imagination
is quite a part of reality
says Larry Eigner   and history
will be revisionist   ALL history
WILL be revisionist   all power temporal
power exists in TIME
"your time is up, Mr. Power"
and there he goes
with all his little
longings & belongings   there he goes

11

gates waterfalls shifting horizons
plastic halberds gentle fugitives
una Beatrice on the ramparts of Carcassonne
in black miniskirt more like Juliette Greco
is she thinking of "Raymond the Cathar Count of Toulouse"
fat chance she's gazing at sudden
flock of paragliders in the sky
while the guide drones on & I think of
"fictitious employment by no means uncommon in France"
he means government employment
fictitious government employment
but then government is fictitious too
as are the governed much of the time
look for yourself in this pebble or pencil

12

the only good knee   is a live knee
(how incontestably true)
& we do be fond of these limbs that take us
across lands old & new & enormous waters
(which at times make one feel a bit like a vole
facing infinity)   & return us to calmer things
"oriented" "at home" simply just where it is
(draped over her shoulder   green eyes confident:
"we are going to the studio!")
or "the study of gratifying discourse"
(inscription on Chinese scholar's cottage
two hundred years ago)
the way the waters' voices speak
slow erudite surprises   yarns in your arms

"draped over her shoulder" — Zophiel the Cat, who stayed in Boulder Colorado and was much missed at rue Wilson.

13

just where it is is with you
whom I found fifteen years ago
empty & sad I was   as one of Simenon's tales
pretty much heading across the river & into the trees
(my particular brand of sentimentality)
a wanderer twixt the two worlds
of Bar Trance & Brain Tundra   reluctant to dance
not even in the manner of William Holden in Picnic
but who can tell the story of true astonishment
not even Guido who did try   but with him I say
that I saw in my lady's eyes a light
that brought a new spirit into my heart
"awakening there a cheerful life"
— so, Happy Birthday, Janey! signed: Yours, Biped Al.

"not even in the manner of William Holden in Picnic": how Ted Berrigan once described his dancing style. Guido: Cavalcanti. "awakening there a cheerful life": "sì che vi desta d'allegrezza vita" (Mark Cirigliano's translation). "Biped Al": a "spell-check" donnée (fortuitous present).

14

now does he know how to beam? contented?
grow fuzzy? nothing wrong with fuzzy
blissful? feel some place
keep stupid demons at bay
let them go or go on
hammering nothing in Nothing Land —
this be quite different
from crazy hot soul of sudden beginnings
cluttered & ever 'novel' inside
yes that did make for impetuous bellows
violent staggerings   irritating ruins
before it all settled into rose debris;
so locate old hotel before books close
on trundling troubadours. semicolon

15

give up your ampersands & lowercase 'i's
they still won't like you
the bosses of official verse culture
(U.S. branch)   but kidding aside
I motored off that map a long time ago
yet have old friends
still happily romping in the English lyric
and Reverdy! dear Reverdy! so much of him rhymes
it must be   poésie   ma chérie . . .
looks at the stacks of books on the floor
gods help us, dear poets
pass the salt pass the mustard
hike the present
or the hypothetically honest horse-drawn past

16

bygone masks of the night: dream, sentence, voices, air
undulating desire   but then what was there for lunch
"MOOTHWATERING HAMBURGUERS"?
do we take it the basic unit of "the new poem"
is the menu? OK I'll take it
one flight down with a daffodilly
for my love
& if that's too silly
I'll hit myself over the head with my billy
club o let the chemicals bubble
when this you see you see a PANEL
of edited accidents   "cumshaw"   cumshaw?
"small gift offered in thanks or as inducement, gratuity"
now isn't all this just too atrocious

"MOOTHWATERING HAMBURGUERS" — sign outside fast-food restaurant in Palma de Mallorca. "cumshaw" — kam sia: Xiamen dialect, port in SE China: "grateful thanks." Entered English in early 1800's.

17

draped in defiance & bewildered hair
not up to the waves of the task
ready for the big mallet   yet still chanting
"what vast sky wagons? what balloon yard?
what order to this?"
praying for door back to scale
begin the beguine may body begin
to turn the big barrel climb mountain
regain some sense of basic human
ever esurient for flash of meaning
our minds too orderly
in ways too predictable
so fill in the blank
between fedora and wingtip shoes

---

esurient — exhibiting hunger or greediness (Latin *esurire* = to be hungry).

18

as we glance out from our machine
time leaps ahead, slips away
into clumsy but sensitive entity's
invisible notebooks   but imagination
consists of desire   "professional desire —
it lit me, by god   from heavy top to toe"
who was that now was it my dear
irrational suspect, Perennially Dangerous
Adolescent? maybe however some'a dese young'uns
a bit too 'techno' for jaded old taste
(rolls back down, perplexed
by field of too much stuff)
ah short meander best meander
verbarium empty, once again

19

certainly privileged to have an
interior existence one likes
well . . . doesn't mind? sometimes even enjoys?
hard not to be bored by oneself
just another incoherent refugee
once radical high and true   oh long ago
in pow! pow! converse
been there what's the rush   wipe the screen
sway deep shade, opaque   bleak lacunae for sure
wrinkly, repeatable   thought to rip up
the book of small odes but was again charmed
by its miniature world so couldn't do it no
couldn't do it   now back to think on
idealized historical conduct vs. tendresse

---

tendresse = tenderness (Fr.)

20

came down the old oaken stairs he must also have trod
who wrote "old and young, we are all on our last cruise"
and "to know what you like is the beginning of wisdom
and of old age" or up those stairs again, to read: "the old
appear in conversation in two characters:
the critically silent
and the garrulous anecdotic"   Cousin Louis
who first met his Fanny here   thanks to Cousin Bob
who was the more dashing   the model for Alan Breck
and perhaps the dark Master of Ballantrae
when first we came here in August the pigeons next door
said coo-coo coo-coo   coo-coo coo-coo
but now in November it's only coo-coo-coo
coo-coo-coo   so, time to go, soon

21

oft turning others' leaves
calm is the sea; the waves work less and less
oh that my heart could hit upon a strain
would strike the music of my soul's desire
what joy seems half so rich from rapture won
as the loud laugh of maidens in the sun
when selfish greed becomes a social sin
the world's regeneration may begin
now slides the silent meteor on
shake hands forever my silly ghost
desire! desire, I have too dearly bought
with price of mangled mind thy worthless ware
an endless wind doth tear the sail apace
it is some picture on the margin wrought

Composed out of lines by Philip Sidney, Henry Howard, Nicholas Breton, John Clare, Ada Cambridge, Alfred Tennyson, Michael Drayton, Thomas More, William Drummond, and Thomas Wyatt.

22

"that the ants seem to wobble
as the morning sun catches their shadows"
not with us "too much" at all
not with us very long at all   the sun the ants
the wobbling shadows   all too hung up we be
on a civilization devoted to the speechless stare
punctuated by mindless speech
(& WHO is likely to read
these headthrob grumblespeak lyrics?)
"because they do not understand that cacophony
is at least as intricate an art   as harmony"
& she cries out in her dream "where are you going?"
infinitesimal moods for milliseconds
kindly provide a theme for   these variations

"that the ants seem to wobble / as the morning sun catches their shadows" — EP, Canto LXXX, p. 105 in *The Pisan Cantos* (London: Faber & Faber, 1949). "because they do not understand that cacophony is at least as intricate an art as harmony" — Basil Bunting, "The Lion and the Lizard," p. 30 in *Three Essays* (Durham: Basil Bunting Poetry Centre, 1994).

23

"I wish that life were an opera
I should like to live in one" said
Stevenson, Robert Louis
& les Surréalistes du Mid-Ouest
showed up at a reading
by the Reverend Robt. Bly   in Chicago
to (at least momentarily) estop
his woodnotes wild
with a large, vigorously &
accurately propelled
cream pie
"beauty will be convulsive" et cetera yes chérie
we must needs beg to differ with rare Ben
& let the Lybian lion hunt them butterflies

"les Surréalistes du Mid-Ouest" — "the Surrealists of the Midwest." They know who they are. Last two lines refer to Ben Jonson's "the Libyan lion hunts no butterflies" (To a Friend, an Epigram of Him).

24

only & always as old as who I'm talking to, no, with
then, how old am I when talking myself? to? with?
pondering practical martial origins of various ferocities
of man way past brain   that dark reviewed
tunnel doodles out of cognition igloo
thus head learns fictions
material life & arms o.k. but am I a dream
hurled & become a figment in groundswell
a noise of things settling on shelves
prattling selves   quavered elliptics
history shifting, sudden, us too
"surf's up, mister!"   o.k. I kill trees
it's barrel time, dear   time to watch
poppy fields billow in staunch wind

25

faintly flapping horizon of Symbolist project
fused in cosmic azure (French pronunciation)
brief clouds merge and pass
away away   into other vapors
"Hyperbole! from my mémoire
Triumphantly you rise today, grimoire"
ah, Stéphane Mallarmé
after a lifetime in classroom hell
translated Poe, but his students
never learned any English
neither did two of mine who attempted
yet another translation of the dice-toss
enshrined now in   exalted lacquer box
we have to think French to read him

"grimoire" — "a) piece of mumbo jumbo; illegible scrawl; unreadable scribble; b) magician's book of spells" (Collins-Robert French / English Dictionary). "in exalted lacquer box" — Mallarmé shared Whistler's and Manet's love of Japanese art and artifacts.

26

crackle crackle "good" "history"?
verify tales of each ego?
crackle crackle cerebral twitch
who slipped on the caviar?
who broke the hammer clavier?
& that was by Stupid Staggering Desirée
(Jean Baudrillard's favorite group) (who he?)
(I think he invented The Meter)
(well take him back to the meter office)
& that is so bad it's really kinda great
crackle crackle screeches whistles & ululations
(you say communists, bro? those really happen?)
hand me the righteous indignation   but first
let me negotiate this corniche

---

corniche — road built along cliff-lined coast.

27

walls dwellings built, streets paved
with stones from old ruined fortress
rue Wilson was the Grande Rue
first came modernism of subject matter
then came modernism of form(s)
followed by wiseass postmodernism
present company not excluded
those crepes were great
the tap is running
the lights just went out where are the candles
did we take some candles on board Mr Bosun
 aye aye Captain Dustball
but no land in sight it's a long haul
to daffodil land and galactopoiesis

"those crepes were great / the tap is running" — translation of this book's epigraph.
"galactopoiesis" — pertaining to the secretion of milk; but perhaps, and why not, to a "galactic poetics"?

28

lover walks out on friend   what a mosquito!
other friend almost dies in fire
"the phone was busy   so I was sure he was there"
firemen would not believe it at first
she insisted   he was brought out
greeted her with big smile a week later
totally wired hooked up still unable to speak
surrounded by terror we are yes indeedy
days of rocket up then straight down
when the good times don't roll no mo'
or they don't roll the way they used to
"Fings Ain't Wot They Used to Be"
sunny afternoon, London: Mr. Norman & Mr. Corso
imbibing Scotch in my study   Big Bad Boys Together

"Mr. Norman & Mr. Corso": the late Frank Norman, ex-convict, author of "Fings Ain't Wot" etc., successful East End musical directed by Joan Littlewood in the late Sixties; and Gregory the Herald.

29

in fragile days on frightful parapet
space sustains quest! eat art, Stéphane!
inside a stagecoach don your cuirass
sink into head's reanimated folds
torsos anthologized by gaze in days
of . . . thin black wind streaks into machine:
"space light on pocket students . . . dig j
oker dolly idol dirge censor . . . moose dada
maw finery nada soggy moan . . .
a-and as for my favorite christians
they're Fletcher Christian
Linda Christian   and The Magic Christian"
thanks Bill   now inscribed in grimoire
not easily deciphered by Proud to Be Dumb & Brawny School

"eat art, Stéphane" — Mallarmé, of course, who not only ate and drank it but was art. "thanks, Bill" — William S. Burroughs. Quite a treat, to have both these guys on the same page.

30

stalking the elusive ego? a bit like gravity
no one's ever seen one
nor do we really know how it works
"Vous etes Américain?" "Oui —
de l'Amérique de John Lennon"
geese honk on river, moped kids roar by
people are fond of the world's smallest dogs
a low-slung wire-haired bottlebrush kind
that likes to wear its eyes completely covered
since it can't really see anything anyway
& we've been here for years
wow, or "pouf!," as they say here
years like they used to make
not present souped-up blur-speed corporate model

"Vous êtes Américain?" "Oui — de l'Amérique de John Lennon." — "You're American ?" "Yes — from John Lennon's America." "& we've been here for years" — de facto, five months.

31

steer resolutely into the Dada channel
but hoist old pre-Raph flag now & again
as in "those lovely days of youth
when so often we thought
we'd die from laughing together"
wrote Madame Sévigné   those days are here and now
more than ever they were in my belle jeunesse
swans either dignified or hilarious
when upside down looking for alimentation
blue heron swoops overhead   blessings so many
ways beyond 'counting'   long had we sought
for nutts amid the shade   & though we're all busy
in this world building towers of Babel said Cousin Louis
life is a permanent possibility of sensation

"pre-Raph" — pre-Raphaelite. "belle jeunesse" — literally "beautiful youth": the original quote in French is "Cette belle jeunesse où nous avons souvent pensé crever de rire ensemble." "long had we sought for nutts amid the shade" — John Clare, *Nutting*. "Cousin Louis" — R.L. Stevenson.

32

now for some questions about As I Was Saying:
was As I Was Saying a pseudonym for Major Dustball?
or was he a member of the Cacademy of Amurkan Poets?
was As I Was Saying known? known to whom? known in France?
was As I Was Saying a positive profane development
(like "pie-ganism" in the UK)?
or was he just a fake jesus on horseback in buckskins
(like Buffalo Bill)?
was As I Was Saying a diffident dissident? a syllabubus?
a synopopsis? a fraggyloductus?
was As I Was Saying pumped full of vitamins,
ready to roll on the Eurostar?
where did he come from, this As I Was Saying?
where did he go?

"a fraggyloductus" — dream language; semantic signification unknown.

33

waiting   waiting for a loved one to return
waiting for air raid sirens
waiting as in the old French popular song
"J'attendrai"   waiting   repeating the word
boring as waiting can be   "Bored Again"
nice anti-fundamentalist bumper sticker
and so time curls slowly around
yet another bad anecdote   blue hour
a look both frightened and brave yes
we can make things fall from the sky
post-USA poets will ponder our programming
& its consequences in the third millennium
"remote ends are a dream" said Alex
the one with heart in his name

"said Alex" — Aleksandr Herzen: 1812–70, Russian revolutionary thinker and writer. "Herz": German for "heart".

34

be serious yes
can you / can't you be serious
yes and no
"the only important thing is to be
somebody's favorite composer"
come on somebody let me give you a hug
then let's sneak away
from old fill-in-the-blank school rhythms
on a ship in a storm
you're not going to wait for the verb
& when they asked the member of the English department
if there were any poets in the department:
"They don't have elephants
in the zoology department, do they?"

"the only important thing . . .": "I remember what [John] Cage once said to me when I was a very young man and looked him up for tutoring and advice. He asked me what I wanted with my music, and when I did not know what to answer, he asked me if I wanted to be a respected composer. Somewhat confused I answered, yes, I suppose so. Then he said, don't try that, the world is full of respected composers that nobody cares about. The only important thing is to be somebody's favorite composer." — Sten Hanson, Swedish poet & composer (member of Fylkingen group), in "Word Score Utterance Choreography," eds. Bob Cobbing & Lawrence Upton, London: Writers Forum, 1998. "on a ship in a storm" — my father, J.A. Hollo, on the comparative merits of English vs. German. "& when they asked" — thanks to Don Byrd for the anecdote.

35

scurry down bleak corridors in Gare du Cauchemar
conflicting arrows point to a spot in the floor
this is the way to your train, left, no, right
straight down, no, straight up
so, my dear, you'll just have to ROCKET out of here
as will the entire species in three hundred years
has someone said this before you? not to worry,
they'll do so again and there's no reason whatever
for this to be fourteen lines
or lines at all, come to think of it
right now I just want to get home to my desk
to translate another play of drab awfulness
which on the evidence of a show of "new art" we just saw
is the esthetic of these pretentious boonies

"Gare de Cauchemar" — "Nightmare Station," more specifically, the Gare de Lyon in Paris.
"show of 'new art'" — piles of rugs roped together; overblown photographs of nothing much; the umpteenth thousandth fake 'minimalist' surface . . .

36

and there was the 'art opening' in Moret
old gutted church floored with gravel
we were taken on a tour of the two young women's works
everyone stopping to listen to detailed explications
(French pronunciation) with copious quotes and references
to the works of French thinkers
spoken at levels of animation and velocity quite beyond
our capacity to follow
assembled Moretians classically polite & attentive
that was a year ago we twinkled at each other   still do
though there have been times not so twinkly this year
once again season turns leaves tumble off trees
once again happy birthday dear favorite painter
whose work speaks for itself!   and sings, and dances, too

37

consider “considerate”
best not to consider it too much
what was I after? the Colossus of Rhodes?
always adored   the mouse that roared
in zee canyons of Nueva York
gosh yes as the man said writing
allows you to weep and laugh all by yourself
& yes why not “chart the power codes” too
don’t you wish you knew who I’m talking to
or that I did or they did
oh she was just a little colossus
moaning in the dark   “it was so dark
in Sarvan Vistay”   but sky over Baghdad
’s now lit up again by expensive explosives

“writing allows you to” — Ramón Gomez de la Serna, “Greguerías”. “it was so dark” — line from a Swedish poet his co-translator Gunnar Harding and I used to giggle about back in the seventies.

38

returns, twilight-summoned, the master of dolorous speak
now click here for dazzling version of nothing
but hearts moated by joyful pessimism
sing with watery creatures, sleep in leaky boats
curtains on eyelids, dark laughter heard falling
out over ivy, with music, cut to tracer bullets
earth trembles under mysterious house on Closed Eyes Road
closed form is coffin, Pentagon is closed form
expensive explosives engulfed by fracturing stone
punctuate swarm of questions, “it’s all opaque”
watch the cerebral thermometer disintegrate
globules of mercury, angle of hand on keyboard
sparks of silence & nonsense fly up the chimney
longing: a kind of loitering, with no intent

“it’s all opaque” — Basil Bunting, in print and conversation. “longing: a kind of loitering” — response to Thomas A. Clark’s “longing is a kind of lingering.”

39

no "word count" in poetry
there used to be a "line count"
but nowadays even that
's become a little dubious   what's a "line"?
is it just pieces?
yes it's just bits and pieces
did G.A. Custer's ghost
flit through their conversation
(Fanny and Louis at Grez)?
but even so   a change
from the world as murder & alimentation
cats eat birds birds eat worms worms eat us
between words   silence
in the silence   a face

This poem consists of seventy-five words, arranged on fourteen lines. "did G.A. Custer's ghost": Robert Louis Stevenson met his wife-to-be Fanny Osbourne in the village of Grez-sur-Loing in July 1876, not long after Custer met La Muerte at the Greasy Grass on June 25. So, the answer is, presumably, yes.

40

how about just a few words
decoratively arranged on the page
with plenty of espace
between them around them
above and below, in good old
Mallarméan flotation mode?
lids on houses   mist over arches
of invisible speech to cast more light
"keylight?" on human window
thread of night   flash of jasmin
chickadee in the rain
away from guard rail identity
and all those bloody nations
in their implacable hats

"espace" — space (Fr.).

41

rare bright sunny December day in the Isle of France
WHY do I sit here & worry about a dead friend's book
due out 2 months ago? and WHO
are these hulks at cave mouth
waiting for brains to catch up with their stomachs? *)
flashed on a screen of ciel as bleu as my laptop's
"your query was all noise words, or blank
please make sure that at least one word
in your query is not a noise word"
but that was how we first summoned
faint image of life from dour spark
'noise words' relate things to one another
"because before between but" yes! BUT! & yes, BECAUSE!
*) probably right-wing members of United States Congress

"Isle of France" — Île de France, the administrative department surrounding Paris. "ciel" — sky, "bleu" — blue (Fr.).

42

streets of water sadness, self's knotty beast
and its unreadable mysteries
wrapped in above head, pilgrim of empty air
on days of pale silhouettes grappling through past
certain wor(l)ds have elusive time
it is what gets gazed upon
against the sky
but now move in on the question
beyond pages squandered
on long gone mirrors, memory coins
treacherous operettas
now say hand, street, soul
say friendly vegetable, profile of cat
summer tobacco, circling birds

43

In the jingle-jangle mornings I went following you
& you & you & you   (a love letter to the word "and")
"You see here before you," Guillaume said, "me"
Laments, Consolations   And what is not a quotation?
"Words, m'dear, words, not pretty pictures"
The leaves are detaching themselves
Letting gravity do its job
Go ahead, read Mr. Rumi, read Mr. Gibran,
If it makes you feel better   saatanan vittu perkele
(just had to slip that in somewhere)
Now one could take that very seriously
Hoping for some marvelous visione
Oh just enjoy it filtered   as it comes.
"Best oatmeal," said Harry Smith, "I ever had!"

"saatanan vittu perkele" — roughly, Finnish equivalent of "sh*t p*ss f*ck hell." visione: vision (It.) Harry Smith — the filmmaker, musicologist, magus, collector of cat's cradles and many other things. "Best oatmeal" — at Marie's on North Broadway, Boulder, Colorado. With Allen Ginsberg, another dear ghost.

44

time and desire their offspring devour
in heaven's forgetful snooze
that's from The Paleface Love Call Waltz
excuse me but which English are we now speaking
there's a poet writes these little machines
I must admit I quite like them
partly because I remember his smile
it is a nice smile   a famous smile
but right now I'm reading a French book of poems
in which the only proper noun is Raworth
"la lune noire de Raworth est rectangulaire"
so Tom has a dark moon? and it's rectangular?
hmm   specific weights of words different
in French poetic lexical table of elements

"la lune noire de . . ." — from Claude Royet-Journoud, Les natures indivisibles (Paris, Gallimard 1997). Claude is not the poet referred to in the preceding lines, although he, too, has a very nice smile.

45

some of the French no longer writing poems like that
celebrate the new year by trying to kill some birds
then silence swells   the product picks someone
democracy sinks   are we legends of grace?
who wanted to know that, what did you order,
who purchased these herbs   whom have the fires eaten?
the director turns "I must rule someone"
his umbrella a rose
the bank of his thought so unique a barrel
under a desk in the desert
between the jungle and the head
between this need and some other
falls the pleasure operator's
whisper: a valve of wonder

46

and these may well be
"snippets of impossible interiority"
"and that certain images be formed in the mind
                                        to remain there"
"or the bugs in Mrs. Jevons' hotel"
or coots, "foulques," small black diver birds
that rocket up   then straight down
on the pond near Grez
                    whence came the town's building stones
yes time is a voice goes a-roaming
on those soirées that leave small holograms
in the old brain cellos
(and no, that is not a typo,
even though first thought was cells)

"snippets of . . .": from a review of another poet's book by Steve Evans. "and that certain images . . .": Ezra Pound, *Pisan Cantos,* p. 30. "or the bugs . . .": ibid., p. 32.

47

and where is FORTUNE DUBOISGOBEY
woke up this morning to his echoing name
"author of sensational novels
with titles like 'The Severed Hand'
whose works occupy many columns
of the British Library catalogue"
the dusty rat barrel Paradiso of books
that were meant to be read fast
they were written fast   & they were gone real fast
EMILE GABORIAU! XAVIER DE MONTEPIN!
"in moments of effort one learns to do
the easy things people like"
said Cousin Louis who was a fan of those guys
they worked so hard   and so fast

Information on 19th century French pop authors from Louis Stott's "Robert Louis Stevenson & France" (Milton of Aberfoyle, Creag Darach Publications, 1994).

48

now back to States whose President
is bullied by the viciously lame
— cultural demons, embodied in ignorant power heads
(sadly, including his own) —
into facing sex mores Inquisition
unable to tell them "That, you sanctimonious slugs,
is none of your business!"
as the Scot poet psychologist who died playing tennis
once told innocent questioner plagued by internal rakshasas:
"Just tell them to FOCK OFF!"
watch out in the lands of fanatical hypocrites
smiling, unsmiling, they radiate spite
when this you read, liable you become
to conspiracy charges filed with their fiendish Goddy

"Scot poet psychologist who . . ." — R.D. Laing. author of a.o. "The Bird of Paradise" and "Knots." "rakshasas" — hungry demons.

49

the mouth had that turn that says lucky at cards
unlucky in love "no hay caminos, hay que caminar"
ah yes all the elegance twisting thro' our murderous empires
and their insistent vibraphone style
it reverberates in the evening air
as we circumambulate the church in Larchant
thirteenth century, burned & ruined for good
in the sixteenth by one Count Montgomery
former captain of Henri the Second's Scots Guards
after he happens to kill Henri "by mistake"
i.e. by driving a lance through his eye in a tournament
but as Cousin Louis once pointed out
"a man is never martyred in any honest sense
in the pursuit of his pleasure"

"no hay caminos, hay que caminar" — "no roads? keep walking!" (Sp.). Attributed to St John of the Cross.

50

ah Guillaume this aviation morning
the trees abloom with sirens
along avenues of ancient crimes
airworthy heads sail on slowly
chessmen chesswomen humming rose gas songs
(ah, those upswept hat brims, Goethe, Buffalo Bill)
while squawking bugles herald ragged centurions
risen from elderly fires in frozen starlight
now who could stay linear for more than five seconds
no need to call for cerebral backup
as life growls on through heaped-up space
rubbery distant othernesses
nor is key house but it lets you in
to evening's grace and a cup of coffee

51

yes 'twas an Arcady, le temps both weather and time
tread softly when you sneak across the border
find quiet spot to curl up, gaze
at chance to think
                              in work & think time
on close farness   structures curled back
in vaporous melody of life and lives,
breeze through the grand accordion of frames
watch reflections flounce
prattling selves, quavered elliptics
sink into head's reanimated folds
but don't forget where you keep your heart
and whom the fires have eaten.
mist over arches of invisible speech

52

Finnish word dream   clacks and alliterates:
"kolpakko, kapakka, kalpa"   tankard, tavern, épée
no doubt from early reading
of *The Three Musketeers* in Finnish
with footnotes that said "French pun: untranslatable"
and if I hadn't been born there
that would just be catacomb gibberish
wouldn't you rather dream of
Heidegger's Being and Frankenstein's Monster
hey what's wrong with Heidegger's Being
it's the ing, stupid
but there's not that much wrong
with Frankenstein's Monster, either
only the creature knows its awful secret joys

53

now no more late night city street drives
looking for A Lodging for the Night
at least not for a while   instead
early wet snowy drive home along Sheridan Avenue
big sign facing the road says
"Scoop Chinese Food: One Dollar"
ah Barcelona mornings in the Barrio Gótico
which English are we now speaking
the day and the hour are ends in themselves
said Aleksandr Herzen   not a means
to another day or another experience
a heart moated by joyful pessimism he was
he believed that remote ends were a dream
& that faith in them was a fatal illusion

"A Lodging for the Night" — Cousin Louis's wonderful story about the great 15th century poet François Villon.

54

joys sorrows but in miniature
candent flinders   none of this heavy stuff
like "tragedy — the protein of consciousness"
don't ask me who said that
fools like me can read the Tarot
but only God can make a carrot
what crowing eccentricity!
the director turns
surveys pale silhouettes
"I'll tell you what to do
while you're waiting for the bus
when the bus comes you're on your own"
legends of grace? sealed & farouche
now slides the silent meteor on

"candent" — glowing from or as if from great heat (first used by John Clare in 1577). "flinders" — splinters or fragments; probably of Scandinavian origin. "I'll tell you what to do . . .": Ted Berrigan in a Kerouac School workshop, 1978.

55

rebellious servants vandalized the viburnum
but venerable masons tended the heights
now those are timeless lines
from the quill of "poet humorist translator Anselm Hollo"
apostrophized thus by cultural workers
at the Daily Camera a pretty humorous name for a paper
founded back in the days when Rocky Mountain Joe
clambered these steep rocks with tripod & flowing locks
& Oscar Wilde recited the memoirs of Benvenuto Cellini
to Leadville miners ("the most elegant males
in the universe" said Oscar)
& they asked him to bring that Mr. Cellini along next time
when told that the dapper swordsman was dead and buried
in his native Italia they wanted to know "Who shot 'im?"

56

you're born and you grow and as you're growing up
things never quite happen in the right way
and you never get enough of everything
and then suddenly you're a little bit older
and you're getting too much of everything
and then you're quite a bit older
and everything hurts a little
then, alas, you die
                                        yes Ted yes it is very much like it
but you are the master of intelligent conversation
and no emotional slither   consummately gentle
stops and starts
                                    and rain makes us sad
because it reminds us of the time   when we were fish

The first eight lines are a verbatim quote from Ted Berrigan's Kerouac School workshop in 1978. Ezra Pound praised Mina Loy's poems for their "intelligent conversation vs. emotional slither." "it is very much like it" — Gertrude Stein. "and rain makes us sad" — Ramón Gomez de la Serna.

57

Just heard myself say
"That's as good as a Guggenheim,
Man!" But can't remember
What it was that was as good as a Guggenheim
Saw Peggy Guggenheim once, in Venice
With her little dogs in white tennis shoes
I mean she was wearing the shoes
But the dogs were nice & white, too
Write write delete delete
Some things there are that are unreadable
Poor Stuart Merrill   to take him out
Of the formaldehyde was a big mistake
But you read his works didn't you? Yes,
I did. And now you've read this, too

58

it was good the labor of building a citadel to the muse
that blows from the green fields and from the clouds
and the result was elevating thoughts
tunnel doodles out of cognition igloo
hope your floorboards settled   why are you mattering?
another speaker figures in you   composted & composed
yet stuck or struck for ever with an English tone or tune
that SOUND hits the EYEBALL — here comes the GHOST!
& as for the omission of essential grammatical elements
essential to whom is the question to ask
why should best minds groan under most distress
asked William Drummond & centuries later
Allen Ginsberg tried to answer that question
sway deep shade opaque   smoke between stars

"it was good . . .": from "The Enemy of the Citadel" by Max Jacob, as translated by Ted Berrigan. Lines 2 and 3 from Wordsworth, "The Prelude." "that SOUND hits . . .": "The human eyeball has a resonant frequency of 18 cycles per second . . . the eyeball may vibrate in sympathy to low-level waves causing a 'serious smearing of vision.'" — Guardian Weekly, 16 August 1998.

59

now this is getting a bit noir is it not
back here in the sauvage West
(still such a pretty savage)
but yes we do live in fear of an age
of the absolute rule of absolute greed
for absolute power (yes of and of)
wielded by bodies that live sans human souls
lumps devouring digesting and being digested
not what the "founding fathers"
(boorish little land "owners" that they were)
had in mind   this is bye-bye America
this is to put it mildly Hell
Cassandra remember her little Cassandra
her wail doth echo in these open spaces

"wielded by bodies . . .": "Now bodies live without the souls of men / Lumps being digested; monsters in our pride" — George Chapman, Hymnus in noctem.

60

oie blanche white goose in French "an innocent young thing"
not so young this one but certainly innocent
& not deserving of barbarous funnel torture for liver
distention the Gallic mangeurs so fondly practice
in Nemours supermarket mine eyes beheld a coq au vin
whole chicken crammed into bottle with dim reddish liquid
hail Damien Hirst! thy art doth put one off one's food
if that manner of food it be
nature herself will inform us Tertullian wrote
whether before gross eating and drinking we were not
of much more powerful intellect more sensitive feeling
than when the entire domicile of men's interior is stuffed
with meats inundated with wines and fermenting with filth
pull down thy arrogance French mangeur   pull down

"Hail Damien Hirst!": British artist who has exhibited cross-sections of cow carcasses immersed in formaldehyde. Tertullian (ca.160–240 CE) quote from his *On Feasting or Abstinence against the Carnal-Minded.* "mangeur"— eater.

61

impetuous bellows for attention
human or vole they all want attention! want
the gods and goddesses to descend & cuddle
them. yes. well. reality always tough
so we had romantic realism social(ist) realism
surrealism superrealism and they're all the same
mostly poor excuses for getting something down
on canvas paper film and tape
bees above ants ants above worms worms above plants
as above so below yesyes you heard that one before
his helmet now shall make a hive for bees
so why don't you kick nicotine & write some "Clean
and Well Literature"— eh? all right
here's a cookie: go sit in the corner

"bees above ants" etc.: Jain classification, hierarchical according to number of sensory organs. "his helmet now"— George Peele, Polyhymnia. "so why don't you . . .": Tom Raworth's book of poems *Clean and Well Lit* was listed as "Clean and Well Literature" on the Barnes and Noble website (10 February 1999). "all right / here's a cookie" — "You have to recognize the demons, or else they'll annoy you like mosquitoes. But if you acknowledge their existence, if you say, 'All right, here's a cookie: go sit in the corner,' then you can go about your work, and you don't have to go into a deep depression because of it." — James Broughton, interviewed by Jack Foley on KPFA, 1997.

62

yes Kai by historical happenstance
the jazz saxophone is indeed anglophone
"flying machines is perfect"
but when is that sentence correct
lines and lives to be reinserted
who can wait for the verb as we fly
through the accordion of frames
the if is the yew the holly the houx
"Mr. Andronicus?" "No, it's Sardonicus"
card in wrong slot all pains and sorrows
in miniature let's go visit the foot
how are you foot oh I'm O.K.
I bear the traces impressed on me
by Mr. World and Ms. Life

"yes Kai": Finnish poet Kai Nieminen who rhymed the two words. "Mr. World and Ms. Life": "I am finally faced only with the following question: to what extent have I succeeded in transposing into language, with the greatest precision, the traces impressed on me by world and life?" — Austrian poet Friederike Mayröcker (Mail Art).

63

has he returned with outrageous opinions?
oh no I find the place as beautiful as ever
apart from its tolerance of Salem's grim offspring
sometimes do wonder about all these folks
with their new houses new cars new children
they are of course willing to shed their blood & others'
in defense of their . . . their way of . . . life . . . ? yes? no?
but I'm glad to have shared some of the century's ride
with Armand the Scholar-Translator of *The Tablets*
his wild tenderness   serious fun   friendly learnedness
& (as the English used to say) "no side"
last painter to stay at the old Chevillon
was the American Walter Palmer   in 1914
"last one out turns off the lights"

"Salem's grim offspring" — the bafflingly resistant vicious strain of narrow- minded Calvinism that still afflicts U.S. American political discourse. "Armand" — Armand Schwerner (1927–1999), author of *The Tablets,* one of the century's major serial poems, in which he assumes the persona of "the scholar-translator." "last painter" — of the late 19th / early 20th century crowd at the Hotel Chevillon; since its renovation in 1994 it has once again become a retreat for artists and writers. 1914 was, of course, the year World War One began.

64

She of the White Hands flutters with doves
 around old Tour de Gannes
on foggy Grez (yes, gray!) mornings
past always more present when elsewhere
FRENCH POET SEES GERONIMO CANTER
    THROUGH JURASSIC PARK
so many places remembered
"the way the road turns
it's special"   trees arching over
on the way to the quarry ponds
in memory's Chinese boxes
you walk along you stop
you have little balloons with question marks
appear above your head
where was that?   was that me?

"She of the White Hands" — Blanche of Castile (1185–1252), queen of Louis VIII of France and regent during the minority of their son Louis IX, "Saint-Louis." During the later years of her son's reign she held court at Grez in a fortified castle whose only remains now are a few walls and the "Tour de Gannes," a ruined sandstone tower just off the present rue Wilson. "the way the road turns" — phrase remembered from Finnish poet Pentti Saarikoski's *Trilogy*.

65

fix some matter, eh? sit down in delight
to further it up   in photon-music's air
an anthology there
of laughing you — will it swell to a movie?
no, no drugs. just a kindly tome
of vintage conundrums submitted to you-all's future
by this morning's super performative
CROCUS   holding up through the afternoon
it's kept me seriously rolling
on with culture & major works
totally unwound   thanks to the French
sing with watery creatures
sleep in leaky boats   be a myth in the land
(let national disgrace proceed apace)

66

graceful awkwardness the mode
most suited to the disarmament of matter
in delirious over-amped atmosphere of Y2K US
the gift to be simple   it lives in a dimple
you don't say yes and it is bound for international
nay intergalactic acclaim
no question   any questions
well then let us recline
on the riverbank and watch
White Mama Goose of Grez
as fubsily majestic
she sails under the bridge
upstream and away
her honk reverberates   in evening air

"fubsy" — chubby and somewhat squat (U.K.).

from Braided River: New and Selected Poems 1965–2005

to Janey

from *The Man in the Treetop Hat (1968)*

First Ode for a Very Young Lady

Shamming accuracy
I was going to say
    she is spherical . . .

She is not,
she consists of
    two spheres

joined together
by not much of a neck
and six
    symmetrical protuberances
ears, arms, legs —

plus a small knob
in the center
    of the smaller sphere,
the one on top.

But this
    laborious
description of her shape
gives you no idea.
    She's round!

She's simply
round, and moves
in a manner
    not unlike rolling —
slowly . . .
    advancing
while remaining seated
very upright

towards
what attracts her
    attention, right now
the silent
    television set:

and there she is,
on the screen —
in full
        though slightly muted
                color . . .

It is
        without question
the best program
        of the day.

Of course,
I am thirty years older
and so
        our relationship
is deceptively easy:

countless
complications
will follow —

I hope
        they will,
I wish for decades
        of trouble with you
my daughter

wish it
        in the teeth of
                our monstrous days:

that the screen's
daily images
        of incessant war
and destruction

will fade
        and be superseded
by faces and forms
        of another degree

worthy of you, your
happy geometry.

A Lion or a Flower (for Mayakovsky, I Thought)

To all appearances a flower
on a stem
from the floor, behind that
to all appearances hotel or
boardinghouse window
rising, lonely
with his eyes in its petalled
head, dark, thickly
burning against the orange
at this late hour, and yet
the people, in passing, had to
smile. But we knew, about
windows at night in passing, so many
we had called out to only
to find it wasn't there anymore
only acid dust bottles and where
was the room the staircase?
In passing while looking for,
but it had gone back to the old house
or looking for what, for more
for a flower, a lion maybe
to make them smile in this city
at this late hour
at the cement mixers, at the dead
workingmen fast asleep in his eyes.

And How It Goes

Zoo-day, today
with the 2 young

"What animal
did you like best?"
"That man"

She's three, more perfect
than any future
I or any man
will lead her to

but now, to the gates
& wait for the boat
by the Regent's Canal

we stand in a queue
all tired, speechless

A line from Villon
sings into my head:
"Paradis paint"
"A painted paradise
where there are harps & lutes"

Yes and no children
but who say such pretty things
for me to inscribe
in one of my notebooks
with the many blank pages
marking the days
when I feel as forsaken as
balding François
who also found
in himself
the need to adore

as different as my stance is
here, in a queue of mums & dads
down the green slope
to the canal

— when he wrote to the Virgin
hypocrite, setting his words
to the quavers
of his mother's voice

le bon Dieu
knows where he'd left her

At least
I'm holding her hand
she's here, my daughter
he is here
"my son

the lives of the poets
even the greatest, are dull
& serve as warnings"

To say this, suddenly
here, in the queue
would no doubt be brave

He's half asleep,
clutching a plastic lion

"The thing is, they could not
get out of themselves
any better than these
who also wait
for a boat
— o that it were drunken
on what wild seas —
they didn't
even try, just griped about it
or made little idols
for brighter moments . . ."

The boat has arrived
and there,
the elephant's trumpet,
farewell

Her weight on my knees
His head on my shoulder
                    here
                    we
                    go

We, best-loved animals
one, two, three
      and as illuminated
      as we'll ever be

from *Spring Cleaning Greens (1973)*

In Northernmost Michigan

there is this old Finn
sits on a lakeside park bench
with a bottle of wine
looking out over the land-
scape of his youth

only it isn't
the landscape of his youth
but an amazingly life-
like simulation
on this other planet

from *No Complaints (1983)*

Fool's Paradise

"You
live in a Fool's Paradise . . ."

"Yes! It's *home*!"

Cells grow tree
and in it,
heavy cicadas

They finite
We gone

*

Stop, dear Mozart:
You're making me cry

*

"Sure *I* killed a bunch of Chinese —
they're *tall* —
them Veetnamese are *small* —"

Handsome man in his thirties
clean and with it   pickin' up a sixpack

looks perfectly capable

but is given to these fits of weeping

*

Ginkgo tree
was here
before dinosaurs

*

Sometimes I feel like an idiot boychild
longing for Mama Ocean

Oh would you ride with the religious?

Oh no I'm just an old crank

Now that the old confusions
have been moved out and junked
the heart looks rather empty

"Boy, you gotta carry that weight"
I remember it well   that song

and mushrooms have been here all along

*

Watch it
go by

"Oil is an act of God"
"Come Home to America"

"You always laughed at those things
it took a little time   but you laughed"

Someone in movie   Some remarkable dreck
I step into, slip

"You've sublimated that into 'oops-a-daisy'"

Dreaming, deprogramming then awake
convulsed with rage-mirth at suave golem-blather
chewed ends of blond-gray Fu Manchu
grown out of stoned middle-aged chin

Object speaks
Object has spoken

in irritable parentheses

*

Smash bad faith (pretense) says the feathered speaker
sweet shoes goofy grace and heartbreak kid
What happened to us Fred   My little arm hurts
in the great Dracula organ roar of existence

*

Queen Anne's Lace out my window, Virginia
I don't have to go to the bloody store every day

But where else is there to go in this bloody place
or any other place in this bloody society
this bloody monolith of "store"

And when I say bloody I mean bloody   Like Joseph Spero
mob *store* operator in Kansas City
"accidentally exploded" a while ago

"After all, the old bum is your father"
as Buster Keaton pointed out a while ago

*

In the great return engagements
between the nineteenth and twentieth centuries
we'll experience many surprises

As for the news, it's still punched in and out
by obedient punks   I know, I was one
for almost a decade

Until one day on a very ordinary bus
suddenly deprived of impressions   I became aware
once more   Of the painful and weary
and tired of all sensational beauty tips tricks and freebies

It was the time of early to mid-period Rolling Stones
Their diction was excellent then   It was a help
as was Herbert Marcuse

*

There's this Assyrian rite
survives in southern Italy:

a year after death,
you dig up bones

and take them home,
and polish them, and talk to them.

"Dear Aunt Maria,
Dear Uncle Gesualdo" et cetera
All night, all day
you polish them, talk to them,

then put them back
in the ground.

*

Buenas dias, Argentina.
Buenas dias, Cambodia.

Buenas dias, Russia.
Buenas dias, America.

*

Stars   Stars   All around

The airborne laser lab

    New god of all good Soviets
                good Americans

Some of them some of us positive roses

Like those blooming in wild Russian jungle garden
around this house now

There's obvious love in some houses

But Queen Anne's Lace no way out cowboy hats no way out

It's time time again to come out of the cave

(and go to the store)

*

James Dean
now dead
as long as he was alive
to himself

An amusing distinction

*

"So you really want to know how it is with me?"
As some poet might say in that strange place
known as translation
in muffled gutturals one strains to hear
the other side of massive airlock glass

Well, everything's pretty great really
but for poverty illness mortality   and so on

Language it   Think   Thing big
Big Sentence

Then let no more remain
than of Doc Hipponax

Doc Hipponax

Hip Dog

*

We tend to think the world sort of stands up
while all it really does is roll around

Women's laughter through crickets and tree frogs

*

Hum hum twilight's
Halloween, year's
dusk   Every day   Diodoros
of Aspendos

redeems the culture vultures

Sleazeville Collegeville Pentagon

Hospital follies   A long cold drive

And bathroom mirror says
"Old man, some bloody *sense*!"

(Remember the Professor
whose name translates as garbage?)

Diodoros   Two teeth left, barefoot, grinning
"Broad beans? Sure, I'll have some"

with the blue eyes of a bay scallop
at this best when alone and confused   At large

*

Hum hum   "You gotta serve somebody"
Ah, the new self-righteous righteousness:

"They behaved like sickening pigs"
What a way to speak of your elders

But when the new self-righteous righteous
speakers and singers look up
they see their "Lord"

When they look down
they see shit on their shoes

"What a self-indulgent jackoff!"
I hear you say

But I do not understand those phonemes

Because I am Diodoros
of Aspendos   Pythagorean
of the last days   Disguised as a Cynic

*

This faded purple box of five thousand
"Standard Swingline Staples Number S.F. Minus One"
has lasted me through
a marriage or two
almost a dozen addresses phone numbers
defunct checking accounts
seven years and some months
and I still have a couple of hundred left

*

Max Jacob: a moment's thought to
Max Jacob

Just a little artist
caught in the roiling of time hands grabbed him out of—

believed in weeding, they did,
and he was a weed

flowered beyond and above
the greatest French garden

was plucked and destroyed by those hands in black gloves:
regulation SS, acronym for SchutzStaffel

"Protective Squadron." Protective of what?
Of another little artist, a weed

grew like killer kudzu all over Europe
was burned off her face not much later

Both their seeds still circle the planet.

*

Pissing on open grave of last morning's mouse
trapped in the house

Three a.m. Sweet Briar Virginia

Quiet   Madness   Insomnia   Tequila

Old Charles Laughton horror movie "Strange Door"

Dust whale vacuum cleaner in corner and now
it's one hundred degrees and I understand nothing
though still attentive just like the cat

to grotesque collective regressive manifestation:
some doddering lopsided smiler
our future leader?

Pea-brained predatory type
repeated several thousand times over   gleeful   jumping
up, down   blowing whistles   punching
little balloons in the air

back pockets stuffed with truly oily bills

mad baby grins   bubbling   manic brain soup

"America   Behave   Or Be Damned"

That's Baptist billboard

You take deep breath   And drive on by

*

Sure's been nice to meet all you people
the complicated simple
the simple complicated
the complicated complicated
the simple simple

Not as exciting as it was for your ancestors
or was it   confronting Red Cloud's negotiators

Just like you, like them, I've come to the end of the push:
the Beach Boys' concert

Finn Swede German Pole
and various smaller fractions Anglo Dutch and Martian
citoyen du monde

by the light of your campfires
                    shopping malls
                    museums
                    and a few good bars

No way to go now but out

Let's figure it out

*

"Right side of face hurts more than the left"
Another pointless statement

Thousands upon thousands of those
made in this life   until it is over

Music fades in and out

Beat stays the same

*

Now "le beau reste"
as our French sisters say   *ah oui!*
where do we go from here?

Round the page

We'll just go gamboling round the page once again

and then

let's kill

all the bad guys

let's have

all the good guys

over for dinner

"What's for dinner?"

"Bad guys"

Ralhar (2004)

The Long Hiss of Time

the way they pop up now
late in this life
the dead & the living
technicolor   black & white

different parts of the brain
begin talking to each other
in a new way
small children reappear

& now they are either dead
or alive as film directors
record producers high tech designers

but some ancients are still present too
even more ancient than this, this brain life
— still hesitant before typing that single comma

looks out the window thinks squirrels
are not very contemplative
but the cats watching them
are

30 Oct 04

"different parts of this brain" — paraphrase of Andrew Duncan on Jeremy Prynne: "different parts of his brain began talking to each other in a new way."

So you start out you come across some writing
You fall in love with at first sight
It says what you feel you always wanted to say
Exactly that way   & it seems so easy to say it that way
You write some of your own that is more
Or less like this writing you have fallen in love with
Then there's a shift

& you fall in love with some other writing
& again & again & then some mean elder
Says oh he he just writes
Like everyone whose writing he's fallen in love with
& you remember that you still remember that
40 years later & feel foolish for remembering
That Mean Thing

---

listen
                    to the long hiss of time
given a functional
time-reverse machine
who wouldn't mind
a second childhood

one would be better equipped
to deal with one's parents

but being a poet it's hard
to imagine a society
that wouldn't think one a parasite

or as archaic as
let's say a   "mule skinner"

poets, poems = telepathic
landing pads

so here one sits
                                                            "airside"
waiting for long-ago vessel
sailed into one's dream last night

29 October 04

"airside" — analogous to "poolside"; term first observed at Heathrow airport.

On Reading Certain Novels

halfway through this "family saga"
I no longer care to keep track of who is who
as they go on darting about and "having" "conversations"

affirming our kinship with all that walk fly crawl
that's what they're doing
that is all they're doing

it is enough
no matter what order they're doing it in
& who is whose nephew uncle mother mistress or niece

it's like a big treetop full of twittering birds
& I was so lucky to find my little branch long ago
at quite some distance from the rest

Thirty years later
back in Ann Arbor
Music sounds much the same

"Thirty years later"
sounds insane!
Who can be that old!
Here, in Mr. Greek's Coney Island
On State Street, Ann Arbor
(the "Athens of the Midwest")

Yes, Ha-Ha Yoga
Was the discipline then:

Get a little high, then get a little higher

Are they "fond"
those memories
Or did they just get a little fonder?

for Andrew and Susan Carrigan

---

wind gusts changes sky from blue to white
above carpet of crabapples under the tree
flickers flicker through air

tremendous lightning strike two nights ago
gave me the flesh of the hen for half a second
then water poured from the sky

          — no, I'm not turning into a "nature poet"
but the little green house you built for me
does make me notice a few more things in the universe
to add to my "Notes on the Possibilities and Attractions
   of Existence"
               and I never imagined I could be so unjealous
of my loved one's art
               even when it takes her away from me
for many evenings and mornings and nights inbetween
but o I make myself a joy of it
                              to see her again

---

see laughing delegates
gobble your granola

deftly screw then unscrew you
from their history

later walk into dust storm
contemplatively

unless you really want to kill
someone, a gun

is just another expensive
ultimately disappointing object

quite unlike a patch
Love planted.

o hold me tight — !
Signed,
Old Bones

28 October 04

From the Sayings of Chairman Ted

"People that are feeling wonderful
will tell you that God is love,
which is not much help
when you've stepped on a tack
or something. On the other hand,
people who've just stepped on a tack
will tell you that life is shit,
which you frankly don't believe very well
when you've just had a milkshake.
If you want to say that God is love,
you should throw in
a few milkshakes at least,
so one will understand
where you got this feeling."

"Chairman Ted" — Ted Berrigan, in one of his lectures at Naropa University.

These Bookshelves a Forest of Poetry

Thelonious in a glade
"Just You, Just Me"

Well   love is love   God
Just a word

The old ram's still alive
The beautiful lion cub died

(why did it take me so bloody long
to get to be any good at all?)

    Read for how it's DONE
    Not what it SAYS

PEOPLE tell stories
GOD does NOT tell stories

    but PEOPLE DO

        all the time

IX:04

Cat Pome

Epitaphs? Eulogies?
For the ones I loved, still love —
I resent their departing,
always too soon. So what can I say?
For the ones I hated, still hate —
well, I wish them too bon voyage.
In very general terms.
For the ones I never felt
anything much about,
it makes too little of a difference
for me to force myself to say anything.
But, ah, Phinney: you were a pal
impeccable to the end
in your little tuxedo!

IX:04

"But, ah, Phinney" — nineteen-year-old female feline, one of the gentlest and bravest of her kind, passed away in the Fall of 2004.

Ever Poem

hard to figure what people think "works"

ever
if ever
how ever
when ever
never ever
ever ever
ever & ever & ever

does it not all depend on how fussy you want to be

oh
I'm just
standing here
thinking

hard to figure what people think "works"

II:04

Ralhar

well . . . I guess dying
will be
just one of those

not-a-whole-lotta-fun
"things to do"
but autumn
is when

I would like to come back
if I could
to watch
the stars come out

& RALHAR!

my loves

with all of you

Ralhar — old Occitan — to babble, to joke; origin of "to rail (against)," but also of "raillery."

Mardi

Ay, sí: "The other place"
Where the most abstruse
(Intimate?)
Connections are made

The "impossibly private"
Versus the
"Oo-ee, baby"
School of thought

Ah, Tuesday
Mardi — here you are
So now I'll be able
To live for ever: walk

From the Chateau Impermanence
To The Temple of Emphasis and Motion
No rain in my space suit
"Oh don't you wish"

"Ah, Tuesday / Mardi" — the scribe has always liked this personification of Tuesday, and her French name in particular (it resonates with Kerouac's "Mardou" in The Subterraneans).

Lyckan

Stand by the door of the old orphanage
in Visby, north in the world

where last night we watched
this watery globe

roll back and away from the sun
"A tiny tick just walked across my arm"

Talk to small Swedish tuxedo cat
in the blustery morning

tell her you better not mess
with that big bumblebee

Go back in   Coffee is ready
Good morning, Janey!

"What are those weathervanes?"
"They're WHALES"

"Lyckan" — Swedish for "happiness," "good fortune." Cognate of "luck," but primary meaning is happiness (which now tends to sound sappy in English).

"How is it far if you can think of it?"
It's still far. Sometimes too far. Too far
To even think of —
So let's do the outer space shuffle
On this inner space shuttle

& think of some more something
In small but sweet helpings . . .

"O dear love I'm so glad
You did not have to escape
To that Plywood Motel!"

Signed, The American Pebble

No, you can't sign that — who are you, anyway?

"I'm The American Pebble, author of
The 100 Best-Loved Poems of the American Pebble"

for Philip Whalen

---

riding the thermals all the time BORING
sometimes you just flap   caw caw   but yes
we would like for something
much bigger than us

to be conscious
& live much longer
than we do

that's how we get religion

she is indeed une ancienne
& makes our thoughts stumble
back to the past

back to long-gone freckled boogie nights
lost scarves & drunken couplings

"Is this where you wanted to go, sir?"

"une ancienne" (Fr) — an old flame.

Moving the books was like moving brain cells
— vittu helvetti pissa kakka —
Now those be powerful words
The words any five-year-old
In the land of my "origin" used to

Used to use to enrage their elders
          (still does, probably)

But "only" five million persons will say
"Did you HEAR what that kid just said?"

Definitely an item from the Forbidden Apartments

Ah yes 'tis important to find
Your "self"
Consistently interesting
In a consistent spirit of self-mockery

---

it is 9 p.m. and you're not up for it
not up for writing this essay on the "major" poet
not up for answering a "minor" correspondent
not up for a roll in the hi with your love, aye aye aye
you feel like Sir Dragon Rider on your windowsill
     most cobweb-overgrown
who is this?   why is you telling you this?
what does you care what you is up for?
"oh I think I'll just go to Yurrup
my miniature desktop Yurrup: a miniature Fifties Citroën
a miniature Highland bull a miniature lighthouse
perched on a stack of diskettes"   aye
the way she came down the stairs, the erstwhile Rockette
one evening   in the old incoherences

"the old incoherences" — the last two lines refer back to a Sixties poem of mine, "The Coherences."

"I cannot be making a mistake
about the fact that I have just had lunch"
French onion soup, in fact, at "Le Français"
like pasta, one of those foods
that involve moments of apprehension:
stringy cheese floats on top
and my crude pasta strategy
simply to cut it up with fork and knife
won't work, since you're supposed to eat it
with a spoon. Subsequently, feelings of satisfaction
and satiety when one has managed to ingest it
without getting too much cheese on whiskers or clothing;
BUT "Perhaps no person can be a poet, or even enjoy poetry,
without a certain unsoundness of mind"

"I cannot be . . ." — Ludwig Wittgenstein, On Certainty. "Perhaps no person . . ." — Thomas Babbington Macaulay.

---

walking down oldtime hotel lobby corridor
high ceiling white half-paneled walls tall doors chandeliers?
I've been in this building before! it is intricate & I know
there is a pleasant cafe
in a brightly lit spiral core section up ahead
now man looks like truncated tubby Ezra P
comes up alongside on my left trying to hand me
small white & red pamphlet, I need to pee
so signal to him to give it to Jane (to my right)
we're all just really striding along CUT
I get up slip on rug bang leg damaged in March
against chest of drawers SHIT SHIT SHIT
CUT back to sleep, next morning wonder,
where is that place? where is any "place"?

---

was born coiffed (né coiffé)
not mute as a carp (muet comme une carpe)
old bones I hoped to make (faire de vieux os)
with some heart in the belly (coeur au ventre)
outlived the midday demon (le démon de midi)
a fine fly (une fine mouche)
without faith or law (sans foi ni loi)
on the straw (sur la paille) sometimes
at times not there (je n'y suis pas)
but not of the same tobacco (du même tabac)
a lone horseman (cavalier seul)
trying to catch the cadence (attraper la cadence)
to the great never (au grand jamais)
found myself with not a cat (pas un chat)
was a white cabbage (chou blanc)
scraping the bottoms of drawers (les fonds de tiroirs)
by the light of the one
that stays awake
(la veilleuse)

for Alice Notley

Composed entirely out of literal translations of French idioms. Their actual meanings are not always apparent. "La veilleuse" — night light.

---

brain hovers above keyboard
cat slips in curls up
nothing comes to mind
then something comes too
they do a pas de deux
and that (if you ask me)
is la méthode
— so, no more epic awe code!
dig the streets!
come on up out of your whale!

wade ashore! hear gravel crunch!
use lots of exclamation points!
warble with ironic witch
'til dawn does closely fold you in

"'til dawn . . .": paraphrase of a line by Edward Arlington Robinson.

---

wave motion green as text
can't even begin to imagine not hanging
on to these tatters while counting nights and days
says the wanderer but you have to wrap them around
some sort of core   fanfares of long gone
cheerful hours candles stand on a drum
draws knife edge across thumbnail
can you kill death with this
there are days on the plains when one can see
all the way to the sea
sea's breaking on hefty beach says the wanderer
now gone a million years
hear dusk roar air ash fish hair
rapidamente siempre rapidamente

rattle like arrow-shafts in a quiver
wizard bliss mighty music all very well
& good says the wanderer but are they
catching up with us well they don't sound
as good as we did
exeunt omnes
the place hasn't changed all that much
the human being is punched in the nose
he or she must have
in order to ensure that every viewer
gets the message
o seethe with this sound

lull tomes   ports of lore

for Tom Raworth

---

excellent excellent
what could be more excellent
than the memorable
the memorable? what is it
what is it that's so memorable?
was it something he said?
yes yes that's it! it was something he said!
he said "look up at the sky"
that's what he said he said
"look up at the sky"
so that's what I do when not thinking
about how to save the art
from Elephantiasis Americanus
I look up at the sky

"that's what he said" — he: Allen Ginsberg. I think he was quoting one of his gurus who had told him to do this whenever he felt "down."

The Royal Hunt of the Sun just a memory
in this soap opera life   as are The Phantom
& Mandrake — "loser" superheroes?

& "love oh love oh foolish love"
it's the same old brain
wallowing in ambivalence

I've lived here forty years
but she says Anselm I think
you're still a little naïve
about America

and I say well yes Holy Jayzuss I guess I am

just like Genghis Khan's man
what choice did he have?

small shaggy rider on small shaggy horse
but to pick up the reins

18 Nov 04

That mouse that mouse
I'm sure was very dear
It came out of its little house
In the compost pile
And our cat ate it
It is now part of the cat

Who also is very dear
Muchos dolares
In veterinarian's bills
Due to his fight with another cat
Who a while back intruded
On his hunting ground

I.e., the compost pile.
We hate that other cat!
Well, we don't really
We're too nice to hate

But we sure wish he could be disarmed

The tastemakers will go on
Until they need pacemakers
They always do

And as for the secret history
Correction: histories
Of la poésie américaine
No one repeat no one
Will ever get it "right"
It will be revised   and revised again

Yes lives of quiet desperation
Quote unquote said Douglas Oliver
As we walked the quiet streets of Nemours

Read his poems
He got quite a few things "right"

Douglas Oliver (1937–2000), one of the United Kingdom's most excellent poets of the second half of the twentieth century.

Satyricon

Thinking about successions . . .
Here comes a message from Aubrey Beardsley
(forwarded by EP): "Beauty so very difficult"
Damn straight! As is the sublime, think of Mozart
They buried him sub lime

And when they told Maurice Ravel "your requiem
For the WW1 dead is too cheerful"
His comeback: "The dead are sad enough
      in their eternal fire"

After Papa Doc   came Baby Doc
Now Baby Shrub has succeeded Papa Shrub (twice!)

And when the people no longer speak anything but teevee
And you don't even have a set in your hut —

Signed, Proud to Be An Aberration of the Sixties

Going Home

"We're going home"
said convicted robber
Robert Carroll Coney, seventy-six,
when with his common-law wife
he departed
the Angelina County jail
in Lufkin, Texas

after a judge found
that his confession
to a 1962 robbery
had been extracted by sheriffs
who crushed his fingers
between cell bars.

Coney had served
forty years.

IX:04

for Carl Rakosi

puzzled
        watching people
                use this weird gesture
probably learned from television

FORGIVE ME, FOR I AM ANCIENT

though I can still remember my time
with the young masters of "inappropriate" laughter
and frequent enjoyable use
of "fatigue management tools"

    caught in a time warp the senator
    puts both feet in his mouth
    then cringes in desperate loop

"resting comfortably" equals "unconscious"

            ah, Language

"fatigue management tools" — recent (2003) U.S. Air Force term for amphetamines.

A Double for Jack Collom

Sort of a tough day, this, albeit sunny —
All the leaves positively shooting off their trees —
Where are my glasses? Where's my bag of tricks?
If you think this is me talking, you may be right
But I too would rather listen to Karl
Who speaking of Heinrich had this to say:
"I love him as much as his works
And do not mind his political weaknesses —
Poets, you see, are queer fish, and must be allowed
To go their own ways. They should not be assessed
By the measure of ordinary or even extraordinary men."
Thank you, Karl. I love you too, across the centuries.
You my man. As is Heinrich, who unfortunately
Loses more in translation than you do.

But you, dear Jack, and I can read him in German
and hope to share his self-savaging wit
in Dichtkunst and Kunstdichtung
ah to motor along the beaches of Boulder with you
in a convoy of heroic young figures on skates
past twenty-five foot plexiglass prairie dog
with flashing red eyes above twenty-eighth street
then return to our stille Kammer
to dream up more verbal outrage
here in the going-under of the evening land what a
    botched job
terraforming Earth in our image has been
but as long as we keep on throwing out the baby
of sentimentality with the bath water of shlock
there is hope and I don't know about faith but love for sure

Karl — Karl Marx. Heinrich — Heinrich Heine. Quote gleaned from Eleanor Marx's memoir. Dichtkunst — art of poetry; Kunstdichtung — art poetry. stille Kammer — quiet chamber. going under of the evening land — literal translation of original title of Oswald Spengler's "Decline of the West."

a lot of commotion kerplunk and galumph
death birth marriage pluridirectional fuss
no time to pursue thread of night   flash of jasmin
or the age of chivalry's ever attractive awfulness
message just in from Sir Andrew Aguecheek
"I'm a great eater of beef,
and I believe that does harm to my wit"
sorry can't help you time to give up those steaks I guess
"writes love poems in exchange for steaks at the local grill"
"YI! WE MUST BE IN ARR-HENTINA!"
aye, meat eats meat, some meat survives to just die and rot
blue heron, theatrical, walks fine line
amid the overall music of the line
all that to say and wish a good night before going to bed

"Sir Andrew Aguecheek" — Twelfth Night I, sc iii, 92. "amid the overall music" — Doug Oliver: "The best way to show stress patterns in a line is to obtain a fundamental frequency intonation contour using glottal electrodes and then try to work out how the hell you can identify the stresses amid the overall music of the line."

after a third go-around with The Emperor
now it's Don Pablo "skinnydipping in the scent of blue"
in 1936 but quite in line with contempo
reading practice: "cutting the scent of silence
in a tree of dormant candles"
masks of mad joy surges of colocynth genius
green eyes in black furry face — no, that's Zophiel the Cat
"dust hiding under the jangling bed
smells like a burnt wooden shoe . . .
and the amorous song of the raven
frightened by its shadow
shattered into a thousand pieces"
but now it's Buddhist year 2542
so, no Y2K panick here

1999

"with The Emperor" — poet Paavo Haavikko, his nickname in Finnish PoMo circles: I had completed a third version of a selection from his work (the first two were published in 1968 and 1991). "now it's Don Pablo" — Picasso: collaborating on a selection of his poems edited by Jerome Rothenberg and Pierre Joris. Lines between quotation marks are from these works. "colocynth" — "bitter apple": gourd family, purgative.

They sit on some of the furniture
and talk about houses, talk about rooms
and try to remember exactly
what they looked like, those houses and rooms.
Then they argue about it.
They sit on some of the furniture
but have other furniture they never sit on.
That other furniture
they worship. Outside
a recent (still alive) Poet Laureate strides
down main campus promenade with pensive mug,
black polo shirt, matching shorts (toga better?)
under old trees, thinks of how to go Rilke
one or two "better". Et cetera

O to be in Nueva York
now that April's here
or some other utterly GONE place
trains sough through the night
on waves of old world debris
tuxedos in dining cars
shiny polyglot flesh
gazes of glowing inclination
incoming message reads
"he barely escaped with this life"
yes you manage to escape from one box
only to find they're trying to cram you into another
or else they say Oh you don't want to be in this box?
Well then, they say, you don't really EXIST

A Bit of Hades (2004)

Faintly a brabble all cadence no words
rolls on in the night you wish you were
"The Tenant of Wildfell Hall" stilted and lovely
under the stars   but no stars here
look   a humvee has landed
                    on the roof below
a traffic light spider
        marches across the ceiling
many ideas   shine in the dark
the nights do get long the man said he was right
flat on your back you listen to the stations
of your body   FM AM short wave
what happened to long wave
that's what you'd like to ride   a long long wave

---

down down into the city of the dead
no more cars on crumbled avenues
grass grows through the asphalt's cracks
drizzle turns everything pale
green around darker patches of moss

reel along in the murk slide down steep hillside
into dark quarter lit by trashcan fires
tall buildings stores boarded-up dim lights
in upstairs windows

where has he gone   ask the men on the corner
ah they say the old boss man yes? yes he up there
on the top floor last house on the corner
you say you knew him when he was a big shot?
well no one's a big shot here

---

can only love you like a sister she says
in mute sorrow the Master of Toggenburg
tears himself loose swings his steed
graveward he roils   to commit large acts in the holy land
when he returns
                    "she you seek to god is given
veiled before him bows   yestermorn the bride of heaven
    sealed her marriage vows"
reel along in the murk remembering poem by Freddy Schiller
    Englished by Connie Naden (1858–1889)

"and a little hut he raises looking towards the glade
where the convent darkly gazes from the linen shade:
waiting from the morn's first blushing till the sunset shone
silent hope his features flushing sat he there alone"

& whythehell do I remember this bullshit when I've just died

"The Master of Toggenburg" — faux-medieval ballad by German poet Friedrich Schiller, translated by American poet Constance Naden. Toggenburg in Switzerland is renowned for its excellent breed of goats, popular among U.S. breeders. The anything but goatish Master of Toggenburg has become a German byword as an example of amorous loyalty pushed to absurd extremes. My mother would say "Don't be such a Toggenburger" when I pined for my high school sweetheart.

reel along in the murk
when sudden light floods the cobbles
in front of your muddy boots
        it's a door
                    & no it's not Jayzuss
        not Pallas Athena
                                not your Mum
but a large sea bird in late summer sky

& things find you
water and crystal
                    & kinds of glass
through which you drop down and feign death
                    until danger has passed
            among curious and not unattractive noises

Remembering how Paul Blackburn Made Those Old Troubadours Sound

"Old age not for sissies" — pas de question!
"May you stay
        forever young" — a big fat lie. Pas de question.
"Don't be so literal" (well, maybe he is
        that literal kind of poet. Perceval,
        if you wish, so dumb he seems brilliant).
Where were we. Ah, my lady, it is your birthday tomorrow
& I wish for you all the happiness humanly possible
        in this totally fucked-up world. I know,
        "fucked-up" is not polite parlance — does,
        in fact, indicate an impoverishment of the author's
        language — yet
        I think, my lady, you will agree it is not
                entirely inapposite, non? HOwever. It is,
has been, & one hopes, will be for a while longer
my incredible good fortune to share lives
        with you, My lady,
        & only the gods know what you, as they say,
        "get out of it"
but I do know that you are my Paradiso
(my secular paradiso: Oh, I'm so secular!)
& that I can't even begin to express my gratitude
        in any but this, the most private yet public way,
        mon amour
        who slept next to me on a narrow cot
        while I made my way back from the devastated
        yet deeply bewitching cities of the dead
                through many a night.
        And in my conscious moments, my love for you
        knew, & knows, no bounds, except for those
prescribed by present, early twenty-first century,
        impossibility
                to live
                        for ever
                                with you

2003 / 2004

from Notes

Braided River

The title of this book comes from something Peter Warshall, poet, biologist, peaceful eco-warrior extraordinaire once said in a talk at Naropa University: "Life's not a tree but a braided river."

Fool's Paradise

Diodoros of Aspendos was one of the few survivors (who often masqueraded as cynics) of the anti-Pythagorean purges in the 6th century BCE. They were active in politics, and their opposition to accepted religion caused them to be persecuted from existence in Magna Graecia. Orthodox followers of Pythagoras never partook of beans.

In its cento-like passages, this poem incorporates brief quotes from films, television, radio, Robert Grenier, Lorine Niedecker, Don Marquis, John Sjoberg, Laurie McElroy, Ludwig Wittgenstein, James Schuyler, Walter Benjamin, Edmund Spenser, Bob Dylan, and probably others.

Guests of Space

to Janey
and all our artist and poet friends

Guests of Space I

Guten Tag Herr Schopenhauer Bonjour Monsieur Cioran
good morning Mr. Swift how are you Mr. Burroughs
once again history the unstoppable proves you right
species no better than smart rat (maybe not even as smart)
evolutionary leap? my foot, my foot in three-foot hole
but let all peaceful mutants leap for spring
calloo callay, while they still may —
watch it! don't twist that ankle!
don't step into that three-foot hole!
"and wisdom has not come" "against wisdom as such"
oh, it is apt to give a gopher tantrums!
anecdotal befuddlement. infinite terminators.
toujours a mountain eased a previous you;
should it feel easier, writing? I don't think so. No.

"and wisdom has not come": "Wisdom has not come, says Pollagoras. Speech keeps strangling itself, but wisdom has not come." — Henri Michaux, *The Old Age of Pollagoras* (trl. by Laura Wright). "against wisdom as such" — Charles Olson, in *Against Wisdom as Such,* pp. 260—264, *Collected Prose*: "I take it that wisdom, like style, is the man — that it is not extricable in any sort of a statement of itself . . ." "gopher tantrums" — minor "Ghost Tantras."

---

here have I summed my sighs, playing cards with the dead
in a broke-down shack on the old memory banks
e'en though my thoughts like hounds
pursue me through swift speedy time
feathered with flying hours
but could have sat there for many more hours
listened to poet friends reading
words by an absent friend whose work we love
in the name of Annah the Allmaiziful,
the Everliving, the bringer of plurabilities
concretized, concertized, temporally minute

progressions of actions, swirling mists of the past
"you have a lot of stuff here, you know?"
"yes   now run on home"

"here have I summed my sighs": Samuel Daniel, *Delia*: Sonnet I. "e'en though my thoughts like hounds": conflated lines from Delia, Sonnets V and XXXIV. "in the name of Annah": James Joyce, *Finnegans Wake.*

Once you've said something, you can't unsay it
Once you haven't said anything, it remains unsaid
and anything you can't say, well, it's unsayable
All right now that we got that out of the way
we need some particulars
but where did I put them, where are my particulars?
"Here they are, sir." Oh, thanks. Today's mail:
3 books of poems, 1 cigar catalogue
the poems look great, so does the catalogue
"But aren't you trying to quit?"
Mel Tormé died, Charismatic didn't make it today
the fifth of June nineteen-ninety-nine
And in a restaurant called The Europa Ninety-three
warlords consult on a respite from murder and mayhem

"in a restaurant called . . ." Located on the border between Macedonia and Kosovo, the "Europa" was *bought* by NATO for a meeting between Yugoslav and NATO military commanders.

---

i.m. Hannes Hollo

Fought the hungry ghosts here on Earth
"What is man?" asked the King
Alcuin's reply: "A guest of space." And time yes time:
The past lies before us, the future comes up from behind
Walking on Primrose Hill or Isle of Wight beaches
Iowa City streets scrambling up snow-covered deer track
To Doc Holliday's grave in Glenwood Springs
His helmet now shall make a hive for bees
He fought the hungry ghosts here on Earth
Strong & resourceful on his best days,
Patient kind and *presente*
Returning those with him to here & now
But just as we settle in with our Pepsi and popcorn
THE END rolls up   too soon   always too soon

"'What is man?' asked the King": Pippin, son of Charlemagne, 9th century C.E. "His helmet now . . .": George Peele, *Polyhymnia.*

---

and of course it won't do, it won't do at all
Herzen again: "Suffering inescapable,
infallible knowledge
neither attainable nor needed"
sound of swans' wings
over the quarry ponds at Grez
look up! the departed sail on
to some picture-book Norway
and Mr. P old ga-ga cantor
among the ruins of Europe
writes to his missus "where are they?
where are they?" old "genius" snows falling
on his head in his head
(no, it won't do, it won't do at all)

"Herzen again" — Aleksandr Herzen (1812–70), Russian revolutionary thinker and writer, "the one with heart in his name."

Private they are, the sums of grief, "impossibly private"
"There probably is some intelligence at work here"
"Yes, but I don't want to know what it is"
Elizabethans considered a nosebleed a symptom of love
But if 'n the wind don't blow through it   it don't make it
& what if the 'personal' prove as tiresome as the 'public'?
Mawkish messages to the dear departed? No
That is not given to you to do
Nor can you really get behind idealized forebears
Getting wiped out while attacking some barn
"Did you say *barn*?" In the glorious South or any other
Cardinal direction. & now this old Cardinal
(Universal Life Church) hums
Cani capilli mei compedes   "Gray hairs are my chains"

Against meaning, lunatic, real,
Possible in appearance, you work a line,
Be like a larger logic to defy
The dumbly trembling unities
(quotation fringe is blue)
Your self helps us from prose & down
Into an orange: "Hail my effort, you people"
"Stand and deliver!"
But stubborn world is time & airy dung
Insists on legible distance, inhabited heaps
"As Lacan points out"
Never mind what Never mind Never mind
Sing the old huddles (persons bowed down
With age or heavy wraps

& should I buy this *Scientific American*
to see how the quest for immortality is going?
got the one on space exploration
. . . such incredible hardships ahead . . .
calling twenty-nine-ninety-nine in this old English
but we are just learning to walk
and time is a voice goes a-roaming
"just a chickadee in the rain"
Green House almost ready now
oh they too have their troubles
the belovèd intuitive abstract expressive painter
the ever-distracted monkish poet
musing upon the Malevich square on Hitler's upper lip
and the fact that "questo" does not mean "quest"

---

the human being talks it talks
and talks and talks   even to
itself   so "hating speech" what was
that about? no speak no talk no read no write
now that sounds like the dead except
some of them do read them-
    selves into our ears
day and night
    when The Slinger passed on
    it left me restless
    the way one was restless
    after a teenage rendezvous
"driving somewhere, fast
with the windows rolled down"

"so 'hating speech'" — a reference to Robert Grenier's notorious statement "I hate speech."
"driving somewhere, fast": my daughter Tamsin's memory of Edward Dorn, from when she was 5 years old.

"would that it were otherwyse"

        one eyebrow raised
        Sir Thomas listens to his quill

(check Wyatt quote) (can't find,
it's not a Wyatt quote) (so what,
it's you   trying to sound like him)

    o would that it were otherwyse
    friends did not have to die

Andrei Voznesensky, in Iowa:

"TRAH-DZHED-DEE OV ARTIS EEZZ: ARTIS HAFF TO *DIE*"

bye-bye Fielding
bye-bye
Falstaffian
fun

Fielding — Fielding Dawson, master of USAmerican poetic prose: 1930–2001.

I'll write a poem about nothing
absolutely nothing
not about myself
or youth or love or any person
I'll write it riding along
half asleep in the sun
and then I'll send it to a friend
signed, William of Aquitaine
nine hundred years ago
and ever since we've raged
in shirts red black and blue
we've raged still do
in our dream rooms asking the air
mad questions about nothing

The Duke of Poitou's poem can be found on page 7 of Paul Blackburn's *Proensa: An Anthology of Troubadour Poetry.* For the shirts, see Ted Berrigan's *The Sonnets.*

Equipped with human heart's dizzy gyroscope
In the yellow submarine we lived oh my darlings
Is it now all just imaging?
No more imagining   in The Momentous Events
In Small Rooms Hotel   the brain is?
"Don't remember the time I was born
Don't want to remember the time I die"
Old troll stands in secret memory garden
Gazes at mirror globe's beloved faces
Through time they move as "guests of space"
Yes that we are he thinks remembers Alcuin's answer
When Pippin son of Carolus asked him "what is man"
& Cousin Louis: "You will always do wrong
You must try to get used to that, my son"

"human heart's dizzy gyroscope" — Tristan Tzara, *Poem for a Dress Designed by Madame Sonia Delaunay.* "Old troll" — "Moomin Papa" in Tove Jansson's great *Moomintroll Saga.* "Cousin Louis" —Robert Louis Stevenson.

My first computer:
Poor old workhorse machine
Just an advanced version of the clay tablet
Archaic box, you still work
Humming that hum I found so irritating
22 years ago
            (used to say "this thing's
            no smarter than an amoeba")
Waiting for me to write
A word and then another
And another
But I shouldn't have said what I said just then
Because only a few days later
It went from hum to loud groan   And died

There's words, and there's hair
And hair and hair . . . Would you know
Evocative if you saw it?
Or have you not had the Enigma
Reversal Experience?
"What's that? What's that?"
They cringe and snarl
It has to do with the minutely sensational
Say I, with what's little enough but enough
As when you turn the radio on
And it is the right music
Even when It introduces sadness
And one understands little
Of what's going on

---

and thus we woo our wit with gentle memoranda
birthday thoughts about mother long gone
& her madcap cocaine-addled sister
Aunt Karin I never knew, her son cousin Peter
ever wistful but such a smile   now gone too
dusk road games   dust road fumes
REALITY IS WET today
"How big is the mind?
How could we avoid dissolving
in our own private oceans?"
asks Randolph Healy dear Irish poet
beat, beat   "It's a strange, strange world we live in,
Captain Jack"   and who was that and why
(look up at the sky, bro, look up at the sky)

"(look up at the sky, bro, . . ." — Allen Ginsberg's recommendation for states of mild depression.

all that fifties-style
wretchedly splendid
better living through chemistry
when people said things
like "haven't I seen you somewhere before"
always worried about hitting exactly wrong note
hence tall strung-out conversations
with hypothetically beautiful persons
remember those? but now
I am pissed off at you old sport
even though you are dead
to my regret & possibly even yours
no longer hanging on to tatters of poetic mantle
or moth-eaten unacknowledged legislator's wig

Addressed to no one in particular; a composite (possibly even self-) "portrait."

You
are not the Countess of Tripoli

And I
am not dead yet
unlike Jaufre Rudel
So now I can tell you about
The most interesting metrics of The Horse
To wit, the *rack,* the *fox trot,* the *amble*
Four-beat gaits with each beat
Evenly spaced gliding and smooth
In perfect cadence and rapid succession
The legs on either side move together
The hind leg striking the ground
Slightly before the foreleg!
Vraiment,
Poetry can be so many more things
Than what people mostly believe it is.

And there were years when nobody died.

"Countess of Tripoli," "Jaufre Rudel" — "Jaufre Rudel [. . .] fell in love with the countess of Tripoli without ever having seen her [. . .] because of his desire to see her, he took the cross and put to sea. He took sick on board the vessel, and at Tripoli they thought he was dead and carried him to an inn. When it was known to the countess, she came to him, to his bed, and took him in her arms. [. . .] Then he died in her arms." — Paul Blackburn, *Proensa.*

Guests of Space II

When in a mood of fair-
Ground music mortality   Drift
Down Feral Boulevard
Wearing your sentimental formal
To the bar called "The Far"
Sit down to a think
I won't be back
You won't be back
He She It won't
Nor will We You They
In the Twenty-First's air
And none of them
Will ever want to hear
From whom they haven't heard *of*

---

make big fat sounds
list the two or more places
where you'd like to be
at once and more than once
where questioning every question
hasn't killed all questions
(at least not yet)
and all is long damp hedgehog love
on a perennial sunny tourist morning
then go there ASAP
and send me a postcard
that postcard will be this poem
wish you were there already
wish I was here

---

perhaps we exist
as the notes of the string exist

back when all was continuous chuckles
a trembling fringe of cryptonyms
hermetics winking in the magic tree
sweet as Bizet's *Fair Maid of Perth*
ah but those lovely *hoarse* 15th century horns
(now it's cool again to be "passionate")
old man thunder rolling o'er the hills tonight
the open window full of logic you tell yourself
that via this literality
you may recover a semblance of body
"certain things happen
& continue, they exist in us
by a species of recurrence,
they fall   vividly into our days & nights"

Epigraph and last four lines from Ezra Pound's *A Walking Tour in Southern France* (ed. Richard Sieburth).

---

from up there on the ridge
the successful manufacturer of vacuum cleaners
surveys the valley: ah,
all those little lights —
each one of them a "home"
with at least one of
his dear machines!
it is festive
it is the festival of Saint Retail
that ends every good U.S. American's year —
martinis über alles!
but bellicose poem no buy dinner
but the sea slug remembers everything, you hear?
It remembers Everything

"but the sea slug" — sea slugs have been immensely helpful to human memory and dopamine receptor research.

Now that was pretty simple-minded wasn't it.
A dog barks in the dark. It's simple-minded.
It probably belongs to some simple-minded person
who cannot understand what the dog wants. The dog wants
some simple-minded attention,
that's all it wants. 2. ~~So softly stirs~~
3. So stubborn are the boots
walking an old man. His matter hesitates
where there are doors among the glaciers
furred with brine. O softly stirs, when he goes out,
the next-door cat, pees on the holy book
under his pillow. So the old guy grits his teeth
and wishes for that song "She Is a Country Woman"
to call him back to the bars of? Late Modernism?

What's current? I mean misheard?
Currently misheard? Shelf dancing? Alpine badminton?
Now write a sampling on one leg
Of composed being with shaky eyelids
Who tells you "I am in the art, but molecular
Only by dint of a visiting pillow;
I am the author of *Author.*"
Now shall we agree, say I, before the bar is toothpicks
That poetry is a chicken in good mud-tennis weather?
Such tube-lit discourse. Ten dollars a waltz.
No tidy archery. So sell me that bumper, no, I meant
The mouse calliope, yes, that's it! The ego
Seriously in tears at the holy beneath
Dangerous furry feelings — beware the hole punch
Of darkness, shrunk from the world.
So. One mouse calliope, please.

In this world of snickering squirrels
Who gives a hoot for Jesus in a box
Or was it his brother? the one not begot
By Zeus. One much prefers
Even the obvious, but if you must be obvious
Keep it brief — with maybe a witty touch.
Lissen, lemme tellya sumpn, says Lemmy
Caution, the tough guy of many French movies
I don't give a rat's ass if you don't
Think that's funny. You don't think that's funny?
Them squirrels sure think it's funny.
He sure was a caution, that Lemmy,
He was. And an Italian mile is a thousand paces,
So is a verst on Mother Russia's roads.

Lemmy Caution — Runyonesque character in pulp novels by British author Peter Cheyney. French filmmakers based a number of thrillers on Cheyney's books, with craggy Algerian-French actor Eddie Constantine as Lemmy, who also appeared (as Lemmy) in Jean-Luc Godard's *Alphaville*.

Past middle-aged, I enjoy the Middle Ages (some-
What) in Visby, Gotland. In Visby, Gotland
in the Baltic Center for Writers and Translators
the fire alarm goes off three times a night
without fail. A brace of Mormon missionaries describes
their Utah religion to a group of Medieval Swedes
one of whom wants to know "But where is this AMERICA?"
Jane finds a sheet of paper in her night table drawer:
"Writers are at their best when they have no idea
what they are doing." It says this in Swedish,
attributes it to Nelson Algren (in Visby, Gotland).
Shouldershooting Duck: A Manual is a book
I find in Visby, Gotland but do not buy.
Be here now. Then be there, then. In Visby, Gotland.

"An ancient land animal"   Man in wheelchair
comes rolling out of old folks' home
I hold the door open for him

He looks at me, says "WIND'S PICKIN' UP . . ."
rolls on down the slope to the parking lot

not heading for any car! but the good old Open Road
— I'm beginning to have my doubts

when a nurse comes charging after him
an air of disapproval about her

she turns him around and pushes . . .
I help her pull the chair back up the slope

They perform a successful reentry

"So a lot of time has passed   But without
the imagined future having come to pass"

"'An ancient land animal'" and "'So a lot of time . . . to pass'": Carla Harryman, discussing the part of "Reptile" in her *Memory Play*. I was assigned that part in a reading of the play one summer at Naropa in the nineties.

Bright sunny "garden" apartment
A euphemism for basement, like
The one in San Fran
Where late the L=A=N=G=U=A=G=E poets sang
But bigger bay
Window out to street
Sitting with someone in some
"Waiting excitement"
Big black limousine or hearse?
Pulls up, hey it's my mother
Amy!, elegant in black with black
Toque or perhaps medium-brimmed hat
Veil in back, gets out
We embrace, she (sort of) groans

---

my mother was not The Great Mother
your mother was not The Great Mother
even though they were pretty great
there were times when they were not so great
but they were just human beings
like you and me
and that goes for all The Great Fathers too
that said "a short discussion followed
during which Tony Lopez raised poignant questions"
but I wasn't there and I bet you weren't either
but in weird dreams
recumbent incoherence
our parental molecules   long dispersed
do make the odd return appearance

Glazed with alcohol, old sailor
Reels into me on Stockholm street — "Heyy, you old fucker!
How are ya! Remember the times in Veracruz?"
(And he is not "Stetson" and I am not T. S. Eliot)
What *would* you say to the ones you lost if they appeared
Before you as themselves, as who they *were,*
Not merely these phenotypes
That surface now and again in bodies, faces, in ways
They gaze back, mirror your own puzzled look?
Uh, welcome back? Long time no see? Where have you been,
And how? Or oh, it's been so long . . . But that
Is what those puzzled eyes do say
Before they turn back to the living
(Who needs to dwell more than half a second in Hades)

Tracking down some of the (now unreadable) books of my youth
Proves nonproductive   So now to get back to where
Fabulous meets Nebulous? But no they've booked passage
With ANT TRAVEL, INC.: an agency
Whose motto is IN DOG WE TRUST
& playing with fire when it burns Yeatsianly low no good

"Don't have a home in this world any more"
Some ways he never did have much of a one
Mon *fils* but who am I
To say what the world is

"What was it I just remembered?"
"The 10,000 little resentments"

Felt a little like crying   Or maybe burning a couch
Like some of the ignorant human spawn of this burg

They discussed the Code of the West
"Plan your moves   Pick your place
Don't make any threats   Don't walk away ever"
Enter in black fur coat
Mournful eccentric   Songs of lamentation
Evening at Donnelly's Pub in Iowa City
Thirty-plus years ago
"You look just like Frankenstein's Monster!"
What to do but grin back at him
With bad original teeth: "I AM HE!"
And this is way too literal
So hand me that drug of Egyptian origin
Mentioned in the *Odyssey*
Before the guys with the torches arrive

"They discussed . . ." — reference to a recurring line in Ted Berrigan's *The Sonnets.* "'Plan your moves . . ." — text in a collage made by Ted and Alice Notley from the 1970s.

IT WAS ALL RIGHT
or, What I Learned from Kenneth Koch

It was all right to be funny   all possible kinds of funny
It was all right to be erudite
All right to use as many words of the English language
        as you could possibly come up with
All right to be elegant   all right to be rowdy
But never all right to be pompous
It was all right to be modern   and postmodern and premodern
All right to be all of those at the same time
All right to be for intelligence and kindness
        and against hypocrisy and dumb power
All right to believe in your wishes lies and dreams
All right to tell what you had never told anyone
All right to be a poet   a lover   a lover of words
All right   it was all right   thank you Kenneth
Thank you for *Thank You and Other Poems*
So many   other   poems

Hundreds of prisoners of the motor car
grind past this office window every minute.

A league is an hour's walk.
A lecture is an hour's talk.

A *li* — a hundredth of a day's march.
No one's counting but you.
And an uphill *li* is shorter
but takes longer
than a downhill *li*.

Millions are dying! Millions being born!
And here he sits worrying about his sick cat.
That's all right, Anselm,
says the central committee
of a million gods. We're counting you, too.

Traveling into the past on the Internet
I see an old friend from forty years ago
Now dead five years. He hasn't changed a bit.
Or listening to a tape there are lots of feathers
Another friend's feathery voice
Stilled in a mix of blood and French gasoline.
Deserters both of them, one from Hitler's army
The other from consensus reality:
"When he was good he was just mildly insane
When he was bad he was out of his mind"
& into another we could not know.
And this is one of those "long ago" poems.
They did give me courage: I still run
On some of their *essence.* They were fine *déserteurs.*

"essence" in French — gasoline. The friends: Anton Fuchs, Austrian novelist and short story writer, 1920–1995. Piero Heliczer, American poet and filmmaker, 1937–1993.

On the tenth of March, two thousand and three
Bix Beiderbecke
would have been a hundred years old
just like
Carl Rakosi,
then still alive.

Did Carl and I ever listen
to Hector Berlioz?
I do remember
listening to the *Symphonie Fantastique*
with Gregory Corso, up in his little room
with a view of London's Primrose Hill
where Sylvia Plath walked with her young . . .

"Time is a great teacher,"
said Hector Berlioz,
"but unfortunately
it kills all its pupils."

So the Ants Made It to the Cat Food

---

now that some of the young ones
have taken to writing
like Eugene Jolas and Elsa von Freytag again
(if not quite as vigorously)
(pass the thesaurus, said the dinosaurus)
we may once again enjoy the "oh I see
(s)he just found out about that" experience
ready for the impending product
besieged by books looks at a book:
"this I have read" looks at another:
"this I should read"   picks a book off a pile
"now where in the hell did this come from?"
memory browser stumped   old owl
just a slip of a girl

"Eugene Jolas and Elsa von Freytag-Loringhoven" — early 20th century avantgardists; see Jerome Rothenberg's anthology *Revolution of the Word* and biographies of William Carlos Williams.

---

cannon goes boom boom   canon goes round and round
every decoding's another encoding
& when the teachings haven't
quite   sunk in . . . it may be quite interesting
but could be more interesting
just isn't interesting enough
"admired, he lets his work
warp back into itself
for this, he admires himself"
but where is she? what happened to herself?
then there's the awkwardly dwarfish
sculpture of Mr. Robert Frost
in front of Colorado's "Old Main"
slung a little too low for pigeons to shit on

---

lives deaths “A Life”
three days with A Life
of one who painted meticulous magic
in 1930s Paris, Antibes
great c l a r i t a s   more than in anyone’s cantos
. . . rough seas lately but . . . “I can hear birdies” . . .
now Rudy’s gone to join Edwin in death pond
old Hem one hundred
he steeled my heart for heartbreak
cursor flicks across screen
“shut your eyes hard
against the recollection of your sins
do not be afraid
you will not be able to forget them”

“three days with ‘A Life’ ” — Amanda Vaill’s biography of Gerald and Sarah Murphy. “now Rudy’s gone” — Rudy Burckhardt; “Edwin” — Edwin Denby. “old Hem” — Ernest Hemingway. “‘shut your eyes hard . . .’” — R. L. Stevenson.

....rue Blue
where we stopt between rattling journeys
...................................noon street people
..................like seaweed mocks the water
.................................glide swirl oratorio
....................in the world’s pretty pinions
..............................long company of time
...........“and the Cristo came back as a fly
with a million eyes” ....
daylight crackles ....behold the garden
pale record of selves...............................
....just an asterisk
.....................................this is an asterisk
(example of asterisk)................................

"Successions of words so agreeable"
Yes they are yes they are
So agreeable successions of words are agreeable
& a great deal of it all was Greek at first
Before it was Roman the way it still is
Ah the simplicity of those lives
Oh no there are no simple lives
So many hours per place
So many ladders of grief
Now is this all about the great themes as listed:
Death! Truth! Meaning of Life!
Love! Romanticism! Loss! Reality! Consciousness!
Symptoms of universe we be
And we pray for an end to idiocy

"'Successions of words are so agreeable'" — Gertrude Stein. "great themes as listed" — on Gale Research poetry web site. "Symptoms of universe" — Alan Watts: "We are the symptoms of the universe."

"The range of cultural & historical reference
& information in the mass and popular media
is remarkably limited"
French popular writers have a thing
about fucking on top of motorcycles:
the beast with 2 backs
doing a hundred and twenty
But I am just learning to talk
"How could we avoid dissolving
in our own private oceans?"
Life squiggles on
perchance to leave a record forlorn
private impossibly private
(I thought it was Red Bug Dermatitis)

"'The range . . .'" and "'How could we avoid . . .'" — USAmerican poet Charles Bernstein and Irish poet Randolph Healy in e-mail tertulias. Tertulia — Spanish for regular, informal, literary, or artistic gathering. Last parenthetical line refers to the scribe's case of shingles.

Why am I reading this ill-written tome
About the lousy life of a 19th century hoodlum
With a big knife? Because
It just might help me understand
A particular strain of USAmericano "mentality"
That resists Evolution
Tooth and Nail   Handgun and Literal Bible
(irritable parenthesis: big knife too messy now)
The Protocols of Elders of WASP
But now to think of a better subject
Irwin Catullus who passed away
Three years ago to this day
He cultivated a different strain, the one
That brought me here   To be a guest of this space

"a 19th century hoodlum" — Jim Bowie. "Irwin Catullus" — Allen Ginsberg; "to this day" — April 5 (1997).

---

inkling   in/kling   ink/ling
Norse "enkel" equals single equals simple
Middle Dutch "enckelinge" — a falling or
    diminishing of notes
Middle English a whisper, a murmur, low speaking
a hint, an intimation
                "To inkle the truth"
actual instance of speech
years lost in the alleys of making
minimal unities of meaning
possible in a line
Eluard: the Earth is blue like an orange
& I'm just a tepid heart inhabiting The Blossom
with tactful terrorism. The tear-stained screed

Things people say
"I think you're a very lonely man" said one
Another one said her friend said
"He's just a sentimental lumberjack"
I must have reminded her of Jack Kouack
Sentimental sí Lumberjack NO
More like a jolly garden gnome
And as for lonely no I don't think so
More like lonesome which is American
As American as applejack by the quart
A favorite among Iowa Writers' Workshop
Lumberjacks   A dead or dying breed
Can't believe I am saying these things
People say   These things, these things

---

so the ants made it to the cat food
but then you scrape them into the compost

one day we'll set out under solar sail
to the systems of fifty new planets
discovered this year

who knows if we'll do any better
than these ants you think
then contemplate vast grids upon grids
shifting and twisting
clashing and jelling flowing apart exploding

shrinking   to this little blob of cat food
in the kitchen sink
oh it gives one the flesh of the hen
comme on dit en français.   cat disappears into bush

"comme on dit en français" — as they say in French.

PRODUCING UNSALEABLE FOR . . .
HOW DEE DO . . .
THAT POETRY'S SMART TWADDLE MY MAN
LE PARADIS N'EST PAS ARTIFICIEL
PRETTY LOT. DO A THERE.
SO ABOUT, OR THEY THEN?
WELL SHE PRETTY, AND OF
IS. WE MODERN,
PREMODERN. THE THE. WHAT'S THE DIFF?
SELF-RIGHTEOUS ASSHOLES
BENT ON THEIR POWER & THAT.
OF THEIR HIDEOUS OFFSPRING.
ALL CAMPS. HELL ARTIFICIAL TOO
ON LITTUL BOOL.

"le paradis n'est pas artificiel" (Fr.) — "paradise is not artificial": Ezra Pound, in response to Baudelaire's *Les paradis artificiels.* "bool" — boule (Fr.) — ball (globe). This is a "treated graffito" sonnet.

All of last year's farewells
in this Piranesi
parking lot
"Seems we can't get to the right level"
"Hope to see you again"
Bye-bye Haa Tsay Aytch See Art Man
"Vissi d'arte, vissi d'amore"
Whence this Italian that keeps creeping in?
Old Ez? Joe C? Piero? old bones
remember young bones now old, too
have lived for art and lived for love
how many to a pillow sprouting wings? en la memoria
He sure was one funny monocle
a living breathing *House of Usher* played as high comedy

"Bye-bye Haa Tsay . . ." — H. C. Artmann, the postmodern Austrian troubadour, wit, bon vivant, great terrible lovable guy, d. 2000 C.E. The last two lines refer to him, as well.

& then we went
Alice and Doug and Jane and Anselm
(small sample of us featherless bipeds
who measure conscious existence in paltry decades)
to have some diner at the old inn
with its sign to inform us that Victor Hugo
had "descended" there   for a night or two

And that was only a little more
than two turns around the sun
                                        ago   ago
And the gods have slain many since then
and so have the people
                                        Yes, so have the people
the riders of the purple rage

"History always written by the victors"
(Confederacy sure disproved that adage)

"to have some diner" — "diner" to be pronounced in French, approximately "diné."

---

this is not the bear this is a picture of the bear
's big head   stunned then deleted

newspaper story: Old Grizzly "Falls Creek Male"
aged 22 years   for 15 of those avoided traps
outsmarted humans killed dozens of cattle
"worth up to a total of $200,000"
finally trapped given lethal injection
April 18 in Bozeman Montana

he did not know that those cattle were MEANT for food
for humans who couldn't kill a cow if they tried
were MEANT to send the rancher's kids to "college"

were MEANT to perpetuate one of stupidest cultures
ever constructed on this planet

this is not the bear this is a picture of the bear

Speech balloon above head reads “Does poetry help?”
The answer to that is only if you can turn your head
Three hundred and sixty degrees, then turn it
Faster and faster, so it becomes a fuzzy blur —
In other words, if you’re an owl! But you’re not an owl,
You’re a person. Persons need house,
But persons need persons more. “SHUT UP DOG!”
Who was that? He’s right. Ah, life:
“Sometimes I see it as a straightforward
Linear equation
Drawled with a pendant and a rumen
Transfiguring the circulation of the worm.”
That was a quote from our new Poet Laureate,
Somewhat improved by “seven up or down.”

“‘seven up or down’” — Oulipian method of replacing nouns in an existing text by other nouns occurring in a dictionary “seven up or down” from the original ones.

The Guy in the Little Room

In the back of your mind is this little room, and in that little room is this guy, and that guy, if you read lots of poems all the time, that guy will learn everything about poetry, about form, and shape, and when you make your poems, that guy will take care of all the technical details. All you have to do is write those poems. But that guy, you got to feed that guy plenty of material all the time, or else that guy will start raising a giant ruckus in the back of your head, and you'll think you're going crazy. It's only because you're not keeping that guy busy, you know. And that's true — believe me.

— TED BERRIGAN

So now they have pressed
Their singular gods into service again
"A pillar of fire by night A pillar of smoke by day"
Twenty-four hours before that massacre
In the city garden not far away
I saw that wing-lamed crow
Pursued by the landlady's sweet-faced cat
Shooed it away and the bird
Managed to flap over the wall
Into the garden next door where Ted Berrigan
Composed a "Poem Written in the Traditional Manner"
Forty years ago: "I summon
To myself sad silent thoughts,
Opulent, sinister, and cold."

So it's a return engagement between
The Short-Sighted Corporate Greed Heads
& The Nothing-to-Lose Religious Fanatics

Unbridled capitalism
Versus "adolescent disease
Of humankind" (Arthur C. Clarke)

"The days of fun and waste are over"
"Someone has hanged himself in a rectangular emptiness"

Yes people are scary
People who fall in love with a singular god
Are really scary
50 million dead in World War Two
The end of honorable warriordom
If ever there was such a thing (10 million in WWI)

now that the empire done struck back
how come everybody's feeling like merde
head full of rubble is that a metaphor no
sounds like a headache to me
statuesque angel drifts by how nice but no
it is hauling a banner that says
NO IDEAS BUT IN HAMBURGERS!
should one pretend to be very pained
when one is simply fed up and grouchy
"there is some shit i will not eat"
yes that's a quote oh boy I used to wonder
how anyone could end up looking
like winston churchill
but he was an angel

compared to these neo-beowolves
yes evil is live spelled backwards, by dog
is that him over there
waving his hefty defense budget
"fat free! flat rate!" stop cluttering my mind!
was that the author yes he just left the room
was it the obvious author yes
with expensive precision weapons
to defeat the enemies
we need more of
like we need more of more itself
unless we can manage
to be ousted from the joust
of pawns against pawns

When you're feeling
about as
bad as your
average

English translation
of Goethe you must
go see the
Parrot of Penance

and he will
say unto you
"Way around it?
Way around it?

There's never been any
way around it"

---

what are your daily inspiration needs
(you don't know that you know that)
but childhood's insect musketeers
as they thrust parried danced
on those transparent pages
they sure were fun
their authors wrote
to please their champions
and made you feel like a champ
hegemonic   mildly imperialist
but you didn't know those words then
nor did those authors
but nothing will ever take you back
to a place   a time   a child

---

feel like evil spirit
ride the black horse wear the black hat
regret just about every thing
be a good boy be a good boy
regret just about every other thing
once in a while rejoin the human club
with a touch of the whip a shot in the arm
be Siegfried ice cube old cold fish
dream a little dream with me
cat woman bird woman
faint whiff of extended family
long ago far away   so love
where are you marauding tonight
in the vast bog of terminology?

Would it be sentimental to state
That the wild apple tree's red blossoms
Give me shivers of joy?
Well, have you ever heard
A mountain lion burp?
Sort of abruptly?
Me neither
But now, on the digitized didjeridoo
We have The Dolly Lama
Who deserves a big hand
Unlike the poet who writes things
Like "the air's faithful oblong"
Assignment: Look at these lines
Again in a hundred years

By the end of the day
I will have said all
I had to say
This day   to loved ones
Friends associates grocery checkout persons

And quietly   in my head
Even to those little gangsters
In their sentimental suits
Who run the show

And seem very fond of
The Kiplingesque expression
"At the end of the day" (harrumph)

Trying to indicate that they just know
What something they call The Outcome will be

Such an Expensive Dream

---

first they asked for your *Ausweis*
then they took you to Auschwitz   Kosovo! Kosovo!
the way the species now does what it does
is the way it has always done it
& the way the species will do what it will do
will probably be the way it is doing it now
exactly the way it has always been doing it
Kosovo! Kosovo! yes, the species: a serious underachiever
may well go on flunking Conflict Resolution 101
until the end of time
in the great continuous absolutely unstoppable
weave of sad memories medium of human existence
"a murderous dream, confetti falling
helplessly into the fissured past"

March 7, 1999

Ausweis (German): "identity" card (or "papers"). "'a murderous dream . . .'": from Rachel Loden's poem "Premillennial Tristesse" in her book *Hotel Imperium*.

---

because our lives were so short
we had to imagine One more patient than we
perhaps even one reborn every year
so we celebrate the man who reenacted Osiris
"cherchez la femme" yes quite possibly Mary
of Egypt   upon whom the Roman Empire
did *not* build its monotheistic monolith
& the zealots are of course always with us
the poor miserable and vicious zealots
Palm Sunday. Kosovo. NATO. Clinton
now tries to atone for Andrew Jackson?
stop Milosevic's Trail of Tears?

(after the innocent and the ugly
here comes the *bewildered* "American")

March 8, 1999

"(after the innocent . . ." — now, in 2007, it looks like we're back to the ugly, all right.

---

old "red" years now quite forever over?
along with postwar lyricism & doggèd cynicism
some breathless absinthe
some invigorating celluloid
much theoretical hovering above baleful
phantom formulations   poignant drunken lies
the ephemeral the recurrent the eternal
"Good Lord, if our civilization
could sober up for a couple of days
it would die on the third day from remorse"
the tribes are back in old cutthroat mode
freed from the yoke of Pax Communista free
to hunt among stones
to count the bones among stones

March 12, 1999

"*the ephemeral* . . .": E.P's whilom "plan" for the *Cantos*. "'Good Lord, if . . .'": Malcolm Lowry, quoted by Albanian poet Genci Mucollari in e-mail from Tirana April 1, 99. "to hunt among stones": Charles Olson, "The Kingfishers": "I hunt among stones."

Now Cormac has sent word: "To all the lands
of civilization, beset by barbarians and by war,
bring us your books and works of art.
We will keep them safe in Hibernia
until the danger has passed —
even if it takes centuries!
From palaces and monasteries
the treasures have come —
first a trickle, soon a flood
Word of mouth was once our ally.
Now it is our enemy. Corsairs prey upon our ships.
All they want is gold and silver
to melt it down. The books
they throw overboard. We must have help."

This was the news from Prince Valiant, Sunday October 23, 1999. I started following his adventures 60 years ago.

"A strong tendency toward silence
. . . the poem holds its ground on its own margin"
Says Paul Celan   Yes, even if only in elegies
Addressed to our previous selves
On the troubles of The Naturally Immoderate
That persist even after you have become Moderate
Cut to dogs at banquet dressed up as people
Card I was going to send to my sister a decade ago
She gone now, shrunk away, into another dimension
But the cartels and monopolies still mutate and grow
Oil-slick amoebas over a universe they wish to appropriate
Thunk go the rubber bullets through hissing tear gas
While delegates snooze at long tables
In December's Seattle convention hall

"Thunk go the rubber bullets" — fired by riot police at demonstrators in Seattle protesting the policies of the World Trade Organization, early December 1999.

The bread was cardboard
The circuses simulacra on a screen
In hilaritas tristis, in tristia hilaris

Strange to see our moneyed classes dressing up
As ants   so they can resent the impecunious
(Nay, "improvident" in their book) grasshoppers

The question arises out of the bubbling
Pot of questions (note: I do not call it a "cauldron")
The question arises why do I bother to write
These things
                    But so does the question why
Taxes we pay are used to finance slaughter
Slaughter and waste instead of hugs embraces
Friendly arguments about birds identified
Or even better   misidentified

"Oh man did you see that toucan"

"In hilaritas tristis, in tristia hilaris" (Latin): "Sad in gladness, glad in sadness" — Giordano Bruno.

If we could miniaturize
Our species

To prairie dog size
We'd be much better off

Never met a prairie dog I didn't like
Even though they can't read or write

They live in big cities
And they have "coteries"

Which means
They're good at setting boundaries

Unlike their present overfed co-inhabitants
Of the United States of America

Who let themselves be ruled by a gang
Of vicious thieves

---

if it's not propaganda, what is it?
if it's not brainwashing, what is it?
if it's not a capitalist oligarchy, what is it?
this ain't funny   not funny enough
how to stay funny enough
let's just go out and die
under the stars in the snow
driven by these little molecules
are you asleep are you alone
life a Riemann bottle
can't get in can't get out
but the music does tinkle on
driven by these little molecules
"see what you got, tomorrow"

Suits for the dead
Lawsuits for the dead
In war world's whirlpool
                              sluggish explosions
          hope apathy whine roar

"I mean, how many vases do they have in there?"
Rumsfeld, "drawing laughter from reporters"

          "We live under a system by which the many
          are exploited by the few
          and war is the ultimate sanction
          of that exploitation" said Harold Laski

Written while recreating a death
          attended to over the telephone

Ah, America   Such an expensive dream

Rumsfeld — 21st century U.S. warlord, commenting on the looting of Iraq's national museum.
Harold Joseph Laski (1893–1950), British Labour democrat.

Ah, America   Such an expensive dream

"My dream a crumpled horn"

          Listen to the wind

To keep the peace, prepare for war
          say the warlords

Little melodious raptures no help
          & war creates
                                        more warlords

So here you sit
Dear micro-speck of star dust

To keep the peace, prepare for war

And who, among
these throngs of deaf souls
would care to hear
your cry

"'my dream . . .'": a line from Ted Berrigan's *The Sonnets,* possibly borrowed from Conrad Aiken. Last four lines paraphrase Rilke.

---

mule deer fawns
cavorting in the backyard
backyard paid for
fawns a bonus

imperial president
cavorting on the deck of expensive killing vessel
paid for by you and me
president no bonus

young humans dying
in a country occupied
to the tune of millions of dollars a day
paid for by you and me

"mit der dummheit kämpfen die götter selbst vergebens"
"with stupidity even the gods struggle in vain"

Ah, to be a "National Poet"
wouldn't that be fun?

No I don't think so
They shot the last one
In the nineteenth century

& even less so
In the twenty-first
Where "spectacle overcomes thought"

& Xtianity so-called
's a perversion
Of the renegade rebbe's teachings

Shock & awe   Shlock & dread

Into the valleys of idiocy
They ride, our lords

---

for Harris Schiff

Boots on a treadmill   "Do not lean on this wall
It is not secured to the floor"
Do not lean on this heart
It is not secured to the brain   Boots on a treadmill
Well, here comes another book of poems . . .
What are the findings?   Boots on a treadmill
Stagger on yes bloody well stagger on
George Orwell's four motives for writing:
Sheer Egotism   Aesthetic Enthusiasm   Historical Impulse
The desire to record things as they are
For posterity   & last but not least
Political Purpose — the desire to push the world
In a certain direction
Stagger on yes bloody well stagger on

The Tortoise of History

for Janey, to the end of time

Foreword

Could Anselm have possibly foretold
that *The Tortoise of History,* this peculiar compilation of old and new
musings, revisitations, letters to past and future, love notes
 to friends — and to me

was an inevitable foreshadowing of *this* day, when I, his Janey
would stop the endless fuss, unplug the phone, sit quietly
 for 20 minutes,

and then settle into *his* chair, in *our* kitchen
and read this book — aloud, in *his* cadence
and *really* take in

this "message in a bottle"?

— Jane Dalrymple-Hollo

Part 1: The Tortoise of History

Wildly Tangled

wildly tangled dream:
festivities
with current presidente
quite a nice guy really

old face old cat in mail

wind drives propaganda
so have a last capitalist
cigarette
in this lame old plutocracy

everybody
seems quite happily occupied
by their precious little lives

but She Who Must Be Obeyed
She Who Laughs at Your Jokes

love them both as one
as best you can

Quake

The ocean sure is a BIG tub

the continents
                                        none too solid

they growl!

                    TECTONIC GRIND

"say something?"

LA TERRA TREMA

but not right here
not right now

I love your hair
                    atop your dancer's body

absolute loveliness
                    in a quaking world

Don't Tell Me

Don't tell me you can't
love the dead
sometimes I love the dead more
than the still living

there was a time
one sounded as
"authoritative"
as any so-called media

(in my case
shortwave radio person
for ten cold war years)

and they all
old amigos
young apprentices
do still sound that way

not the same but
                    just that way

Why Not

put the book mark
at the wrong page

She Said

Don't fret   she said
it's all right

a human
is not a machine

Art History

Someone comes along
gives that tedious old thing
a new twist   or
breaks its neck

the old questions
don't change:

what do you want me to say?
what do you want me to do?

Home

for jdh

When we drove across
all those states
away from your old hometown
and you were crying

for good reason
(familiar familial strife)
I tried to console you
and worried about how to do that

until I thought I knew
and told you we're going home now
even though then
we had no idea
where home really would be

Some Ways

Some ways you know more
than ever before

some ways
it has become

even harder
to convey that increase

City Of

City OF, says Alice
that's what they all are, the cities
OF
they're OF
OF pain OF love OF life OF hurt of dying
OF memory   ach   yes   OF mamma mia

"Why Read So Much?"

Why read
so much?

to see
what others

may have
found out

and we
would not

want to
miss

before
we die

Time

Too slow
when you're
not here

Dasein

Lightness, my foot —
the incredible ONSLAUGHT of being!

feeling floaty
all right as long as
it's a "controlled" float

but what if it isn't?
reading Marx and Spinoza
dust to dust
you soon will be too

life in the folds
which do not unfold
contradictions
nothing but

"an exhibition of REAL HUMAN BODIES"
i.e., plastinated corpses

it is hard to please the dead

old man looking for his youth
in another
very different body

"Desire?"
"Where do we stand on desire?"

"We don't stand
we just sit
or lie down
dreaming"

(quietly screaming
in our sleep)

Somewhere

Between the cat and the tree
must be my country

and the finch
singing above us

about the world
that suffers
and yearns

Who Said He Could Do This

Half a century trying
still not sure why
he ties his shoelaces funny

Boulder, Colorado

"That's such *inappropriate* behavior"
— woman in antique shop
to small white terrier

after it charged outside
to bark at
big Labrador

"There Is Room in the Room That I Room In"

Said (I believe) Ted Berrigan
          and there IS room
                    in the rooms that we room in

for work and works
          of art
                    and of course myriad objects

needed and / or believed to be so
          and talk and touch and looks
                    there is room for us

who may feel large sometimes
          if not downright great
                    but also truly quite small

                         as I told you one night

Who Would Have Thought — Santa Gaṇesh!

Lovely Parvati's par-
thenogenetic son
bravely guards
the door to her bath

gets his head lopped
by angry Shiva
always angry
but now repentant

replaces lost head
with an elephant's —
yes Virginia there is a
Santa Claus

but here's a Santa Ganesh:
his ride is a mouse
not an eight-legged horse
or sled pulled by reindeer

his gifts open doors
through mind and illusion
        in heads and bodies
        ever refreshed

        so hail to the Universe
        ever refreshed

100-Year-Old Poet

Modigliani
        first name Amedeo
                didn't live long enough
to paint you
        this morning
                (or one of many mornings)
stretched out
        beside me
                to tell the truth, he, Amedeo

did not live long enough at all
        to meet & paint you
                but Hollo (first name Anselm)

has lived long enough
        to see you there
                unfortunately

he is not a great painter
        but he is
                your 100-year-old poet

Nothing

nothing is too
        unimportant
                to write about

nothing is too
        important
                to write about

there really is
        nothing
                to write about

except for
        you
                over there

Rides with Bob Creeley

"The man who really knows
can tell all that is transmissible
in a very few words"
— SAID OLD EZ

Young Bob's few words hit home oh did they ever
        plain and ironic
                always aware
        how insecure
words' ground can be

        both noir and humane

light flashing through dark trees
                by the side of the road

mind & heart stop for a fraction
        time slows

then Thelonious
strikes the next note
and the next

and you wonder how you could ever not
have known that
this would be
the next word
unexpected yet perfect

but you didn't know
or you forgot

and the poem takes you
to a love of the kind wisdom

refuses to abandon
the endlessly
contradictory
human heart

for grand abstractions

so we make it through hours of talk
and laughter and blizzards
on our way on the road
heading east to the rising sun

to rescue she who walks into the sea

before the waters close above her

a tall woman
but not that tall

and then we all trudge back
to the General Store
for some terrible coffee

Bugs Killed Our Tree

b u g s   k i l l e d   o u r   t r e e

The Less Known

Always thought of d'Artagnan
as the little guy
can change the gears
of history

If even just a tad
with a little help from his friends

well   how true can that be
this is not unimportant

guess we were
a wee bit aroused
seeing those guys jump around fighting
with long knives which is what the Cheyenne & Lakota

called Custer's cavalry

Yes Custer wore his hair Mousquetaire fashion as did

Cody Hickok Omohundro

& the less known
Rocky Mountain Joe

Rainy Night

Missing and losing

More ancient than loving

Animal Time
                  so short

          never
          enough

Ah, let it come down

New Year's Poem

          Cats
     are wiser
               than humans

especially present
               human chieftains

so here's wishing you

          cat wisdom
     up
          (note:
               NOT down)
     the years

including the one
               coming up

Crocus

Hello yellow
crocus she says
snaps a picture   looks away   turns to see
the deer that later swallows the crocus
oh well   Spring
will spring

More So Than Before

Love the cluster of Johnny-Jump-Ups in front of my green house

love the words chalked on a pillar
of the university's library:

> TO YOUR POCKET I WOULD SCURRY
> IF THE COLD RAIN FELL AND SHRANK ME SMALL

no idea if that's a quote from popular song
or children's book
or spontaneous anonymous ejaculation
to the unknown muse

but hey it's hard not to feel that it's got something
same something those Johnny-Jump-Ups
sitting atop a crack in the pavement got

which is really all
the scribe of these lines is doing too

sitting atop a crack in the pavement
brought out and sustained by sun and rain

and if you think that's too sweet, well, not to worry
bitter antidotes are easy to find

Broken Flowers

See her sleep
feel no crazy

pack obsession
DA!   what?

not phone wildly
        or oligarchly
just un poco company

just go feel forever
before the dark

anyone home?
old cat in snow

wind drives molecules —
you the ones?

this me years ago
says the cigarette

lame old prick
        blurs into hills
light has brushed

poetic, what?

un poco cheek
rest desert flame on moss

or shyly dream
inspiring tufts

drummer, remember

African Gray Parrot with a Brain the Size of a Walnut Understands a Numerical Concept Akin to Zero

Yes my dear that may well be true
but I do wish
this pleasant early June evening breeze
would evaporate
all the terrible servants of Mammon
masquerading as servants of the "American People" —
in a kind of reverse "rapture," i.e.,

tomorrow morning they just wouldn't BE here anymore

Ah it is late
in the game dear hearts
dear hearts it is late in the game

and how will the untold be told?

will the bugs remember?

or in a dog's or cat's brain a small flicker
            that there were these "humans" once

no no says the Doge of Dogs
no no says the Caesar of Cats

no   to quote your great singer Tom Lehrer
"We'll all go together when we go"

Listen to the Long Hiss of Time

Given a functional
time-reverse machine
who wouldn't mind
a second childhood

One would be better equipped
to deal with one's parents
but being a poet it's hard
to imagine this society
that wouldn't think one
a parasite
or as archaic as
let's say a "mule skinner"

The Way They Pop Up Now

late in this life
the dead and the living

Technicolor
or black and white

different parts of the brain
begin talking to each other

small children reappear
and now they're either dead

or alive as film directors
record producers high tech designers

but some ancients are still present too
even more ancient than this brain life

looks out the window
thinks squirrels are not very contemplative

but the cats watching them are

Mirlitonnade

fous qui disiez
plus jamais
vite
redites

(SAMUEL BECKETT)

you fools who said
never again
hurry
say it again

A Valentine

Love
play a song
for jaguar
and tree

and you and me
and all that lives
and loves
to be

"Growing Old Together"

to Nathaniel Tarn on his 80th

Came to the Empire
got to know and love many
of its inhabitants

watched it being
at least some of the time
what it claimed to be

now old
we feel privileged to watch
its waning

The Bugs Sang Grand

"The bugs sang grand"
— CHARLES OLSON, MAXIMUS II.8

You're not Billie Holiday
you look a bit like Billie Holiday

but you don't really sound like Billie Holiday
so what are we supposed to do about you?

a "fresh" face an old face
a face familiar from back and beyond

(well, I thought that
so I guess I have a right to say it)

"mistaken identity" "amnesia"
good old noir plots

smoke rises

on earth
smoke rises

the untold stories
the untellable ones

You Were Talking (1967)

"You were talking
talking
not looking at me at all"

ephemeral light effects
lack of oxygen in the brain
other space travel symptoms

the doll
back from the "Doctor's"
with a new head
"it is not the same"

I had been away
where no one could know who I was

your eyes
coiling my mind
back into my head

The Pika

So aren't we all
the trembling fawn
or baby rat

entering
re-entering
this terrifying place

so place is it
but time is it too

deceptive results
of efforts to extend
what we believe are our senses

the Pika
can only live
above 6,000 feet

it does not know
any better place

75

It ain't the middle of life
            but I'm still
                        lost in the woods

Formal Prosody

Never ever needed
more formal prosody
than what Thelonious
teaches

and as it goes on
it just needs more
of that
rapt attention

The Stars

The stars
do not
"blink out"

oh no   it's UP
they puff
quite monstrously

and then

they EXPLODE

As

The music
goes on
as long as
you can stand it

A Place Is a While

Over there up
                    on the hillside
walking uphill
in the dark

anything rather than nothing

little lost homesteaders on this web

there is room in this room that we room in

myriad objects

the Poet and the Centipede

a place is a place

a place is a while

After They've Gone

yes

yes

yes

we spoke of

you

& you

& you

& you

Still

Still as alive as the pygmy hippo
in the Liberian forests of the night

but shall end up owing many
letters to the dead

Reading Joanne Kyger

Such poems
          of gentle sadness

not the sadness
          that makes you want to burrow
          into the ground
          jump off a tall building
          slit your wrists

                    no not that kind
                    but one of gentle rain
                              falling
                              softly
                    on memory gardens
                              in your brain

Hunchback Mountain

Small caves in the mountains
not much time left to find them

not enough lifeboats
20 hours
until the fish start to eat us

all right let's go to heaven BEFORE we die
the rich will always be with us

indulging in the usual
religious rape & pillage

the prophets a figment of bad imagination
and love a labor indeed

of having to shovel
the loveless out of the way

all right let's go to heaven
BEFORE we die

"Twenty hours until the fish started to eat us"
— EGYPTIAN FERRY DISASTER SURVIVOR

Late Night, Old Surprises

Doctor Faustus sits in his kitchen
facing Black Feline Angel
on the opposite stool
who looks at him, sends telepathic message:

"No, old friend, you're really not Dr. Faustus
and I'm not Mephistopheles
and you don't really want to be Richard Burton, do you?
Nor do you want her to be Liz Taylor — do you?"

all right, I say
all right, old friend
(she does not look like Liz at all
but just enchantingly herself)

never mind, I say, us oldies
just have to hang on
to our lives
and true loves, too

Noir

Dream dreams dream
dream dreams a samba perennial

you me him her
"Staples beginning to rust in otherwise fine copy"

the back of the electric fan's head
looks like a Wyndham Lewis

but "God" does not look like a Wyndham Lewis
"God" does not look like anything at all

(god
& dog
don't
vote)

Hunter Thompson said he was a
"road man for the Lords of Karma"

"He stomped Terra" said his son

Oh it makes an ill musick la vida
and only lasts a pissing-while

Running

Running
                    to meet
running
                    away

that's what we do

Sitting in Peaceful Lamplight

reading a book on how to become a better person

Zophiel the cat touches my leg and asks me

"Why don't you write a book about becoming just a pretty good person

& by the way what happened to my late-night snack?"

At Civitella Ranieri

To rise out of the mist each morning
into a version of *The Peaceable Kingdom*

feeling as dumbly content as Mr. Hicks's lions
for the first hour or two, and then

to confront the beauty of Umbria
and person — correction: persons — all
concerned with improving
the intelligence of the species
of ape we are —

          is a gift and delight that occurs
          in few civitellas of this planet

this planet — such as it is now,
still struggling on,
trying to leave a record

perhaps no more permanent than the head
now lost   of Ruggiero Cane,
("Khan" = Condottiere)
who returned from his wars
to rebuild castle and fiefdom

later resuscitated —
and truly renewed — by Ursula,
saintly person, whose love still sustains us

here — among persons
of light and delight

The Bard of the Pyrenees

Young poet Raoul Lafagette
arrives from the provinces
like a latter-day d'Artagnan
bearing letters of introduction
to important persons
among others the Democratic Deputy Eugène Pelletan
and the poet Théophile Gautier

On hearing of manuscript verses
the democratic deputy favors his visitor with a résumé
of his views on human progress:
"Why do you write in VERSE?
No one cares for it now. It is little read, and not at all sold.
In the childhood of humanity
verse had its raison d'être.
The first songs are hymns, outbursts of terror
or of enthusiasm. But in our age
of SKEPTICAL MATURITY
and republican independence
verse

is a superannuated form. We prefer
PROSE,
which by virtue of its freedom of movement
accords more truly
with the instincts of democracy."

Whereupon followed a demonstration
of the same principles
from the spectacle of external nature,
in which the crystal is the type of the poem's line
and "the masterpiece which dominates this hierarchy"
— woman — with her undulating grace
is the analogue of prose.

Young Lafagette, enlightened but unconvinced, does not
tear up his manuscripts,
but carries them a few days afterward
with a letter of introduction from GEORGE SAND
to the house of THÉOPHILE GAUTIER

author of the exquisite
ENAMELS AND CAMEOS
who receives the young man with paternal kindness
but after reading the two pieces of verse
submitted to him by the neophyte
speaks as follows: "Your verses
are 40 years older than yourself. They are
too old, therefore —
that is to say, too young.
Poets sang in this manner in 1830. NOWADAYS
we desire a more compressed, more concrete poetry.
Lamartine was a sublime bard,
but his vague effusions are no longer
to our taste. Musset is a great poet
but an exceedingly bad model.
Read HUGO much, he is the true master."

"And Théophile Gautier?" timidly murmurs
the visitor. "And me, too, a little,
if it pleases you to think so," replies Gautier,
smiling. "You are a poet
and must not abandon poetry. Only I advise you

to make three or four thousand verses
and before you publish anything
burn them."

Note: Raoul Lafagette (1842–1913) returned to the French Pyrenees and pursued the advice of both interlocutors. In front of the town of Foix's mayoral offices stands on a plinth a marble bust with the inscription "Raoul Lafagette, Bard of the Pyrenees."

See What You Got, Tomorrow (2002)

If it's not propaganda, what is it?
If it's not brainwashing, what is it?
If it's not a capitalist plutocracy, what is it?
The politics universally incorrect

Catnip yes it nips the old cat &
"How will anyone understand those poems of yours
Unless they're stoned?"
A crazy princess asked me twenty years ago

This is the phase of early a.m. phone calls
Observing this, I am
What a dumbo flap flap dark peacocks rise in the wind
Home at three a.m. from eight hours

Proofreading offshore contracts (San Fran '81)
Drank myself to sleep feeling lonely as shit
Then even more so
This ain't funny not funny enough

How to stay funny enough back then
Not even a fish for company back then
A sad sack for sure
Let's just go out and die under the stars

In the snow
Driven by these little molecules
Rilke molecules Billy Yeats molecules
Yes I had a son whose molecules gave out before mine

I was not good to him   Not good for him
He was as they say hard to take
Once tried to kill me and the feeling was mutual
So did my "folks" and that feeling was mutual too

So now I am grateful for kindness
So now I try to understand power
You help to keep this network thriving says the radio
And some of the poor sons of bitches

Out there are creating a terrible beauty
Some of them ready to kill for their "god"
In a persistent drunken trance
Wishing to live forever

But not here and now
Are you asleep are you alone
And the cigarettes keep jumping out of the pack
Life a Riemann bottle:

Can't get in can't get out
Estrange it Estrange it
Yeah fill 'er up Jack lessgo
Gosh yes the music does tinkle on

(Bertolt Brecht:)

And the ones
They stand in darkness
And the others
In the light

The ones well lit
Oh yes we see them
The ones in darkness
We do not see

Looking at the Old Hand

for Simon Pettet

looking at the old hand
I almost lost and
its old bones and veins

I print your messages
dear friends
and feel the love and

accept it with
all my heart and brain which
still feel like they're working

Two Strange Little Vessels

one a tiny wooden chest from the once-upon-a-time

small town of Hameln

whence the Pied Piper of Hamelin

was said to have lured all the town's rodents away

by playing a magical tune on his pipes

but sadly the town's children heard it too

and followed the Piper where?

nobody knows for sure

the other a small bowl with what looks like an Etruscan design

of two birds identical except for their coloration

(I'm sure it is not "genuinely" Etruscan)

and, and a small

nonallergenic

metal flower

complete with roots

it is a garlic flower

for healing

provenance unknown

AND a small book from Crown Point

Press of some etchings

by the late

Mr. John Cage

HAPPY BIRTHDAY JANEY!!!!

James Butler A.K.A. Wild Bill Hickok's Final Stream of Consciousness

holy shit i shouldn't have had that big shot of whiskey but what the hell i'll just sit down here with my back to the bar this is just a halfassed mining camp "deadwood" give me a break i survived chicago new york and that crazy buffalo bill and his buddy buntline and their goddamn wild west shows . . . . . .

Blue Moon

Being dead, Steve Carey, wonderful poet
can't sign his *Selected Poems*
to me

These days I find myself
ordering only books by poets
who are

being
dead

Another One Gone Too Soon

"Like RIVETS"
said Ken Smith
about my lines

don't know if
he really approved

but now it's
way too late
to ask him

2010 A Spring of Departures

Would you mind

POPPING UP

again?

You can't just

disappear

or can you?

The Tortoise of History

The tortoise of history
keeps stomping along

it carries
on its back

all the prophets,
visionaries,
"great men"

It is almost blind

but its legs still work

Part 2: Hipponax, His Poems

"I ain't got no future, but Lord, Lord, what a past."

— BILLIE HOLIDAY, AS QUOTED BY GEORGE MELLY

William Carlos Williams ends Book 1 of his *Paterson* (New Directions 1992, p. 40) with a quote from John Addington Symonds's two-volume *Studies of the Greek Poets,* prefacing it with an "N.B.":

"In order apparently to bring the meter still more within the sphere of prose and common speech, Hipponax ended his iambics with a spondee or a trochee instead of an iambus, doing thus the utmost violence to the rhythmical structure. These deformed and mutilated verses were called *choliambi,* lame or limping iambics. They communicated a curious crustiness to the style. These *choliambi* are in poetry what the dwarf or cripple is in human nature. Here again, by their acceptance of this halting meter, the Greeks displayed their acute aesthetic sense of propriety, recognizing the harmony which subsists between crabbed verses and the distorted subjects with which they dealt — the vices and perversions of humanity — as well as their agreement with the snarling spirit of the satirist."

There is an echo of this quote, one that Williams found relevant to his search for a new measure, in the final lines of Book 5, the last complete installment of *Paterson* (p. 236):

> We know nothing and can know nothing
> but
> the dance, to dance to a measure
> contrapuntally,
> Satyrically, the tragic foot.

This was not my first introduction to the Ephesian inventor of the "limping foot," who lived and made poems around 540 BC. I had read what remains of his work in a book by the late Finnish poet Pentti Saarikoski, a contemporary and a friend, who in 1959 published a collection of poems titled *Runot ja Hipponaksin* runot *(Poems and the Poems of Hipponax).* Saarikoski, one of the major European poets of the twentieth century — even though he was far from tame enough for "Nobels" or "MacArthurs" — was also a prolific translator from classical Greek as well as from modern classics, including Joyce's *Ulysses*. While he went on later to write two powerful postmodern "epics" (*What Is Really Going On* and *Trilogy*), in his 1959 volume he demonstrated his interest in how brief a poem may get and still be a poem — whether its brevity is due to the ravages of time (as in the case of many ancient Greeks) or to the author's desire to explore the possibilities of the laconic.

No "complete" poem by Hipponax survives. All we have is ninety-two mostly short quotes, in the works of later authors on history and its metrics and mores, chosen for being exemplary in one way or the other. Obviously, a fragment that was chosen as a "technically interesting" example of Hipponax's "lame or limping foot," the *choliamb,* may lose much of its raison d'être in translation:

what a mob

or

libations and innards of a wild sow

may not seem all that evocative, or merely evocative, hovering just below the threshold of "interesting." One might say that "The Collected Poems of Hipponax" as they can be found in the Loeb Classical Library's *Herodes, Cercidas, and the Greek Choliambic Poets (Except Callimachus and Babrius),* edited and translated by A. D. Knox, late fellow of King's College, Cambridge (1926), are an aleatory (or "stochastic") work composed by Clio, Muse of History, employing her own secret chance operations formula, in a tradition later brought to full bloom by John Cage and Jackson Mac Low, and also in "cut-ups" in the related lineage of Tristan Tzara, William S. Burroughs, and Brion Gysin.

The arrangement of the fragments in the Loeb edition is chronological, i.e., in the order of the approximate dates of the extant papyri and other texts in which lines attributed to Hipponax appear. Saarikoski's Finnish versions follow this arrangement fairly closely. I have created an "intuitive" display of the pieces, consisting of four parts (or poems, if you wish), under the headings:

"Careless Love" (check out Dr. John's recorded version of that American classic)

"What a Mob" (consisting of angry, vicious, and slanderous material)

"Screech Screech Here Come the Ghosts" (Or, "People Who Died") (see Ted Berrigan's poem, Jim Carroll's song)

"Still Waiting for My Winter Coat" (lines dealing with the ever-present needs and wishes of the unhoused and impecunious)

The four sections reflect what little is known about the poet's life.

From Pliny the Elder's *Natural History* we learn, in a passage dealing with the annals of Greek sculpture, that Hipponax was a satirical poet of Ephesus (c.

540 BC) who became involved in a feud with the sculptor Bupalos. The reason for this feud seems to have been a woman, Arété, whose affections Bupalos alienated from Hipponax. Either before or after (we don't know) Arété rejected Hipponax for Bupalos, the latter created a three-dimensional caricature of the poet, presumably in marble or some other stone. One wishes this piece of sculpture had survived; in Mary Renault's novel *The Praise Singer* (1978), a fictional autobiography of Hipponax's far more successful contemporary Simonides, we find the following description of the poet's appearance:

"He limped in one leg, which he had broken as a child, so that it was shorter than the other. The foot turned in, and his rocking gait had twisted his whole body, making his shoulders tilted. I thought it no wonder he should be bitter, for princes would not want to see him about their courts . . . That his clothes were dirty, I put down to his having no wife; but I thought that in a city not short of water, he could have washed himself. He ate noisily, and was helped twice." (p. 38)

Here, the "limping" measure is understood as the poet's translation of his physical handicap into a new poetics.

Whether or not Hipponax was physically repulsive and unsanitary, he certainly often found others to be so. He became notorious for his irreverent and slanderous verses, and after Ephesus became a Persian colony (presumably when Hipponax was still young and feisty), the new vice-regents of the city found him undesirable and politically incorrect and banished him:

"He did not go far, just north across the headland to Klazomenai. Now and then we would get news of him, or someone would bring back one of his poems . . . They grew more savage; we heard rumors of someone he'd caused to hang himself. He did not live very well, however, and came down to cadging from strangers in the harbor, or begging alms from people whose enemies he had reviled. He died, they say, lying in rags in the marketplace . . . One or two citizens, I've heard, poured oblations upon his grave, thinking his spirit would do mischief if not appeased." (*The Praise Singer,* p. 41)

"Careless Love" is the tale of Hipponax's infatuation with Arété, her rejection of him in favor of the sculptor Bupalos, and his subsequent indulgence in negative emotions. In "What a Mob" we see scattered 2,400-year-old reflections from Hipponax's verbal laser beams as they were aimed at dribblers, gluttons, imitators of Homer, corrupt judges, dumb painters, witches, sadists, masochists, con-men . . . "Screech Screech Here Come the Ghosts" is a similarly patchy frieze of elegiac matter. "Still Waiting for My Winter Coat" gathers the ancient street poet's prayers, complaints, and curses, echoed later in the works of François Villon and our own Charles Bukowski. Pentti Saarikoski, in notes to his translation, mentions Callimachus and Catullus as poets who regarded Hipponax as a master (and presumably still had access to a body of his recorded work).

Knox's and Saarikoski's translations have served as source texts for these versions. Like Saarikoski (who cites the Knox edition), I have tried my best not to stray too far from Knox's post-Victorian literalness, while also relying on Saarikoski's knowledge of classical Greek to guide me. Since mine is not a scholarly translation, more like a transcription — or if you wish, a "version," — I refrain from encumbering it with footnotes.

While giving Hipponax my best shot, I have sometimes wondered what on earth compelled me to engage with this oh-so-long-dead (white? probably coppery, and certainly ornery) male who was so obviously of the slash-and-burn persuasion in his private / political life and work, yet prone to feeling sorry for himself; whom Mary Renault suspects of having provided such eloquent negative poetic testimony on the character of one of his enemies that the latter was scapegoated by the citizens, not a pleasant process; who sounds as if he didn't like his species fellows very much — any more than they cared for him — ?

The answer is, I think, simply that "Now and then . . . someone would bring back one of his poems" from his ragged exile at Klazomenai, and that in the twentieth century, now half a century ago, an admired and beloved friend (whose own life was not lacking in Hipponactean themes) brought what is left of them to my attention. Then, there was that intriguing quote in *Paterson* by William Carlos Williams, whose understanding of American idiom and measure went far beyond the literal.

I Careless Love

on my way to Arété I saw
the heron fly just right

"all right all right all right"
I thought

and I did stay with her
all night

*

lamp-
light on her face

above mine

*

her slave stumbled and broke
the cup so we drank from a

bucket   I had the first drink
then Arété   downed the rest

*

baked goods from Amathusa
bread from Cyprus a bucket

of honey (a gift from the flower-
eaters) sweet Rhodian

ointment a garland of damson
flowers & mint aahh mmm

*

pierced the stopper
with a thin tube

*

soothed
my nostrils

(peanut oil)

*

greased
my keel

*

her lips
voracious

as a heron's beak

*

I love you more than I
love anyone else I swear

this to you by this
head of cabbage

*

silky
slit

*

stepping
proudly

like an
arch-

necked
horse

*

o but why did you take to your bed
that arsehole Bupalos?

*

man carved out of stone

*

threatens to render me senseless

*

told them to punch Hipponax in the mouth
told them to throw rocks at Hipponax

*

got away thanks to the seven-
leaf cabbage (Pandora's offering
at the Thargelia before *she* copped it)

*

here hang on to my shirt
while I bop Bupalos right

in the eye for I am ambi-
dexterous and my aim is

perfect

*

thought it was him
so let him have it

*

ripped his cloak
slashed him
down the middle

*

she rents out her tongue
for eighty bucks

*

you want her?
I'll let you have her

dirt cheap
her nose a bell
with snot for a clapper

why bother to wrap it up
(it isn't fresh partridge, exactly)

*

another game?
with those loaded dice?

you must be kidding

*

no more warming your
chilblains at my embers

*

so fooling The In-Bred of Erythrea
Bupalos feeds at the trough

(Arété
beside him)

*

then they shrieked at each other

*

hips out of whack
no teeth only one eye

she sure knows how to pick ’em

*

may Artemis strike you down
or Apollo

(I don’t care)

II What a Mob

when they catch Phrygians
the Soloeci sell them to Miletus

where they need slaves for their mills

*

what a mob

*

was that a fart or a croak?

*

they drool
like a sieve

*

Kikon you hideous glutton son
of Amythaon your head may be

crowned with bay leaves but your
forecast doesn't look good

*

starve him and whip his gonads
pelt him with rocks in the meadow

beat him with twigs like a scapegoat

*

hold it Mimnes I don't think it is
such a good idea to paint the snake

on the side of that trireme with its
tail at the prow its head at the stern

if the snake bites his leg the brawny
helmsman will roar "count me out"

*

galloping upsidedown you lay there
after she snipped the cord

*

sing Muse of Mrs. Eurymedontiades
who needs no cutlery to wolf her food

shout Rabble vote for her death by stoning
by the Sea ever-restless

*

a hypocrite
the judge who condemned you
a paterfamilias
smirking at whores

*

with three witnesses he returned
to the bootlegger's place and found

a man who having no broom was busy
sweeping the floor with a broomstick

*

then she said in a strange tongue
now I'll clean your disgusting

arsehole she beat me with twigs
like a scapegoat caught between

two boards I hung above dung
beetles came to the feast

*

(handy invective)

one who barfs at the feast
old sow fed on slops

cow pie's sister
Ephesian porker

bag of puréed squid

III Screech Screech Here Come the Ghosts (Or, "People Who Died")

screech screech
here come the ghosts

*

Myson whom Apollo
called the wisest of all

*

pillaged along the road to Smyrna
through Lydia past the burrow of Alyattes

past Gyges' grave mound past
Ardys' splendid slab and Sadyattes' tomb

the mighty conqueror
his belly pointing west

*

his chariot powered by white stallions from Thrace
he charged the walls of Troy and was slain

*

a better judge than Bias from Priene

*

bright Cybebe
Bendis from Thrace

daughters of Zeus

*

he lived in Smyrna
the wrong side of town

halfway to Hades

*

and how did he get to Kypsos

*

libations and innards of a wild sow

*

black fig-tree

*

sister of the vine

*

clean cock and balls

*

happy the hunter

IV Still Waiting for My Winter Coat

called on Hermes
strangler of dogs

brother of thieves
a.k.a. Kandaules

(in Scythia):
PLEASE HELP ME OUT

*

ah . . . to wear a mantle
of mountain sheep's wool . . .

Hermes lord of Cyllene
great son of Maia

Hipponax begs you:
send me a winter coat

*

for I am starving

*

unfunny he who drinks his lunch

*

now that was good advice

*

last night while I lay sleeping
someone made off with my clothes

lay in a room on a pallet buck naked

*

o teeth
you

that used to reside
in my jaw

*

picked tarragon out of a dented bucket
hands shook trembled

like the toothless
when the north wind blows

*

Zeus
Emperor of Olympus

Big Daddy

*

no scrumptious feast of partridge and hare
no sesame pancakes

no fritters drenched
in honey

nor yummy Lebedian figs
from far-off Kamandolos

*

for Hipponax:

> 1 coat
> 1 shirt
>
> 1 pair of sandals
> 1 pair of winter shoes
>
> > (and 60 gold bars
> > to hide in the wall)

*

still waiting for my shaggy greatcoat
to keep me from freezing in winter

and for that pair of winter shoes
to save my poor feet from chilblains

*

Plutos must have gone blind
he's never found his way to my house to tell me

"greetings dear Hipponax
see here I brought you this bag of silver"

*

o great Athena
please grant me a gentle master

one who won't beat me

*

I bow to Hermes
wait for the sun to rise

*

in his bright shirt

Last Poem

In the Autumn of 2012, as Anselm re-connected his brain to body after his second brain surgery, he began to piece together his experience during recovery. Translating thought to word to page was a frustrating, even anguishing process, but I was delighted to see his "just the facts" account taking form as poetry. In some dimension somewhere, perhaps there still exists an Anselm as he was then on a crisp Boulder day: tearing up and down 14th Street chasing his racer red walker (the one with wheels); grinning, impatient, hopeful, free.

— TAMSIN HOLLO

---

wild dreams

getting dressed   in odd tweed suit
to catch train in helsinki   call up papa mama
to hurry up "train is leaving at ____"
it appears we're still living in soviet days
and some kind of petition is to be presented in moscow
for the freedom of some unjustly imprisoned person
but the weather is glorious and everybody in good spirits
except for my folks   they respond grumpily
a la "do you realize what time it is?" and "no, dear, we're not
going anywhere"
and "i" had been so enthusiastic about this trip
with my dead mother and father and sister

Dreamt while imprisoned for circa 2-1/2 months in otherwise quite congenial rehab home, an expression of wanting to go Elsewhere.

2 (earlier)

in a stall not unlike one you keep your horses at night
there is a challenger next door
behind a small square opening
just about eye level
and i notice there is a wooden beam on the floor of the stall
it is my task to kick that beam through the small square hole
as soon as my challenger's face appears
but wait there are 2 of them and there is water below them
enough said I emerge victorious
(Jane's tape for further details!)

I never was any good at athletics / sports. It swelled my chest with pride.

3

I get up and get dressed in order to catch
an airplane to Bucharest
because I have received an invitation
from the press attache of Romania
to go there
I show it to a taxi driver
who is helpful and deciphers it
so off we go   and are soon stopped in front of an impressive door
I realize I have no Romanian currency
but a few dollars will do
I check the board and recognize the name second floor
enter ancient elevator and ascend
I ring the doorbell   there's no response
finally I turn the handle on the door it opens
to a vacant but well furnished apartment
nobody home here   well   I make myself comfortable
before retiring on a couch I entertain myself changing the décor
    on the walls
and so I wake up in the morning   still alone
then there's a jump-cut and I'm with Jane and Tamsin

Who totally pooh-pooh the whole idea, attributing it to Andrei C.

Editors' Note

Contents

Across from the title page in many of Anselm's books readers find a list of his books. The latest iteration of that list we could find is in *Guests of Space* (Coffee House, 2007). We followed that list, the poetry section, only adding two titles, both of which were published after his death: *Last Poem* (2013), which first appeared in *The Poetry Project Newsletter* No. 236, and which was subsequently published the same year, "Printed at the Harry Smith Print Shop, Summer Writing Program: Week 4 2013. The Jack Kerouac School of Disembodied Poetics, Naropa University, Boulder, Colorado," and *The Tortoise of History* (Coffee House Press, 2016). Despite the publication dates, we have put *Last Poem* last, because it really was last.

The one exception to the above scheme concerns *Motes & Paramecia.* Though *Motes* was published without *Paramecia,* and *Paramecia* wasn't published until *Sojourner Microcosms,* Anselm's lists consistently indicate that he considered them one thing, since he always calls *the* publication *Motes & Paramecia* (except when *Motes* is *Notes,* which we take as a typo). Therefore, we have treated *Paramecia* as a section of *Motes,* and called the combo *Motes & Paramecia.* The work thus appears here as it does in Anselm's book lists.

We realize that Anselm published a number of volumes that were for whatever reason not included in his list, and therefore not included here. Luckily, most of the poems from those books (at least the post-early 60s ones) made their way into the volumes we did include. As far as the rest are concerned, we hope to be able to follow this publication with another, called provisionally, in our minds at least, The Selected Uncollected.

Editorial Principles

Since Anselm tended to republish poems multiple times, sometimes modifying them as he went, we chose to use the first version published in one of the titles on his list. We have then omitted reappearances of these poems in later volumes, except in a few cases, when he either changed them drastically or recontextualized them by including them in sequences. Since this a reader's, not a scholar's, edition, we felt free to follow our intuition here. That said, we have made use of subsequent appearances when it was time to decide whether an apparent typo really was one, or whether there was a stanza break between the end of one page and the beginning of the next.

We have also regularized texts, following Anselm's own practice when he republished poems in his various volumes of selected poems, including his last two, *Notes on the Possibilities and Attractions of Existence* (Coffee House, 2001), and *Braided River* (Salt Publishing, 2005). We have tried to make *The Collected Poems* read smoothly. Not, of course, by altering the sense of his poems in any way (we hope), we have tried hard never to do that, but by using the same kind of dashes, quotation marks, and so on, throughout.

We have included Anselm's prefaces, epigraphs, dedications, and notes, in an attempt to be as complete as we can. On a few occasions, early in the book, we were able to include poems he published in his own calligraphy, or handwriting, he had such nice handwriting it's hard to tell the difference.

Any mistakes, omissions, etc, are of course all on us. Please let us know if find anything in need of correction.

Acknowledgments

People who must be acknowledged: Jane Dalrymple-Hollo, Josephine Clare, Tamsin Hollo, and Kaarina Hollo, for trusting us, and so much more; Clara Burns, for creating a wonderfully helpful finding aid for Anselm's archive while it resided at "HH"; Kai Eckholm, for many things; Jerome Rothenberg, Tom Marshall, Andrew Schelling, and Brad O'Sullivan, Smokeproof Press, for loaning us copies of Anselm's books; Ken Mikolowski, for answering questions concerning the activities of the Alternative Press; Amanda Rybin Koob, Director, Library and Archives at Naropa University; Lynda Claassen, Nina Mamikunian, Jennifer Donovan and everyone else, UC San Diego Special Collections, which houses the Archive for New Poetry, and also all the good people in UCSD's Interlibrary Loan Department; Michael Rothenberg (for sharing his experiences assembling Philip Whalen's *Collected Poems*); Michael Tencer, for sending us a pdf of the spoof issue of the *English Intelligencer*; Victoria Verzunova, for her concrete poetry expertise; Kuei Chiu, collection development librarian, U of California, Riverside; Alison Fraser, Rare & Special Books Collection, SUNY-Buffalo Libraries; Freddie Alexander and Angus Wark, National Library of Scotland; Brian Sherwood and Mukund Miyangar, The British Library; Courtney Chartier and E. Kathleen Shoemaker, Stuart A. Rose Manuscript, Archives, & Rare Book Library, Emory University; Heather Cole, Brown University Library; Patricia

Sundman, Archives and Special Collections, University of Connecticut Library; Robin Wheelwright Ness, Special Collections, John Hay Library, Brown University; Ana D. Rodriguez, Rare Book & Manuscript Library, University of Illinois at Urbana-Champaign; Cara Gilgenbach, Special Collections, Kent State University; Jenna Silver, University of Iowa Special Collections; Kirstin Johnson and Dave Butler, University of Illinois Music & Performing Arts Library; Katie Armstrong, University of Arizona Special Collections; Kate Collins, Duke University David M. Rubenstein Rare Book & Manuscript Library; Betsy Pittman, University of Connecticut Archives & Special Collections; Stephanie Fletcher, Ryerson & Burnham Libraries, The Art Institute of Chicago; Melanie Hardbattle, Special Collections and Rare Books, W.A.C. Bennett Library, Simon Fraser University; Lisa Wettleson, Department of Special Collections, University of Wisconsin-Madison; Tim Hodgdon, Louis Round Wilson Special Collections Library, The University of North Carolina at Chapel Hill; Alastair Johnston, Poltroon Press, for gifting us a copy of the very scarce *Wreck O'lections*; Iben Brodersen, Special Collections, Music and Theater Collection, Royal Danish Library; Valerie C Stenner, Special Collections, Morris Library, University of Delaware; Laura Wait and to Bob Hagerty, Laura for sending slides of her artist's book *Retablo, or Flares in the Dark*, and Bob for remembering enough of the text for us to be able to identify which poem of Anselm's was used; Pat Nolan, for some Anselm stories, and for publishing our working bibliography at the New Black Bart Society website so that interested Anselmites could comment on it; Jeffrey Cyphers Wright, for help dating Hard Press items and for sending us all kinds of wonderful Hard Press postcards and zines; Linda Quirk, Special Collections, University of Alberta, for searching the Black Sparrow Press archive for a MS Black Sparrow was to have published and/or for hints of it, a MS which Anselm listed as one of his books in Maya (it wasn't to be found); Tom Peters, The Beat Book Store, Boulder, for trying to chase down a very rare imprint for us; and others whose names escape at the moment . . . as Freddie Mercury almost put it, You brought us fame and fortune and everything that goes with it, we thank you all.

—YG and JBR

First Lines Index

Coffee House Press began as a small letterpress operation in 1972 and has grown into an internationally renowned nonprofit publisher of literary fiction, essay, poetry, and other work that doesn't fit neatly into genre categories.

Coffee House is both a publisher and an arts organization. Through our *Books in Action* program and publications, we've become interdisciplinary collaborators and incubators for new work and audience experiences. Our vision for the future is one where a publisher is a catalyst and connector.

LITERATURE
is not the same thing as
PUBLISHING

Funder Acknowledgments

Coffee House Press is an internationally renowned independent book publisher and arts nonprofit based in Minneapolis, MN; through its literary publications and *Books in Action* program, Coffee House acts as a catalyst and connector—between authors and readers, ideas and resources, creativity and community, inspiration and action.

Coffee House Press books are made possible through the generous support of grants and donations from corporations, state and federal grant programs, family foundations, and the many individuals who believe in the transformational power of literature. This activity is made possible by the voters of Minnesota through a Minnesota State Arts Board Operating Support grant, thanks to the legislative appropriation from the Arts and Cultural Heritage Fund. Coffee House also receives major operating support from the Amazon Literary Partnership, Jerome Foundation, Literary Arts Emergency Fund, McKnight Foundation, and the National Endowment for the Arts (NEA). To find out more about how NEA grants impact individuals and communities, visit www.arts.gov.

Coffee House Press receives additional support from Bookmobile; Dorsey & Whitney LLP; Elmer L. & Eleanor J. Andersen Foundation; the Gaea Foundation; the Matching Grant Program Fund of the Minneapolis Foundation; Mr. Pancks' Fund in memory of Graham Kimpton; the Schwab Charitable Fund; and the U.S. Bank Foundation.

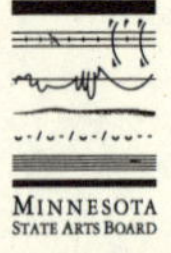

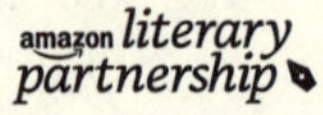

The Publisher's Circle of Coffee House Press

Publisher's Circle members make significant contributions to Coffee House Press's annual giving campaign. Understanding that a strong financial base is necessary for the press to meet the challenges and opportunities that arise each year, this group plays a crucial part in the success of Coffee House's mission.

Recent Publisher's Circle members include many anonymous donors, Kathy Arnold, Patricia A. Beithon, Andrew Brantingham, Anitra Budd, Kelli & Dave Cloutier, Mary Ebert & Paul Stembler, Eva Galiber, Jocelyn Hale & Glenn Miller Charitable Fund of the Minneapolis Foundation, Roger Hale & Nor Hall, William Hardacker, Randy Hartten & Ron Lotz, Dylan Hicks & Nina Hale, Carl & Heidi Horsch, Amy L. Hubbard & Geoffrey J. Kehoe Fund of the St. Paul & Minnesota Foundation, Kenneth & Susan Kahn, the Kenneth Koch Literary Estate, Cinda Kornblum, the Lenfestey Family Foundation, Sarah Lutman & Rob Rudolph, Carol & Aaron Mack, Mary & Malcolm McDermid, Daniel N. Smith III & Maureen Millea Smith, Robin Chemers Neustein, Alan Polsky, Robin Preble, Rebecca Rand, Grant Wood, and Margaret Wurtele.

For more information about the Publisher's Circle and other ways to support Coffee House Press books, authors, and activities, please visit www.coffeehousepress.org/pages/donate or contact us at info@coffeehousepress.org.

About the Author

Poet and translator **ANSELM HOLLO** was born in Helsinki, Finland, in 1934. In 1958 he moved from Vienna to London to work full time in the Finnish section of the BBC World Service. He was in the foreground of the small press movement of the early 1960s, writing, giving readings, and publishing widely while also freelance translating poetry and prose from Finnish, Swedish, German, and French into his chosen language—English. By 1965, when he participated in the International Poetry Incarnation in London's Royal Albert Hall, he already had close connections with a number of the leading lights of the Beat Generation, Ginsberg and Corso in particular. His early translations of Ginsberg (into Finnish) and, with his wife Josephine, Corso (into German) were hugely significant in their European reception. After moving to the USA at the end of the decade with Josephine and their three children, he became an itinerant professor, teaching first at SUNY Buffalo and the University of Iowa and then at various other institutions, while meeting and making friends with poets across America. In 1989, he and his second wife, Jane, moved to Boulder, CO, to begin his professorship in the Writing and Poetics Department at Naropa University. In 2001, he was honored by poets associated with the SUNY Buffalo POETICS listserv as the "Anti-Laureate"—a parody of the "official" Poet Laureate that year.

Hollo was the author of more than forty books of poetry, including *Notes on the Possibilities and Attractions of Existence: New and Selected Poems 1965–2000* (2001), which won the San Francisco Poetry Center Book Award; *Corvus* (1995); *Finite Continued* (1980); and *Sojourner Microcosms: New and Selected Poems 1959–1997* (1997). He also published a book of essays, *Caws and Causeries: Around Poetry and Poets* (1999). His many translations include works by Paavo Haavikko and Pentti Saarikoski, for whose *Trilogy* (2003) he was awarded the Harold Morton Landon Translation Prize by the Academy of American Poets. Anselm Hollo passed away peacefully in 2013; his final work, *The Tortoise of History,* was published posthumously in 2016.

About the Editors

JOHN BLOOMBERG-RISSMAN is a mashup anthropologist (*No Sounds of My Own Making; Flux, Clot & Froth; In the House of the Hangman*), editor (*Barbaric; Vast & Wild,* with Jerome Rothenberg; *The End of the World Project,* with Richard Lopez and T. C. Marshall), and photographer. He has been reading Anselm Hollo for over fifty years.

YASAMIN GHIASI is a graduate of Naropa University, and obtained her MFA from Milton Avery Graduate School of the Arts, Bard College. A former student of Anselm Hollo, she lives in Boulder, Colorado.

The Collected Poems of Anselm Hollo was designed by
Bookmobile Design & Digital Publisher Services.
Text is set in Adobe Caslon Pro.